The Orchards of Eastern England

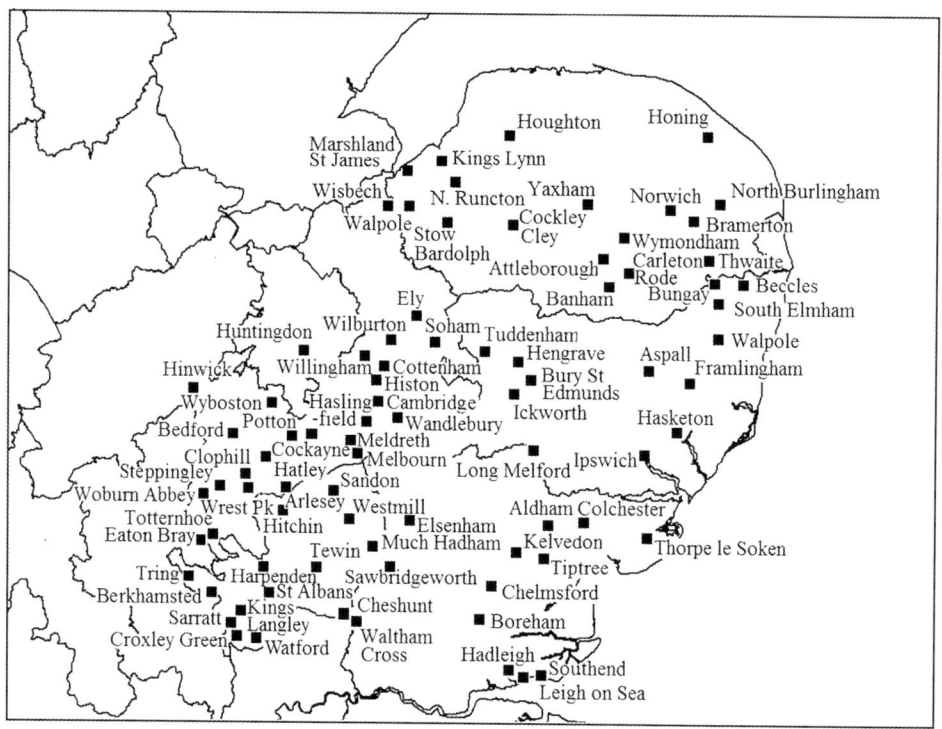
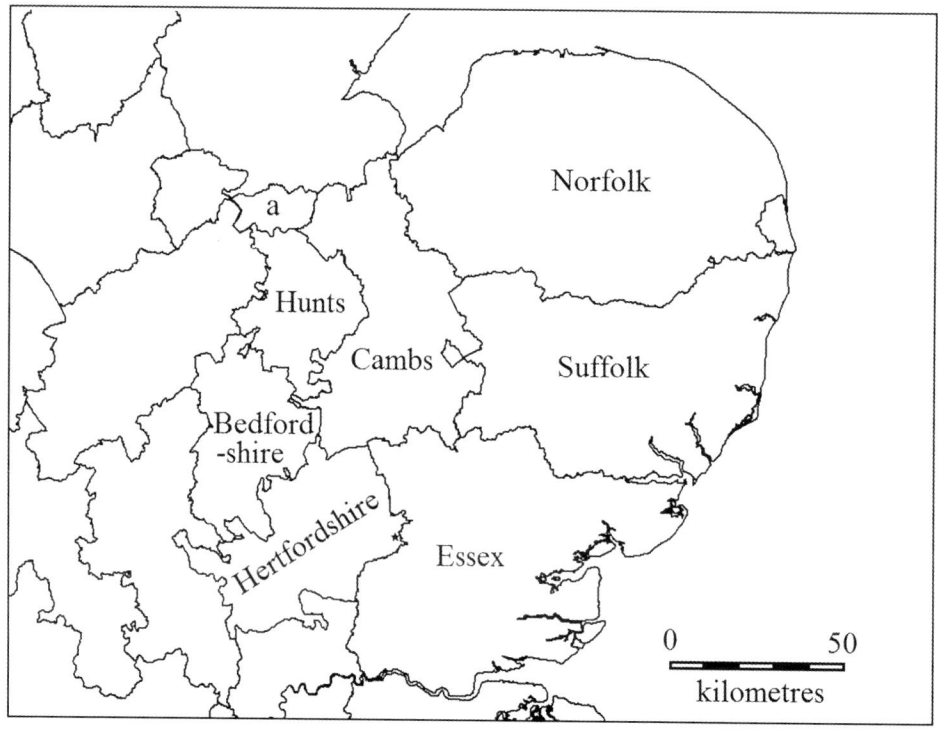

The eastern counties, with nineteenth-century boundaries, showing the principal places referred to in the text ('a' is the Soke of Peterborough)

The Orchards of Eastern England

History, Ecology and Place

GERRY BARNES AND
TOM WILLIAMSON

UNIVERSITY OF HERTFORDSHIRE PRESS

First published in Great Britain in 2021 by
University of Hertfordshire Press
College Lane
Hatfield
Hertfordshire
AL10 9AB

© Gerry Barnes and Tom Williamson 2021

The right of Gerry Barnes and Tom Williamson to be identified as the authors of this work has been asserted by them in accordance with the Copyright, Designs and Patents Act 1988.

All rights reserved. No part of this book may be reproduced or utilised in any form or by any means, electronic or mechanical, including photocopying, recording or by any information storage and retrieval system, without permission in writing from the publisher.

British Library Cataloguing in Publication Data

A catalogue record for this book is available from the British Library

ISBN 978-1-912260-42-3

Design by Arthouse Publishing Solutions
Printed in Great Britain by Henry Ling Limited, Dorchester

Contents

List of illustrations   vii
Acknowledgements   ix
Abbreviations   xi

1 Orchards, landscapes and history   1
2 Farmhouse and commercial orchards before c.1850   28
3 The 'orchard century', c.1850–1960   55
4 Garden and institutional orchards   88
5 Processing: cider, jam and canning   119
6 The recent history of orchards   147
7 Fruit varieties and the nursery industry   171
8 The significance of orchards   206
9 Conclusion   239

Bibliography   245
Index   253

Publication grant

This book was produced and published
with the financial support of
The National Lottery Heritage Fund.

Figures

Frontispiece.	The eastern counties	ii
1.1	A typical 'traditional' farmhouse orchard	2
1.2	A modern commercial orchard at Bramerton, Norfolk	3
1.3	A 'veteranised' apple tree	6
1.4	'Bush'-pruned, open-centred Bramley's Seedling tree in the East Anglian Fens	13
1.5	Orchards as a percentage of county area, from the Agricultural Census	16
1.6	The depiction of orchards on the Ordnance Survey first and second edition 6-inch maps	17
1.7	The distribution of orchards in eastern England, c.1900	18
1.8	Eastern England, showing soils, topographic features and areas discussed in the text	23
2.1	A typical small farm orchard shown on a map of 1730	33
2.2	A reconstruction of the plan of an orchard at Thwaite in Norfolk in 1734	36
2.3	Plan for an orchard at Hasketon, Suffolk, 1814	38
2.4	Veteran cobnut stools at Saxmundham, Suffolk	38
2.5	Poultry in a farmhouse orchard	43
2.6	A map of a farm at Flaunden, west Hertfordshire, c.1700	48
2.7	The Caroon cherry	50
3.1	Orchards in Eaton Bray, Bedfordshire, in 1880	58
3.2	One of the surviving 'Prune' orchards at Eaton Bray, Bedfordshire	59
3.3	Workers in the orchards of Wilkin and Son's jam company, Tiptree, Essex, c.1910	61
3.4	A train on the Wisbech and Upwell 'Tramway' in the 1950s	63
3.5	Old orchard on former county smallholding, Blofield, Norfolk	68
3.6	Jeacock's Farm, Tring	68
3.7	Bramley's Seedling orchard, Marshland St James, Norfolk	72
3.8	Alexander Whitehead, founder of the Cox's Orange Pippin Orchard company	74
3.9	Workers in the COPO orchards at Cockayne Hatley, Bedfordshire	76
3.10	Orchard at Clophill, Bedfordshire	84
4.1	Detail from a map of Hoxne Hall, Suffolk, 1619	89
4.2	Channons Hall, Tibenham, in Norfolk, as shown on a map of 1640	90
4.3	Somerleyton Hall, Suffolk, and its gardens in 1652	92
4.4	Old espalier pear tree in the kitchen garden at Cockley Cley Hall, Norfolk	97
4.5	Heated wall at Kimberley Hall, Norfolk	98

4.6	The Apple House at Bromham, Bedfordshire, 1903	100
4.7	The orchard at the St Elizabeth's Centre, Much Hadham, Hertfordshire	113
4.8	The orchard at The Oval, Harpenden, Hertfordshire	114
4.9	The small orchard at Steppingley Hospital in Bedfordshire	116
4.10	The orchard at Girton College, Cambridge, planted around 1895	117
5.1	Norfolk Beefing apples, ready for baking into 'Biffins'	120
5.2	The 'Cyder House' at Aspall, Suffolk	126
5.3.	Plan of the 'Cyder House', and plan and elevation of the cider mill, at Aspall, Suffolk	126
5.4	The orchards at Aspall, Suffolk, in 2017	135
5.5	Gaymer's cider factory at Attleborough in Norfolk, photographed from the air in *c.*1955	137
5.6	Chivers' 'Victoria' factory at Histon, Cambridgeshire	141
5.7	Wilkinson's jam factory, Tiptree, Essex	144
5.8	The orchards at Tiptree today	144
6.1	The decline of the orchard area in the post-war period	147
6.2	Planting a new community orchard at Great Wymondley, Hertfordshire	163
6.3	A recent orchard at Sarratt in Hertfordshire	163
6.4	An old farmhouse orchard preserved, but integrated into a garden, in Suffolk	168
6.5	A modern, intensively managed commercial orchard in Wisbech St Mary, Cambridgeshire	170
7.1	Map of 1833 showing Mackie's nursery ground in Lakenham, Norwich	176
7.2	The surviving remains of Rivers Nursery at Sawbridgeworth in Hertfordshire	183
7.3	Mackie's nursery at Bracondale, Norwich, *c.*1855	184
7.4	One of the catalogues produced by Daniels Brothers of Norwich	185
7.5	Orchard workers at Lane's of Berkhamsted in Hertfordshire	187
7.6	Lane's Prince Albert	188
7.7	Laxton's 'Superb'	190
7.8	Plan of orchard and list of fruit trees, Carleton Rode, Norfolk, 1758	195
8.1	Veteran apple tree at Saxmundham in Suffolk	208
8.2	Veteran apple tree, broken by a gale, at Wymondham in Norfolk	210
8.3	Derelict cherry orchard, Sandon, Hertfordshire	212
8.4	Derelict cherry orchard, Rickmansworth, Hertfordshire	212
8.5	Tewin Orchard, Hertfordshire	213
8.6	The Norfolk Beefing	217
8.7	Old apple trees can carry rich collections of lichens and bryophytes	224
8.8	Interception trap, used to capture flying insects in biodiversity surveys of orchards	226
8.9	Fieldfares are regular visitors to orchards in the autumn and winter months	232
8.10	The orchard at Clintons, Much Hadham, Hertfordshire	234
9.1	Old farm orchard	243

Acknowledgements

The research we present in this book was undertaken as part of a much larger project, Orchards East, which ran for four years from early 2017. Our gratitude must go, first and foremost, to the National Lottery Heritage Fund, who generously provided not only the financial resources for the project, and for the publication of this book, but also much advice and useful guidance, especially from Claire Adler, Sylvia Collier and Erin O'Grady. We are also immensely grateful to the University of East Anglia for providing additional resources, as well as accommodation for the project officers, Howard Jones and Rachel Savage. We would particularly like to thank Howard and Rachel, and also the core members of the project team: Gen Broad, Rowena Burgess, Andrea Lovick and Paul Read. Bob Lever and Martin Skipper provided invaluable identifications of fruit during detailed orchard surveys; Monica Askay, Anna Baldwin, Louise Crawley, Martin Hicks, Peter Laws, Steve Oram, Val Perrin, Neil Reeve, Lorna Shaw, Jackie Ulyett and Sally Wileman supplied encouragement and advice more generally. The biodiversity surveys discussed in Chapter 7 were carried out by Gen Broad, Agneta Burton, Colin Carpenter, Jane Carruthers, Martin Collier, Adrian Knowles and Julia Masson, with additional identifications by Tony Price, Peter Vincent and Mark Welch. Thanks also to the members of the various county Environmental Record Centres – Brian Arbon, Ian Carle, Ben Heather, Tom Hunt, Jane Mason, Andy Mercer, Sam Neal, Phil Ricketts, Lorna Shaw and Jackie Ulyett – for map digitisation and other assistance.

Some of the archive research, and particularly that into the history of the Aspall Cyder company, was undertaken by Patsy Dallas: financial support for the latter work was generously provided by the company and Barry Chevallier. Additional documentary research was undertaken by Carol Champion, Martyn Davis, Bridget Howlett, Martin Smithson, David Stannard and Clara Zwetsloot, with extra information from Stephen Coleman, Kate Harwood, Margaret Roberts, Anne Rowe, Di and Neville Stangroom, and Peter Woodrow. Thanks also to Cliff Amos, Cherry Carter, Michael Clark, Alina Congreve, Sharon Copple, Jenny Cousins, Joanna Crosby, Claire Males, Margaret Pomfret, Sue Raven, Alison Rubens, Claire Smith, Neil Wiffen and the staff of the Bedfordshire, Cambridgeshire, Essex, Hertfordshire, Norfolk and Suffolk Record Offices, the Public Record Office at Kew, Attleborough Heritage Centre, Dacorum Heritage Centre (Berkhamsted), the Royal Horticultural Society Library and the John Innes Library (Norwich).

We would also like to thank the many owners and managers who kindly allowed access to orchards throughout the region, including Fiona Andrews, David Bain, Clare Boscawen,

Celia Boyle, Dawn Britten, Peter Byass, Caroline and Peter Chenery, Lord Chomondeley, Penny Daffarn, Roger and Anne Dudley, Terry Elphic, John Everett, Lorraine Geddis, Tony Gillet, Lady Rose Hare, Stephen Hayes, John Hill, Martin Hicks, Stephen Howes, Colin James, Liz James, Emma and David Lawley, Bob Lever, Oliver Mann, Glenn Muleady, Helen Nistala, John North, Liz Pryor, Roland Randall, Georgina Roberts, Mark Robertson, Alan Roscoe, Keith Saunt, Yvonne Smith, Wendy Szelong and Andrew Tann.

Above all, we would like to thank the staunch band of Orchards East volunteer surveyors, without whom the project, and this book, would not have been possible: Henry Adams, Steve Addy, Liz Anderson, Lynn Ballard, Hugo Barker, Marilyn Basketter, Sheila Baxter, Emma Bird, Chris Birt, Sarah Bott, Bryony Brierley, Jane Brook, Alison Brown, Clare Browne, Malcolm Bruce, Andrew Bulman, Don Burford, Agneta Burton, Liz Carlin, Richard Carter, Colin Clare, Will Cockerell, Carol Coleman, Marlys Collins, Ian Cook, Andy Culshaw, Martyn Davis, Bernice Davison, Sarah Day, J. Devonshire, Sarah Dickie, Ines Everett, Simon Fisher, Sue Fleet, Sue Flower, Robin Forrest, Rosemary Forrest, Simon Fowler, Sue Friend, Laura Garrod, Barry Green, Sue Green, Tom Griffin, Julia Grover, Tony Grover, Anne Hall, Colin Hall, Jane Harrison, Kate Harwood, D. Hayes, Melvyn Helsey, Oliver Hendrie, Wendy Hendrie, Bridget Hetford, John Hills, Kathryn Hindley, John Hook, Philip Hookway, Sarah Hookway, Naomi Horrocks, Bridget Howlett, Steve Hulse, Deryck Johnson, Glyn Jones, Henry Kilvert, Marian Land, Millie Ling, Mike Macartney-Filgate, Rob Mann, Jilly McNaughton, Sue Meek, Julia Merrick, Jenny Milledge, Jane Millership, Tom Moat, Jackie Moss, Ellen Muirhead, Mike Muirhead, Peter Oakenfull, Nick Packer, Mary Palmer, Sue Parker, Andrew Partridge, Joel Petts, Laura Powell, Tony Powell, John Quenby, Tracy Richards, R. Richardson, Tina Rowland, Phil Salter, Clive Scott, Martin Smithson, Ann Sparrow, Deborah Spring, John Stinchcombe, Rob Street, Trish Street, Simon Tarrant, David Taylor, Jane Tomkins, Keith Tomkins, Jane Turner, A.J Vrylundl, Adrina Walmsley, David Warren, Elizabeth Waugh, Steve Whitby, Izzy Whiting, Lucy Whittle, Andrew Williams, Kevin Wilson, Vicky Wing and Karen Wright. Many thanks also to the many individuals who provided formal oral-history interviews or offered information or reminiscences on a more informal basis.

The photographs, maps and diagrams are the authors', with the exception of Figure 1.2, Rosemary Forrest; 1.4, Bob Lever; 2.2, Patsy Dallas; 3.6, Dacorum Borough Council; 3.7, Carole Coleman; 3.8, 3.9 and 4.6, Clara Zwetsloot; 3.10 and 8.8, Howard Jones; 4.3, Suffolk Archives; 4.7, 6.3 and 8.4, Rachel Savage; 4.8, Agneta Burton; 4.10, Girton College, Cambridge; 5.1, Daniel Jones; 6.2, Cherry and Derek Carter; 6.5, Alamy Photos; 7.1, Louise Crawley; 7.2, Julian Walker; 7.3, Norfolk County Council; and 8.5, Judith Dainty.

We would like to thank the following for permission to reproduce images of material held in their collections: Attleborough Heritage Centre (5.5); Bedfordshire Record Office (3.8, 3.9 and 4.6); Dacorum Heritage Centre (7.5); Hertfordshire Archives and Local Studies (2.1, 2.5 and 8.10); Norfolk Record Office (4.2, 7.1, 7.8 and 8.10); Suffolk Archives (2.3, 4.1 and 4.3); and Tiptree Jam Museum (3.3 and 5.7).

Abbreviations

BRO	Bedford Record Office, Bedford
CRO	Cambridge Record Office, Cambridge
ERO	Essex Record Office, Chelmsford
HALS	Hertfordshire Archives and Local Studies, Hertford
HRO	Huntingdon Record Office, Huntingdon
NRO	Norfolk Record Office, Norwich
PRO/TNA	Public Record Office/The National Archives, Kew
SRO, B	Suffolk Record Office, Bury St Edmunds branch
SRO, I	Suffolk Record Office, Ipswich branch
SRO, L	Suffolk Record Office, Lowestoft branch

CHAPTER ONE

Orchards, landscapes and history

Introduction

This book is one of the outcomes of a large Heritage Fund project, Orchards East, which began in early 2017 and continued, through the multiple disruptions of the Covid epidemic, until the end of 2020. The project was concerned with all aspects of the orchard heritage of the eastern counties – defined as Bedfordshire, Cambridgeshire, Essex, Hertfordshire, the old county of Huntingdonshire (including the Soke of Peterborough), Norfolk and Suffolk. It involved a range of practical activities, including the planting of new community orchards and the teaching of necessary skills such as grafting. It also featured a major regional survey of orchards, carried out by volunteers; detailed studies of the biodiversity of selected orchards; oral-history interviews; and extensive research in a range of local and national archives. This book presents the results of all these investigations. It examines the history of orchards and fruit-related industries in the eastern counties, investigates the current number and condition of orchards in the region and attempts to evaluate the importance of the orchard legacy, in terms of biodiversity, history and culture. Although it touches on many fields of academic interest, it is primarily a history of orchards in the landscape: how their numbers and extent changed over time, how they affected the wider environment in the past and how they may benefit it today, and in the future.

Remarkably little has been written about the history of orchards as features of the English landscape compared with, for example, ancient woods or hedges. The history of particular types of fruit, especially apples, has received much scholarly attention, most notably in the works of Joan Morgan,[1] but little research has been undertaken into the orchards in which they were grown. Although orchards have been present in every village and beside almost every farm since at least the early Middle Ages, the principal histories of rural settlement in England – including Taylor's *Village and Farmstead* and Robert's and Wrathmell's *Region and Place* – conspicuously fail to discuss them.[2] Moreover, while some recent writers on ecology have given orchards a measure of attention, our greatest historical ecologist, Oliver Rackham, specifically excluded them from his monumental

---

1 See, in particular, J. Morgan and A. Richards, *The New Book of Apples* (London, 2002).
2 C. Taylor, *Village and Farmstead: A History of Rural Settlement in England* (London, 1983); B. Roberts and S. Wrathmell, *Region and Place: A Study of English Rural Settlement* (London, 2003).

History of the Countryside, and most general studies of ecology and wildlife ignore them.[3] All this is somewhat surprising given, as we shall see, the great interest in orchards and old fruit varieties that exists among the general public, and the presence in most parts of England of extensive, active and knowledgeable networks of orchard enthusiasts.

Until comparatively recently, well within living memory, orchards were a common sight throughout England, a familiar part of the environment. Not all were of any great antiquity. Some, located beside old farmhouses and filled with tall, spreading trees, had been in existence for centuries (Figure 1.1). But many were commercial enterprises, or were planted close to hospitals, colleges or other institutions to provide food for the residents, and were creations of the late nineteenth or twentieth centuries. Many, indeed, were modern – intensively managed fruit farms comprising closely spaced, low-growing trees, rather different from our romantic image of an orchard (Figure 1.2). Historical interest does not reside in antiquity, however, and even these relatively recent additions to the environment are an important aspect of our culture and our landscape, and worthy of the historian's attention.

Figure 1.1 A typical 'traditional' farmhouse orchard, with tall, spreading trees on vigorous rootstocks growing in unimproved permanent grassland.

---

3   O. Rackham, *The History of the Countryside* (London, 1986), p. 65.

Figure 1.2 Bramerton, Norfolk. Closely planted apple trees on dwarfing rootstocks, typical of post-war commercial orchards and 'fruit farms'.

Examples of all these kinds of orchard, and of others, can still be found throughout England. But in almost all parts of the country orchard numbers have fallen, steadily and to an often catastrophic extent, since the 1950s. This has been for a variety of reasons, including foreign fruit imports, the decline of small farms, changes in agricultural subsidies, the rise of the great supermarket chains, urban expansion and house building on 'infill' sites in rural villages and, perhaps most importantly, changes in lifestyles and in attitudes to food.[4] And not only have we lost the majority of our orchards over the past half century but the wide range of fruit varieties once grown in them has also dwindled. Most shops now sell only a limited number, many with recent origins. This is not simply a matter of losing some odd-looking fruit with strange, evocative names – D'Arcy Spice, Dr Harvey, Norfolk Beefing. It also means that a diverse range of tastes has been lost to our experience, almost unnoticed.[5]

---

4   A. King and S. Clifford, 'The Apple, the Orchard, the Cultural Landscape', in S. Clifford and A. King (eds), *Local Distinctiveness: Place, Particularity and Identity* (London, 1993), pp. 37–46; S. Clifford, 'Save Our Orchards: One Insight into the First Two Decades of a Campaign', in I.D. Rotherham (ed.), *Orchards and Groves: Their History, Ecology, Culture and Archaeology* (Sheffield, 2008), pp. 32–42.

5   King and Clifford, 'The Apple, the Orchard, the Cultural Landscape', pp. 73–5.

It is hard to overstate the significance of the wholesale decline of English orchards, their replacement by arable fields or housing, their conversion to gardens or pony paddocks. For centuries orchards were an indispensable aspect of everyday life, a central part of our culture, valued not only for their fruit but also for their blossom, so cheerful a sight after the long winter months. Indeed, as we shall see, orchards – especially in the sixteenth and seventeenth centuries – were used as important elements in the gardens and designed landscapes laid out around the homes of the social elite. In part this may have been because orchards also carried symbolic meanings or, at least, would have evoked among contemporaries memories of the biblical and classical texts that framed early modern culture. As Liz Bellamy has recently pointed out, not only was the 'forbidden fruit' in Genesis commonly, if erroneously, described as an apple, the pre-lapsarian garden of Eden was itself, in part, depicted as an orchard, planted with 'every tree that is pleasant to the sight, and good for food'.[6] Various classical myths of a golden age of plenty and abundance make similar references, with Homer's description of the grounds of King Alcinous rendered, in George Chapman's translation of 1616, as 'a pretty orchard-ground … of near ten acres'.[7] Orchards were not only represented as but to a large extent really were beautiful places of relatively gentle, leisurely production, clearly distinguished from wider arenas of bitter agrarian toil.

From the perspective of the landscape historian, and perhaps that of the cultural geographer, orchards have another significance. Particular areas of the country – because of their soils, climate or access to markets – developed dense concentrations of orchards, which became a defining aspect of their local landscape: the cherry orchards of Kent; the cider orchards of Devon, Herefordshire and Somerset. Again, this is something that many landscape historians, including those involved in official bodies such as English Heritage, have been happy to ignore, in spite of a professed interest in 'landscape character' (which emerged towards the end of the twentieth century) and in spite of the fact that orchards in such areas were deeply woven into the fabric of local life, their presence both encouraging and stimulated by particular local industries such as cider-making.[8]

The suggestion that orchards have been neglected by historians and geographers should not be taken too far, however. An important study of the fruit-growing heritage of the county of Sussex was produced by Brian Short and colleagues in 2012; a number of important books have been written on the history of West Country orchards; and orchards have received some attention in the volumes of the *Cambridge Agrarian Histories of England*

---

6   L. Bellamy, *The Language of Fruit: Literature and Horticulture in the Long Eighteenth Century* (Philadelphia, 2019), p. 16.

7   G. Chapman, *Chapman's Homer: The Iliad and the Odyssey*, ed. Jan Parker (Ware, 2002), Book 7, l. 155.

8   S. Rippon, *Historic Landscape Analysis: Deciphering the Countryside* (London, 2004); J. Lake, 'The English Pays: Approaches to Understanding and Characterising Landscapes and Places', *Landscapes*, 8/2 (2007), pp. 28–39.

and Wales, most notably those dealing with the early modern period.[9] But, for the most part, the history of fruit growing and orchards has been the preserve of the amateur and, while many of the works produced have been well-researched and scholarly,[10] few have attempted to tie the subject firmly to wider narratives in social, landscape or environmental history. And, in the absence of rigorous enquiry, as we shall see, much that is written about orchards, and much that is widely repeated in conservation circles, is arguably based more on modern myth than on historical reality.

Rather more rigorous, but nevertheless limited, attention has been paid to the significance of orchards for biodiversity.[11] This arises principally from their combination of old, herb-rich pasture and 'veteran' specimens of tree species that, while not themselves indigenous, have close native relatives. Orchards, it is suggested, have much in common with wood-pastures – that is, grazed woodland featuring ancient trees – but with an important difference.[12] Fruit trees age more quickly than other trees and within decades rather than centuries become 'veteranised' – that is, filled with the cavities and rot required by a large number of rare organisms (Figure 1.3). Lichens, mosses and fungi are also significant features of some old orchards. But studies undertaken from a botanical or zoological perspective have often lacked a historical dimension, and conflicting claims about the importance of orchards as habitats can arise from an inability to distinguish the ancient from the not-so-old. Moreover, the importance of orchards as habitats is intrinsically tied to the ways in which they developed over time – their life stories – which are in turn connected to modes of exploitation and management – in other words, to the human world.

For it is important at the outset to emphasise that orchards, while sometimes described as 'semi-natural habitats', inhabit the world of culture more than that of nature. This is probably the main reason why Rackham, in his numerous studies of historical ecology, conspicuously failed to address them. Orchards have limited resilience and need to be maintained by interventions more radical than the management systems usually required to sustain habitats. In particular, fruit trees are comparatively short-lived – apple trees will seldom exceed an age of 120 years, cherries 80 years and plums 60 – and have

---

9   B. Short, P. May, G. Vine and A.-M. Bur, *Apples and Orchards in Sussex* (Lewes, 2012); M. Gee, *The Devon Orchards Book* (Wellington, 2018); J. Thirsk (ed.), *The Agrarian History of England and Wales, Vol. V, 1640–1750* (Cambridge, 1984).

10 E.g. M. Roberts, *The Original Warden Pear*, rev. edn (Bedford, 2018).

11 I. Rotherham, 'An Introduction to Orchards and Groves', in Rotherham (ed.), *Orchards and Groves*, pp. 6–10; K. Alexander, 'The Special Importance of Traditional Orchards for Invertebrate Conservation, with a Case Study of the BAP Priority Species the Noble Chafer *Gnorimus nobilis*', in Rotherham (ed.), *Orchards and Groves*, pp. 12–18; A. Henderson, 'Lichens in Orchards', in Rotherham (ed.), *Orchards and Groves*, pp. 76–85.

12 Alexander, 'Invertebrate Conservation', pp. 13–14.

Figure 1.3 A 'veteranised' apple tree in the kitchen garden at Cockley Cley, Norfolk.

limited powers of regeneration. Active replanting is required if an orchard is to survive beyond the lifetime of a significant proportion of its original trees. Without this, and without regular measures to control the development of scrub between the trees, it will rapidly become something else. A neglected orchard, if grazed by livestock or mown, will become a paddock. If completely left to its own devices it will soon develop into secondary woodland. Orchards are fragile, their existence dependent on constant human attention and use.

The origins of fruit trees

Apples, which belong to the genus *Malus*, appear to have been first domesticated in Kazakhstan and neighbouring areas. The main genetic ancestor of the thousands of domestic cultivars we know today is *Malus sieversii*, the principal species of the local forests. However, recent research suggests that other species, including the crab apple (*Malus sylvestris*), which is native to Britain and western Europe, have also made a major genetic contribution.[13] Wild apples were part of the diet of people living in Britain since at least the Neolithic – one of the earliest finds of preserved pips, dating to around 3800 BC, comes from a settlement site at Dixie in Devon.[14] It is probable that the domesticated apple, however, was introduced during or shortly before the Roman period.[15] It was certainly widely cultivated in Anglo-Saxon orchards – 'orchard' is itself an Old English word (variously rendered as *ortgeard*, *orcerdleh* and *orcyrd*).[16] By the Middle Ages the presence of different types or varieties of apple is attested by the use in documents of terms such as *Pearmain* and *Costard*. In the eastern counties one of the earliest documentary references to apples comes in a deed from Runham in Norfolk, dating to 1204–5, which describes how Robert de Evermere held the manor for, among other payments, an annual render of '200 pearmains'. In the same year Walter de Evermere paid a debt to the exchequer for lands in Rackheath, Norfolk, in the form of two measures of red wine and 200 pearmains yearly.[17]

The origins of the domesticated pear are probably similar to those of the apple. There are a number of wild species of pear – more than 20 in Europe, temperate Asia and north Africa – and the domestic pear *Pyrus communis* shows in its genetic composition the influence of several, including *P. eleagrifolia*, *P. spinosa*, *P. nivalis* and *P. syriaca*. Pears were

---

13 Morgan and Richards, *New Book of Apples*, p. 9; A. Cornille, T. Giraud, M.J.M. Smulders, I. Roldán-Ruiz and P. Gladieux, 'The Domestication and Evolutionary Ecology of Apples', *Trends in Genetics*, 30/2 (2014), pp. 57–65.

14 <https://cotswoldarchaeology.co.uk/company/about-us/25-highlights/highlight-4/>, accessed 8 March 2021.

15 Short *et al.*, *Apples and Orchards in Sussex*, p. 51.

16 J.R. Clark Hall, *A Concise Anglo-Saxon Dictionary*, 4th edn (Cambridge, 2000), p. 269.

17 F. Blomefield, *An Essay towards a Topographical History of the County of Norfolk*, 2nd edn, vol. 2 (London, 1806), pp. 241–6; vol. 9 (1809), pp. 446–51.

certainly domesticated in the classical world – Theophrastus (371–287 BC) specifically distinguishes between wild and cultivated forms, and Pliny's *Natural History* records over 30 varieties. Like the domesticated apple, the pear may have been brought to Britain by the Romans.[18] The Old English *pere* or *peru hu* is derived from Latin *pera* or *pira*.

As we shall see, apples and pears were the most important fruit grown in farmhouse orchards, but filberts, cherries and plums were also cultivated there, and the latter two fruit became more important as commercial orchards developed through the seventeenth, eighteenth and nineteenth centuries. Plums are a diverse group that includes greengages, cherry plums, damsons, mirabelles and others, and they are classified in equally diverse ways by natural scientists and horticulturalists. The European plum (*Prunus domestica*) probably originated in the Caucasus as a natural hybrid of the cherry plum or Myrobalan (*Prunus cerasifera*) and the sloe (*Prunus spinosa*). Most domesticated plums are cultivars of this species, including mirabelle and greengage. Cherry plums were themselves widely planted in England, although usually as a rootstock. The damson, a domesticated version of the bullace (*Prunus insititia*), is distinct from all of these.[19] Although the latter is indigenous, domestication almost certainly occurred abroad, so that both of the main plum types are introduced. The stones of domesticated plums have been recovered from a number of Neolithic sites in Europe and, while the date of introduction to England remains uncertain, the fruit was certainly grown in the Anglo-Saxon period: the word 'plum' comes from the Old English *plume*.[20]

The cultivated forms of cherry are derived from the sweet cherry (*Prunus avium*) and the sour or morello Cherry (*Prunus cerasus*), which is primarily used for cooking. *Prunus avium* is native to much of Europe, including Britain, and was cultivated from at least 800 BC in Asia Minor.[21] Sour cherry is also native to much of Europe as far as south-west Asia, although not to Britain. It is a natural hybrid of *Prunus avium* and *Prunus fruticosa*. The cultivation of both may not have begun in England until after the Norman Conquest (there is no Old English word for cherry), but by the late thirteenth century Matthew Paris was able to list cherries among the fruit that had cropped badly in the poor weather conditions of 1257.[22] It is often suggested that sour cherries were introduced to England as late as the sixteenth century by Richard Harris, fruiterer to Henry VIII, who:

---

18 G.J. Silva, T.M. Souza, R.L. Barbieri and A.C. de Oliveira, 'Origin, Domestication, and Dispersing of Pear (*Pyrus* spp.)', *Advances in Agriculture*, 20 (2014), pp. 1–8.

19 J. Janick, 'The Origins of Fruits, Fruit Growing and Fruit Breeding', *Plant Breeding Review*, 25 (2005), pp. 255–320, at p. 282.

20 J.E. Spangenberg, S. Jacomet and J. Schibler, 'Chemical Analysis of Organic Residues in Archaeological Pottery from Arbon Bleiche', *Journal of Archaeological Science*, 33/1 (2006), pp. 1–13.

21 Janick, 'Origins of Fruit', p. 281.

22 J.A. Giles (trans.), *Matthew Paris's English History from 1235 to 1273*, vol. 3 (London, 1854), p. 255.

Fetched … out of the Lowe Countries, Cherrie grafts, & Peare grafts, of diverse sortes: Then took a piece of ground belonging to the King in the parish of Tenham in Kent, being about the quantities of seven score acres; whereof he made an Orchard, planting therein all these foraigne grafts. Which Orchard is, and hath been from time to time, the chiefe Mother of all other orchards for those kindes of fruite in Kent, and of other divers places.[23]

While possible, such a late introduction from Europe seems intrinsically unlikely, however, and it is, on present evidence, probably best to assume that both types of cherry were being cultivated in Britain by the thirteenth century.

Filberts and cobnuts feature in many surviving orchards and were widely planted in the past. While often confused in the popular mind, they are in fact quite distinct. The filbert (*Corylus maxima*) is a type of hazel originating in the eastern Mediterranean around Turkey. Cobs, in contrast, are cultivated varieties of the native hazel (*Corylus avellana*). Cobs are roughly spherical in shape, Filberts more elongated.[24] Confusion arises in part from the fact that hybrids between cobs and filberts can occur, but mainly as a result of loose nomenclature. The famous 'Kentish Cob' is actually a filbert and traditionally in the eastern counties the two terms are used so loosely as to be interchangeable. Lastly, walnuts featured in many orchards in the past, even small domestic examples. They were of two species, the common or English walnut (*Juglans regia*) and the black walnut (*Juglans nigra*). The former, in spite of its name, is not native to this country, but originated in the Middle East, and has a complex history of genetic diversification and diffusion in Europe.[25] It was widely cultivated in medieval Britain. The black walnut, in contrast, was introduced from North America and not until the seventeenth century. Today, numerous cultivars of both species are grown.

Orchards contained, and often still contain, various other kinds of fruit. The medlar (*Mespilus germanica*), from south-west Asia and south-eastern Europe, and the mulberry (*Morus nigra*) – introduced in medieval times, possibly earlier – were occasionally grown, but mainly in the grounds of the social elite and more usually in their gardens than their orchards. Moreover, many orchards produced, in addition to the 'top fruit' grown on the trees, soft 'bush fruit' such as gooseberries and blackcurrants, which were cultivated either around the periphery or in lines between the trees. Less familiar fruit might also be present, such as barberry (*Berberis vulgaris*), the leaves and berries of which were widely used

---

23   Anon., *The Fruiterer's Secret* (London, 1664), unpaginated.
24   Suffolk Traditional Orchard Group, 'Cobnuts in Suffolk', <https://issuu.com/suffolkbis/docs/stogan__6_cobnuts_in_suffolk_v3_aug?ff=TRUE&e=25146667/41601866>, accessed 8 March 2021.
25   P. Pollegioni, K. Woeste, F. Chiocchini, S. Del Lungo, M. Ciolfi and I. Olimpieri, 'Rethinking the History of Common Walnut (*Juglans regia* L.) in Europe: Its Origins and Human Interactions', *PLoS ONE*, 12/3 (2017), <https://doi.org/10.1371/journal.pone.0172541>, accessed 7 March 2021.

for cooking but also, well into the eighteenth century, medicinally.[26] Such plants will be discussed in passing but, being less durable than the trees themselves, will not be accorded a significant amount of attention in the pages that follow.

Grafting, pruning and pollination

As already intimated, over the centuries many different varieties of the principal types of fruit have developed, with their own particular tastes, appearances and uses. For the most part, however, these are unable to sustain themselves unaided. The majority will not 'breed true', so that a pip from, say, a Cox's Orange Pippin will not grow into a tree bearing fruit of this variety. Instead, every pip will represent a new genetic variation.[27] While most of these, like other chance variations arising from sown pips, stones or seeds, will be hard, bitter, or at best bland, some seedling trees, growing by chance from discarded fruit or fruit waste, will produce new forms of fruit that are attractive and useful. Other new forms may emerge as 'sports' – that is, as genetic mutations arising on the tree itself – in the form of a branch bearing fruit (and sometimes leaves) different from those on the rest of the tree. In recent centuries, moreover, fruit breeders have also deliberately developed novel types by cross-pollinating established varieties that display desirable characteristics. Whatever the manner in which they first arose, new varieties – not only of apples, but also of other fruit – could usually be propagated only by a process known as 'grafting'. Pieces of 'scion wood' – small sticks – are cut from a tree of a desired type and carefully spliced onto a dependable 'rootstock', one or two years old. Propagation could also be achieved by 'budding'– by taking a single bud from the plant and slipping it under the bark of the rootstock, a technique generally more effective with apples than with other fruit. Budding can be carried out in the summer, but normal grafting is a winter task. Both are difficult operations, only effectively executed by people who have been properly trained.[28]

Rootstocks come in a variety of forms. In the case of apples, early writers made a distinction between 'crab', or 'wilding', stocks and 'paradise'. The former produced tall, vigorous, spreading trees: as Ralph Austen put it in 1653, trees that are 'free from canker and will become very large trees and will last longer than stocks of sweeter apple trees and will make fruits more strong and hardy to endure frosts and cold weather in the spring'.[29] These were the main rootstocks used in orchards before the late nineteenth century.

---

26 G. Barnes, D.G.O. Saunders and T. Williamson, 'Banishing Barberry: The History of *Berberis vulgaris* Prevalence and Wheat Stem Rust Incidence across Britain', *Plant Pathology*, 69/7 (2020), pp. 1193–202, <https://bsppjournals.onlinelibrary.wiley.com/doi/abs/10.1111/ppa.13231>, accessed 8 March 2021.

27 Morgan and Richards, *New Book of Apples*, pp. 11, 18, 296–8.

28 R. Garner, *The Grafter's Handbook*, 6th edn (London, 2013); K. Mudge, J. Janick, S. Scofield and E. Goldschmidt, 'A History of Grafting', *Horticultural Review*, 35 (2009), pp. 437–93.

29 R. Austen, *A Treatise on Fruit-Trees, Showing the Manner of Grafting, Setting, Pruning, and Ordering of them in all Respects* (Oxford, 1653), p. 104.

'Paradise' stocks, in contrast, produced dwarfing or semi-dwarfing specimens, which could be more closely planted. Although sometimes used in early orchards, these were more a feature of gardens, especially the walled gardens of the wealthy.

In the Victorian period a significant range of intermediate rootstock types, including Doucin, Kelziners, Ided and Laune de Metz, were developed, partly for use in the fast-expanding commercial orchards.[30] With growing concern about the proliferation and variability of rootstocks, and about the particular susceptibility of some to disease, there was much discussion about how this range might be limited and rationalised, and in 1871 the Superintendent of the Royal Horticultural Society's Chiswick garden, Archibald Barron, set up an apple rootstock trial, looking at the characteristics of 18 different types.[31] But it was only in the early years of the twentieth century that a number of improved, more disease-resistant rootstocks were developed, recognised and standardised at the East Malling Research Station in Kent ('M' rootstocks), latterly in conjunction with the John Innes Institute, then based in Merton ('MM' rootstocks). Apple rootstocks M1–M16 (with M1–M9 originally referred to as Malling Types I–IX) were issued between 1912 and 1914 and M17–M24 in 1924. Further releases occurred over subsequent decades, with MM116 appearing as recently as 2001. Many of these rootstocks remain in use, variously producing dwarfing, semi-dwarfing and vigorous trees: among the most popular are 'MM106' and 'M25', which produce small, semi-dwarf trees and tall vigorous ones, respectively.[32]

Pears were originally grafted onto wild pear rootstocks but, increasingly, from at least the late seventeenth century, onto rootstocks of quince.[33] Most cherries, plums and other fruit are similarly grafted, on rootstocks selected for their suitability for the location in question, although some, such as greengages, can be grown 'true' from seed. In the field, the old graft – where the scion wood was originally fixed to the young rootstock – is usually visible low down on the tree, as a line separating barks of slightly different colour or texture. But mature trees could also be 'top-grafted': branches could be removed and new scion wood inserted, instantly creating a mature tree bearing a new variety of fruit.

Although rootstocks have a critical influence on the 'vigour' of a tree – how fast and how tall it will grow – this is, and was, also a consequence of the variety of the graft, especially in the case of apples. Some apple varieties, including several well-known ones, such as Blenheim Orange or Bramley's Seedling, are triploids. That is, rather than each cell having two sets of chromosomes, inherited from the father and mother, as is usually the case ('diploids'), they have three.[34] Most triploids exhibit particularly vigorous growth,

---

30 P. Blackburne-Maze, *The Apple Book* (London, 1986), pp. 45–9. In practice, most were described as types of 'paradise' stock.

31 Blackburne-Maze, *Apple Book*, pp. 48–9.

32 R. Sanders, *The Apple Book* (London, 2010), p. 158.

33 As at Wrest Park in Bedfordshire in 1693: BRO, L/31/295.

34 H.V. Taylor, *The Apples of England* (London, 1948), pp. 39–42.

almost independent of the rootstock. Bramley's Seedling, for example (for many decades our most popular cooking apple) always towers above neighbouring trees in an orchard, even when grafted onto a semi-dwarfing rootstock.

Triploids have another characteristic, although one shared with many diploid varieties. They are not usually self-fertile, and therefore require another similar variety to pollinate them, one that comes into blossom at the same time. Indeed, even self-fertile varieties generally do better in the presence of a compatible partner, one that flowers in the same season and is thus, in the parlance of horticulturalists, in the same 'pollination group'. Many of the large commercial orchards that developed in the nineteenth and twentieth centuries contained extensive blocks of varieties unable to pollinate themselves effectively, such as Bramley's Seedling or Cox's Orange Pippin. They were thus interplanted with a smaller number of pollinators (often, in both cases, Worcester Pearmain).

To maximise production, fruit trees were and are pruned: that is, the growth is cut back in a selective manner. Pruning is a complex business and, once again, only the essentials (already familiar to many readers) are relevant to our main theme. Of particular importance is the 'formative pruning' used to shape the tree in a manner that will increase the number of fruit-bearing limbs, make it easier to pick the fruit, prevent trees overshadowing neighbours and (in modern commercial orchards) facilitate spraying.[35] This takes place when the tree is young – it can begin before it has been planted out in the orchard – and is a rigorous process: 'It is usually necessary to prune standards very hard in the first few years of life in order to obtain the right sort of growth. The aim should be a symmetrical, well-balanced tree.'[36] Sometimes the intention was to create various types of 'standard' tree – the kinds of tall, spreading form typical of farmhouse orchards. But, in other contexts, it might be directed towards the production of 'half-standards', in which there is a shorter trunk, or 'bush' trees, where the branches rise from a short bole, less than a metre high. All are the consequence of carefully selecting what to cut and remove and what to retain. In particular, upward growth can be restricted by removing the leading shoot, directing growth into 'scaffolding branches', while further cutting back of these, just above an outward-facing bud, will produce a new branch growing away from the tree.

In some standard trees pruning was simply used to ensure the dominance of the 'leader', thus ensuring a tall trunk from which side branches rose at intervals. But sometimes the tree was pruned so that the main branches all grew from the same point, pollard-like; this is a style widely found in farmhouse orchards but also in commercial cherry orchards, for cherry trees grow with particular vigour, making harvesting difficult if they are not carefully pruned. A variant of this form of pruning was the 'open centre' system, adopted in many commercial orchards:

---

35   R. Bush, *Tree Fruit Growing*, vol. 1 (London, 1951), pp. 101–20.

36   A.H. Hoare, *The English Grass Orchard and the Principles of Fruit Growing* (London, 1928), p. 117.

Figure 1.4 Upwell, Norfolk. A typical example of a 'bush'-pruned, open-centred Bramley's Seedling tree, of the kind characteristic of the older commercial orchards in the Fens.

> [It] involves the removal of all crossing branches and the keeping of the centres more or less free from growth. This last-mentioned type of tree has many advantages. Its airy, uncrowded condition makes for greater natural freedom from disease, and it is certainly more easily sprayed than a crowded, unpruned tree.[37]

This type of pruning was often applied to trees of 'bush' form, especially in the commercial orchards of the Norfolk and Cambridgeshire Fenland. Here, low-growing forms were probably favoured because of the prevalence of vigorous Bramley's Seedling trees, which, if grown as standards, might be toppled by high winds in this open landscape of damp soils (Figure 1.4). But, as in other contexts, the presence of low-branching trees also reflects the fact that these orchards were not usually grazed by livestock, just as the long stems of 'standard' trees indicates that they were planted in areas which were so used, typically farmhouse orchards. Indeed, in general terms different kinds of pruning were the result of decisions based on a range of such practical considerations – how the orchard was used, the local environment and the type of tree. But it was also a function of the intensity of

---

37 Hoare, *Grass Orchard*, p. 120.

management. The farmer, for whom the orchard was a source of fruit for the household and for whom the money made from the sale of any surplus constituted only one part of his income, usually had less time to spend on intensive pruning than the manager of a commercial concern whose main focus was on fruit production.

This was even more true of the kind of routine pruning that was continued after the 'formative' stage had passed. Pruning was, and is, now directed towards the maintenance of the overall 'architecture' established in the early years, by getting rid of any developing branches which threaten to disturb or distort it, as well as towards the removal of basal 'water shoots' and any limbs that are dead or diseased. Moreover, production can be increased by trimming away the flat, scaly buds that develop into foliage, leaving the rounder and furry buds growing on the offshoots or 'spurs', which will develop into fruit. In more general terms, regularly thinning the tree increases the proportion of branches exposed to the sun, encouraging blossom and thus the amount of fruit produced, helping the fruit to ripen and increasing the circulation of air and thus, perhaps, reducing the impact of pathogens. In the case of older trees, pruning also serves to reduce the weight of branches and the pressure on the trunk, preventing loss of limbs or even the collapse of the tree.[38] While pruning was thus an important aspect of management, however, it should be emphasised that – at least for some varieties of some types of fruit – regular 'maintenance' pruning was and is by no means essential. Many apples, in particular, if growing in favourable conditions and not over-shadowed by neighbours, and if suitably pollinated, will continue to crop abundantly, year after year, even if left completely to their own devices. One of the authors owns the remains of a small orchard in which the old apple trees have not been pruned for at least 25 years, but still crop profusely. This said, inadequate pruning of old trees can render them more susceptible to wind damage.

In gardens, trees on paradise stocks (and sometimes others) were also pruned, but often in such a way that they grew in a single plane, against a wall or on a frame of wire. Sometimes they took the form of a 'fan', with branches rising and spreading from a low point, not far above the ground; sometimes they were 'espaliers', with a straight vertical stem supporting a series of neatly parallel, horizontal branches. In commercial orchards, where the use of dwarfing rootstocks became steadily more important from the late nineteenth century, trees might be similarly trained, or rigorously pruned to form 'pyramids' in which the main leader was dominant and, moving up the tree, the radiating branches decreased in size to produce a narrow 'Christmas tree' form, with the lowest little more than 40cm above ground level. Compact trees were attractive to commercial growers because they could be closely spaced and the fruit was easy to pick but, for obvious reasons, they made it impossible to use the orchard as a place to keep livestock. Other compact forms were developed in the middle decades of the twentieth century, such as 'cordons', in which regular pruning maintains the tree as a single low-growing trunk with very short

---

38   Hoare, *Grass Orchard*; Morgan and Richards, *New Book of Apples*, pp. 293–8.

side branches; 'spindle' forms, similar but as much as 2m in height, were widely adopted in commercial orchards from the 1970s.

Mapping orchards in Eastern England

Most people would not associate orchards and fruit growing with the eastern counties, and think instead of Devon, Somerset, Gloucestershire, Herefordshire and Worcestershire in the west of England, and Kent in the south-east, as the classic 'orchard counties'. But government statistics present a more complex and perhaps surprising picture. In 1871, when the earliest official agricultural surveys recorded the density of orchards in each county, the prominence of these western areas was indeed marked. But over the following decades the gap between east and west narrowed significantly and, by the post-war period, was much less noticeable (Figure 1.5). We shall, in Chapter 3, explore the character and the causes of this expansion, and in Chapter 6 chart the contraction of fruit growing in the east after *c*.1960, which returned some of the western counties – and, to a lesser extent, Kent – to their position of primacy. But we should also note that in all periods county averages tend to obscure the details of localised clusters of orchards, and that even in 1871 some districts in the east, such as the Fens around Wisbech or parts of south Bedfordshire, could boast densities as great as any in England. Indeed, the principal reason why the east of England makes such a good area to study the history of orchards is precisely because their numbers, and also their character, not only displayed marked changes over time but also significant variations from area to area. This makes it possible to examine with some degree of granularity the kinds of factor that gave particular encouragement to their development.

Yet it is surprisingly difficult to map the distribution of orchards across the whole of the eastern counties at an individual level, even for quite recent periods. Tithe apportionments and their associated maps – drawn up under the terms of the tithe commutation act of 1836, and mainly dating to the period 1838–42 – are available for the majority of parishes in the region, although with some significant *lacunae*, especially in areas affected by large-scale parliamentary enclosure during the previous decades.[39] Tithe apportionments were essentially surveys of land use, made to assist in the commutation of tithes to fixed rental payments, but in the eastern counties they do not systematically record orchards. This is in marked contrast to the situation in counties such as Devon or Herefordshire, where 'orchard' is regularly employed as a land-use category in the 'State of Cultivation' column, alongside 'arable', 'pasture', 'wood' and so on. The difference reflects the fact that, in general, orchards were of much greater economic importance in the west than in the east of England, where orchards were instead categorised in terms of their other main productive function, as 'meadow' or 'pasture'. As we shall see, there are some parishes in the eastern counties where 'western' practice was followed, but they are fairly few in number. The apportionments do, however, sometimes include 'orchard' in the 'Description of Lands and

---

39 R.J.P. Kain and H. Prince, *The Tithe Surveys of England and Wales* (Cambridge, 2006).

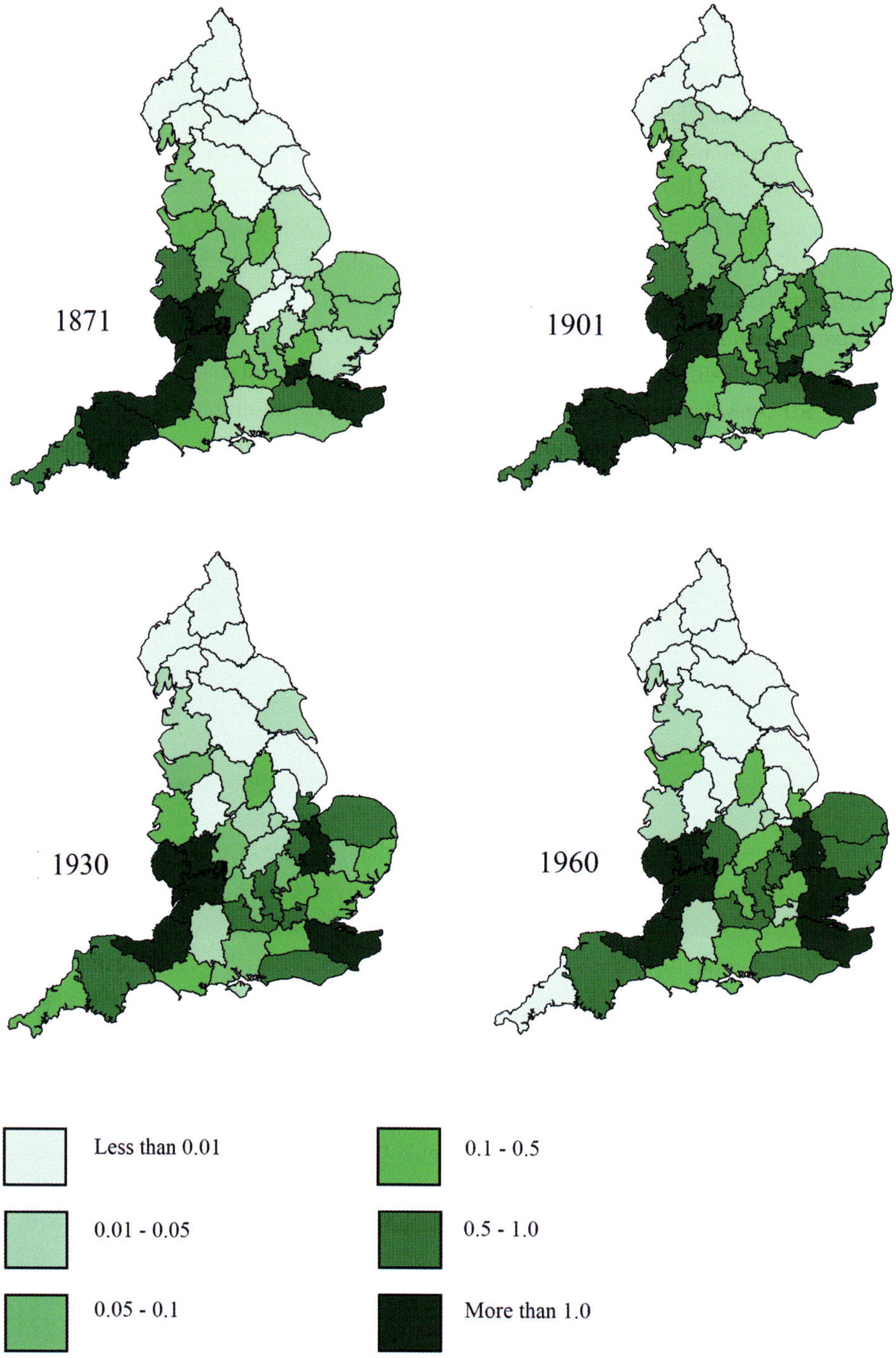

Figure 1.5 Orchards as a percentage of county area, from the Agricultural Census. The figures omit unproductive and domestic orchards and those on holdings of less than an acre. Between c.1870 and 1960 the relative importance of fruit growing in the eastern counties increased steadily.

Orchards, landscapes and history 17

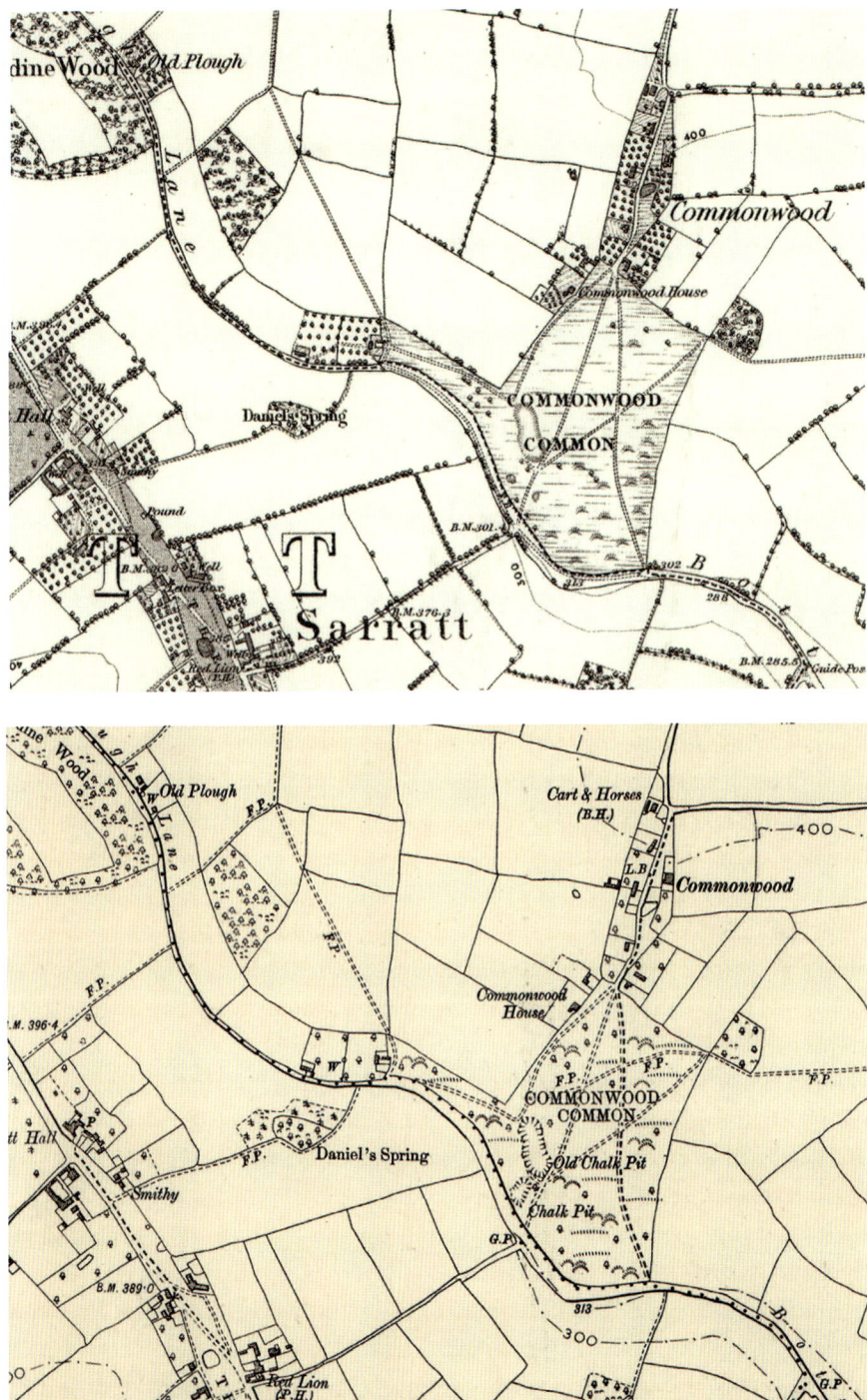

Figure 1.6 Sarratt, Hertfordshire. The depiction of orchards on the Ordnance Survey first edition 6-inch map (1870s), and on the second edition (1897). The orchards are shown more schematically on the latter, as they are on subsequent revisions of the OS maps, and are easier to distinguish from other forms of planting.

Figure 1.7 The distribution of orchards in eastern England in c.1900, based on the Ordnance Survey second edition 6-inch maps. Note the concentrations of commercial orchards on the Norfolk–Cambridgeshire border; in central and south Cambridgeshire; and, less distinctly, in west Hertfordshire and south-west Bedfordshire. Significant clusters can also be discerned in south-east Hertfordshire and south-east Essex.

Premises' column, as the name for or description of an individual parcel – comparable to the names given to individual fields – but it is unclear, in the case of particular parishes, how consistently this was done, or how many orchards might be subsumed within vague descriptors such as 'yard', 'close' or 'garden &c'. The tithe documents can, therefore, sometimes be used to ascertain the numbers and distribution of orchards within some parishes, albeit with varying degrees of confidence, but not to map the distribution of orchards across the region as a whole in the middle decades of the nineteenth century.

The Ordnance Survey 1:10,560 (6-inch) and 1:25,000 (25-inch) maps are much more comprehensive in their coverage and demonstrably depict orchards down to a size of less than 0.1 acres (0.04 hectares). The first editions of these maps, dating to the late nineteenth century, cannot easily be used to map the distribution of orchards across the whole of eastern England, however. This is in part because they were surveyed gradually, so that in some districts the maps date from as early as 1864 and in others to as late as 1886; and in part because these excellent surveys attempted to represent every individual tree present in the landscape above sapling size, with the result that it can be difficult to distinguish between orchards and other relatively regular areas of planting. The second edition 6-inch and 25-inch maps, however, were mainly surveyed over a shorter period – between 1895 and 1905 – and depict orchards schematically and more clearly, with tree symbols arranged in an artificially regular grid (Figure 1.6). Figure 1.7 is thus based on the second edition Ordnance Survey 6-inch and 25-inch maps. It was meticulously compiled by the various county Local Environmental Record Centres, with resources from the Heritage Fund – a monumental undertaking. It provides a reasonably accurate picture of the general distribution of orchards as this was around the turn of the twentieth century.

But here we must emphasise something that we noted at the outset. Not all orchards were, or are, the same. Firstly, the overall scatter Figure 1.7 depicts is made up, for the most part, of small domestic orchards attached to farms, parsonages and other middle-class residences. These produced not only food for the household, including residential servants – whether this was eaten immediately, raw or cooked, or stored for later use – but also, on most farms, a surplus for sale in local markets. Domestic orchards, that is, represented one of several income streams exploited by the farmer, although generally one that was less valuable than livestock or arable crops.

Secondly, a small proportion of the orchards mapped were associated with country houses – the homes of the landed gentry or great aristocrats – and were often larger, and contained a more diverse range of fruit. A few still formed important parts of the pleasure gardens, as had usually been the case a century and a half earlier. Country house orchards, although never as numerous as those associated with farms, have a considerable cultural significance and are also among the best documented in the historical record. They will thus be afforded extended treatment in Chapter 4, together with another broad type. Institutional orchards may be defined as those associated with places such as workhouses, colleges and psychiatric hospitals, and which supplied the food required by their residents. They were never very numerous but have survived, in relative terms, rather well, and today account for some of the most impressive and extensive orchards remaining in eastern England.

Thirdly, and overlapping and merging to a significant extent with farmhouse orchards, were commercial orchards: that is, those that formed the main business, or a major part of the business, of their owner or tenant. These account for the noticeable clusters on the map, as well as many of the sites constituting the more diffuse background scatter. The concentrations in Cambridgeshire and the Fens are immediately obvious, but those in western Hertfordshire and south Bedfordshire are also clear; rather less dense clusters in south-east Hertfordshire and south-east Essex can also be discerned. It is sometimes suggested, or implied, that commercial orchards are recent additions to the landscape and of little importance in terms of history or biodiversity but, as Figure 1.7 shows, in all these districts a major fruit-growing industry had become established by the end of the nineteenth century. Moreover, orchards of this kind planted at a later date, in the course of the twentieth century, also form a part of our landscape history. Much of Chapter 3 is thus concerned with how commercial fruit growing expanded in the period after 1900.

Charting this later history in spatial terms poses a number of problems. No source comparable to the second edition 6-inch and 25-inch Ordnance Survey maps exists that allows us to comprehensively map the distribution of orchards across the eastern counties at any later date. The various revisions made to these maps over the following half-century, while adopting the same convention for showing orchards, were produced for different areas at intervals too varied to allow roughly contemporary distributions across the entire region to be plotted. In urban or other rapidly changing areas revisions might be frequent, and for much of the region studied here, even the more rural parts, several revised maps were produced between 1937 and 1950. But for small but significant parts of Eastern England the maps were revised only once, in some cases as early as 1920, and occasionally not at all: parts of south Suffolk, and much of Essex, are especially poorly served in this respect. Moreover, in the 1930s and 1940s the Ordnance Survey made only selected revisions before republication, and it is unclear whether these included details of orchards. Although the smaller-scale 1:25,000 (2½-inch) Ordnance Survey maps for the eastern counties were all published within a few years of each other, in the late 1940s and 1950s, these are likewise difficult to use to plot the distribution of orchards. They were surveyed at too small a scale to include many of the more diminutive domestic examples. More importantly, they were not the result of a comprehensive remapping of the country but were instead compiled from earlier surveys and revisions made at 1:10,560 (6-inch) scale, updated to varying extents with the help of aerial photographs. As a result:

> The 1:25,000 maps reflect quite different sources of information from different dates, often on the same sheet, reflecting their terminology as a 'Provisional edition'. For more populated areas where the larger-scale National Grid survey had taken place, the latest, more detailed six-inch to the mile mapping could be used, photographically reducing detail down to 1:25,000. For other areas, the best available source mapping could be decades earlier, supplemented by less detailed map sources, including Second World War bomb-damage surveys, and military and road mapping in the 1940s.[40]

These later maps – the various revisions of the 1:10,560 and the 1:25,000 series – can be used to chart the changing distributions of orchards within limited areas of the eastern counties, but not across the region as a whole. We should also note that the maps produced by the Land Utilisation Survey of the 1930s and 1940s – so useful a source for many purposes – are similarly of limited use for plotting the distribution of orchards, as the earliest of these maps placed them in a single, undifferentiated category with gardens and market gardens.[41] We can, however, use all these sources, together with the agricultural

---

40   National Library of Scotland, 'Ordnance Survey, 1:25,000 maps of Great Britain (Regular series) – 1937–1961', <https://maps.nls.uk/os/25k-gb-1937–61/info1.html>, accessed 20 May 2020.

41   L. Dudley Stamp, *The Land of Britain: Its Use and Misuse* (London, 1948), p. 113.

statistics regularly published by the government in the course of the twentieth century, to obtain a broad, overall view of how the numbers and extent of orchards in eastern England have developed up to the present day.

Contexts: environment and geography

In order to understand how orchards developed over time – and, in particular, why certain areas of the eastern counties came to have a significant fruit-growing industry while others did not – we need to first examine briefly the wider landscape and environmental contexts in which orchards developed, and to identify the kinds of conditions that favoured, or discouraged, the successful cultivation of fruit. The region has the most Continental climate in the United Kingdom, with warm summers but often cold winters, and with low overall precipitation, especially in the summer months. Only in a few areas – western Hertfordshire, parts of north and central Norfolk – does average precipitation exceed 800mm and in much of the Fenland of Cambridgeshire and Norfolk, in south-east Suffolk and in eastern Essex it is less than 600mm.[42] This is important, because fruit trees will not thrive in ground that is regularly waterlogged. But extremes, rather than averages, were the key factor limiting fruit cultivation. Indeed, the extent to which the fruit crop was precarious must always be remembered, and explains why in many contexts orchards formed only one part of the owner's (or tenant's) income stream. Warm, sunny summers provided ideal conditions for ripening fruit but spring and summer droughts could affect the harvest and, if severe, could damage the fruit crop in a variety of ways, some quite unexpected. In April 1685 Sir John Wittewronge of Rothamsted in Hertfordshire recorded in his diary:

> This May there was a very fine bloom of Apples etc but the great drought brought such an exceeding many caterpillars (the most ever remembered) that there is like to be little or no fruit, they eat up not only apple leaves and other fruit but some Oaks also.[43]

Further problems came in June, in the form of 'thunder showers on the 27th which with the caterpillars spoyled all our apples, peares and other orchard fruit'.[44] High winds at blossom time could also ruin the crop – in May 1687 Sir John recorded how, after a late start, by 'the first weeke in May both Apple blossom and other things came forwards amain, & before the middle of May there was the greatest bloome of Apples that ever I saw in my Orchards

---

42 D. Wheeler and J. Mayer (eds), *The Regional Climates of the British Isles* (London, 1997); E. Barrow and M. Hulme, 'Describing the Surface Climate of the British Isles', in M. Hulme and E. Barrow (eds), *Climates of the British Isles, Past, Present and Future* (London, 1997), pp. 33–61; <www.metoffice.gov.uk/climate>, accessed October 2019.

43 M.H. Williams and J. Stevenson (eds), *'Observations of Weather': The Weather Diary of Sir John Wittewronge of Rothamsted 1684–1680,* Hertfordshire Record Society 15 (Hertford, 1999), p. 18.

44 Williams and Stevenson, *'Observations of Weather'*, p. 20.

but were much damnifyed by the extream tempestuous winds the 11th and 12th instant'.[45] But the most serious threat was, and is, posed by late frosts, which can damage blossom and, in extreme cases, reduce yields to nothing.

To a significant extent, any problems posed by climate could be ameliorated by choosing the right site for planting, a topic to which writers from the seventeenth century onwards devoted much attention. In particular, every effort had to be made to avoid 'frost pockets', such as those which might develop in deep and narrow valleys: 'Let the fruit planter look first for open country, as valleys are a snare for the unwary'.[46] This was less of a problem in the eastern counties than in many parts of England. Extensive tracts of land, especially in the Fens, were dead level, while elsewhere the topography is for the most part gently undulating. Only in parts of Essex and Hertfordshire, and especially in the west of the latter county, do deep valleys which regularly act as frost pockets occur, and a cursory perusal of the maps soon reveals that these were simply avoided by planters. Climatic factors were also mediated by soils and geology, subjects to which writers on fruit cultivation have also paid much attention. Heavy, poorly draining clays were not good for fruit trees, because of problems of waterlogging, unless they lay on sloping ground; in the twentieth century drainage in such situations might be further improved by using pipe drains. In contrast, chalky soils, or those formed in sands or gravels, were too freely draining, leading to the possibility of summer drought. They also tended to leach nutrients rapidly, leading to attacks of chlorosis that could seriously reduce yields. Nevertheless, such soils are easy to cultivate and there was general agreement that sandy soils, at least, could be used to grow fruit, provided the right steps were taken, such as applying potash to remedy potassium deficiency.[47]

Loams – that is, silty soils intermediate in consistency between sands and clays – have long been considered the best growing medium. Arthur Hoare in 1928, for example, recommended a 'strong, even-tempered and good-holding loam'. A light, sandy clay might also be suitable, if it were 'not over-cold nor wet – i.e. waterlogged'.[48] The Hertfordshire farmer and agricultural writer William Ellis even suggested in 1732 that some clays – he had in mind the sandy clays of the Chiltern dipslope – made the best ground for orchards.[49] The ideal conditions, however, were found where loams or light clays overlay some freely draining substrate. In the 1920s Hoare thus advised the would-be grower to look for planting sites 'in the neighbourhood of chalk', although not actually on it.[50] Loamy, water-retentive soils overlying other permeable formations, such as the Upper or Lower Greensand, were also recommended. In such locations fruit trees could be

---

45   Williams and Stevenson, 'Observations of Weather', p. 47.

46   Hoare, *Grass Orchard*, p. 28.

47   N.B. Bagenal (ed.), *Fruit Growing* (London, 1939), pp. 27–31.

48   Hoare, *Grass Orchard*, p. 45.

49   W. Ellis, *The Practical Farmer or Hertfordshire Husbandman* (London, 1732), p. 104.

50   *Grass Orchard*, p. 37.

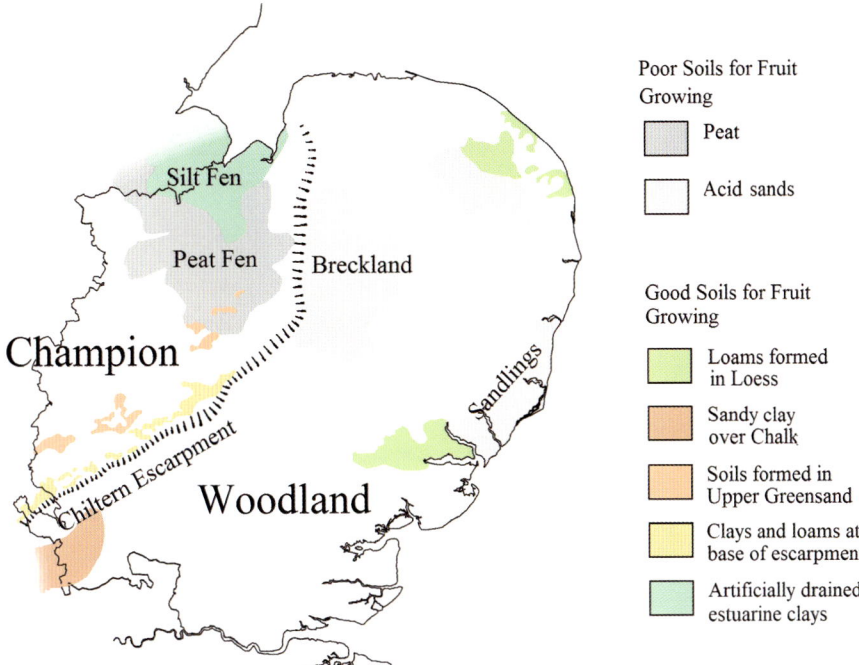

Figure 1.8 Eastern England, showing features and areas discussed in the text: the chalk escarpment, soils particularly suitable and unsuitable for fruit-growing, and 'Woodland' and 'Champion' areas.

assured sufficient water for summer growth, but the porous nature of the underlying geology guarded against waterlogging. All the main kinds of fruit tree benefited from such conditions, but the cherry to the greatest extent because it is 'a surface rooting tree', prone to suffer from both excess water and 'from a too-rapid drying out of soil moisture'.[51] Plums, in contrast, flourished when planted on rather heavier soils, 'fairly heavy calcareous loams', although again where these overlay a porous substrate. Apples and pears also did well in such circumstances.[52]

The eastern counties provide a number of these desired locations (Figure 1.8). The geology of the region is dominated by the long chalk escarpment of the Chiltern Hills and their more muted continuation to the north-east, the 'East Anglian Heights', which together run in a gentle curve all the way from Hertfordshire and south Bedfordshire to west Norfolk.[53] Immediately to the north and west lies a wide but intermittent band of calcareous loams and clays, varying in width, formed by glacial weathering of the chalk

---

51 Hoare, *Grass Orchard*, p. 41.
52 Hoare, *Grass Orchard*, p. 42.
53 J.R. Lee, M.A. Woods and B.S.P. Moorlock, *British Regional Geology: East Anglia and Adjoining Areas*, 5th edn (London, 2015); J. Catt (ed.), *Hertfordshire Geology and Landscape* (Welwyn, 2010).

escarpment and the later deposits lying above it. These overlie permeable rocks – earlier chalk formations or patches of Upper Greensand – and the conditions thus provided encouraged, in particular, the development of the commercial orchards of south Cambridgeshire and south Bedfordshire. Beyond this band of amenable soils, further to the north and west, the hills and vales of Bedfordshire and western Cambridgeshire are dominated by Jurassic clays, overlain by glacial boulder clay. However, a discontinuous band of light, slightly acidic soils overlying the Lower Greensand formation runs, roughly parallel with the chalk escarpment, from the Greensand Ridge in Bedfordshire to the southern edge of the great basin of the Fens, continuing on to the islands of high ground within the Fens, especially around Stretham, Haddenham and Ely. These locations, as we shall see, also afforded opportunities for profitable fruit growing.

The Fens themselves, which account for a substantial portion of eastern England, are divided geologically into two very different areas. To the south, the Fen basin is filled with peat, and this area largely remained as waterlogged common land until it was enclosed and reclaimed in the course of the post-medieval period. Here conditions were too acidic and the soils too unstable for orchards to flourish, except on the 'islands' of high ground just noted. To the north, however, the basin is characterised by silts and clays that were largely under cultivation by the thirteenth century. The strong loams to which they give rise do not overlie permeable rocks and lie at or below sea level, but orchards could nevertheless be protected against serious waterlogging by the complex network of drainage ditches, connected by mechanical pumps to the arterial channels. The district around Wisbech still remains the most important fruit-growing area in eastern England.

To the south and east of the Chiltern escarpment the chalk slopes away and is, for the most part, buried beneath later deposits, Tertiary or Quaternary in age. In west Hertfordshire these take the form of the sandy clays usually termed 'clay-with-flint', ensuring loamy soils with good drainage at depth. The area around St Albans and Hemel Hempstead became, at an early date, important for its cherry orchards. Elsewhere much of the land is occupied by soils less congenial for fruit growing – the heavy boulder clays of east Hertfordshire, north-west Essex, central Suffolk and south Norfolk, and the waterlogged and acidic London clays of south Hertfordshire and south-east Essex. Yet even here areas of loamy soils or light clays with reasonable drainage can be found – as, for example, in the valleys cutting through these clay deposits, or in parts of east Norfolk or north-east Essex, where Pleistocene Loess overlies freely draining Crag.

More details of soils and geology will be given in the pages that follow, when particular fruit-growing districts are discussed in more detail. But we must be careful not to place too much emphasis on natural factors, on soils, drainage and climate, in investigating the history of orchards. When nineteenth- and twentieth-century writers such as Hoare discussed the best places for planting they did so with commercial rather than domestic production in mind. While environmental conditions might be critical where the maximisation of profit was the main concern, fruit trees – especially apples and pears –

will produce a reasonable crop on most soils, and most farms had an orchard attached. As William Ellis put it in 1754, ostensibly quoting a West Country correspondent, orchards were best planted on soils comprising 'a deep and fat Earth, not a stiff cold Clay, or binding Gravel, or a light, sandy or hollow Earth; yet with good Husbandry, if it run not into the Extremes of any of these, Fruit-Trees may prosper reasonably well in it'.[54] To a large extent, the distribution of orchards shown on Figure 1.7 thus simply reflects the distribution of farms and patterns of settlement. It was only the clusters of commercial orchards that, to a significant extent, were structured by environmental circumstances particularly conducive to fruit growing. But even the distribution and chronology of these specialised areas cannot be explained entirely in terms of environmental influences. Other factors, economic, technological or institutional in character and only tangentially related to the environment, were also crucial.

As we shall see, before the twentieth century orchards were more likely to be planted by small landowners than by large, and by freeholders or those holding on long leases than by those suffering insecurity of tenure. It was also impossible to plant fruit trees on any scale on common land, or where properties comprised numerous small unhedged strips in 'open fields' that were subject to rights of communal grazing. Enclosure was a precondition of large-scale fruit production. In fact, settlement patterns, landholding systems and enclosure history were intimately connected. If we ignore the Fens – reclaimed and drained at varying times in the medieval and post-medieval periods – the landscape of the eastern counties can in broad terms be divided into two, the line of separation roughly following that of the chalk escarpment (Figure 1.8). On the escarpment itself, and across most of the extensive tract of land lying to the north and west, lay 'champion' countryside. From early medieval times farms were concentrated in large nucleated villages and their arable land took the form of numerous small, unhedged strips, which lay intermingled with those of neighbours and scattered across two or three great 'fields'. Farming was governed by strongly communal routines, administered by a village assembly or manorial court, which also regulated the management of any areas of common grazing and meadow land. In such circumstances orchards could be established only on the limited area of land attached to the farmstead itself – the 'toft' – within the village. In the open fields the village livestock, grazing together after the harvest or when the land lay fallow, would have made short work of any young trees established on individual strips, while on the common land grazing pressure was continuous.[55]

---

54 W. Ellis, *The Compleat Cyderman: Or, the Present Practice of Raising Plantations of the Best Cyder Apple and Perry Pear-Trees* (London, 1754), p. 14.

55 G.C. Homans, *English Villagers of the Thirteenth Century* (Cambridge, MA, 1941), p. 21; Rackham, *History of the Countryside*, pp. 164–79; B. Roberts and S. Wrathmell, *An Atlas of Rural Settlement in England* (London, 2000); T. Williamson, R. Liddiard and T. Partida, *Champion. The Making and Unmaking of the English Midland Landscape* (Exeter, 2012).

Open fields and associated commons began to disappear – to be converted into consolidated blocks of private property, free from communal regulations – from the late fourteenth century. They continued to be enclosed, at varying rates in different districts, over the following centuries. Nevertheless, around half of the 'champion' land in the eastern counties still remained open until the advent of enclosure by parliamentary act in the eighteenth century simplified and accelerated the process. Indeed, a surprising number of parishes remained unenclosed into the mid-, or even late, nineteenth century, and these were particularly numerous on the kinds of loamy soil found at the base of the chalk escarpment, or over the Lower Greensand, where orchards were later to expand. These reasonably fertile and easily worked loams often featured villages with higher proportions of small landowners than those lying in the neighbouring clay vales, individuals for whom enclosure brought relatively few benefits and significant costs. These were also the kinds of people for whom, once enclosure had been accomplished and if the environmental and economic circumstances were right, commercial fruit growing was an attractive option.

To the south and east of the chalk escarpment rather different landscapes could be found, the transition between the two sharp towards the south-east, in Hertfordshire and Essex, and more gradual – comprising a broad transitional zone – moving north into Suffolk and Norfolk. This extensive area was characterised by 'Woodland' countryside, to use the term often employed by early modern writers. Here, settlement was more dispersed or scattered than in the 'champion' lands to the north and west and, although compact villages could be found, many farms and cottages stood alone, were strung irregularly along roads, clustered in small hamlets or scattered around the margins of greens and commons. In some areas, much or most of the farmland lay from earliest times in hedged closes, fully in the control of individual proprietors; only areas of common grazing were subject to communal regulation. Elsewhere, the medieval landscape comprised a complex mixture of small open fields and hedged closes, but the former tended to disappear at an early date through informal, 'piecemeal' enclosure. By the eighteenth century the areas lying to the south and east of the Chiltern escarpment were mainly landscapes of hedged fields.[56]

Patterns of settlement, systems of landholding and the character of field systems had an important influence on the development and distribution of orchards. But in the emergence of specialised fruit-growing districts of greater significance was the existence of a nearby market, or good transport links to one. There was no point in growing a surplus of fruit for sale if it rotted before reaching its destination. This issue will be treated in more detail in subsequent chapters, but suffice to say at this stage that the eighteenth, nineteenth and twentieth centuries witnessed a steady growth in urban markets and progressive improvements in transport systems. At the end of the seventeenth century

---

56 E. Martin and M. Satchell, *Wheare Most Inclosures Be. East Anglian Fields, History, Morphology and Management*, East Anglian Archaeology 124 (Ipswich, 2008); T. Williamson, *Environment, Society and Landscape in Early Medieval England* (Woodbridge, 2013), pp. 125–47.

Norwich was still the second largest city in the country, with a population approaching 30,000.[57] While the principal county towns, and the ports of King's Lynn and Yarmouth, were also significant places, none could boast populations exceeding 10,000. All were dwarfed by London, lying outside the region but within a few kilometres of its southern boundary, which by 1700 already had a population of well over half a million. While the towns and cities of the eastern counties certainly represented from an early date important markets for agricultural produce, including fruit, London was clearly in a league of its own. But in the course of the eighteenth and nineteenth centuries markets on a similar scale emerged in the industrial areas of the Midlands and north of England, far from the eastern counties. Moving ripe fruit any distance along poor roads was beset with problems and the first districts to engage in large-scale commercial production were thus located where suitable soils lay within easy reach of either London or a major port with good access to these more distant markets. The development of the canal network in the second half of the eighteenth century had little impact on the eastern counties, and transport by narrow boat was anyway slow. But, as we shall see, the arrival of the railways revolutionised fruit transport, allowing access to key markets in the main areas of industrial growth. This led to a marked expansion of commercial orchards in eastern England and the appearance of entirely new areas of specialised fruit production.

---

57 P. Corfield, 'From Second City to Regional Capital', in C. Rawcliffe and R. Wilson (eds), *Norwich Since 1550* (London, 2004), pp. 139–66, at p. 142.

CHAPTER TWO

Farmhouse and commercial orchards before c.1850

The ubiquity of farm orchards

The dense 'background' scatter of orchards apparent almost everywhere in Figure 1.7 was not a recent development. Even a cursory examination of maps and documents shows that by the sixteenth and seventeenth centuries orchards could be found almost everywhere in the eastern counties. They were a normal feature of the farms of yeomen and husbandmen, while smaller groups of fruit trees were regularly associated with lowly cottages. Even in the Middle Ages an orchard appears to have been a standard feature of a yeoman's farm. In 1386, for example, John Coppyng granted William Draper a 'Messuage and 12 acres, with buildings, orchard, hedges' in Hockering in Norfolk; at Great Melton in the same county in 1391 there is a reference to a tenement with 'orchard and garden and 1 rood'; while at South Elmham in Suffolk an 'apple orchard' is mentioned in a document from 1322.[1] Indeed, the formulaic wording of many post-medieval legal documents betrays an underlying assumption that no house of significant size would lack a collection of fruit trees. In 1574, for example, the manor of Abbots Ripton in Huntingdonshire was granted with '40 messuages, 20 cottages, 60 tofts, 2 dovehouses, 60 gardens, 60 orchards'; a deed of 1656 refers to 'three messuages, three gardens and three orchards … in Wetheringsett and Brockford' in Suffolk; while one from Brent Eleigh in the same county, from 1670, refers to '2 messuages, 2 gardens, 2 orchards'. Many more such examples exist.[2]

Orchards, the trees they contained and the fruit they produced appear in the documentary record in a multiplicity of contexts. When early modern farmers drew up their wills they left their farms to their sons, or sons-in-law, but also made provision for their widows, which frequently included a proportion of fruit from the orchard. Sometimes heirs were left with the task of devising an equitable division, as in the case of Henry Hyde of Eccles, in Norfolk; his will, drawn up in 1592, instructed his wife and son-in-law to 'parte the fruite that shalbe growing in my backhouse yarde at Hempstead'.[3] In 1597 John Battell

---

1 NRO, EVL 189, 455X1; EVL 396/2, 461X4; MC 44/63, 500X3; Sheffield City Archives BFM/1232.

2 G.J. Turner (ed.), *A Calendar of the Feet of Fines relating to the County of Huntingdon, levied in the King's Court from the Fifth Year of Richard I. to the End of the Reign of Elizabeth, 1194–1603* (Cambridge, 1913), p. 175; SRO, I, HD 1538/151/13; SRO, B, 1754/1/124.

3 NRO, NCC Will Register Apleyarde 411.

of Eastwood in Essex left to his wife 'during her widowhood, yearly out of my orchard six bushels of the best apples, if they be growing there'; while the will drawn up in the following year by William Baker of Great Chishall in the far north of the same county (and now in Cambridgeshire) left to Alice his wife 'the use of my twist [intertwined] walnut tree in my garden' and allowed her to take nuts from the orchard and to 'choose 2 of the apple trees in my orchard and gather the apples'.[4] Orchard fruit featured as elements in rental payments and similar agreements not only in the Middle Ages, as at Wood Norton in Norfolk in 1290,[5] but also, on occasions, into the eighteenth century. In 1701 part of the payment for a piece of land in Downham Market in Norfolk comprised '3 lbs. potatoes and the fruit of three fruit-trees each year to Thomas Buckingham and his wife for their lives'.[6] Evidently, most farmers would have agreed with the advice offered by Thomas Tusser, who farmed at Cattawade in south Suffolk in the middle of the sixteenth century and who published his *Hundredth Good Pointes of Husbandrie* in 1557:

> Good fruite and good plenty, doth well in thy loft,
> Then lay for an orcharde and cherish it oft.[7]

Indeed, as noted, even small cottages usually had some fruit trees growing beside them, sometimes provided by local landowners as an act of philanthropy. In 1736 the agent of the Marsham estate in Norfolk was instructed to buy '6 aple trees & 2 cherry trees to set in Ann Watsons yard & 2 apel trees in Jexes orchard at 8d a piece'.[8] In October 1834 the noted horticulturalist Andrew Knight informed Lord Bristol of Ickworth in west Suffolk that he had sent him a consignment of fruit trees, including 'fifteen … very little pear trees, which I will request you to give to your Cottagers to plant in their gardens, being confident that they will in a very few years, amply repay their care of them'.[9] Fruit and nut trees were even sometimes planted in churchyards for the good of the poor, as at Briningham in Norfolk in 1750, where a number of walnut trees were established, or at Woodston in Huntingdonshire, where a list was made in 1759 of the 'Fruit Trees as they stand in a row from the door' of the church.[10] Orchards, in short, were closely associated with settlements of all kinds in the pre-industrial landscape and formed part of the daily experience of most if not all of the population.

---

4 F.G. Emmison, *Elizabethan Life. Home Work and Land. From Essex Wills and Sessions and Manorial Records* (Chelmsford, 1976), pp. 31 and 194.
5 NRO, DCN 44/128/3.
6 NRO, SF 431/19, 308X5.
7 T. Tusser, *A Hundreth Good Pointes of Husbandrie* (London, 1557), fol. 12.
8 NRO, MC 602/53.
9 SRO, B, 941/56/25.
10 NRO, PD 625/2; PD 646/1.

All this said, early surveys suggest that not every farm necessarily possessed an orchard, as opposed to a few fruit trees. A survey of the manor of Wilburton in Cambridgeshire, drawn up in 1636, records 'the dwelling houses, orchards, gardens or yards in the Town with the number of acres, roods and perches that each of them contain'.[11] Eighteen of the village farms, in addition to the manor house and parsonage, had an orchard, several of them more than one, but 19 were described as having a 'yard' or 'homestead' only. The orchards were, on average, larger than the latter, although the difference was not great – an average of 3 roods 29 perches against 3 roods 5 perches. Of course, it is unclear how 'orchard' is being defined, and likely that the 'yards' and 'homesteads' themselves contained some fruit trees. We should also note that there were whole districts where domestic orchards were, by the end of the nineteenth century, relatively thin on the ground. Many farms on the acid clays and gravels of south Hertfordshire lacked one, presumably because of the inhospitable nature of the soil. More importantly, as a comparison of Figures 1.7 and 1.8 illustrates, there were few on the chalk escarpment of the Chilterns and its north-easterly continuation, the 'East Anglian Heights', on the acid sands of Breckland or on the 'Sandlings', the area of heathy land running along the Suffolk coast; or, to a lesser extent, on the light soils, variously calcareous and acidic, of north-west Norfolk. To a large extent these gaps in the overall distribution simply reflect the fact that, due to problems of water supply, large areas of land in these districts were devoid of settlement. But even where farms were to be found, a high proportion seem to have lacked a full-sized orchard. Nor was this a recent development. In c.1900 Tuddenham in West Suffolk, for example – an area characterised by the sandy, freely draining soils typical of Breckland – contained only a single small orchard in its entire 2,664 acres (1,078 hectares). A survey of the manor drawn up in 1766 describes in some detail 15 separate farms, only one of which had an orchard.[12] In part this paucity was probably a consequence of the fact that none of these freely draining, drought-prone soils – variously very acidic or alkaline in character – were very suitable for growing fruit trees. But it may also have been a consequence of social and tenurial factors. By the eighteenth century most districts of poor, light soil were already dominated by extensive landed estates, the properties of which were largely leased out as very large farms, many extending over 500 acres (200 hectares) or more.[13] These were tenanted by well-to-do 'gentleman' farmers and run, in effect, as industrial grain factories. Such men had a more single-minded focus on arable production than the smaller tenants or freeholders who occupied the majority of farms in the eastern counties. In addition, the fact that they held the land on relatively short leases provided little incentive to plant fruit trees, which took several years to mature.

---

11   CRO, R/106/091.

12   SRO, B, 507/1/48.

13   S. Wade Martins and T. Williamson, *Roots of Change: Farming and the Landscape in East Anglia, c.1700–1870* (Exeter, 1999), pp.76–80.

With these notable exceptions, orchards appear to have been common almost everywhere. Yet, in most districts before the nineteenth century they did not take up a very large area of land. The majority of farm orchards covered between half an acre and an acre (*c*.0.2 and 0.4 hectares), but many were smaller. A sale of properties in Milden in Suffolk in 1819 included a Great Orchard covering 3 roods and 6 perches (*c*.0.3 hectares) and a Little Orchard covering a mere 34 perches (*c*.0.1 hectares).[14] Some even smaller examples are recorded. One extending over only 15 perches (0.04 hectares, or 400 sq m) was sold in Great Henny in the same county in 1669.[15] Below this size, capable of containing perhaps a dozen trees, collections of fruit trees may not have been described as 'orchards' by contemporaries. Given the size of the holdings of which they formed a part, all this means that in most areas orchards comprised significantly less than 1 per cent of the total farm acreage. In Suffolk, for example, a 144-acre (58-hectare) farm at Preston in 1690 had an orchard covering around half an acre, or *c*.0.4 per cent of its total area; on a holding at Whepstead in 1771 the orchard accounted for 0.8 per cent of the total area; at Layham in 1794 the figure was 0.4 per cent; at Worlingworth in 1758, 0.4 per cent; at Monewden in 1656, 0.75 per cent; on 'Mr Long's Farm' in Gisleham and Rushmere in 1726, 0.4 per cent.[16] Similar figures come from the adjacent county of Norfolk, such as the 0.4 per cent on a farm in Loddon and Heckingham in 1767.[17] Across most of Essex and east Hertfordshire the situation was the same. On a farm at Great Dunmow in Essex in 1759 the orchard comprised 0.2 per cent of farm area; on a holding at Manuden in Essex, *c*.1760, 0.7 per cent.[18] Much and Little Hadham in east Hertfordshire are particularly well-mapped parishes, and various properties there had orchards covering around 1 per cent of their area in 1759; *c*.0.5 per cent in 1767; 0.4 per cent in 1789; 0.7 per cent in 1793; and 0.5 per cent in 1814.[19] Farms in the neighbouring parishes exhibit very similar proportions. The orchard accounted for *c*.0.3 per cent of the land of Nuthampstead Bury Farm in 1835;[20] 1 per cent of a farm in Meesden in 1835;[21] 0.5 per cent of a farm at Colliers End in Standon 1767;[22] *c*.0.7 per cent of Green Farm, Standon, in 1774;[23] 0.4 per cent of Marshalls in the same parish in *c*.1730;[24] and *c*.0.5 per cent of Young's

---

14   SRO, B, 1754/1/370B.

15   SRO, B, 613/411.

16   SRO, B, Acc 2123/1; 1167/12; HD 1187/A2/3; SRO, I, HD 417/40; SRO, L, 741/HA12/D4/6; 274/28.

17   SRO, L, 41/HA12/D4/19.

18   SRO, I, HD 417/46; ERO, T/M 457/2.

19   HALS, D/Z44P1; D/Ecn P1; 7/486; E/Ecn P2; Acc 2164.

20   HALS, D.1171B0.

21   HALS, D.1171B.

22   HALS, D/EB/1768/P1.

23   HALS, A 2838.

24   HALS, 83281.

Farm there in 1768.²⁵ All these figures, we would emphasise, relate to the areas of the farms in question. Orchards constituted a considerably smaller proportion of the total land area of the parishes in which they lay, for this included woods, common land, parks and roads. In most parishes, orchards made up significantly less than 0.5 per cent of the total land area.

The areas just discussed were all areas of relatively dispersed settlement and early enclosure, lying to the south and east of the chalk escarpment. In the 'champion' districts lying to its north and west, where the extent of enclosed land was less and dwellings more tightly packed in nucleated villages, the proportion of the farmed area occupied by orchards was sometimes lower. A survey of the holdings on an estate of 4,583 acres (*c.*1,855 hectares) in Ramsey, Huntingdonshire, drawn up in 1700, recorded only 9 acres of orchards, just 0.2 per cent of the land described.²⁶ Bedfordshire was a mainly 'champion' county, and the agriculturalist Thomas Batchelor described in 1808 how:

> The orchards are in general very small in this county. There are a few that may contain a 100 fruit trees of various kinds, and new ones of an acre or two may be occasionally met with, planted sometimes in squares of about seven yards between each tree, but there are frequently no other orchards than what are included in the gardens, consisting of four or five trees.²⁷

But even in such districts the average proportion of farm area occupied by orchards was often in excess of 0.5 per cent. The 20 orchards recorded in the 1636 survey of Wilburton, a parish of some 2,610 acres (1,056 hectares), collectively covered nearly 0.9 per cent of the farmed area.²⁸

As we shall see, there were individual parishes and districts in which, by the eighteenth century, orchards were larger and more numerous. But for the most part the early modern landscape was characterised by small farm orchards producing fruit for domestic consumption and a small surplus for sale. This might be disposed of locally or taken to a nearby urban market. In December 1798 Randall Burroughes, a 'gentleman' farmer who operated two large farms in Wymondham in Norfolk, recorded in his journal how 'the apples this year were sold in Norwich at 6 shillings per sack & 28 sent in and I gave six shillings to the man viz [gap] of Wicklewood who sold them. I reserved about fifteen sacks of the best at home.'²⁹ In some cases the orchard crop appears to have been sold to a local 'middleman' for disposal – individuals such as Mary Bone, who purchased quantities of apples and walnuts from Thomas Ripingall of Langham in the same county in the early nineteenth century.³⁰

---

25 HALS, A 2831.
26 HRO, R40/4/1/1.
27 T. Batchelor, *General View of the Agriculture of the County of Bedford* (London, 1813), p. 438.
28 CRO, R106/091.
29 S. Wade Martins and T. Williamson (eds), *The Farming Journal of Randall Burroughes of Wymondham, 1794–99*, Norfolk Record Society 58 (Norwich, 1995), p. 113.
30 NRO, WKC 5/277/2; MC 120/45.

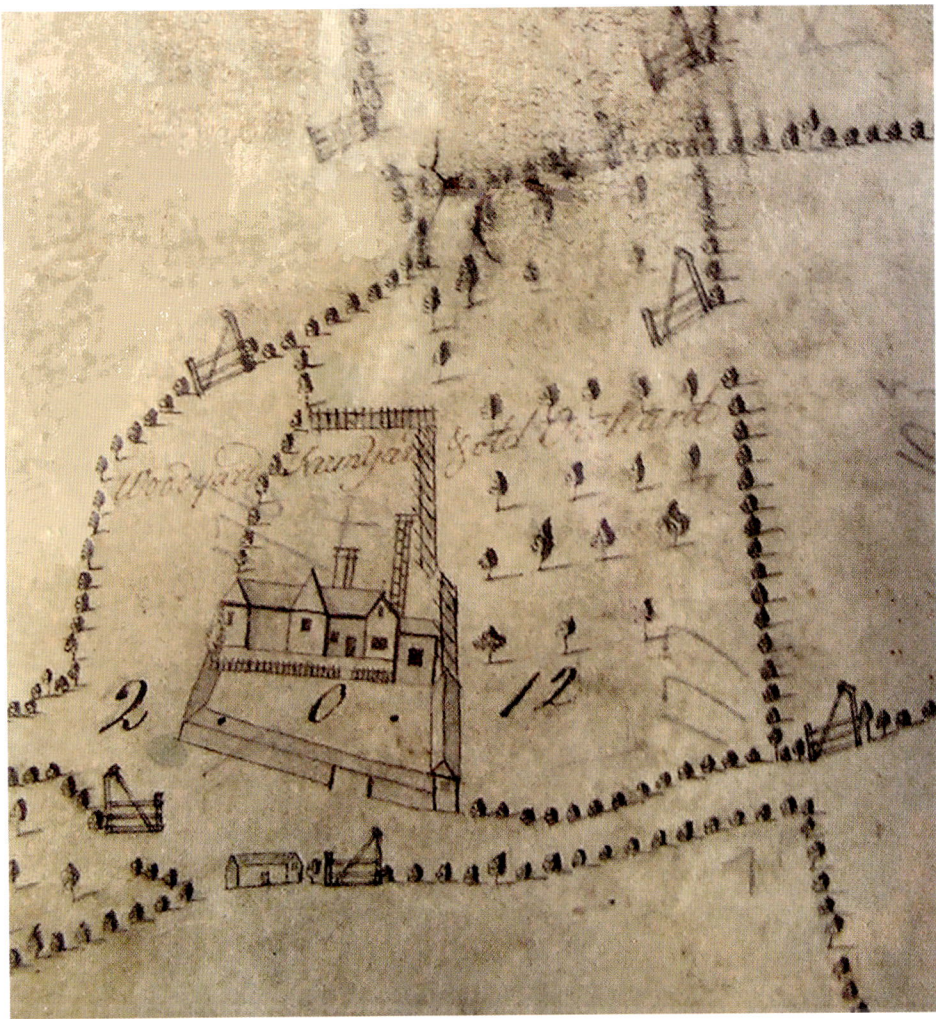

Figure 2.1 A typical small farm orchard shown on a map, surveyed in 1730, of Boxted Farm, Hemel Hempstead, Hertfordshire. Hertfordshire Archives and Local Studies AH/680.

The layout and management of farm orchards

Map and documentary evidence leaves no doubt that farm orchards were almost invariably situated in close proximity to the house and often immediately adjacent to the garden (Figure 2.1). This preference was partly dictated by practical considerations. Such an arrangement made it easier to inspect the condition of the growing crop and to move harvested fruit to the kitchens or fruit store. But it may also indicate the way that owners derived pleasure from blossom, fruit and birdsong, and thus wanted to have the orchard in view or at least easily accessed from the house. It also probably reflects the fact that fruit was a valuable crop, subject to predation from wildlife and easily pilfered by humans.

Indeed, some owners even paid nightwatchmen to guard their orchards. In 1828 Henry Roberts and George Pratt were employed by John Burr of Kempston in Bedfordshire 'to watch some Fruit Trees standing in a close in his Possession at Kempston. For several Nights we have slept under one of [the] Trees in a small hut made with a few hurdles and straw, for the purpose of keeping us dry from the Weather'. They (and their 'little dog') were attacked by a group of men armed with cudgels, one of whom demanded of Roberts:

> Whether the apples were mine I told him they were my Master's. He then asked me whether I was paid for looking after them I said Yes. He then said to the other men jump up and they got up into the tree. He then said shake away. I then heard a great many apples fall. Two men stood all the time at the entrance of the hut with bludgeons in their hands. I heard one man say shovel them in, when they were picking up the apples. The apples were put into either sacks or bags …The leader who seemed to order and direct the others then said I want fourteen or fifteen bushels for I have got a horse and cart here.[31]

In addition, the fruit trees, especially young ones, were vulnerable to damage caused by hostile intruders. Vandalism was in some cases perhaps motivated by a simple desire to settle a private score but it might also be a manifestation of the same class antagonism that sporadically encouraged the maiming of farm animals.[32] It is unclear why, for example, in 1822 Andrew Chambers, William Hardwicke and Joseph Partridge maliciously damaged apple trees belonging to John Austin of Bedford.[33] A desire to protect fruit and trees from damage presumably explains why many orchards were securely enclosed by fences, rather than by hedges alone. In 1720 the incoming tenant of Stonehill Farm in Tetworth, Bedfordshire, for example, agreed to 'pale in the orchard and plant it with fruit trees'.[34] Where, as was more usual, orchards were surrounded by hedges, writers on fruit cultivation emphasised the importance of maintaining them in good condition, to prevent cattle from entering and 'cropping the tender Twigs of the Fruit-Trees, and rubbing against their stems, and unruly People destroying the Fruit'.[35]

Orchard trees, and their fruit, were also vulnerable to wind damage. Shelter belts formed by one or more lines of plum trees were often planted around the perimeter of the orchard (they grew more rapidly than the apples and pears within it, quickly providing them with a measure of protection). Traces of such arrangements sometimes remain today in the form of dense concentrations of suckers growing within the perimeter hedges of old

---

31 BRO, QSR/25/1822/345.
32 C.J. Griffin, '"Some Inhuman Wretch": Animal Maiming and the Ambivalent Relationship between Rural Workers and Animals', *Rural History*, 25/2 (2014), pp. 133–60.
33 BRO, Bor BF4/67/106–8.
34 BRO, FE 335.
35 Ellis, *The Compleat Cyderman*, p. 16.

farm orchards, as at Wood Farm, Hempnall, in Norfolk. Some early writers recommended taller-growing trees for shelter, William Ellis in 1754 advising the planting of elm, poplar, aspen or 'the Perry-Pear' in perimeter hedges.[36] But these needed to be kept trimmed or pollarded, and on occasions removed altogether, to prevent the fruit trees from being too much in shadow to flourish (care had to be taken more generally to minimise the shade thrown by neighbouring trees: in February 1798 Randall Burroughes of Wymondham recorded how one of his men was employed cutting down 'an elm that grew on the drain before the study window & by its shade greatly injur'd the orchard').[37]

We have relatively little information about the layout of early farm orchards, or about the balance of the different kinds of fruit grown within them. In his *A New Orchard and Garden* of 1618 William Lawson suggested that 'the form most men like in general, is a square', and advised that 'trees should be well spaced', at a distance of 20 yards (18.2m), in order to provide the room which they needed to mature. He also recommended surrounding the orchard with a hedgerow planted with filberts.[38] Gervase Markham, writing in 1613, also recommended a square orchard, divided into four quarters by walks. He thought that the trees could be planted just twelve feet (4.2m) apart, 'sufficient enough for their spreading', and in 'such arteficiall rowes that which way soever a man shall cast his eyes yet hee shall see the trees every way stand in rows making squares, alleyes and divisions according to a man's imagination'.[39] These were to be surrounded by a boundary composed of more closely spaced plum trees to provide shelter, in the manner just noted.

The orchard described by Mary Birkhead in 1734, at her daughter's house at Thwaite in Norfolk, seems to have been laid out following the advice of Markham (or some text derived from him). It comprised 'an acre of land very near square. The trees planted in rows look which way you please' (i.e., they formed lines both along the rows and diagonally). But in other ways its plan echoes Lawson's ideas, as the trees were planted '36 foot one way and 26 the other' (11m and 7.9m).[40] More interesting is the fact that the inside of the perimeter fence was planted not just with filberts as Lawson recommended or with plums as Markham suggested, but with a diverse range of fruit, including several sorts of plum, quinces, barberries and unspecified 'nuts'. On one side – probably the north, so as to provide shelter from the wind and limit the amount of shade cast on the other, lower-growing trees – there was a single row of six walnut trees. Moreover, instead of having all the filberts relegated towards the boundaries, there were filbert bushes placed between the

---

36 Ellis, *Compleat Cyderman*, p. 13.
37 Wade Martins and Williamson, *Farming Journal of Randall Burroughes*, pp. 95–6.
38 W. Lawson, *A New Orchard and Garden* (London, 1618), pp. 14, 23.
39 G. Markham, *The English Husbandman* (London, 1613), pp. 36–7.
40 NRO, BRA 926 122. This analysis and subsequent discussions of Birkhead and her orchards are largely based on the research carried out by Patsy Dallas in 2014 and published in P. Dallas, G. Barnes and T. Williamson, 'Orchards in the Landscape: A Norfolk Case Study', *Landscapes*, 16/1 (2015), pp. 26–43.

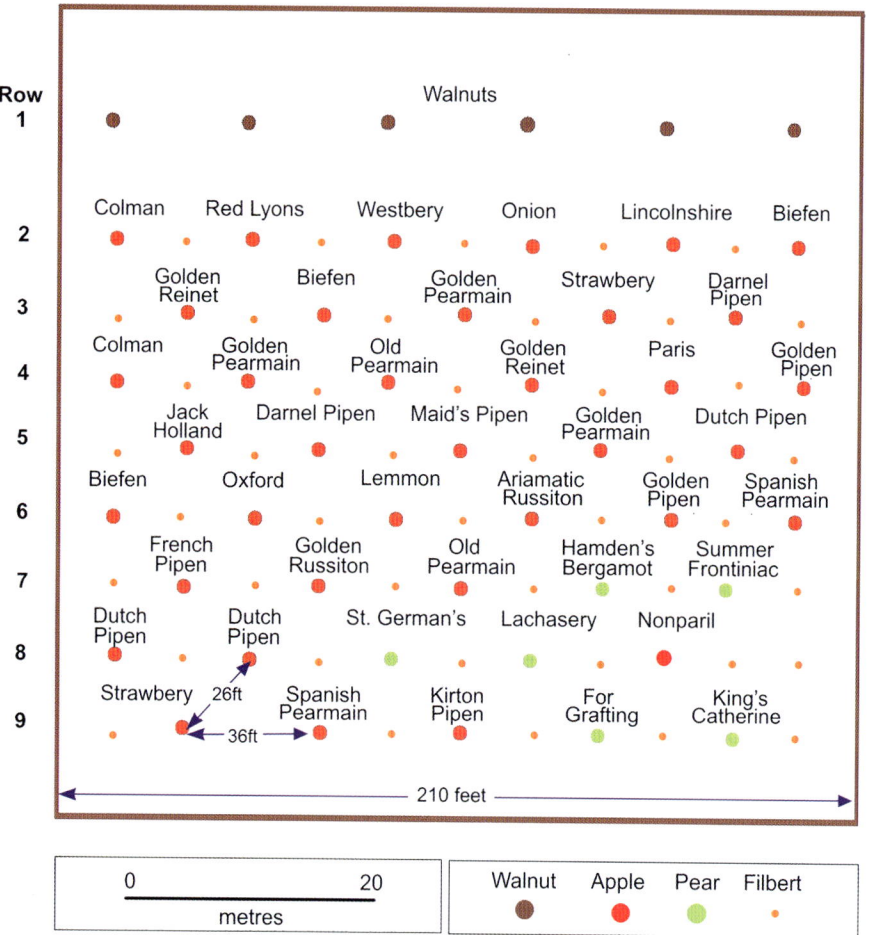

Figure 2.2 A reconstruction, by Patsy Dallas, of the plan of the orchard described by Mary Birkhead and owned by her daughter at Thwaite in Norfolk in 1734.

trees in the grid formed by offsetting rows of odd and even numbers of trees. In all, this one-acre orchard contained 44 fruit trees, together with the filberts and the six walnuts, and had a wide assortment of stone fruit and berries set against the fences around its margins (Figure 2.2).

Birkhead was one of the 'middling' sort, rather than a member of the landed elite, although she was certainly well connected in social terms. The daughter of a minor gentry family, the Gostlings, she married Matthew Dixon, a London artist, in 1692, a few years after he had purchased a farm in Thwaite.[41] He died in 1710 and in 1723 she was married

---

41 M. Edmund, 'Nicholas Dixon, Limner; and Matthew Dixon, Painter, Died 1710', *The Burlington Magazine*, 125/967 (1983), pp. 611–13; NRO, BRA 926/120.

for a second time, to John Birkhead, a wealthy lawyer from Clerkenwell in Middlesex.[42] There were several children from her marriage to Matthew Dixon but the one who owned the orchard just described was probably Anne. The family properties in Thwaite were not extensive. They were mainly inherited by Alice, another daughter, who married John Gamble of Bungay in Suffolk in 1723, and a century later, when the tithe apportionment for Thwaite was drawn up, Hannah Gamble owned a total of 101 acres in the parish.[43] All this suggests that the orchard described by Mary Birkhead at her daughter's house was probably broadly similar in character to those associated with ordinary farmhouses. But at this time much of the family property was rented out to a tenant, together with the farmhouse originally purchased by Dixon, and the orchard associated with this is also described in Birkhead's memoranda book. It was considerably larger and less regular in shape than her daughter's, with 12 rows of varying length, containing in all 152 trees.[44] Here there were more pear trees, interspersed within the rows of apples, but filberts, walnuts, cherries and plums were again placed along the margins of the plot.

Whether this concentration of stone fruit and berries – as well as walnuts and filberts – towards the orchard boundary was normal practice is unclear. Certainly, the plan of an orchard published by the nurseryman George Lindley of Norwich in 1796 has only filberts on the edges, with plums, cherries, quince, medlars and mulberries included in the body of the orchard.[45] Covering 1.48 acres (0.6 hectares) and containing 77 trees spaced 9 yards (8.2m) apart east–west and 16 yards (14.6m) north–south, Lindley's orchard would have allowed more space between the trees than was the case with those at Thwaite. But an orchard at Hasketon in Suffolk, planted in 1814, is in many ways similar to those described by Birkhead. A plan shows that it measured 40 yards east–west and 134 north–south and was planted with seven rows of nine trees, mainly apples, but with some pears and plums, two walnuts, a quince, a sweet chestnut and a medlar. The trees were spaced at 14 yards (12.8m) along the rows but the rows were only 7 yards (6.4m) apart. On the west side there were a further 20 closely spaced apples and pears, planted at intervals of 5½ yards; there were also one or two irregularly placed trees within the body of the orchard, bringing the total number of trees to 89. In addition, the orchard was surrounded on all sides by rows of 'filberts, Spanish nuts, damsons and bullaces', beyond which was a grass walk (Figure 2.3).[46] Within surviving examples of farm orchards the disposition of the older trees – planted long after these sources were produced – suggests a broadly similar range of spacings, usually between 6m and 8m each way, as at Home Farm, South Elmham, and Lampardbrook Farm, Framlingham, both in Suffolk, and Oaklands Farm in Wymondham,

---

42   Broome parish registers, NRO, PD 303/2.
43   Thwaite parish registers, NRO, PD 716/1; tithe map and apportionment for Thwaite St Mary, NRO, DN/TA 536.
44   NRO, BRA 926/122.
45   NRO, COL 9/96.
46   SRO, I, V5/11/4/.2.

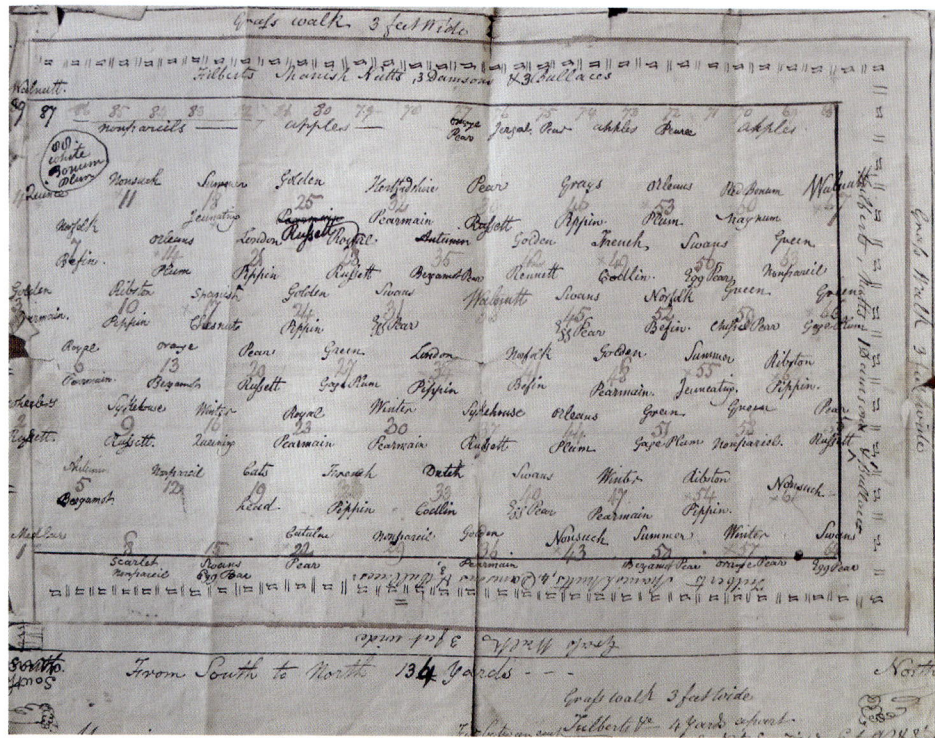

Figure 2.3 Plan of an orchard at Hasketon, Suffolk, drawn up in 1814. Mainly planted with apples, but with some pears, plums and other fruit, it was surrounded by rows of 'filberts, Spanish nuts, damsons and bullaces'. Suffolk Record Office (Ipswich) V5/11/4/2.

Figure 2.4 Veteran cobnut stools, planted around the margins of the orchard at Parkgate Farm, Saxmundham, Suffolk.

Norfolk, or around 6–8m in one direction and 10 or more in another, as at Home Farm, Stow Bardolph, Norfolk. Remaining farm orchards are, like those described in our sources, almost invariably dominated by apple trees, and in some examples the remains of peripheral plantings of cobnuts can be found, as at Ivy Cottage, Wreningham, in Norfolk or Parkgate Farm, Saxmundham, in Suffolk (Figure 2.4).

Documentary sources suggest that apples were almost always the most common fruit planted in farm orchards, usually accompanied by smaller numbers of pears (mainly culinary types and often long-keeping 'wardens'). Other kinds of fruit were poorly represented, except in the borders. In the main body of Mary Birkhead's daughter's orchard at Thwaite in 1734 there were 38 apples and seven pears; that on the family's tenanted farm in the same parish contained 113 apples and 39 pears, together with a single cherry (although in both cases nuts, plums and cherries were planted on the boundaries).[47] At North Runcton rectory in Norfolk in 1719 there were 14 apples but only two pears listed; in 1784 the orchard at West End Farm in Wormley, Hertfordshire, contained 18 apples but only two other trees, both walnuts, while all the trees in the orchard at Ayot St Lawrence parsonage in Hertfordshire in 1806 were apples.[48] At Hasketon in Suffolk in 1814 apples outnumbered pears by more than three to one, although here around 16 per cent of the orchard trees comprised plums and other fruit.[49] In the orchard attached to the parsonage at Westmill in Hertfordshire in 1710 there were ten apples, six pears, three quince and four 'Spanish Nuts', while in William Wilshere's orchard in Hitchin in the same county in 1811 the six apples were accompanied by three pears, a cherry, a damson and an apricot.[50] Apple trees more clearly dominated in his garden, where there were 17, together with one pear, a single standard apricot and five damsons (of which four were described as 'bad'). But gardens normally featured a rather larger proportion of other kinds of fruit. All the 15 trees in the 'New Orchard' at Carleton Rode in Norfolk – again, probably at the parsonage – in 1758 were apples, but plums, pears and cherries were to be found growing beside the walks in the garden, along with two almonds and a mulberry (although even here nearly half the trees were apples).[51] Similarly, while the trees in Birkhead's daughter's garden in Thwaite in 1734 were mainly apples and pears they also included six plums and a cherry, together with a vine and a single apricot; while in the garden of the family's tenanted farm there were 17 apple and pear trees but also numerous plums and at least ten cherries.[52] Cherries might thus be present in the gardens of small houses but only rarely were they planted in significant numbers among the apples and pears in the orchard, probably because their tall, spreading habit impacted on neighbouring trees, but there were exceptions. Richard

---

47 NRO, BRA 926/122.
48 NRO, PD 332/20; HALS, DE/Bb/E27; D/P10 1/3.
49 SRO, I, V5/11/4/.2.
50 HALS, DP/120/3/1; 61181.
51 NRO, PD 254/60.
52 NRO, BRA 926/122.

Du Cane of Little Coggeshall in Essex planted 11 cherries and eight apples in his 'Grange and Dairy Orchard' in 1735.[53] The dominance of apples in the orchards of farms and rectories, the secondary importance of pears and the tertiary significance of other fruit presumably reflects the extent to which these different products could be successfully stored without having to be preserved, bottled or converted to jam.

Filberts and cobnuts were also a feature of many small orchards, as we have seen, again because they could be easily stored. Mary Birkhead described in 1734 some specimens she had propagated for the orchard at her former home at Thwaite: 'I set Filberts they came up and made trees much sooner than from suckers but they all proved nutty, some as bad as hedge nuts, some as good as Filberts, one I call the cluster nutt I value very much, it is a round large nutt, grows on a cluster.'[54] Walnuts were generally present only in small numbers and were more often cultivated elsewhere, away from the house and gardens. The orchard owned by the Dixon family in Thwaite in the 1730s contained five walnut trees, but a further 23 grew in the Home Meadow.[55] In 1817 the farmer Thomas Ripingall of Langham in Norfolk recorded the sale of walnuts grown in his orchard and his meadows.[56] Indeed, walnuts appear as hedgerow trees quite frequently in timber surveys from the eighteenth and nineteenth centuries, albeit generally at low frequencies, making up 0.8 per cent on a property at Finchingfield in Essex in 1805, for example.[57] But they could be more numerous where particular owners planted them enthusiastically, forming 5 per cent of the trees at Navestock in the same county in 1772.[58] In these contexts walnut was probably mainly planted for its wood, highly valued before the large-scale import of mahogany from the Americas began in the early eighteenth century. It was also widely used for gunstocks. Growing walnuts in hedges, rather than in the farmhouse gardens or orchards, could cause problems, however. William Ellis warned that 'boys and others' would damage hedges while trying to steal the fruit.[59]

Whatever the precise balance of apples and other fruit grown in farmhouse orchards in the post-medieval period, what is striking is the sheer diversity of varieties present. The 37 apple trees planted in Mary Birkhead's daughter's orchard at Thwaite in Norfolk in the 1720s, for example, included no fewer than 21 different varieties (in addition to six of pear: Figure 2.2). Such diversity was partly a consequence of the fact that apples (and to some extent pears) were consumed in a variety of ways, and partly reflected the desire of owners to enjoy a long fruiting season. Much of the fruit grown was probably stored or preserved

---

53   ERO, D/DDc E15/3.
54   NRO, BRA 926 122, 373X2.
55   NRO, BRA 926/ 121 and 122, 373X2.
56   NRO, MC 120/45.
57   ERO, D/D Pg T8.
58   ERO, T/A 783.
59   W. Ellis, *The Timber Tree Improved* (London, 1738), p. 63.

for use through the winter, either on the tree or in a cool outbuilding or store room, where varieties such as the apple Winter Majetin could be left to improve through the winter months and where culinary pears would keep until spring.

Farm orchards served a number of additional functions in the domestic economy. Beekeeping was an important secondary activity and was discussed at length by both Lawson and Markham. The placing of hives or skeps in the orchard ensured both pollination of the fruit and the production of significant amounts of honey and beeswax: when William Baker of Great Chishall in Essex died in 1598 he left to his wife Alice '1 hive of bees standing in my orchard'.[60] Maps occasionally suggest that the ground between the trees was cultivated, presumably for vegetables or soft fruit – examples include a survey drawn up in 1752 of Denton and Alburgh in Norfolk – but inter-planting was mainly a feature of commercial orchards, or small cottage gardens, and the overwhelming majority of farm orchards were under permanent grass.[61] This was often cut for hay, to judge from tithe payments, as for example at Shotesham in Norfolk in 1649, where George Gooch paid a shilling for tithe hay in his orchard.[62] Indeed, when tithes were commuted in the years around 1840 the apportionments often describe orchards as 'meadow' rather than as 'pasture' in the 'State of Cultivation' column, in those cases where the commissioners made such distinctions. Orchard hay is referred to, directly or obliquely, in a variety of other kinds of document. Sir John Wittewronge of Rothamsted in Hertfordshire described in his diary how on 29 May 1686 he began to mow hay in the 'hopground orchard', and on 8 June 'Carried in 4 indifferent Jogs [loads]' from there; while on 14 June he 'Brought a good load from Lazarusses Orchard'.[63] The will of Margaret Haward of Writtle, drawn up in 1729, mentions apples, walnuts and plums in the orchard, and 'one hay cock' standing there, worth £9.[64] In 1708 the rector of Fowlmere in Cambridgeshire paid 'Old William Thrift' for a day spent mowing the orchard and carrying out the grass.[65] All this is in spite of the fact that some agricultural writers, including Arthur Young, thought that regular removal of hay caused damage to the fruit trees by depleting the soil of nutrients.[66] The fact that orchards produced enough grass to be worth mowing for hay suggests the presence of widely spaced trees. A dense and continuous canopy would have cast significant amounts of shade, even in spring. It is, however, likely that the quantity of hay produced varied over the life of an orchard, with the grass growing more abundantly when the trees were young

---

60 Emmison, *Elizabethan Life*, p. 194.
61 NRO, MC 1744/1.
62 NRO, FEL 476, 10.
63 Williams and Stevenson, 'Observations of Weather', pp. 34–5.
64 Emmison, *Elizabethan Life*, p. 265.
65 P. Brassley, A. Lambert and P. Saunders (eds), *Accounts of the Reverend John Crakanthorp of Fowlmere. 1682–1710*, Cambridge Record Society 8 (Cambridge, 1988), p. 112.
66 A. Young, *General View of the Agriculture of the County of Hertfordshire* (London, 1804) p. 143.

than it did later, as they matured.

Orchards were also frequently grazed, whether routinely or only after the hay harvest. In the eastern counties sheep seem to have been pastured there more often than larger stock such as cattle or horses, presumably because of the potential damage the latter could cause to the trees. Indeed, agricultural leases – such as one for a farm in Rushden in Hertfordshire dating to 1687 – sometimes instructed tenants to keep cows out of the orchard.[67] The close association of sheep and orchards appears in many ways in the documentary record. In 1678, for example, Mary Jenkins of Chalgrave in Bedfordshire was indicted for driving a sheep into her orchard from the adjacent field and hiding it there, claiming that she thought it was 'a lost drove sheep & hopeing to be rewarded for the care she took of it', and that her offer to sell it to her neighbour William Page was only 'a jest'.[68] Where cows were kept in orchards, elaborate measures were sometimes adopted to limit the damage they might cause. Arthur Young described at the start of the nineteenth century how, in the orchards on the Dengie peninsula in Essex, 'they buckle a circingle round the body across the chine, and to this attach a sort of halter on the head, which passes between the legs, to keep them from raising the head high enough to browse the trees'.[69] Pigs were also sporadically kept in orchards and fed on windfalls – in 1612 a property in Diss in Norfolk was conveyed 'with part of an orchard or hogs' yard'.[70] They presumably had a ring put through their nose, or were very carefully supervised, to prevent them disturbing the ground too much and thus damaging the roots of trees. Sometimes they were fed on other food strewn across the ground beneath the trees: on 17 November 1797 Randall Burroughes reported that 'the hogs were employed in picking up the potatoes in the orchard', although it is possible that these were tubers left after a crop sown between the trees had been harvested.[71] Geese and other poultry would have done little damage and their presence presumably explains the ponds in orchards that are frequently shown on early maps and which in some cases survive today. In 1706 the rector of Fowlmere in Cambridgeshire paid Thomas Watson 2s 6d for 'casting ponds in orchard'.[72] The grazing of livestock suggests, once again, the presence of tall 'standard' trees on vigorous rootstocks, of the kind that still characterise the older planting in surviving examples of farm orchards (Figure 2.5). As noted in the previous chapter, trees on dwarfing stocks, and/or trained in 'bush' fashion, would have been vulnerable to grazing, even by small stock such as sheep or even geese. Such trees were mainly, although not exclusively, a feature of gardens – especially those of the wealthy – and of some commercial orchards, rather than of orchards attached to farms.

---

67 HALS, 74499.

68 BRO, HSA/1678 W/54.

69 A. Young, *General View of the Agriculture of the County of Essex*, vol. 2 (London, 1807), p. 132.

70 NRO, MC 257/55, 684X3.

71 Wade Martins and Williamson, *Farming Journal of Randall Burroughes*, p. 92.

72 Brassley *et al.*, *Accounts of the Reverend John Crakanthorp*, p. 142.

Figure 2.5 Poultry can still occasionally be seen in orchards in the more rural parts of eastern England.

In addition to producing fruit, honey and hay, and providing grazing for a range of livestock, it is clear that orchards were also regarded as a useful source of fuel, a perennial concern in many parts of eastern England and elsewhere before improvements in transport systems – the advent of canals and, in particular, railways – allowed coal to be transported into areas lying at a distance from the coast or navigable rivers. Orchards, in short, thus have many parallels with other multiple-use environments, in England and beyond, such as the olive groves in Spain that – as Juan Infante-Amate has demonstrated – were traditionally valued for grazing and as a source of fodder and fuel as much as for the olives they produced.[73]

Orchards were useful features but they took up only a small proportion of farms' land area and the scale of their contribution to the farm economy should not be exaggerated. As well as the tithe from any hay crop taken, the fruit from orchards was usually subject to 'small' tithes, alongside livestock, eggs and hay. Where, as was generally the case by the seventeenth and eighteenth centuries, payments in kind had been commuted to annual payments in cash on an informal, *ad hoc* basis, the amounts paid for orchards were usually small. At Boxworth in Cambridgeshire a tithe of 6s was paid on each cow, 5s and 6d for

---

[73] J. Infante-Amate, 'The Ecology and History of the Mediterranean Olive Grove: The Spanish Great Expansion, 1750–2000', *Rural History*, 23/2 (2012), pp. 161–84.

each lamb and 6s per sow, but the produce from orchards was compounded at 1s, 2s or 4s, depending on size.[74] In 1773 at Barley in Hertfordshire the great tithes brought in £219 8s 7¼d and the small tithes £30 0s 0d.[75] The tithes from wood, pigeons and orchards are listed separately, at £3 0s 0d, £0 6s 6d and £0 10s 0d respectively. At Diss in south Norfolk in the early eighteenth century, according to the historian Francis Blomefield, the rector received 1d per annum 'for every orchard and garden plot': this was the same as he was due 'for every hive of bees … except it be the first year they swarm, and then nothing'.[76] On the other hand, the £8 2s received by Randall Burroughes for the sale of his apples at Norwich in 1798 was roughly equivalent to the amount he received for each of the bullocks that he bought and fattened for a year – a not unreasonable profit from a piece of land apparently covering only 1.5 acres (0.6 hectares), especially given that he retained apples worth more than half this amount for his own use, that the orchard had other uses within the farm economy and that other, unrecorded sales of fruit may have been made.[77] This said, we should remember that, while orchards did not require the frequent and regular inputs of physical work required to coax a reasonable crop from the arable fields, they made a number of demands on the labour of the farmer or his workers, in terms of pruning, the removal and replacement of old or sick fruit trees and the maintenance of boundaries.

Yet, as already suggested, the value of small domestic orchards went beyond the agrarian and economic. Their proximity to the house reflects not simply their aesthetic value but the centrality of fruit in pre-industrial culture, its place in biblical texts and classical myth – the former universally known, the latter widely appreciated at the level of the 'middling sort'. There are signs that orchards were regarded as something of a hobby by their owners, and that the exchange of trees and scion wood between neighbours and relatives helped to articulate social relationships. Orchards were places of family recreation, not merely of production. Mary Birkhead expressed this clearly in her orchard book of 1734, as well as demonstrating the close association there must often have been between the women of the household and domestic orchards. In her description of her daughter's orchard at Thwaite in Norfolk, she notes in passing:

> I have for ten years been at the expence of fencing it round, diging about each tree securing them from Hares, carting fresh Earth … and … now grafting such as stunted after transplanting, the only method I could ever find to cure that evil. But this year I had the pleasure of seeing my two Grand Children run a striving [in competition] which should get most Filberts and such fruit as pleased them, a full recompense for all my past care.[78]

---

74   CRO, P15/28/1.
75   J.C. Wilkerson (ed.), *John Norden's Survey of Barley Hertfordshire. 1593–1603* (Cambridge, 1974), p. 13.
76   Blomefield, *Topographical History of the County of Norfolk*, vol. 1 (London, 1806), p. 20.
77   Wade Martins and Williamson, *Farming Journal of Randall Burroughes*, p. 19.
78   NRO, BRA 926 122, 373X2.

Early production for the market

There were some seventeenth- and eighteenth-century holdings on which orchards occupied rather more than the 0.5–1 per cent of land area that was usual on farms. On two properties at Worlingworth and Rumburgh in Suffolk in 1710 and 1783, for example, the orchard made up 5 per cent of the total land area.[79] This was usually, as here, on comparatively small holdings, an association that was to continue and intensify in the course of the nineteenth and early twentieth centuries. In some cases, indeed, very small enterprises might consist largely of an orchard, perhaps accompanied by areas of vegetable garden, supplying produce for sale at local markets. Isaac Stansby owned two orchards in the parish of Brent Eleigh in Suffolk, around 14 miles (22km) from Ipswich, when he drew up his will in 1719. In this he describes himself as a 'labourer', not a farmer.[80] In 1726 he secured a mortgage of £10 from Robert Colman, a local gentleman, using for security the cottage in which he lived, 'with that part of the house inhabited by James Beeston and 2 orchards and all trees and water spring thereto belonging'.[81] Whether because he defaulted on the payments, or for some other reason, a little later we find Stansby making a new boundary 'to separate that part of his orchard which he still possesses from part he now grants to Edward Colman, gent'.[82] Such small, specialist producers were probably more common than we imagine in the period before the mid-nineteenth century, but there are only a few places where the remains of their orchards survive in the modern landscape, and these date from the very end of the period under consideration here. One example is at Ivy Cottage, Wreningham, Norfolk, which was planted, probably in the 1850s, across the majority of a small 4-acre (1.6-hectare) plot of land attached to an adjacent cottage (which together formed the sole property of a single individual when the tithes were commuted in 1837).[83] None of the original planting exists but the oldest trees – including an ancient Dr Harvey apple tree, an old culinary variety long associated with East Anglia – may have been planted before 1900, and the remains of a perimeter belt of cobnuts still survives.[84]

For obvious reasons, small commercial orchards were most common in and on the margins of the larger towns and cities; printed maps, such as John Ogilby's 1674 survey of Ipswich, show them densely scattered between the houses. Thomas Fuller famously declared in 1662 that it was impossible to tell whether Norwich was 'a city in an orchard or an orchard in a city', so full was it of fruit trees.[85] Even in the Middle Ages urban

---

79 SRO, L, 741/HA12/D4/4; SRO, I, HD 417/37.
80 SRO, B, 1754/3/21.
81 SRO, B, 1754/1/246.
82 SRO, B, 1754/1/248.
83 NRO, DN/TA 173. The orchard is at TM 1571 9841.
84 R. Hogg, *British Pomology: Or The History, Description, Classification, And Synonyms Of the Fruits and Fruit Trees of Great Britain* (London, 1851), p. 107.
85 T. Fuller, *The History of the Worthies of England* (London, 1662), p. 274.

orchards are frequently referred to in leases and deeds, such as the tenement in St Stephens in Norwich described in a grant of 1466 as comprising 'an orchard, a little house and a small piece of land'.[86] In 1781 John Blatch Whaley leased for seven years a property in Colchester comprising land in Maldon Lane with a cottage and 89 fruit trees to 'William Burridge, gardener'.[87] The trees in these small commercial orchards, especially in urban or suburban locations, appear to have been more frequently inter-planted with soft fruit such as gooseberries or blackcurrants, or with vegetables, than those found on farms. A lease for land in Heigham in Norwich from 1684 described it as being in the 'form of a triangle planted with 60 fruit trees and 200 gooseberry and currant bushes'.[88] An inventory of the trees and bushes growing in 1831 on a property on Lower Olland Street in Bungay, Suffolk, occupied by a Mrs Whiskin, lists 678 plum, peach, apricot, nectarine, cherry, apple, pear and bullace trees, 37 nut bushes and 2,040 'currant and gooseberry bushes'.[89]

Some of these small producers developed particular specialities, especially in cherry growing, leading to the often short-lived local fame of certain villages. William Bullein, in his *Government of Health* of 1595, concludes his discussion of cherries with the statement that 'In the country of Kent be growing great plenty of this fruite, So are there in a towne neare unto Norwich called Ketreinham, this fruite is colde and moyst in the first degree.' Perhaps surprisingly, no further reference to Ketteringham's role in this respect has so far been discovered.[90] More enduring was the reputation of the town of Stowmarket in Suffolk as a centre of cherry production, while the area around Sudbury was noted for the cherry known as the 'Polstead Black', after the eponymous village.[91] White's *Directory* for 1845 described how the village of Marham in west Norfolk was also known as 'Cherry Marham' because it was 'formerly noted for its great abundance of *cherries* and *walnuts*'.[92]

What is more interesting than these scattered examples of small commercial orchards are the clear signs that some of the key districts of specialised production that existed by the end of the nineteenth century, and which were noted in the previous chapter, were already emerging by the middle of the eighteenth century and, in some cases, earlier. The most important is the cherry-growing district of west Hertfordshire, where seventeenth- and eighteen-century maps regularly show orchards taking up a significantly greater proportion of farm area than the average of 0.5–1 per cent indicative of domestic production. Over 2 per cent of a farm at Great Gaddesden, mapped in 1756, thus comprised orchards; 1.4 per

---

86   NRO, DCN 45/37/13.
87   SRO, B, HA 519/949.
88   NRO, COL 1/39.
89   SRO, L, 880/D1/96/13.
90   W. Bullein, *The Government of Health* (London, 1595), fol. lxxxiii.
91   E. Kent, *Sylvan Rambles, or a Companion to the Park and Shrubbery* (London, 1825), p. 384; T. Gissing, 'Polstead Cherries', *The Phytologist*, 2 (1857–8), p. 326.
92   W. White, *A History, Gazetteer and Directory of Norfolk* (Sheffield, 1845), p. 620.

cent of Field End Farm, Hemel Hempstead, as mapped in 1764; 3.5 per cent of Heron's Farm in Wheathampstead in 1768; 3 per cent of Jerome's Farm, Redbourn, in 1798; and 2.6 per cent of the farms on an estate in Hemel Hempstead in 1809.[93] Some of the farms in the area had more than one orchard. Cherries were best grown in separate enclosures, because their vigorous growth and spreading habit tended to suppress other kinds of fruit planted beside them. The district did not only produce sweet cherries for the market, although it was most noted for them. In 1804 the agriculturalist Arthur Young described how:

> In the south-west corner of the county, and particularly in the parishes of Rickmersworth [Rickmansworth], Sarret [Sarratt], King's Langley, and Abbot's Langley, Flaunden, Bovingdon and partly in Watford and Aldenham, there are many orchards; apples and cherries are their principal produce. Every farm has an orchard; but the larger the farm the smaller the orchard. Orchards are found chiefly in farms of from 20 to 50 acres. The apples are most profitable; but cherries very beneficial to the poor, in the quantity of employment which they require in gathering the crop, for which the poor are paid from 4d to 8d per dozen pounds.[94]

The cherry district extended into the adjacent parts of Buckinghamshire and, as Batchelor observed in 1808, into the south of Bedfordshire.[95]

The tithe maps and apportionments drawn up in the late 1830s and early 1840s provide further information on the extent of fruit production in the area. Although they do not use 'orchard' as a land-use category in the 'State of Cultivation' column, the term does appear, in some parishes at least, to have been regularly employed as a 'Name and Description of Premises'. The apportionment for King's Langley, drawn up in 1838, records 57 parcels of land in this way, with an average area of 1.25 acres (0.5 hectares), comprising in all around 2 per cent of the total parish land area.[96] In the adjacent parish of Abbots Langley in 1839 there were 49 recorded orchards with an average area of 1.2 acres, here collectively covering 1.2 per cent of the land.[97] In Sarratt in 1840 there were 37 orchards, again with an average area of 1.2 acres, collectively covering 44.5 acres (18 hectares), or 2.9 per cent of the total parish area.[98] In this parish the largest orchard covered 6.3 acres (2.6 hectares); in King's Langley, 5.6 acres (2.3 hectares); in Abbot's Langley, 5.25 acres (2.1 hectares). Almost all the orchards appear to have formed part of a working farm, albeit (as Young implies) generally one of the smaller examples. Indeed, one of the characteristics of this district, in addition to the fact that it lay almost entirely in ancient enclosures, was the large number of small

---

93 HALS, 15597; AH 681; D/EV R2; AH/2772.
94 A. Young, *Hertfordshire* (London, 1804), p. 143.
95 Batchelor, *Bedford*, p. 458.
96 HALS, D/P64/27/1–27/4.
97 HALS, DSA4/63/1–32.
98 HALS, DSA4/92/1–6.

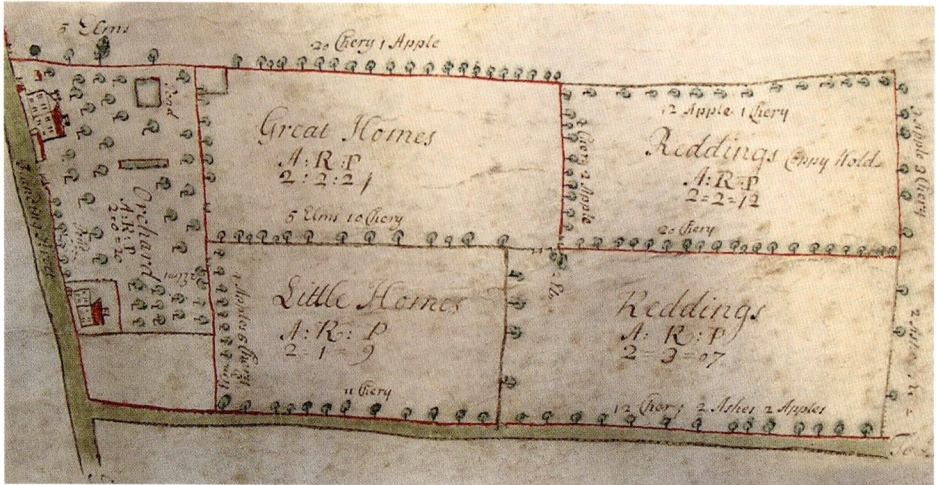

Figure 2.6 A map of a farm at Flaunden in west Hertfordshire, surveyed around 1700, showing the local custom of growing apples and cherries as hedgerow trees. Hertfordshire Archives and Local Studies D/EX905/P1.

farms. Fruit growing thus formed one part of a mixed farming enterprise, something rather different from the small commercial (and often urban or suburban) orchards or combined orchards and market gardens just discussed. As William Ellis suggested, cherries made an attractive crop in the district because they were ready for harvest at a time when labour was abundant, between the hay and grain harvests.[99] In 1864 James Clutterbuck described how the fruit was usually sold on the trees to dealers, realising between 12s and 16s per 'ped', or basket, holding 'about four dozen pounds'. The crop was profitable, but precarious. It was 'very often destroyed in a single night by an untimely frost'.[100]

Typical, perhaps, of the kind of small farm described by Young was an unnamed property in Flaunden shown on an undated map of *c.*1700. This comprised just under 50 acres of land (*c.*20 hectares) but its orchard covered more than 2 acres, around 4 per cent of its total area. The map also shows another feature that appears to have been typical of the district (Figure 2.6): unusually, it names the species of tree growing in the hedges around the various fields, detailing 27 oaks, 18 elms, nine ash and 15 'asps' (aspen), but as many as 59 apple trees and no fewer than 165 cherries.[101] John Norden, writing in 1608, noted the 'south part of Hertfordshire' as one of the areas of the country in which fruit trees were frequently planted in hedges, although he bemoaned the fact that they were disappearing, as the modern generation failed to replace those that had grown old and died.[102] He was

---

99 W. Ellis, *Chiltern and Vale Farming* (London, 1733), pp. 141–2.
100 J. Clutterbuck, *Agricultural Notes on Hertfordshire* (London, 1864), p. 14.
101 HALS, DE/X905/P1.
102 J. Norden, *The Surveyor's Dialogue* (London, 1608), p. 209.

apparently being overly pessimistic: Moses Cook, who lived for a time at Cashiobury near Watford, in the heart of this orcharding district, was still advocating the planting of apple trees in hedges in 1676, while William Ellis, who lived at Little Gaddesden in the first half of the eighteenth century, wrote as if hedgerow cherry trees were a normal feature of the local landscape.[103] It should be noted, however, that cherry trees also produced useful timber, and some examples may have been planted or encouraged with this at least partly in mind. Ellis considered cherry timber to be comparable in durability and strength to that of oak, although modern foresters note its variable quality in this regard.[104] The valuation of trees made at the enclosure of Aldenham in south Hertfordshire in 1803 makes an explicit distinction between 'cherry' and 'cherry timber'; there were also 'cherry saplings'.[105] The planting of fruit trees in the hedges of Hertfordshire appears to have declined from the late eighteenth century, and there is no trace of the custom in the local landscape today.

West Hertfordshire mainly comprises the long dipslope of the Chiltern Hills, a district of light, sandy clays overlying chalk at no great depth, making for the kinds of water-retentive, yet seldom waterlogged, soil which, as noted in Chapter 1, are particularly suitable for fruit trees, and especially cherries. Indeed, gean or wild cherry (*Prunus avium*) grew abundantly in the local woods, thus providing large quantities of suitable rootstocks.[106] The area also lay only a short distance – between 20 and 30 miles (32 and 48km) – by road from London. All this doubtless encouraged an early interest in orchards as a profitable alternative to arable farming, perhaps especially among small farmers in the late seventeenth and early eighteenth centuries, when stagnant population growth reduced the profitability of arable farming, as it did (to a greater degree) on rather similar soils in Kent, to the south-east of the capital.[107] Ellis in 1742 seems to suggest that cherry orchards were by then well established in the district, describing how 'the County of Hartfordshire does certainly more abound in Plantations of the common Black Cherry Tree, than any other in England, and in particular the western parts where I now live, is as famous for the black, as Kent is for the red or Flemish Cherry'.[108] A number of different varieties of sweet cherry were grown here by the early eighteenth century, including the May-Duke or Archduke, which probably originated nearby in Buckinghamshire, and the Caroon, also known as the Hertfordshire Black (Figure 2.7). Ellis was fulsome in his praise of the latter: 'Oh! How rich a Fruit is this Black Kerroon Cherry, eaten in a Morning tasting, off the Tree:

---

103 M. Cook, *The Manner of Raising, Ordering, and Improving Forest and Fruit-Trees* (London, 1676), p. 138; Ellis, *Timber Tree Improved*, p. 64.
104 *Timber Tree Improved*, p. 66.
105 HALS, D/EX 216 B2–4.
106 Ellis, *Timber Tree Improved*, p. 66.
107 B. Short, 'The South-East: Kent, Surrey and Sussex', in J. Thirsk (ed.), *The Agrarian History of England and Wales Vol. V, I, 1640–1750* (Cambridge, 1984), p. 276.
108 Ellis, *Timber Tree Improved*, p. 65.

Figure 2.7 The Caroon cherry, one of the main varieties planted in the west Hertfordshire orchards, as illustrated by George Bradshaw in his *Pomona Britannica* of 1812.

which, for its noble, pleasant Taste, and laxative, antiscorbutic Quality, is most delicious.'[109] In 1864, according to Clutterbuck, the 'Carron' and the 'small Hertfordshire Black' were the mainstays of the local growers.[110]

Another important area of early commercial production was the Fenland of Cambridgeshire and west Norfolk. In the *General View of the Agriculture of the County of Cambridge*, published in 1811, William Gooch described how at 'Ely, Soham, Wisbech &c' there were 'many large gardens, producing so abundantly of vegetables and common kinds of fruit, as to supply not only the neighbouring towns but counties, the produce being sent to a great distance, to Lynn, &c. &c. by water, and by land, affording employ for many hands, labourers, retailers, carriers, &c. &c.'. He added that orchards were 'numerous and large in the same districts as the gardens; the chief growth, apples and cherries; Soham is remarkable for the latter.'[111] These places could all boast very large numbers of orchards by the end of the nineteenth century. The town of Wisbech, as we noted earlier, was the centre of a major fruit-growing area that extended into the adjacent parts of west Norfolk, and, as Gooch implies, was also a major inland port on the river Nene.

The northern Fenland was, like west Hertfordshire, an area of old enclosure and relatively small farms, and with soils well suited to fruit growing – in this case, silty loams kept free from waterlogging by rigorously managed drainage systems. In Wisbech St Peter

---

109 Ellis, *Timber Tree Improved*, p. 130.
110 Clutterbuck, *Agricultural Notes*, p. 14.
111 W. Gooch, *General View of the Agriculture of the County of Cambridge* (London, 1811), pp. 195–6.

the term 'orchard' appears no fewer than 22 times in the 'Name and Description of Land and Premises' of the tithe apportionment.[112] The plots in question were, however, small – only two covered more than 3 acres – and they amounted in all to only 43 acres (*c.*17 hectares), around 0.6 per cent of parish area. In the nearby Norfolk parishes of Emneth and Outwell (1841) there were 33 parcels named 'orchard' covering around 1 per cent of the parish area.[113] In Terrington, to the west of Wisbech, even less of the land area – a mere 0.4 per cent – was occupied by parcels explicitly named as 'orchard', while none at all appear in the apportionments for Wisbech St Mary (1838) or West Walton (1839), both of which were – by 1900 – major fruit-growing parishes.[114] In all these parishes, however, it is possible that other areas planted with fruit trees existed, included in parcels bearing such labels as 'gardens and yards'. In this context it is noteworthy that, in the case of Walsoken, the only place in the immediate area of Wisbech with a tithe apportionment (1842) that specifically distinguishes 'orchard' in the 'State of Cultivation' column, no fewer than 47 parcels are so described, a total of 100 acres (*c.*40 hectares), or 2.2 per cent of the parish area.[115] A significant fruit-growing industry was thus emerging, but the amount of land devoted to orchards was still comparatively small by later standards. It is noteworthy that the tithe apportionments describe some of the larger orchards in this district as 'arable' rather than pasture, suggesting that they were already being interplanted with soft fruit, vegetables or other crops, as was to be the local practice in the following century.

Despite Gooch's comments, there are rather fewer signs in the tithe apportionments that orchards had become a major aspect of the rural economy further to the south, on the Fen islands around Ely and Soham, before the second half of the nineteenth century. The tithe schedule for the latter parish refers to 'orchards' only in the 'Name and Description of Land and Premises' column, rather than as a form of land use: 42 parcels of land are so named but they collectively cover only 57 acres (23 hectares), or 0.5 per cent of the land area, although it is again probable that some examples were described in other ways.[116] The 1843 apportionment for Ely does use 'orchard' as a land-use descriptor but there is a suspicion that some examples were subsumed within the category of 'Garden &c'. Only 20 orchards are specifically described as such, totalling only 0.25 per cent of the land area.[117] A similar picture emerges if we look at the parishes located on the band of Lower Greensand soils running along the southern margins of the Fens, which were later noted for their extensive orchards. In Cottenham, for example, the combined area covered by all the parcels named 'orchard' in the apportionment of 1837 amounted to only 35 acres (*c.*14

---

112   PRO/TNA, IR 29/4/90 and 30/4/90.

113   NRO, DE/TA 10.

114   PRO/TNA, IR 29/4/89 and 30/4/89; NRO, DE/TA 34; PRO/TNA, IR 29/23/52 and 30/23/552.

115   NRO, DE/TA 33.

116   PRO/TNA, IR 29 and 30/4/13.

117   PRO/TNA, IR 29/4/29.

hectares), a mere 0.5 per cent of parish area, whereas by 1901, when the second edition Ordnance Survey 6-inch map was surveyed, there were around 242 hectares of orchard, more than 8 per cent of the parish.[118] At nearby Willingham the apportionment of 1837 records only seven orchards covering around 10 acres (4 hectares), a mere 0.2 per cent of parish area.[119] Although to some extent this low figure may again reflect the definitions employed by the tithe commissioners – where the apportionment records 'garden', the Ordnance Survey surveyors might have seen an orchard – there were at that time clearly only a fraction of the number of orchards that were present by the end of the century, when they covered 284 acres (115 hectares), over 6 per cent of the land area. Here, even more than in the Wisbech district, orchards were more of a profitable sideline or the specialist pursuit of a small minority than the kind of major industry they had become by the end of the century. This said, the fact that a plum variety called the Willingham Gage is recorded before 1800 does, perhaps, suggest the importance of fruit growing in the local economy.[120]

The third main area of Cambridgeshire in which commercial orchards formed a prominent feature of the landscape by the end of the nineteenth century also displays only limited signs of specialisation in the tithe apportionments. The villages lying at the foot of the chalk escarpment in the south of the county were, for the most part, characterised in the early nineteenth century by significant numbers of small farms, many owner-occupied, and extensive open fields survived in most parishes into the nineteenth century.[121] Meldreth and Haslingfield were enclosed in 1820, Orwell in 1837 and Melbourn in 1840.[122] Indeed, the latter still remained open in 1839, when the tithe apportionment described no fewer than 47 parcels of land as 'orchard' in the 'Name and Description of Premises' column. Most were small, however, so that they collectively covered only 32 acres (13 hectares), *c.*0.7 per cent of the parish area.[123] This was, nevertheless, actually a tenth of the *enclosed* land in the parish. The situation was similar in Haslingfield, where the apportionment of 1842 lists 21 orchards covering 17 acres (7 hectares), again *c.*0.7 per cent of the land area. One was presumably the 'orchard of fruit at Haslingfield' that was put on the market eight years later.[124] Some moves towards commercial production on these loamy, calcareous clay soils, ideal for the cultivation of plums, had evidently been made before the middle decades of the nineteenth century, but the industry was still in its infancy.

---

118 PRO/TNA, IR29/4/21.

119 PRO/TNA, IR29/4/85.

120 Information from the excellent EEAOP website, <https://www.applesandorchards.org.uk/cambridgeshire-information/>, accessed 4 November 2020.

121 S. Wittering, *Ecology and Enclosure: The Effects of Enclosure on Society, Farming and the Environment in South Cambridgeshire, 1798–1859* (Oxford, 2013), especially pp. 17–40.

122 W.E. Tate and M. Turner, *A Domesday of English Enclosure Acts and Awards* (Reading, 1978), pp. 72–5, 142–3.

123 PRO/TNA, IR29/4/52.

124 CRO, 296/ B830.

There are clearer traces in the documentary record of the early development of commercial production in some of the other districts in eastern England, where, by the end the nineteenth century, orchards appear to have been relatively dense on the ground. The cluster of orchards in south-east Hertfordshire, for example, seems to have been developing by the early years of the nineteenth century. It was centred on the large parish of Cheshunt, and here the tithe apportionment of 1841 records no fewer than 78 orchards.[125] Most were small, with the largest covering around 5.7 acres (2.3 hectares), but they cumulatively extended over 75 acres (30 hectares), around 1.6 per cent of the parish area. London lay only 14 miles (22km) away by road, and the area was already developing as a major centre for market gardening, with the first of what were to become many glasshouses being erected by the end of the nineteenth century in the hamlet of Turnford, in the north of Cheshunt parish. There are also signs that commercial orchards were developing – well before the end of the eighteenth century – in south Essex, although not apparently in the area around Southend, where, by 1900, they were beginning to be a prominent feature of the landscape and were to become more so over the next two decades. The apportionment for Prittlewell, unusually for Essex, employs 'orchard' as a land-use category in the 'State of Cultivation' column, but only ten examples are listed, covering in all less than 7 acres (2.8 hectares) in a parish of over 6,500 acres (2,630 hectares).[126] The tithe commissioners followed a similar practice in Thundersley, and here only two orchards are mentioned.[127] Instead, orchards seem, in the eighteenth century, to have been more generally scattered in areas close to ports along the Thames, from which there was easy access by river to London. In 1777, when a property in Grays Thurrock called 'Ripleys, otherwise Notts, otherwise Stodies Farm' was placed on the market, the Great and Little Orchard together extended over no less than 18 acres (c.7 hectares).[128] Arthur Young, writing in 1804, singled out 'Burnham, Southminster &c' on the Dengie peninsula – coastal parishes a little way north of the estuary – as places where there were 'many Cherry orchards'.[129]

Conclusion

In the period before the mid-nineteenth century orchards were a common feature of the rural landscape almost everywhere in the eastern counties, a normal adjunct of farms both large and small. But they usually covered only a small area of ground, generally accounting for less than 1 per cent of farm area and significantly less of the landscape as a whole if we take into account roads, commons and woodland. Orchards were usually located beside the farmhouse, partly for convenience and security but also, perhaps, for

---

125   HALS, DSA4/30/2.
126   PRO/TNA, IR 29/12/266.
127   PRO/TNA, IR 29/12/339.
128   ERO, D/DU 218/5.
129   Young, *Essex*, vol. 2, p. 132.

aesthetic reasons. They were dominated by trees on vigorous rootstocks, mainly apples but often with a significant minority of pears. Cherries, plums, cobnuts and filberts were also common features, although less numerous and mostly planted around the margins of the orchard. The majority of orchards were laid to grass and grazed by sheep or poultry and/ or mown for hay, and bee hives were often kept there. Only occasionally are there signs that the ground between the trees was cultivated. Such orchards mainly produced fruit for domestic consumption but also, in most cases, a surplus that was sold locally, making a relatively small but useful contribution to the farmer's income.

The overwhelming majority of orchards were like this. But there were also, from an early date, some examples of more specialised commercial producers, often but by no means always located close to major urban centres. In such orchards, the ground between the trees was more frequently planted with soft fruit or vegetables. There were also a few districts in which, on soils particularly well suited to fruit growing, farms more generally appear, by the eighteenth century, to have expanded the fruit-growing side of their businesses, so that the area of land devoted to orchards rose above 1 per cent, although seldom above 3 per cent, of total farm area. The most important of these was west Hertfordshire, together with the adjacent parts of Buckinghamshire and Bedfordshire, where cherries and, to a lesser extent, apples were being cultivated on a significant scale by the end of the seventeenth century, destined in part for the London markets. Scattered parishes elsewhere lying within easy reach of London had also, by the early nineteenth century, begun to expand their orchards, while some degree of specialisation is also apparent in the Fenlands of Cambridgeshire and west Norfolk, where navigable waterways leading to the coast facilitated the movement of fruit, probably to places as far away as north-east England. But in all these areas the amount of land devoted to orchards – even in *c*.1840 – remained limited compared with the situation at the end of the nineteenth century. And in many of the areas in which, by this time, orchards were extensive, commercial fruit growing had hardly begun, or was continuing at only a low level, at the time of tithe commutations in *c*.1840. In the eastern counties the true development of 'orchard countries', in which fruit growing made a significant impact on the wider environment, was largely a phenomenon of the century after 1850.

CHAPTER THREE

The 'orchard century', c.1850–1960

The orchard century

The 'orchard century' is a convenient term for the period between 1850 and the late 1950s when orchards reached their greatest extent in the eastern counties. Districts in which commercial production was already established by 1850 saw further growth – especially the Fens – but of more significance was the emergence of new fruit-growing districts, such as south Bedfordshire, as well as the more localised eruption of orchards and fruit farms, especially in the inter-war years. This remarkable growth in commercial production – followed, as we shall see, by an even more rapid decline – was the consequence of a complex and interrelated set of factors and influences, of which the most important was the progressive urbanisation of British society. Major conurbations developed in the industrial north and Midlands, London expanded inexorably and most other towns and cities experienced significant growth. The population of the capital, including its outer suburbs, more than doubled between 1850 and 1900. These concentrations of people, many of whom lived with little or nothing in the way of gardens, constituted a substantial market for milk, vegetables, eggs – and fruit. Some of this produce could be supplied locally, from market gardens and small farms on the outskirts or even within conurbations, which in the period before the middle of the twentieth century were much less continuously built up than is generally the case today. But much was supplied by areas particularly well suited to these forms of production, often lying at a considerable distance. Yet urban markets, especially those located well outside the region, could not have been provided with fruit without the development of new transport systems. The main rail line from London to Manchester, passing through the orchard district of west Hertfordshire and just clipping the western edge of Bedfordshire, was completed in the late 1830s; those from King's Lynn, through the orchard areas around Wisbech, to the Midlands, and from London, through east Hertfordshire, to Cambridge, appeared in the following decade. Through the 1850s, 1860s and 1870s railway lines and stations proliferated, and by 1900 few places in eastern England lay more than five miles (c.8km) from a railway station.[1]

---

1 D.I. Gordon, *A Regional History of the Railways of Great Britain, Vol. 5: The Eastern Counties*, rev. edn (Newton Abbot, 1977).

The growth of an urban population and the development of improved transport systems were the key factors encouraging expansion. But other influences were important, including wider changes in the farming industry and in the agricultural landscape; government policy; and the development of fruit-processing industries. Of particular significance was the great depression in agriculture which began in the late 1870s. In America large areas of the prairies were ploughed up as the growth of the rail network allowed grain to be transported to the east-coast ports, where it was loaded onto steam ships and transported to Europe. Wheat prices halved in England between 1873 and 1893, while those for barley and oats fell by a third. This collapse in cereal prices was soon followed by problems in the livestock sector, caused by the development of refrigerated transport ships and the large-scale importation of meat from south America, Australia and elsewhere. Meat prices fell by between 15 and 20 per cent in the same 20-year period, and those for butter and cheese by 15 per cent.[2] Nevertheless, it was unquestionably arable districts that were most badly affected by depression and, for the most part, eastern England was an area of grain production, in which livestock farming took second place in the economy of most farms. In the case of Norfolk and Suffolk, Thompson has calculated that the fall in value of gross farm output between 1873 and 1894 was 14 per cent.[3] Some modern historians have suggested that the parlous condition of agriculture in the late nineteenth and early twentieth centuries can be exaggerated but, overall, this was not a good time for conventional agriculture in the eastern counties. The outbreak of war in 1914 saw some recovery in farming fortunes, but by the early 1920s depression had returned. Although the widespread adoption of sugar beet as a crop helped many arable farmers to remain in business, it was only with the outbreak of the Second World War that prices, especially those for grain crops, really recovered. In difficult circumstances, not surprisingly, many farmers sought new ways of making money from the land. Where conditions were suitable, diversification into milk production, poultry, pigs and eggs made economic sense, as did vegetable and fruit growing, especially for smaller producers who were, in general terms, more adversely affected by the decline in cereal prices than large ones, who were capable of benefiting from economies of scale. Landowners and, as we shall see, county councils encouraged the establishment of small farms and smallholdings, on many of which orchards were a prominent or even dominant part of the enterprise.

The precise balance of these different economic, technological and social influences on the orchard industry changed significantly over time, and in complex ways. But it is convenient for most purposes to make a broad distinction between developments occurring before, and after, the First World War.

---

2 P.J. Perry, *British Farming in the Great Depression: An Historical Geography* (Newton Abbot, 1974); R. Perren, *Agriculture in Depression 1870–1940* (Cambridge, 1995); S. Wade Martins and T. Williamson, *The Countryside of East Anglia: Changing Landscapes, 1870–1950* (Woodbridge, 2008), pp. 11–44.

3 F.M.L. Thompson, 'An Anatomy of English Agriculture, 1870–1914', in B.A. Holderness and N. Turner (eds), *Land, Labour and Agriculture 1700–1920* (London, 1991), pp. 211–40; p. 232.

Before 1914

Urban growth and the spread of the railways led to the development of a major new fruit-growing area in south Bedfordshire, at the foot of the Chiltern escarpment, where numerous newly planted orchards were devoted to the cultivation of 'Aylesbury Prunes', so called because they were also grown in the adjoining area of Buckinghamshire, the Vale of Aylesbury. The 'prune' was not a 'prune' in the usual sense of the word – that is, it was not a dried plum. It was a small dark cooking plum or late eater, a cultivar of the damson, which may have been grown in local farm orchards for many decades before the development of large-scale commercial production.

The tithe maps and apportionments give little indication of an emerging fruit-growing industry in the district, but by the early twentieth century Aylesbury Prune orchards were very large and numerous in a band 2 or 3 miles (*c*.3–5km) wide extending for some 12 miles (*c*.19km) from Weston Turville in Buckinghamshire in the south-west to Stanbridge and Totternhoe in Bedfordshire in the north-east, and including the extreme north-western corner of Hertfordshire, to the north of Tring.[4] Vast areas of orchards existed in villages such as Totternhoe, Billington, Eggington and Slapton: there were well over a hundred separate orchards in Eaton Bray alone by the time the second edition Ordnance Survey 6-inch map was surveyed in 1898, extending collectively over 50 hectares (Figure 3.1). The soils in the area, comprising calcareous loams and clays overlying chalk and Upper Greensand at the foot of the Chiltern escarpment, were well suited to commercial fruit growing, especially the cultivation of plums (Figure 3.2).[5] Such fertile and tractable soils also encouraged the survival of freehold farms and it is possible that specialised fruit growing may have been held back by the late survival of open fields and given a significant stimulus by their enclosure: Eaton Bray was finally enclosed only in 1860 and Totternhoe, the last village in Bedfordshire to be enclosed, not until 1891. But here, as elsewhere, the key development was the arrival of the railways. Most of the fruit was taken, packed in baskets or 'skips', to the railway station at Cheddington, just over the county boundary in Buckinghamshire, or to the halt at Stanbridge, both of which were on the London–Manchester line opened in 1838. Most of the fruit seems to have gone to London but much went north, to Bolton, Manchester, Wigan or Liverpool. The fruit, as in many other districts, was auctioned on the tree: a sales catalogue from 1911, relating to orchards in Stanbridge, Eaton Bray, Northall and Cheddington, describes how trees excluded from the sale would be 'marked by the usual hay, straw or whitewash band'.[6] There is a persistent story that the damsons were used for dyeing military uniforms and hats made in Luton,

---

[4] M. Farnell, 'The Neglected Aylesbury Prune', *Buckinghamshire and Bedfordshire Countryside* (March 1972), pp. 14–16.

[5] C.A.H. Hodge, R.G.O. Burton, W.M. Corbett, R. Evans and R.S. Searle, *Soils and their Use in Eastern England* (Harpenden, 1984), pp. 186–92.

[6] BRO, BML 10/7/12.

58 The Orchards of Eastern England

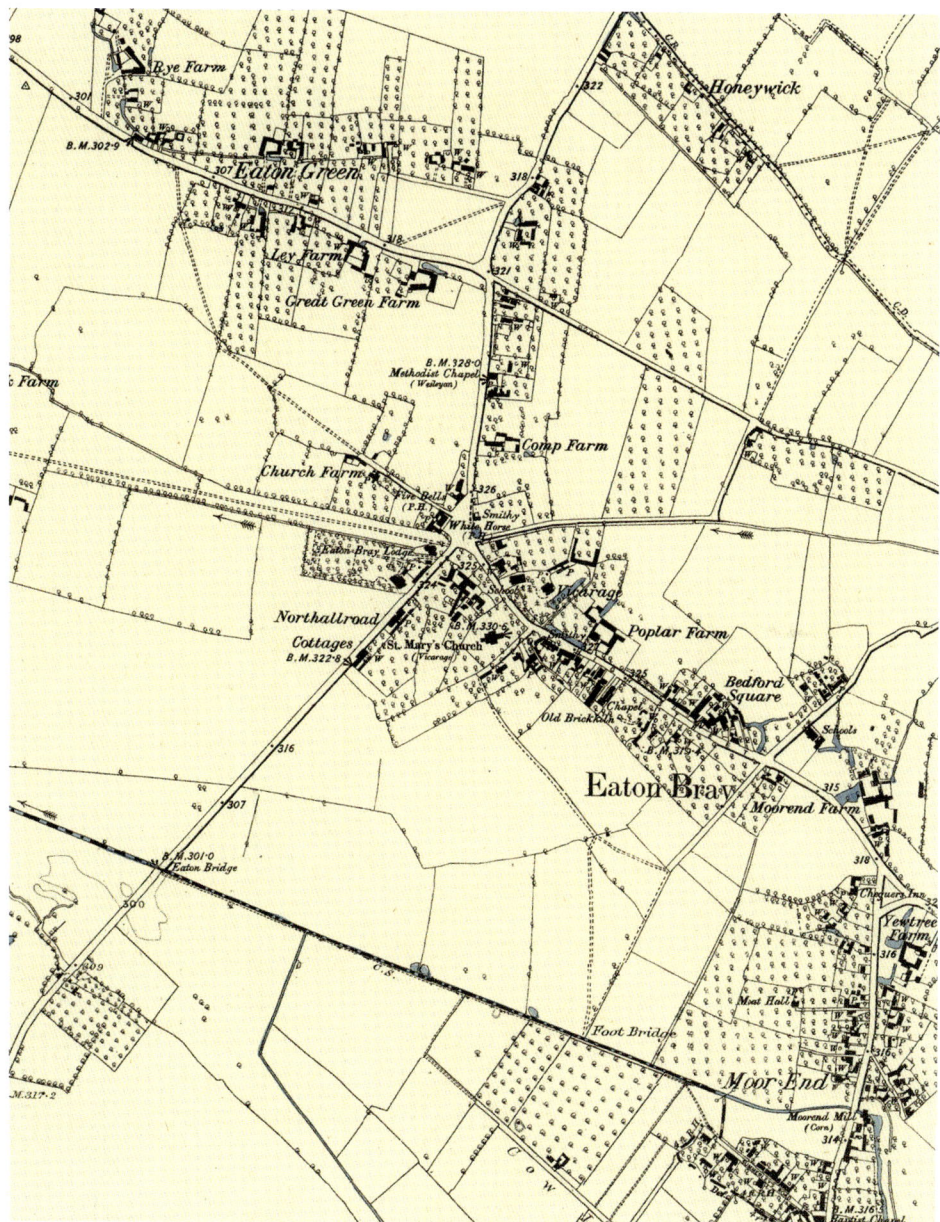

Figure 3.1 Extract from the 6-inch Ordnance Survey map of 1887 showing the density of orchards in Eaton Bray, in the heart of the Bedfordshire 'Prune' country.

Figure 3.2 One of the surviving 'Prune' orchards at Eaton Bray, Bedfordshire.

although no hard evidence to support it. The orchards were largely, if not entirely, laid to grass under the trees; sheep were grazed in many, but some appear to have been used to fatten that other local speciality, Aylesbury ducks.

The south Bedfordshire orchards produced not only Aylesbury Prunes but also apples, cherries and, in particular, other kinds of damson. When the northern portion of the Ashridge estate was placed on the market in 1923, including much land straddling the Buckinghamshire and Bedfordshire border in 'prune country', several of the farms were described as having 'enclosures of Orchard Land planted with Prune and Damson trees in full bearing'. Some were substantial farms on which orchards formed an important but not dominant part of the enterprise. Ivinghoe Aston Farm, for example, was described as an 'important stock and fruit farm' covering 490 acres (198 hectares), of which *c.*2.5 per cent was orchard land. But five were smallholdings largely or entirely devoted to fruit production, each extending over between 7 and 13 acres (*c.*3 and *c.*5 hectares).[7]

There was also a marked expansion in the number of orchards in south-east Essex. To some extent, this was part of a wider development – the growth of the Essex market-gardening industry – for many orchards formed only one part of a larger smallholding

---

7   HALS, DE/By/B1.

business.⁸ Essex market gardens grew celery, asparagus, radishes, onions and lettuces; the larger farms produced peas, cabbages, potatoes, cauliflowers, carrots and early greens. Such enterprises were, unsurprisingly, concentrated in the south-west of the county, in the vicinity of London. But they were prominent all along the band of light, well-drained soils that runs beside the Thames from Rainham to Stanford-le-Hope and Grays Thurrock. The latter parish had more than a fifth of its land area devoted to market gardens and orchards by 1870.⁹ The development of commercial orchards and market gardens was accelerated by the agricultural depression of the late nineteenth century, and by 1900 there were noticeable clusters of orchards in Orsett and in the area around Hadleigh, Thundersley and South Benfleet. All lay close to stations on the London, Tilbury and Southend line, opened in 1856, although an important local market was provided by Southend, already emerging as a major holiday resort. The development of the south-east Essex orchards was still in its early stages at the start of the twentieth century; the following two decades saw a more significant expansion of fruit growing in this district, the number of orchards in the area more than doubling by 1925.

The large orchards at Hadleigh, close to the Thames and a little to the west of Southend, have their own distinct history. They were associated with the Home Farm Colony, which was established by the Salvation Army on the site now occupied by the Hadleigh Downs Country Park. In 1891 General William Booth purchased 900 acres (364 hectares) of land here, comprising Home Farm, Castle Farm, Park Farm and Sayers Farm, in the area between the village of Hadleigh and the estuary, with the intention of giving 'employment (and food and lodgings in return for his labour) to any man who is willing to work, irrespective of nationality or creed'.¹⁰ In less than a year 250 volunteers from the East End were working here. A few years later the writer Rider Haggard described how the colony was 'a place where broken men of bad habits, who chance in most cases to have had some connexion with or liking for the land, can be reformed, and ultimately sent out to situations, or as emigrants to Canada. About 400 of such men pass through the Colony each year'.¹¹ The colony had a diversified economy, with market gardens, a livestock farm and a brickworks, but the orchards were particularly extensive, covering more than 20 hectares by the time the second edition Ordnance Survey 6-inch map was surveyed in 1895 (and nearly 30 hectares by the 1920s). The colony had a jetty from which produce could be taken by barge to London, although much of the fruit and vegetables was sold locally.¹²

---

8   J. Pam, 'Essex Agriculture: Landowners' and Farmers' Responses to Economic Change, 1850–1914', PhD thesis (University of London, 2004), pp. 138–40.

9   Pam, 'Essex Agriculture', p. 138.

10 G. Parhill and G. Cook, *Hadleigh Salvation Army Farm: A Vision Reborn* (Hadleigh, 2008).

11 H. Rider Haggard, *Regeneration: Being an Account of the Social Work of the Salvation Army in Great Britain* (London, 1910), p. 196.

12 Parhill and Cook, *Hadleigh*; H. Rider Haggard, *Rural England*, Vol. 1 (London, 1906), pp. 493–504.

Figure 3.3 Workers in the orchards of Wilkin and Son's jam company, Tiptree, Essex, c.1910.

More localised clusters of orchards developed elsewhere in Essex, especially in the vicinity of major towns such as Chelmsford and Colchester and wherever there were good transport links to London – principally in the area flanking what is now the A12, running diagonally through the centre of the county. There was also a significant cluster on the western border of the county, in the Lea valley between Waltham Cross and Roydon, an extension of the orchard area of south-east Hertfordshire. Of particular interest is the concentration in mid-Essex, in the vicinity of the village of Tiptree, which was associated with the jam factory opened there by Arthur Charles Wilkins in 1885 (discussed in more detail in Chapter 6). By 1906 the family's orchards and small fruit grounds covered more than 800 acres (324 hectares) and were producing some 300 tons of fruit each season (Figure 3.3).[13]

Of more importance than the development of new orchard districts, however, was the rapid expansion of fruit growing in most of the areas where it was already of some significance by c.1850. By the end of the nineteenth century the parishes lying to the

---

13 'Wilkinson's Jam: A Potted History', <www.tiptree.com>, accessed June 2020.

north of Cambridge, on the margins of the peat Fens and on the principal Fen islands, boasted immense acreages under fruit. In villages such as Colne, Bluntisham and Earith (in Huntingdonshire) the second edition Ordnance Survey 6-inch maps suggest that orchards accounted for as much as 8 per cent of land area; in Histon and Cottenham the figure was over 9 per cent and in Impington nearly 12 per cent. Once again, expansion followed hard on the heels of the railways and especially the completion in 1847 of the line from Cambridge to Huntingdon, which passed through the middle of Histon, Willingham and Over, and which provided access, via Huntingdon, to both the London and the northern markets.[14] But, as in the area around Tiptree in Essex, another important factor was the establishment of a significant local processor. As discussed in more detail in Chapter 6, the Chivers jam company, based in Histon, was a major consumer of local fruit, especially plums. Production began on a small scale in 1873, but expanded massively a few years later with the completion of the Victoria Works. In 1894 the company began fruit canning and by 1900 a new factory had been built, which by the 1920s, accompanied by ancillary buildings and fruit stores, extended over more than 7.5 hectares.[15] The presence of the factory unquestionably encouraged the planting of new orchards in the area and was a major factor in the large proportion of plums grown locally.

In the north Fens the orchards around Wisbech also expanded steadily and by the time the second edition Ordnance Survey 6-inch map was surveyed around 1900 there were more than 7 square kilometres of orchards within 5km of the centre of the town, covering around 9 per cent of the land area. Some of this expansion occurred after 1880 – the silt fens had been prime wheat land but prices slumped with the onset of the agricultural depression, encouraging the small farmers here to diversify (many holdings in the area covered less than 30 acres (*c*.12 hectares)).[16] But the first edition Ordnance Survey maps show that orchards were already extensive by the 1880s and a more important factor was, once again, the arrival of the railways. Originally, as we have noted, much of the produce of the silt-fen orchards was transported by boat. The most important markets, however, lay on the western side of England, in the Midlands and around Manchester, and the rapid growth of the industry seems to have followed the construction through Wisbech of the rail line to Peterborough, which opened in 1848 and provided a link to the main lines running north. Within a few years large areas of orchards were being planted by local farmers such as John Cockett.[17] Further improvements in transport came with the opening of the line from Wisbech to Peterborough in 1866, although local fruit-growers continued to lobby for improvements

---

14 T. Kirby, 'Railways', in T. Kirby and S. Oosthuizen (eds), *An Atlas of Cambridgeshire and Huntingdonshire History* (Cambridge, 2000), section 68.

15 'Histon: Introduction', in A.P.M. Wright and C.P. Lewis (eds), *A History of the County of Cambridge and the Isle of Ely: Volume 9, Chesterton, Northstowe, and Papworth Hundreds* (London, 1989), pp. 93–4.

16 Wade Martins and Williamson, *Countryside of East Anglia*, pp. 7–8, 48–50.

17 Stamp, *Land of Britain*, p. 115.

Figure 3.4 A train on the Wisbech and Upwell 'Tramway', photographed in the 1950s.

to the services to northern England well into the post-war period.[18] But as well as being stimulated by the construction of railway lines passing through the area, the expansion of the Wisbech orchards also encouraged the building of a new railway line – the Wisbech and Upwell Tramway. This was opened in 1883 and, in spite of the fact that passenger services took the form of light tram carriages, was of standard gauge, which ensured that standard goods wagons could run along it (although trains on the line were initially limited to a speed of eight miles per hour). The main goods transported were agricultural produce, including orchard fruit in season.[19] The trains would stop and pick up goods anywhere on the line, making it ideal for transporting fruit (Figure 3.4). From the start, it seems, the orchards around Wisbech grew some plums but mainly apples, especially cooking varieties.

In south Cambridgeshire the story was in many ways similar. By the start of the twentieth century commercial orchards were a prominent feature of the landscape in most of the villages lying to the south and south-west of Cambridge. The area is characterised by loamy soils overlying chalk, chalky drift or Upper Greensand at the foot of the chalk escarpment of the East Anglian Heights, broadly similar in character to the soils found at the foot of the same escarpment in Bedfordshire, where the 'prune' orchards were located.[20] Indeed, it is striking that orchards were much less extensive or numerous at the base of the escarpment

---

18   Kirby, 'Railways'; PRO/TNA, RAIL 396/17 and 18.

19   P. Paye, *The Wisbech and Upwell Tramway* (Tarrant Hinton, 2009); PRO/TNA, RAIL 491/831.

20   Hodge *et al.*, *Soils and their Use*, pp. 189–92.

to the east of the river Cam – to the south-east of Cambridge – where the loamy soils lay much more thinly over the chalk, making for poor growing conditions and especially posing a danger of summer drought.[21] The greatest extent of orchards could, by *c*.1900, be found in the parishes of Great Eversden, Little Eversden, Melbourn and Meldreth, where they covered 21 hectares (3.7 per cent of parish area), 28 hectares (8.7 per cent), 61 hectares (3.36 per cent) and 89 hectares (8.75 per cent), respectively. A further seven villages had between 1.5 and 2.5 per cent of their area occupied by orchards: Barrington (2.5), Bassingbourn (1.5), Orwell (2.25), Harlton (2.5), Haslingfield (2.4), Harston (1.7) and Great Shelford (1.8).[22]

As we have seen, there is some evidence of incipient commercial production of fruit in the area in the first half of the nineteenth century but the industry expanded dramatically after 1850. Enclosure, as in south Bedfordshire, may have facilitated this development, but once again the main stimulus seems to have been the arrival of the railways. The rail line from Cambridge to London via Audley End and Bishop's Stortford was opened in 1845, and that running through the heart of the district, from Cambridge to London via Royston and Hitchin, in 1852. In most of the villages the area under orchards had already attained something like its *c*.1900 level when the first edition Ordnance Survey maps were prepared in the mid-1880s, suggesting that the poor prices for arable produce after the late 1870s was only a minor factor in the development of the local orchards. The soils of the locality were peculiarly well suited to the cultivation of plums, although pears and apples were also widely grown. Typical were the four orchards in Meldreth, the fruit in which were advertised for auction in 1889. One was said to contain 'greengages and other plums', pears and apples; another, 'principally greengages and damsons'.[23]

The important cherry-growing district of west Hertfordshire seems to have experienced rather less expansion in the second half of the century. This was in spite of the continued expansion of London and the construction in 1838, through the heart of the district, of the rail line from London to Birmingham. In some parishes there was little apparent change in the orchard area in the second half of the nineteenth century. In Abbots Langley, for example, 47 orchards had occupied around 1.2 per cent of the land area in 1841 and in the late 1890s, when the second edition Ordnance Survey 6-inch map was surveyed, 49 orchards occupied almost exactly the same area.[24] In a few places there was significant expansion, as in the adjacent parish of Kings Langley. Here there were 57 orchards in 1838, with an average area of 1.25 acres, comprising in all around 2 per cent of land area;[25] by the late 1890s there were 59 orchards, but now covering over 3.1 per cent of the land area. But in many parishes there was an apparent decline. In Sarratt, for example, orchards covered

21 Hodge *et al.*, *Soils and their Use*, p. 268.
22 Ordnance Survey second edition six-inch maps.
23 CRO, 296/SP 190.
24 PRO/TNA, IR29/15/1.
25 PRO/TNA, IR29/15/60.

around 18 hectares, or 3.1 per cent of the parish area, in 1840, but by the 1890s the figures were 12.3 hectares and 2.2 per cent.[26] In 1864 Clutterbuck remarked: 'It does not seem that these orchards have been extended of late years, in spite of the access to the Manufacturing Districts affected by the introduction of railways.'[27] On balance, there was probably a slight increase in the orchard area in west Hertfordshire across the second half of the century, but nothing like the growth seen in the other areas so far discussed. It is possible that the gradual industrialisation of the Gade and Chess valleys in the course of the nineteenth century may have reduced the availability of the cheap seasonal labour on which the success of the cherry harvest depended. Paper mills had been an element of the local landscape since the eighteenth century but they proliferated in the course of the nineteenth, especially following the acquisition by John Dickinson of mills at Apsley near Hemel Hempstead in 1809 and at nearby Nash Mills in 1811.[28] By 1826 Dickinson had established a new works a little further down the Gade, at Home Park in Kings Langley, and in 1830 he opened another at Croxley, still further to the south, beyond Watford.[29] By the 1870s paper mills, owned by a variety of businesses, were closely spaced along the valleys of the Chess (at Solesbridge in Chorleywood, Mill End and Scots Bridge in Rickmansworth); the Colne (at Batchworth in Rickmansworth and Hamper Mill in Watford); and especially the Gade (Frogmore, Apsley, Nash, Home Park and Croxley).[30] By 1900 this was the most industrialised part of Hertfordshire and competition for labour both raised agricultural wages and reduced the availability of the seasonal workers on which the fruit harvest depended.[31]

By c.1900 there were around 19,400 acres (7,851 hectares) of orchards in the seven eastern counties, to judge from the evidence of the second edition Ordnance Survey 6-inch maps. This is substantially more than the figure recorded in the government's Agricultural Returns for 1899 – 13,555 acres (5,487 hectares) – indicating that the latter source recorded only the more obviously 'commercial' examples and largely ignored the smaller farm orchards and other domestic and institutional examples (and anyway excluding from analysis all holdings of less than an acre). The commercial acreage had more than doubled since the first figures were produced in the early 1870s, when 6,240 acres were recorded. In 1873 the density of orchards in each county still broadly reflected the presence of the specialised fruit-growing districts outlined in the previous chapter. Hertfordshire and Cambridgeshire thus had 0.27

---

26 PRO/TNA, IR29/15/85.

27 Clutterbuck, *Agricultural Notes*, p. 14.

28 W. Page (ed.), *Victoria County History, Hertfordshire*, vol. 4 (London, 1914); A.J. Ward, *The Early History of Papermaking at Frogmore Mill and Two Waters Mill, Hertfordshire* (Berkhamsted, 2003); W. Branch Johnson, *Industrial Archaeology of Hertfordshire* (Newton Abbot, 1977), pp. 55–61.

29 J. Evans, *The Endless Web* (London, 1954).

30 M. Stanyon, 'Papermaking', in D. Short (ed.), *An Historical Atlas of Hertfordshire* (Hatfield, 2011), pp. 80–1.

31 J.P. Moore, 'The Impact of Agricultural Depression and Landownership Change on the County of Hertfordshire, c.1870–1914', PhD thesis, University of Hertfordshire, 2010, pp. 60–1.

and 0.2 per cent respectively of their acreage recorded as commercial orchards, while all the others had less than 0.15 per cent.[32] By 1899 Cambridgeshire was the premier fruit-growing county, with 0.55 per cent of its land area occupied by commercial orchards. Hertfordshire again came second, with orchards now accounting for 0.39 per cent of the land, reflecting a more general expansion in production, especially in the south of the county, rather than growth in the cherry orchards in the west. Huntingdonshire came third, at 0.32 per cent, a relatively high figure indicating the importance of the fen-edge orchards in the south-east of the county, already described; while in Bedfordshire orchards accounted for some 0.31 per cent of the land area, reflecting the remarkable expansion of the 'prune' orchards. Essex, with 0.24 per cent, Norfolk, with 0.23 per cent, and Suffolk, with 0.3 per cent, had rather lower densities.[33] The area planted with fruit must have been increasing fast at this time, however, for the Agricultural Returns for 1910 record a total of 20,161 acres (8,159 hectares) of orchard in the seven counties.[34] Cambridgeshire continued to be the leading county, now with 1.1 per cent of its land area occupied by orchards; Hertfordshire again came second, at 0.49 per cent; but Norfolk had risen up the table, coming third with 0.43 per cent, largely a consequence of the further expansion of the Fen orchards around Wisbech. Bedfordshire had increased its orchard area to 0.37 per cent, with further growth in the 'prune' district; but Huntingdonshire (0.30 per cent), Essex (0.28) and Suffolk (0.22) had seen less change.

The geography of commercial production in the eastern counties at the outbreak of the First World War was structured by both environmental factors, especially soils and geology, and social and economic ones, especially access to markets. Indeed, on occasions the latter could override any specifically horticultural considerations. The Holwell Bury estate in Shillington, Bedfordshire, which largely occupied an area of fairly heavy clay soils, was put up for sale in 1898 and the *Victoria County History* described in 1908 how 'that portion which includes the old farm-house and buildings has been purchased by Mr Hartley of Liverpool, and is now used as a fruit-growing farm'.[35] William Pickles Hartley ran what became the largest wholesale grocers in Lancashire and began to produce jam in 1871, eventually coming to concentrate almost entirely on this side of his business. His jam factory moved from Bootle to Liverpool in 1886, and by 1912 Hartley's were the largest jam makers in the world.[36] The Holwell Bury farm was conveniently located a little over a kilometre from Henlow Station on the main line to St Pancras in London and in 1901 Hartley's had opened a factory in Bermondsey to cater for the London market. Although mainly devoted to soft fruit such as strawberries, the farm included nearly 40 hectares of orchards, mainly growing plums, in spite of the poorly draining character of the local soils.

---

32   Parliamentary Papers, Agricultural Returns for Great Britain, 1873.
33   Parliamentary Papers, Agricultural Returns for Great Britain, 1899.
34   Parliamentary Papers, Board of Agriculture and Fisheries. Agricultural Statistics for 1910.
35   W. Page (ed.), *Victoria County History, Bedfordshire*, vol. 2 (London, 1908), p. 296.
36   A.S. Peake, *The Life of Sir William Hartley* (London, 1926).

Inter-war developments

The inter-war period saw further expansion in the number and extent of commercial orchards in eastern England. Growth was spectacular in those districts in which orchards were already numerous, and generally most rapid in the immediate aftermath of the First World War. In Norfolk, for example, the area of commercial orchards rose from 5,685 acres (2,422 hectares) in 1910 to 7,989 (3,233 hectares) in 1925, reaching 9,368 acres (3,791 hectares) by 1939; in Cambridgeshire it increased from 5,867 acres (2,274 hectares) in 1910 to 10,522 acres (4,258 hectares) in 1925, falling back only slightly to 10,173 acres (4,117 hectares) by 1939.[37] But those counties in which orchards had been fewer often saw higher percentage growth, which was concentrated towards the second half of the inter-war period. In Suffolk, for example, the area of commercial orchards increased from 2,042 acres (826 hectares) in 1910 to 3,526 acres (1,427 hectares) in 1926, rising to 4,484 acres (1,815 hectares) in 1938; while in Essex the figures for these same years were 2,770, 4,106 and 8,441 acres (1,121, 1,662 and 3,416 hectares).[38] Overall, the area occupied by commercial, or primarily commercial, orchards in the seven eastern counties increased from 20,161 acres (8,159 hectares) in 1910 to 29,875 acres (12,090 hectares) in 1925, reaching over 36,000 acres (14,570 hectares) on the eve of the Second World War. This growth needs to be viewed in the context of a more general expansion in market gardens and smallholdings. This was fuelled, as already noted, by the inexorable growth of urban and suburban markets and continued agricultural depression, but was also a consequence of deliberate government policy.

From the late nineteenth century a series of parliamentary acts, passed in 1882, 1887, 1892 and 1908, empowered but did not oblige county councils to provide smallholdings for local people, either for rent or sale.[39] Between 1908 and 1914 205,103 acres (83,005 hectares) of land were duly acquired in England, on which no fewer than 14,045 smallholders were settled.[40] But it was the First World War that really gave the movement impetus. In 1919 the Land Settlement (Facilities) Act provided a fund of £20m to buy and equip smallholdings for ex-servicemen, rather than for local labourers, and gave county councils increased powers of compulsory purchase. In spite of the adverse economic climate, 24,000 ex-servicemen were resettled in the country as a whole in the immediate post-war years, and as a result the number of government smallholdings more than doubled.

The eastern counties played a major role in the movement. In Norfolk alone between January and October 1919 5,669 acres (2,294 hectares) were purchased at a cost of £101,681, a figure boosted further by the acquisition of the Burlingham estate in the east of the county at the end of the year. By 1925 there were 27,479 acres (11,121 hectares) of county

---

37 J.E.G. Mosby, *The Land of Britain: Norfolk* (London, 1938), p. 183.
38 R.W. Butcher, *The Land of Britain: Suffolk* (London, 1941), pp. 337–8.
39 Q. Bone, 'Legislation to Revive Small Farming in England 1887–1914', *Agricultural History*, 49 (1975), pp. 653–61; Wade Martins and Williamson, *Countryside of East Anglia*, pp. 55–60.
40 C.W. Rowell, 'County Council Smallholdings, 1908–1958', *Agriculture*, 60 (1959), pp. 109–14.

Figure 3.5 Blofield, Norfolk: an orchard planted in the 1920s on one of the smallholdings created on the old Burlingham estate following its acquisition by Norfolk County Council in 1919.

Figure 3.6 Jeacock's Farm, Tring, one of the Hertfordshire County Council smallholdings, was created in 1920 on land purchased from the Ashridge estate. The original timber-clad smallholder's cottage with cartshed/piggery still remains, beside its orchard.

smallholdings – over 2 per cent of the county's land area.[41] Growth was also rapid in Suffolk, where by 1931 there were 13,319 acres (5,390 hectares) of county smallholdings.[42] In that year government finance for the scheme was ended but two years later further money was made available, now with the aim of providing occupations for the long-term unemployed. By 1946 Norfolk had no fewer than 1,896 council tenants occupying 31,928 acres (12,921 hectares).[43] Such developments were by no means restricted to Norfolk and Suffolk. Hertfordshire County Council acquired significant amounts of land for smallholdings under the 1908 Act, especially in Hatfield; on the Putteridgebury estate, close to Luton on the county boundary with Bedfordshire; and in the far north of the county, around Ashridge and Hinxworth.[44] After 1919 their acquisitions were on a more ambitious scale, with major purchases near Tring, in King's Langley, around Hitchin, and including the Baldock estate, with land in Baldock and Clothall. Bedfordshire County Council were no less assiduous, eventually buying land in over 50 parishes.[45] Sometimes smallholdings were dispersed widely across the landscape but sometimes, as in the area around Burlingham in Norfolk, they formed noticeable clusters. In Cambridgeshire, similarly, there were significant concentrations in the parishes of Swavesey, Over, Wimblington, Elm and Steeple Morden.

Some of these smallholdings represented part-time occupations but the larger examples were full-time concerns. Orchards and fruit trees were a major part of many of these enterprises: indeed, the cultivation of top fruit was actively encouraged by central government. Only a few examples of such orchards, fewer still of which contain original trees, survive in the modern landscape. One at Blofield in east Norfolk, planted in the early 1920s on a smallholding recently carved out of the Burlingham estate, features a range of what were then up-to-date apple varieties, including Laxton's Superb (marketed commercially only from 1923), Golden Delicious (first marketed in England in the 1920s), Sunset (first developed in 1918) and Wealthy (first introduced from the USA in 1883 but marketed on a large scale only in the 1920s), alongside longer-established varieties that had, by the twentieth century, become mainstays of commercial orchards, such as Robin pears and Cox's Orange Pippin, Bramley's Seedling and Worcester Pearmain apples (Figure 3.5).[46] More striking is the example at Dunsley on the outskirts of Tring in Hertfordshire, which is still accompanied by its original timber-framed bungalow and combined cartshed/piggery, built around 1920 for the first tenant of the smallholding, Mr Jeacock (Figure 3.6). The

---

41 Wade Martins and Williamson, *Countryside of East Anglia*, pp. 58–9.
42 SRO, B, WSCC 3098/1; SRO, I, ESCC 1194/1.
43 H. Upcher, 'Norfolk Farming', *Transactions of the Norfolk and Norwich Naturalists Society*, 16 (1946), pp. 37–105 at p. 105.
44 M. Bowyer, *'We Have to Deal with the Farmers': Episodes in the History of North Hertfordshire in the 19th and 20th Centuries* (Cambridge, 2010), pp. 46–61.
45 BRO, SH series; AO/C6/25; CS/103/3/6.
46 <https://www.fruitid.com/#main>, accessed September 2020.

original section of the orchard, beside the house, contains a wide range of fruit, including Lord Derby, Allington Pippin, Bramley's Seedling and Annie Elizabeth apples, as well as a cobnut, pears and plums. Compared with what was planted at Blofield, the apples are all well-established varieties with nineteenth-century origins.

The county council schemes were followed, in 1934, by the establishment of the Land Settlement Association. This was a government initiative but was organised under the auspices of the Society of Friends and the Carnegie Trust, with the aim of resettling unemployed people from industrial areas on smallholdings. These typically took the form of large groups of cottages with attached land, organised as cooperatives, which were scattered around networks of straight roads and tracks. Examples were established at Potton and Dunstable in Bedfordshire, Great Abington and Fen Drayton in Cambridgeshire, Newbourn in Suffolk and Wyboston in Huntingdonshire (then in Bedfordshire).[47] Orchards were, perhaps, a less significant aspect of these than of the earlier smallholdings, but were a noticeable feature of some of the settlements, most notably at Wyboston, where several examples still remain.

In addition to those created by local and national government, many new smallholdings, with or without orchards, were established as a consequence of entirely private initiatives in the inter-war years. To some extent, smallholdings of all kinds displayed a rather random distribution. Although the Land Settlement (Facilities) Act of 1919 and the 1908 act gave county councils powers of compulsory purchase, in general they bought whatever land was offered to them by major landowners: in Hertfordshire, for example, the marquis of Salisbury, the Abel Smiths, Earl Spencer, Lord Brownlow and Lord Rothschild all sold portions of their estates.[48] But there was, nevertheless, a tendency for councils to seek land in districts in which market gardens, smallholdings and small farms were already prominent, because of soil conditions, access to urban markets, or historical factors, and these same areas also often saw an increase in private smallholdings in the inter-war years. In East Anglia the greatest concentrations of smallholdings were in and around the Fens and on the fertile loams of east Norfolk, and in Bedfordshire, in the 30 or so parishes in the area around Clophill, Maulden, Husborne Crawley and Sandy, on Greensand and terrace gravels, where a distinct market-gardening district had been developing since the early nineteenth century.[49] Here there were concentrations of county council smallholdings in Flixton, Maulden, Littlington, Meppershall and Clophill, and a Land Settlement colony at Potton. In this district, as elsewhere, orchards sometimes formed freestanding businesses, but they were more usually one part of an enterprise that included the cultivation of vegetables and soft fruit. In 1922 a three-acre plot

---

47   R. Jones and M.A. Dimiz, *Twentieth Century Land Settlement Schemes* (London, 2020); F. Kitchen, *Settlers in England* (London, 1947); L. Belcham, *A History of the Land Settlement Association: With Particular Reference to its Newbourn Estate* (Newbourn, 2014).

48   Bowyer, 'We Have to Deal with the Farmers', p. 49.

49   F. Beavington, 'The Development of Market Gardening in Bedfordshire, 1799–1839', *Agricultural History Review*, 23/1 (1975), pp. 23–47.

in Maulden was placed on the market, described as 'a very valuable enclosure of freehold building or market gardening land', part of which had already been 'planted with Fruit Trees'.[50]

By no means all the new orchards planted in the inter-war years were associated with small farms and smallholdings. Many were developed by large farmers or by members of the local gentry, responding to the continuing poor market for conventional crops. William Seabrook and Sons began as commercial fruit growers in Boreham in Essex in the 1880s, initially specialising in nectarines and peaches but soon branching out into apples. Starting just before the First World War, but at an increasing rate after it, the family planted a large number of orchards in the parishes of Boreham, Hatfield Peverell and Terling. At its peak in the 1950s the firm had 1,150 acres (465 hectares) of orchard and nursery and 200 full-time staff, as well as part-timers, the numbers of which might likewise reach 200 during the picking season.[51] The company also introduced many new varieties, of apple especially, in the late nineteenth and the first half of the twentieth centuries, which they propagated and sold to other producers as well as to the general public. William Seabrook was also a writer, publishing *Modern Fruit Packing for the Market* in 1922, *Modern Fruit Growing* in 1933 and *Fruit Production in Private Gardens* in 1942.[52] Another example was the Cubitt family. They had owned the Honing estate in north-east Norfolk since the 1780s, and in 1907 began to plant an area of 10 hectares immediately to the south of their park with fruit trees. This initial planting was steadily expanded over the following years – with a hiatus during the First World War – and by 1926 orchards covered more than 55 hectares in two main blocks, together with three smaller, outlying areas.[53] The Cubitts' activities were part of a wider growth of orchards on the loamy soils around Sloley, Westwick, Tunstead and Hoveton in north-east Norfolk, partly led by large landowners such as the Petres at Westwick and partly by large freehold farmers.[54] Such localised clusters appeared in many other areas where soils were suitably loamy and well drained. Butcher, writing about Suffolk in 1941, drew attention to the concentrations around Sudbury and Ipswich.[55] Orchards similarly increased in numbers in parts of north-east Hertfordshire and western Essex, where loam soils overlaid chalk on the sides of the valleys cutting through the boulder-clay plateau.

New concentrations of commercial orchards thus developed during the inter-war years, through the expansion of smallholdings or the initiatives of larger proprietors. But, as already intimated, growth also continued in those areas in which orchards were

---

50   BRO, PC Maulden 7/37.

51   N.V. Scarfe, *The Land of Britain: Essex* (London, 1936), pp. 432–4 ; P. Wormwell, *Essex Farming, 1900–2000* (Colchester, 1999), pp. 203–4.

52   W. Seabrook, *Modern Fruit Growing* (London, 1933); W. Seabrook, *Fruit Production in Private Gardens* (London, 1942).

53   Private archive.

54   A. Douet, 'Norfolk Agriculture, 1914–1972', PhD thesis (University of East Anglia, 1989), p. 167.

55   Butcher, *Suffolk*, pp. 337–8.

Figure 3.7 A typical example of a Fenland Bramley's Seedling orchard, Marshland St James, Norfolk. Although planted in the inter-war period, the trees have attained a massive size – a combination of the vigorous habit of the variety and the moist and fertile local soils.

already well-established, and the Fens of Norfolk and Cambridgeshire, together with the chalklands of south Cambridgeshire, easily retained their pre-eminence. By the 1930s the fruit-producing area in the Norfolk Fens was said to extend:

> From Upwell in the south to Terrington in the north, being about a mile in width in the south, it widens rapidly in the neighbourhood of Wisbech and exceeds 6 miles in the north at Terrington. The older orchards are to be found near Wisbech and the more recent extensions in the north, but so far the orchard area does not extend more than half a mile north of the Lynn–Sutton Bridge road. East of Terrington the continuity of the orchards is broken by grass and arable land, but there is a big concentration of orchards on both sides of the Great Ouse in the Wiggenhalls … .[56]

By this stage the Fenland orchards mainly grew apples, and especially Bramley's Seedling, many now destined for the Wisbech canning factories (Figure 3.7). An orchard in Upwell, put on the market in 1943, grew Bramley's Seedling, but also Newton Wonder and Grenadier; a 'capital fruit farm' in Walpole Highway for sale the following year grew Bramley's Seedling alongside Grenadier, Emneth Early, Newton Wonder, Lord Grosvenor

---

56 Mosby, *Norfolk*, p. 183.

and Allington Pippin.[57] Elsewhere in the district Bramleys might be accompanied by combinations including Lord Derby, Lane's Prince Albert and Cockett's Red.[58] All, except the last, were culinary varieties, and all were first developed, or at least marketed, in the second half of the nineteenth century.[59] On the Fen islands and on the southern margins of the Fens, in villages such as Willingham and Coton, orchards likewise continued to expand, with an increasing emphasis on plums encouraged by the demands of the Chivers factory in Histon. In south Cambridgeshire orchards also continued to flourish. In Haslingfield there had been around 7 hectares of orchards in 1840, rising to 24 hectares by the time the second edition Ordnance Survey 6-inch map was surveyed in 1901. By the 1940s this figure had leapt to 59 hectares, around 6 per cent of the parish area.[60] We should note, however, that while the area devoted to orchards more than doubled in the parish the number of separate orchards appears to have declined, from 68 to 50, and most of the expansion was associated with an extensive new fruit farm to the south of the village, Barrington Hall Farm.

To a large extent the distribution of commercial fruit growing continued, in the interwar years, to be structured by environmental factors and access to markets, the former – as most contemporaries agreed – now better understood as a result of scientific advances.[61] It might be thought that the increasing availability of vans and lorries would have led to the spread of commercial fruit growing into new areas, away from rail lines, and it is certainly true that even the smallest businesses often possessed some form of motorised transport, partly because smallholdings often formed one part of a diversified enterprise. The Stone family of Croxley Green in Hertfordshire, for example, operated a coal-delivery business alongside their orchard and by the 1930s had acquired a lorry that was used for both.[62] But the advent of motorised transport seems to have had a limited impact on the distribution of orchards, in part because of the speed of delivery provided by railways. A valuation of a farm in Cambridgeshire, drawn up when a mortgage was being negotiated in 1930, was typical in emphasising the advantages conferred by the proximity of the railway:

> Willingham lies about 10 miles from Cambridge and 1½ miles from Longstanton Station on the Cambridge–Huntingdon Branch of the London Midland and Southern Railway. The parish contains a large proportion of Orchard and Market Garden land much of which has been planted in comparatively recent years.[63]

---

57 CRO, KAR 115/38/40.
58 CRO, KAR 115/38/2/50.
59 <https://www.fruitid.com/#main>, accessed August 2020.
60 Ordnance Survey 1:25,000, Sheet 52/45, revision of 1938–47.
61 Hoare, *Grass Orchard*, p. 34.
62 M. Pomfret, *Stone's Orchard, Croxley Green* (Croxley Green, n.d.).
63 CRO, K515/L/2069.

Figure 3.8 Alexander Whitehead, founder of the Cox's Orange Pippin Orchard company, striking a characteristically patriotic pose on publicity literature from the 1930s. Bedfordshire Record Office X604/33/3.

Indeed, as in the period before the First World War, access to a railway station might outweigh the suitability of soils in choosing a site for a new orchard. In 1922 the Tann family purchased 16 acres at Aldham in Essex to plant with fruit trees not because the soil was suitable for the purpose – it varied from poorly draining clay to stony sand – but because the land lay only a mile and a quarter from Marks Tey station, which was thus easily reached by horse and cart.[64] The attraction of rail transport was increased by specific policies adopted by the principal companies. When the large fruit farm planted by the Oyler family at Great Hormead in north-east Hertfordshire some time before the First World War was placed on the market as late as 1945 the particulars described how 'the vendor has been in the habit of sending his fruit to Spitalfields, the Boro' and Covent Garden Markets. During the last two seasons the Railway Company has collected the fruit from the orchards, put it on the rail and delivered to the markets.' The orchards, covering around 38 acres (*c.*15 hectares), contained 3,800 trees and had the previous year produced 9,000 bushels of apples and about 65 tons of plums.[65]

Idiosyncratic or random factors could sometimes lead to the appearance of large commercial orchards in particularly unpropitious locations. The most striking example is the extensive apple orchards that were planted at Cockayne Hatley in north-east Bedfordshire in the 1930s on poorly draining boulder-clay soils singularly unsuited to fruit growing. In 1929 part of the Cockayne Hatley estate was acquired by John Alexander Whitehead for a 'very reasonable sum' (Figure 3.8).[66] Whitehead had been involved in a number of business ventures in both Britain and the USA and appears to have bought the estate with the intention of planting apples. He aimed at intensive production, using a variety of Cox's Orange Pippin – the familiar dessert apple which had originated around a century earlier – recently developed at the Long Ashton Research Establishment near Bristol, grafted onto rootstocks which produced trees of compact growth not exceeding 8 feet (1.8m) in height (Figure 3.9). Worcester Pearmains and James Grieve, other popular dessert varieties, were planted as pollinators.[67] By 1931 2,000 trees had been planted; two years later the number had risen to 30,000. At this point, however, Whitehead decided on a policy of more rapid expansion and set up the Cox's Orange Pippin Orchard (COPO). He targeted small investors – described as 'treeholders' in his publicity material. For £30 a subscriber could become the proud owner of 90 Cox's and 15 Worcester Pearmains. He or she would receive the profits from the fruit eventually produced, minus cultivation and other costs. More than 2,000 individuals, many of them women, signed up, attracted in part by Whitehead's patriotic claims that they would be, in addition to making money, providing rural employment and increasing the country's

---

64 Oral history interview with Andrew Tann, September 2020.
65 HALS, D/231 254.
66 A. Crossley, *Apple Years at Cockayne Hatley: The History of Coxes Orange Pippin Orchards ('COPO')* (Cockayne Hatley, 1999), p. 6.
67 Crossley, *Apple Years*, pp. 10–18.

Figure 3.9 Workers in the COPO orchards at Cockayne Hatley, Bedfordshire in the 1930s. Bedfordshire Record Office X604/33/3.

self-sufficiency in food.[68] But in 1934 the business model was changed. While trees could still be bought in sets of 50, individuals could also now buy a single tree for 10s and then recruit further members, receiving 4s for every one recruited above an initial two – what we would today describe as a pyramid selling scheme.[69] By 1936 5,000 people had subscribed and £500,000 had been raised. Whitehead purchased most of the remainder of the Cockayne Hatley estate as well as other land in Bedfordshire (and also Stonebury Farm in Hormead and Braughing, east Hertfordshire). He built a large packing shed, workshops and other facilities, and invited subscribers to an annual 'Apple Blossom Day', where they could enjoy viewing their investment. He had a good eye for publicity, making much of the visit of the duchess of Montrose to the orchards in 1936.[70] Visits were encouraged more generally: 'membership entitles the member to visit the orchards, nurseries and gardens at any time, to picnic in the grounds, to be provided with hot water for tea, play tennis, boating on the lake and to generally make one's self at home.'[71]

By 1939 over 2.5 million trees had been planted and more than 200 people were employed in the orchards. But, in addition to the fact that the cold, heavy clays were not

---

68   BRO, X604/32; X604/33/2–4.
69   BRO, X604/33/5–6; X604/ X604/34/1, 9 and 11.
70   BRO, X604/33/7.
71   BRO, X604/34/9.

well-suited to fruit trees, the claims made by Whitehead regarding the future value of the investments were overstated and he siphoned off some of the money into other business ventures. The orchards were profitable in 1936, just profitable in 1937 and then made increasing losses.[72] The treeholders were held to be liable for the losses, and subscriptions dried up.[73] Whitehead then proposed a number of legally dubious forms of further investment, culminating in a claim made in a letter to treeholders in 1940 that the War Agricultural Committee was demanding that large areas of the orchards should be planted with potatoes, and that the costs of 'certain works of cultivation' which were needed had to be met by subscribers at an estimated rate of £1 5s per 100 trees.[74] Unfortunately for Whitehead, his accountant informed the Biggleswade police that all this was untrue. Although the case against Whitehead was finally dismissed in the Old Bailey, the judge ruled that this particular part of the scheme should end, and that Whitehead should return £1,000 he had taken out of the business.[75] A 'Tree Holders' Association' was established to protect investors' interests and at the same time attempts were made to form a new public company.[76] Whitehead, short of capital, tried further means of raising money from 'treeholders' but was obliged to mortgage parts of the estate and, following a particularly bad harvest in 1946, the property was sold to the Co-operative Wholesale Society.[77] This continued to run the orchards until 1974, when they were grubbed out. Only the large brick packing shed, with the COPO name proudly displayed in the gable, remains as physical testimony to this slightly bizarre tale.

The management of commercial orchards

There was a broad distinction, in the management of commercial orchards during the 'orchard century', between those in which the ground comprised permanent grass, grazed by livestock and/or mown for hay, and those in which it was planted with crops. This distinction is blurred and complicated by the fact that in some cases interplanting continued only while the fruit trees were growing; once mature, and with their canopy closing, the orchard would be laid to grass.[78] The cultivation of vegetables or soft fruit between the rows of trees was already common practice in Cambridgeshire and the Fens before 1850, and continued to be a characteristic feature of the area. Typical were three separate properties in Ely, all advertised for sale in 1880. One was described as a

---

72   BRO, X604/34/18, 21, 22, 25.
73   BRO, X604/34/37.
74   BRO, X604/34/35.
75   BRO, X604/34/74; Crossley, *Apple Days*, pp. 30–8.
76   BRO, X604/34/55, 60 and 61; X604/34/57.
77   BRO, X604/34/77; Crossley, *Apple Days*, pp. 38–9.
78   Hoare, *Grass Orchard*, pp. 54–6.

> Fertile and productive garden ground, in a high state of cultivation, planted with a choice selection of apple, pear, plum, and other trees in full profit and bearing. And as undergrowth with gooseberry and current [sic] bushes. Which produce large quantities of Fruit for the London and Manchester markets.

A second was 'A valuable and productive piece of Garden Land well planted with fruit trees and bushes', while the third was 'A productive and valuable piece of Garden Land well planted with fruit trees and bushes in full profit and partly surrounded by a well built brick wall covered with wall fruit Trees'.[79] Six decades later, in 1943, a 3-acre orchard at Upwell contained 'Bramley Seedling, Newton Wonder and Grenadier Apples with Careless and Lancashire Lad gooseberries beneath part'.[80] Further south, on the fen edge, Petit described in 1940 how:

> The small area of Greensand in the parish of Cottenham is remarkable for the intensive production of soft fruits, and of cutting flowers and vegetables. This type of cultivation showed an almost continuous increase in importance from the second quarter of the nineteenth century … . Produce is marketed locally and to a factory at Histon [i.e., Chivers], in the Midlands and to a comparatively minor extent London.[81]

When the owner of one 168-acre (*c.*68-hectare) enterprise at Willingham in Cambridgeshire fell into financial difficulties in 1935, a valuer's report described how,

> with the object of reducing his Labour costs, he has allowed the whole of the orchard land to grass down and no longer cultivates the underlying land for bush fruit, or for such crops as potatoes, sugar beet etc. He has in fact concentrated on the top-fruit trees and these have been well pruned and regularly sprayed.[82]

The farm comprised some arable land but was mostly (114 acres) given over to orchards of apples and plums, in some cases planted in alternate rows.

Inter-planting was especially common in Cambridgeshire and the Fens but was widely practised in other areas, especially in Essex. A valuation made in 1932 of a 'farm of fruit trees' at Buttsbury Lodge, Stock, between Brentford and Chelmsford, recorded 1,050 half-standard Worcester Pearmain apple trees, 155 half-standard Early Victoria (a variety of apple now known as Emneth Early) and 405 half-standard Newton Wonder. All had been planted in 1930 as three-year-old trees, and were together judged to be worth

---

79 CRO, 283/SP 597(ii)).
80 CRO, KAR 115/38/2/48.
81 G.H.N. Petitt, *The Land of Britain: Cambridgeshire and the Isle of Ely* (London, 1941), p. 399.
82 CRO, K515/L/2069.

£483. They were accompanied by 19,912 blackcurrant bushes planted at the same time and valued at £284.[83] An orchard at Rayleigh in the same county in 1924 contained 1,000 trees – apple, pear, plum, damson, greengage, medlars, quince and filbert – all interplanted with blackcurrants, redcurrants, gooseberries and raspberries.[84] The Tann family grew blackcurrants, loganberries and marigolds between the trees in their orchard at Aldham in Essex in the 1920s and 1930s but, as was often the case, on a declining scale as the trees matured. Here, on 16 acres (6.5 hectares) they grew Beauty of Bath, James Grieve, Lady Sudeley, Worcester Pearmain, Cox's Orange Pippin and Bramley's, supplemented in the 1950s and 1960s with Laxton's Superb, all destined for the London market.[85]

Many commercial orchards established in the late nineteenth or early twentieth century were, however, laid to grass, in the traditional manner, and cut for hay, grazed or, in particular, used to run poultry (another expanding sector in the period), bringing added benefits in the form of pest control. One example at Thurston in west Suffolk, advertised for sale in 1878, was described as 'Well stocked with an assortment of fruit trees. This property should appeal especially to poultry keepers'.[86] An advertisement from 1937 for a 'freehold grass orchard' in Nayland, Suffolk, included the statement that 'The fowl house is not included in the sale', while in 1935 an example in Willingham, Cambridgeshire, was said to contain '4 boarded and corrugated iron poultry houses'.[87] In some cases, by the 1940s, fruit growing was combined with quite intensive poultry farming. When Woodside Farm in Haynes, Bedfordshire, was put on the market in 1949, one of the parcels comprised an 'Accredited poultry farm' with incubator house, brooder house and other outbuildings, together with 60 fruit trees and 'other small fruit'.[88] Pigs, too, were also kept by owners of commercial orchards, although seldom in the orchards themselves. A 'productive and well-planted orchard with buildings thereon', put up for sale at Ely in 1913, included a 'brick and slate barn or fruit store, timber and tile stable and loose box, two piggeries, fowl house and lean to cart shed'.[89] The manure from livestock kept, for most of the time, in sheds or sties was easily collected and spread around the trees.[90] Grass orchards appear to have been particularly common in west Hertfordshire and south Bedfordshire, where many were used to graze sheep and also, as we have seen, to fatten Aylesbury ducks.

In addition to all this, bees were often kept in orchards, as in earlier centuries, to aid pollination. In many cases the hives were the property of some third party, but sometimes

---

83 ERO, D/F 33/16/24.
84 ERO, D/DTo/E200.
85 Oral history interview with Andrew Tann, September 2020.
86 SRO, B, HE 500/1.
87 SRO, B, 1432/170; CRO, K515/L/2069.
88 BRO, PK1/4/181.
89 CRO, 283/SP107.
90 Pettit, *Cambridgeshire*, p. 399.

honey production formed another part of the owner's or tenant's business. Leslie Clarke of the Essex Farmers Union suggested in 1948 – in a radio talk for the BBC – that 'Some fruit growers are very bad bee keepers but they all want bees, and lots of them, just at pollinating time, so we have our own expert beekeeper whose job it is to see that members' stocks of bees are built up for strength in the early spring.'[91] Even large fruit farms often produced honey: that at Libury Hall in Munden, north-east Hertfordshire, contained 25 hives when its equipment was listed in 1940.[92] Indeed, whether laid to grass or used for growing vegetables, small fruit or flowers, orchards continued to be multi-use environments, as in earlier centuries. But it was the smallholders who probably exploited alternative sources of orchard income most systematically. Occasionally, even material for Christmas decorations was grown. A number of surviving orchards from this period include holly trees among the lines of fruit and in 1900 James Taber Senior of Little Braxted near Witham recorded in his diary how he had put mistletoe on the apple trees in his newly planted orchard.[93]

By the start of the Second World War, however, the ground between the trees in many commercial orchards was being treated in a different way: it was ploughed, sprayed and maintained as bare earth. This eliminated the need to mow the grass between the trees and reduced competition for nutrients. Control of grass and weeds in this way was part of a more general expansion in the use of chemical sprays, including pesticides and fungicides, that occurred in the inter-war years. They were applied by individuals who were – to judge from contemporary photographs – provided with little in the way of protective clothing, and often with no protective clothing at all. As late as 1949 Leslie Clarke, in another of his radio talks, declared dismissively: 'if your sprayers have sensitive skins get some lanolin or barrier cream from the chemist to protect their schoolgirl complexions'.[94] Hoare in 1928 devoted many pages to the subject of chemicals:

> The control of pests and diseases involves, in a good many cases, the work of spraying the trees with insecticidal, ovicidal and fungicidal washes. Furthermore, the trees are often sprayed with cleansing and 'cover' washes, such as caustic-soda preparations, hot lime or lime and salt.[95]

Trees were regularly tarred, and even nicotine-based sprays were widely used. Spraying, Hoare emphasised, was an 'essential feature of modern fruit-growing', universally employed. He listed the numerous fungal and insect pests of fruit trees, in the case of cherries alone describing the effects of and treatments for Winter Moth, March Moth, Mottled Umber

---

91 ERO, D/F 152/7/1.
92 BRO, BML 10/44/153.
93 ERO, D/DU 2223/2/16.
94 ERO, D/F 152/7/1.
95 Hoare, *Grass Orchard*, p. 161.

Moth, Cherry Black-fly, Cherry Slug Worm, Cherry Fruit-fly, Brown Rot, Cherry Leaf Scorch, Silver Leaf, Leaf-curl, Witch's Brooms, Gumming and Bracket Fungi.[96] The red spider mite was a particular pest in eastern orchards.[97] Denis Knowles, of Oliver's Orchard, Colchester, writing in 1975 about his experiences in the 1930s, described how he and other Essex fruit growers tried various ways of dealing with the problem. 'Denis Carter had tried spraying with lime sulphur every week and this the red spider had not liked, but his trees had not liked it either and they looked awful.' How effective these various treatments actually were, in the period before the Second World War, remains unclear. Knowles described how:

> Orchards before the very effective new sprays were so very interesting as everyone had red spider, some aphis, codlin [moth], borer and other insect pests. Aphelinus would clear up aphis in a matter of a day or so but the weather had to be warm. I kept woolly aphis down by painting on meths.[98]

By the 1950s DDT (dichlorodiphenyltrichloroethane) was coming into widespread use as a way of controlling, in particular, capsid and apple-blossom weevil, together with synthetic phosphorous sprays for eradicating red spider mite.[99] This represented the culmination of the steady increase in the use of chemicals, many clearly as dangerous to humans as to their target 'pests', which was a distinguishing feature of the 'orchard century'.

It is sometimes suggested that, from the start, commercial orchards tended to feature trees grafted on dwarfing stocks, rather than on the tall, vigorous rootstocks that had been usual in 'traditional' farmhouse orchards. In Kent as early as 1908 it was said that 'half-standards, pyramids and also dwarfed or bush trees have in many places taken the place of old standards'.[100] In the eastern counties some commercial or semi-commercial orchards were planted with trees on dwarfing rootstocks even in the early nineteenth century – all of the 149 apples interplanted between the existing standard trees at Wood House, Kelvedon, Essex, in 1831 were described as 'Dwarf'.[101] But the adoption of dwarfing rootstocks was gradual, and the issue is complicated by the fact that the height of a tree can be controlled by rigorous pruning and is not simply a function of rootstock vigour. The orchards of Bramley's Seedlings in Fenland appear to have been managed as low-growing 'bush' trees in the nineteenth century because of the variety's rapid growth and susceptibility to wind damage in this wet

---

96 Hoare, *Grass Orchard*, pp. 193–7.
97 ERO, D/F 152/7/1.
98 ERO, C139.
99 C.P. Norbury, 'Modern Developments in Fruit Growing', *Journal of the Royal Society of Arts*, 100/4881 (1952), pp. 719–34, at p. 726.
100 C.W. Sabin, 'Agriculture', in W. Page (ed.), *Victoria County History, Kent*, vol. 1 (London, 1908), pp. 457–71, at p. 467.
101 ERO, D/DBm E/18.

and open landscape. In most other contexts, a preference for relatively low-growing trees, 2–3m in height, was driven by the increasing use of sprays to control pests, although such an arrangement also made harvesting easier. It was thus mainly a feature of the inter-war years.

When, in 1920, the Ministry of Agriculture and Fisheries initiated a scheme to provide fruit trees for county council smallholdings, the pears were grafted on quince stock and the apples 'on Paradise [i.e., dwarfing] and a proportion on Crab stocks'.[102] At Honing in Norfolk in the 1920s and 1930s the apples – nineteenth-century varieties such as Bramley's Seedling, Lord Derby, Worcester Pearmain, Beauty of Bath, Queens, and Lane's Prince Albert, but including the older Court Pendu Plat and unnamed 'miscellaneous' – were mainly planted on 'paradise' rootstocks, with only a few on crab; all were pruned as 'bush' trees. The pears (Catillac and 'miscellaneous') were on quince stock and likewise bush pruned. With rows spaced at intervals of 13½ feet, this system allowed room for the many thousands of blackcurrants and gooseberries that were planted between them.[103] It is, however, important to emphasise that even the paradise stocks did not produce the kinds of very low-growing tree seen in some modern orchards, but rather half-standards of semi-vigorous habit, and the same was true of new varieties of rootstock, such as the M2 stocks, that were developed at East Malling just before the First World War.[104] To judge from surviving examples from the 1920s and 1930s, it was pruning as much as rootstock type that ensured that trees in commercial orchards grew lower than those in 'traditional', farmhouse orchards. It was only really from the 1950s and 1960s that commercial orchards began to be dominated by trees on extremely dwarfing rootstocks, such as M9, M26 or MM106, or were grown as cordons.

The peak of expansion: the 1940s and 1950s

The advent of the Second World War brought a halt to the expansion of orchards in the eastern counties, although with government concerns about supplies of vitamin C few seem to have been grubbed out and converted to arable production. The principal exceptions appear to have been neglected, overgrown or derelict examples. The War Agricultural Committee in Norfolk, for example, instructed Miss Annie Westgate of Morningthorpe to 'Grub up, remove from site and burn all derelict fruit trees and bushes of the following types:- apples, pears, plums by 15 Sept 1943. Cultivate the land frequently to clean and plough down by 30th Sept 1943.'[105] Occasionally the War Ag committees actually took over a badly run orchard and managed it themselves, as they did neglected farms, but this was unusual. The planting of new fruit trees, fruit bushes, cane fruits and strawberries on any holding of more than one acre was not to be undertaken without written permission, but this was sometimes forthcoming. In early 1942 a Mrs Brayne in south Norfolk was allowed to plant 700 dessert apple trees on the basis that

---

102   BRO, AO N1/1.
103   Private archive.
104   Norbury, 'Modern Developments', p. 721; oral history interview with Andrew Tann, September 2020.
105   NRO, HNR 46/2.

she had paid for them before the war had started.[106] In some districts there was a slight decline in the orchard acreage during the war years – in Suffolk, for example, it fell from 4,737 acres (1,917 hectares) in 1939 to 4,576 acres (1,852 hectares) in 1945 – but overall there was little change.[107] Indeed, the overall area occupied by orchards in the seven eastern counties in 1945 – 36,100 acres (14,610 hectares) was almost exactly the same as in 1935 – 36,111 acres (14,614 hectares). In spite of labour shortages and problems in acquiring equipment, the war was in some ways a good time for fruit growers, as one Essex orchard owner later recalled:

> I suppose one of the chief worries during the war was getting the necessary materials for running the orchard. Also so much time was being spent getting the harvest rations for all the workers and also getting enough pickers. On the other hand there was no trouble selling the fruit, and we got the control price for all the grades … . It did not seem very much but we got it for all apples regardless of quality and this made it a good price … . During the war I sent all my fruit to Witham [Fruit Packers: see below, p. 85] … I was bound to send all my fruit there. They really were very bad and they never had enough boxes and we had bad times putting apples on the ground and all sorts of rubbish. Then they would wrap and pack all apples which was crazy because you only had to put them in a salesmans box and send them to market and get full controlled price.[108]

The longer-term effects of guaranteed prices, however, he thought questionable: 'One unfortunate result of control was that it removed the price incentive to grow, grade and pack to the best possible standard', a complaint that was to be repeated on many occasions through the post-war decades. The war had a number of other effects. The Tann family at Aldham in Essex were, like other growers, obliged to remove many of their Bramley's Seedlings, top-grafting the trunks with Worcester Pearmains, because the market for cooking varieties slumped as the availability of sugar was reduced by rationing.[109]

The immediate post-war period saw renewed growth in the area of orchards in the eastern counties, the total rising from 36,100 acres (14,610 hectares) in 1945 to 44,217 acres (17,894 hectares) in 1955. Around half of this expansion, however, occurred in just one county, Essex, where the orchard area increased by 31 per cent – from 9,185 acres (3,811 hectares) to 13,393 acres (5,420 hectares) – in this ten-year period.[110] Of particular note were

---

106 PRO/TNA, MAF 80/4553.

107 SRO, I, HD 285/2/5.

108 ERO, C139.

109 Oral history interview with Andrew Tann, September 2020.

110 See DEFRA, 'Detailed Annual Statistics on the Structure of the Agricultural Industry at 1 June in England and the UK', <https://assets.publishing.service.gov.uk/government/uploads/system/uploads/attachment_data/file/183104/defra-stats-foodfarm-landuselivestock-june-results-england-1900series111129.xls>, accessed 23 November 2020.

Figure 3.10 Clophill, Bedfordshire. A commercial orchard, now largely derelict, planted in the 1960s on dwarfing rootstocks. Although some conservationists are hostile to fruit trees planted on such rootstocks, because of their short life and failure to achieve veteran status, these trees display an abundance of holes, hollows and dead wood.

developments in the north-east of the county, in the area extending from Colchester north to the Stour and eastward to the coast, where gradual expansion in the inter-war years was followed after 1945 by more significant growth, so that by the late 1950s orchards covered around 7 per cent of the land area. As Norbury noted in 1952, '[i]n recent years there has been a large expansion of acreage in Essex, which county is particularly suited for growing dessert apples where low rainfall conditions are desirable for growing Cox and other dessert apples.'[111] This marked expansion, accompanied by more modest growth elsewhere, ensured that by the mid-1950s the average density of orchards in some eastern counties rivalled that found in the traditional fruit-growing counties of western England (see Figure 1.5).

Much of the post-war growth was associated not with small farms and smallholdings but with large commercial orchards – mirroring to some extent developments more widespread in the agricultural industry towards larger units of production. Over a quarter of the Suffolk acreage by the late 1950s was made up of just seven large businesses, including Risby Fruit Farms, Justin Brooke and F.E. Williamson.[112] On such modern enterprises apples, in particular, were, by the 1960s, usually grown on dwarfing rootstocks, especially M26 and MM106, or even as 'cordons', a method pioneered, in particular, by Seabrooks in Essex (Figure 3.10). The trees were cropped for 20–25 years, then grubbed up and replaced. Many

---

111 Norbury, 'Modern Developments', p. 720.

112 SRO, I, HD 285/2/5.

such orchards were surrounded by distinctive shelter belts comprising trees rather taller than the lines of plums that had protected many earlier examples: sometimes poplar or hybrid willow, sometimes Italian alder (*Alnus cordata*), grey alder (*Alnus incana*) or common alder (*Alnus glutinosa*). The ground between the trees might be managed as bare earth, but from the 1970s there was a growing trend to maintain it as grass, kept short with mowers towed by tractors, with only the area around the base of the trees being sprayed with herbicide.[113]

But in addition to 'fruit farms', as these large enterprises were increasingly called, smaller commercial orchards continued to exist, albeit now often run on broadly similar lines. What is now the Applebee Orchard at Bramerton, to the east of Norwich, was planted by the Daniels family in the early 1930s, mainly with Cox's Orange Pippin apples but with some Monarch, Charles Ross and Bramley's Seedling. These were grubbed out by new owners in the late 1950s and replaced with Cox's and Bramleys on modern dwarfing M9 and MM106 rootstocks, and with Discovery, Golden Delicious, Egremont Russet, Jonagold, Jonathon, Spartan, Grenadier and James Grieve, partly as pollinators. Although covering only some 5.7 acres (2.3 hectares), the business remained profitable for several decades.[114] The Tanns' orchard at Aldham in Essex, planted in 1922, was likewise extensively replanted in the 1960s. Beauty of Bath, James Grieve, Lady Sudeley, Worcester Pearmains and Cox's Orange Pippins were largely replaced by Queen Cox and modern dessert varieties such as Discovery and Spartan on MM106 rootstocks, responding to the popularity of apples with a strong red colour. But there were also smaller numbers of other varieties – Ribston Pippin, Sturmer Pippin, Rosemary Russet, St Edmund's Russet – to ensure that the harvest, and thus the need for labour, was spread over a long period, a particularly important concern for the small producer.[115] In some cases small farms had diversified into fruit growing during the long years of depression but had retained some arable land; in 1952 the Two Saints Fruit Farm in Wroxham, Norfolk, for example, had 100 acres of orchard but 59 acres under arable crops.[116] Small growers thus continued to be important in the 1940s and 1950s, with many now marketing large amounts of their produce through co-operatives or other organisations, such as Witham Fruit Packers, who possessed extensive storage facilities and would collect the harvested fruit from the orchard.[117] But the real expansion in the orchard area through the late 1940s and 1950s was due to the inexorable growth of the large commercial fruit farms.

On holdings of all sizes fruit production was sometimes, as in the pre-war years, combined with poultry farming. Greenacres in Southrepps, Norfolk, was described as a 'fruit and accredited poultry farm' in 1955, while even the great Risby fruit farm in Suffolk

---

113 Oral history interview with Andrew Tann, September 2020.
114 Pers. comm., John Everitt, Applebee Orchard, Bramerton, Norfolk.
115 Oral history interview with Andrew Tann, September 2020.
116 NRO, MC 39/172, 487X3.
117 Oral history interview with Andrew Tann, September 2020.

kept turkeys on deep litter.[118] Some fruit farms also combined, in the long-established manner, growing top fruit with the cultivation of soft fruit such as blackcurrants, although with much of the latter now being planted separately, rather than between the rows of trees, as had been common in the inter-war years. Kirstead Lyng 'Orchard and Fruit Farm' in Norfolk, which was advertised for sale in 1949, covered 43 acres (*c.*17.5 hectares), but less than a quarter of this area comprised orchard.[119] But many enterprises consisted largely or entirely of orchards of top fruit. The entire area of the 158-acre (64-hectare) Golden Apple Orchards Fruit Farm at Roughton in Norfolk, advertised for sale in 1963, was thus planted with fruit trees.[120]

In Britain as a whole the growth in the area under orchards appears to have stalled during the 1950s. Having risen nationally from 257,000 acres (104,000 hectares) in 1940 to 274,000 acres (111,000 hectares) in 1950, the officially recorded area then declined to 234,000 acres (95,000 hectares) by 1960. However, in the eastern counties government figures suggest a slightly more complicated picture. Overall, the area occupied by orchards fell from a recorded 44,217 acres (17,894 hectares) in 1955 to 39,573 acres (16,015 hectares) by 1965.[121] But while some counties experienced a severe contraction – the orchard area in Bedfordshire fell by 60 per cent and in Cambridge by 35 per cent in this ten-year period, both reflecting the grubbing out of orchards at the foot of the chalk escarpment – others held up better. In Suffolk the area of commercial orchards actually increased, from 6,499 acres (2,630 hectares) in 1950 to 7,213 acres (2,919 hectares) in 1955, reaching 7,300 acres (2,952 hectares) in 1960, a late surge in activity that mirrored, if in muted form, that seen in Essex a few years earlier.[122]

Conclusion

In the middle of the nineteenth century commercial fruit growing was still carried out to only a limited extent in the eastern counties. Most orchards were farm orchards and only in a few districts – especially the Fens and West Hertfordshire – was some degree of specialisation apparent. All this changed in the course of the following century. Large-scale urbanisation and industrialisation, improved systems of transportation and wider changes in agricultural economics and the development of local food-processing industries ensured that commercial orchards proliferated. By *c.*1900 several important

---

118 NRO, MC 39/364, 487X3; Accn 1997/146/40/46.

119 NRO, MC 39/134.

120 NRO, MC 39/467.

121 See DEFRA, 'Detailed Annual Statistics on the Structure of the Agricultural Industry at 1 June in England and the UK', <https://assets.publishing.service.gov.uk/government/uploads/system/uploads/attachment_data/file/183104/defra-stats-foodfarm-landuselivestock-june-results-england-1900series111129.xls>, accessed 23 November 2020.

122 SRO, I, HD 285/2/5.

fruit-growing districts had developed and over the following decades orchards expanded more generally throughout the eastern counties wherever environmental conditions were suitable and good transport links to distant markets existed. Much of the initial growth in specialised production was associated with small farms and smallholdings, the numbers of the latter encouraged to an extent by government policies. But over time large fruit-growing businesses accounted for more and more of the orchard acreage, a development that accelerated in the immediate post-war years. This said, small producers remained important well into the 1950s and 1960s.

The intensity with which orchards were managed increased steadily over time, with a growing emphasis on dwarf and eventually on cordon trees and with heavy applications of pesticides and herbicides. While some commercial enterprises were 'grass' orchards, in many examples soft fruit, flowers or vegetables were cultivated between the trees. By the post-war period many featured bare ground or closely mown grass with bare soil around the trees. It is important to emphasise these rather unromantic aspects because orchard enthusiasts usually concentrate their attention on the more picturesque farmhouse orchards, with their tall, spreading trees rising over unimproved grassland. Orchards like this did, of course, continue to exist during the 'orchard century' but in an increasingly neglected state, and they constituted a smaller and smaller percentage of the total fruit-growing acreage. Moreover, while commercial orchards are often thought of as recent additions to the landscape, of little significance in terms of history or biodiversity, some examples are now two centuries old and, as we shall see, even those planted in the middle of the last century can, in a mature and neglected state, now constitute important habitats for wildlife.

CHAPTER FOUR

Garden and institutional orchards

Orchards and country houses before c.1760

So far we have discussed orchards largely in practical terms – as a source of nutrition or profit. But early writers make it clear that they were also valued for their aesthetic appeal, for the appearance of trees laden with fruit, for the birdsong and, above all, for the display of spring blossom. As William Lawson memorably put it, 'whereas every other pleasure commonly fills some one of our senses, with delight; this makes all our senses swim in pleasure, and that with infinite variety, joined with no less commodity'.[1] Lawson was writing in part with an audience of wealthy yeoman farmers in mind, but it was in the more extensive grounds of country houses, manor houses and other wealthy residences that the aesthetics of fruit trees were most clearly of importance. It was in such contexts, moreover, that the greatest range of fruit – in terms of both types and varieties – was to be found.

Before the middle decades of the eighteenth century orchards often occupied a prominent position in the elite domestic landscape, close to the mansion, and fruit trees were also scattered more generally around the grounds. Gardens at this time were 'formal' or geometric in layout, featuring such artificial-looking elements as knots, parterres and topiary, and they were usually enclosed by high walls. Functional aspects of the landscape – such as farmyards – were often located in immediate proximity to the garden, and many of the structures and features found in the latter had both a practical and an ornamental role. Circular 'basons' and linear 'canals', for example, also served as 'stews' in which fish were kept prior to consumption, while dovecotes were proudly displayed within the gardens and elaborately constructed.[2] Such features signalled that the owner was fully involved in the productive life of his estate, and ate more food, and more exotic food, than his humbler neighbours. Orchards fitted in well with the aesthetic of such gardens and large houses often had more than one. A valuation of an estate in Radwell and Norton in north Hertfordshire drawn up in 1650, for example, refers to 'an orchard beneath the house and another above the house both well planted with fruit'.[3] In some cases one may

---

1 Lawson, *New Orchard or Garden*, p. 56.
2 C. Currie, 'Fish Ponds as Garden Features', *Garden History*, 18 (1990), pp. 22–33; T. Williamson, *Polite Landscapes: Gardens and Society in Eighteenth-Century England* (Stroud, 1995), pp. 31–5.
3 HALS, DE/X450/E1.

have been a cherry orchard: a map of Hethel Hall in Norfolk from 1756 shows the 'Cherry Ground' lying within a separate enclosure adjacent to the hall.[4] The tall and spreading habit of standard cherry trees, as we have seen, caused them to out-grow other fruit trees in mixed orchards, making separate cherry grounds a better option where sufficient land was available. Many large houses also had separate 'nut grounds', as at Buckenham Tofts in Norfolk in 1700.[5]

In the Middle Ages many important residences stood on moated sites: that is, they were surrounded by wide water-filled ditches. These served to drain the site and to provide a measure of security against intruders. They also doubled as fish ponds and – redolent of the rather larger water-filled ditches associated with castles – conveyed an impression that the owner was actively involved in martial activities, which were symbolic of social superiority. Well into the seventeenth century moats continued to be acceptable settings for country houses and maps and documents suggest that the central 'island' was occupied not only by the residence and its gardens but also, in many cases, by an orchard. A map

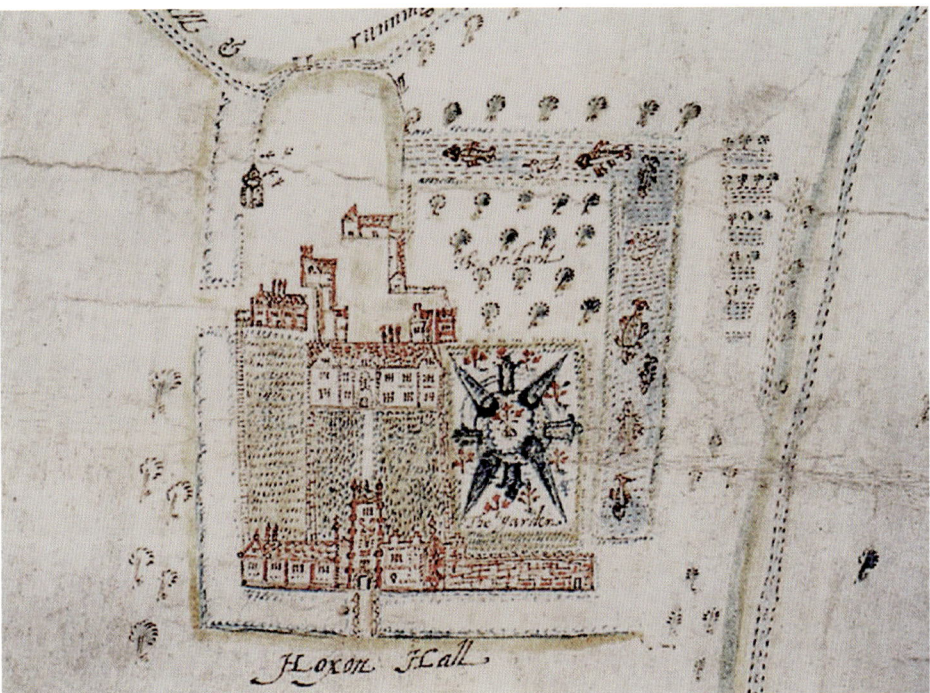

Figure 4.1 Detail from a map of Hoxne Hall, Suffolk, 1619. The house stands on a moated island, accompanied by barns, yards, a dovecote, an orchard and a geometric garden: the strange shapes are the cartographer's attempt to represent topiary from above. The moat is evidently doubling, in the usual manner, as a fishpond. Suffolk Record Office (Ipswich) 110 40 422.

---

4   Private collection.

5   NRO, Petre Box 8.

of Hoxne Hall in Suffolk, for example, surveyed in 1619, shows the house on a moat (filled with particularly large fish) and with an elaborate formal garden to the east, the cartographer evidently struggling with the task of representing, from an aerial perspective, the topiary that grew there; a sizeable orchard adjoined it immediately to the north (Figure 4.1).[6] Similarly, a map of Bedingfield Hall in the same county, surveyed in 1729, shows that the moat – which defined an area of around 4 acres (c.1.7 hectares) – enclosed the house, outbuildings, fish ponds, gardens and an orchard.[7] A lease drawn up for a substantial property in Everton in Bedfordshire in March 1712 bound the tenant to plant the ground between the mansion and the 'mote … with fruit trees for an orchard'.[8]

Several sixteenth- and seventeenth-century writers recommended placing orchards within moats, which would 'afford you fish, fence and moisture to your trees; and pleasure also'.[9] As we have already noted, trees laden with fruit needed to be protected from trespassers, both animal and – in a hungry world – human. In some cases the orchard

Figure 4.2 Channons Hall, Tibenham, in Norfolk, as shown on a map of 1640. The hall stands on a moated site, its orchard within a separate but connected moat enclosing nearly 2½ acres (c.1 hectare). Norfolk Record Office MC 1777/1.

---

6   SRO, I, 110 40 422.
7   SRO, I, HD 417/8.
8   BRO, FE 333.
9   Lawson, *New Orchard or Garden*, p. 14.

was placed within its own separate moat, adjoining and connected to that surrounding the house, as shown on a map of Channons Hall, Tibenham in Norfolk, surveyed in 1640 (Figure 4.2).[10] Such arrangements are sometimes obliquely referred to in documents. A lease for land in Shelfhanger in the same county, dated 1695, thus describes the *Cherryegrounde moate*.[11] Moated orchards, adjacent to moated residences, may account for cases where two conjoined moats – surviving now as an archaeological site, without a house on either island – are found. When, as was increasingly the case in the seventeenth and eighteenth centuries, moats were abandoned, with the mansion being rebuilt on some higher and drier site, the moat was often repurposed as a site for an orchard, as at Croydon Wilds, Croydon, in Cambridgeshire, shown on a map of 1747.[12] A map of Chignall in Essex, drawn up in 1599, shows both the new site of the manor of Beaumont Otes and the old moated site; the latter appears to have already been planted up with fruit trees.[13] The Ordnance Survey 6-inch maps of the late nineteenth century show numerous examples of old moated sites planted with orchards. Whether this use was entirely new or represents the extension of an orchard that, as at Hoxne Hall, already occupied part of the moated island, usually remains unclear.

Orchards, moated or otherwise, were often placed very close to the mansion, at least in the sixteenth century. At Redgrave Hall in Suffolk, the great mansion of the Bacon family, the new garden laid out in 1540 was divided into two sections, the half nearest the house comprising an orchard dissected by walks or *allées*.[14] At Stiffkey in north Norfolk, another of the family's residences, the orchard – which again lay adjacent to the house – was 'pared' in 1570 to create paths of sifted gravel.[15] Lawson in 1618 recommended a square shape for an orchard, principally because this made it easier to lay out walks, and 'one principall end of orchards is recreation by walks'.[16] By the seventeenth century they were often placed at a greater distance from the house, although still forming a prominent part of the ornamental grounds. The gardens at Somerleyton in Suffolk, apparently laid out around 1619, are shown on a map of 1652 and described in a contemporary survey (Figure 4.3).[17] Their plan was clearly based on close observation of contemporary

---

10 NRO, MC 1777/1.

11 NRO, MC 257/6, 683x3.

12 CRO, 288/13–16.

13 A.C. Edwards and K.C. Newton, *The Walkers of Hanningfield: Surveyors and Mapmakers Extraordinary* (London, 1984), Plate 12.

14 A. Hassell Smith, 'The Gardens of Sir Nicholas and Francis Bacon: An Enigma Resolved and a Mind Explored', in P. Roberts (ed.), *Religion, Culture and Society in Early Modern England* (Cambridge, 1994), pp. 125–60, at p. 144.

15 A. Taigel and T. Williamson, 'Some Early Geometric Gardens in Norfolk', *Journal of Garden History*, 11/1–2 (1991), p. 97.

16 Lawson, *New Orchard or Garden*, p. 11.

17 SRO, L, 295 and 942.64 Som.

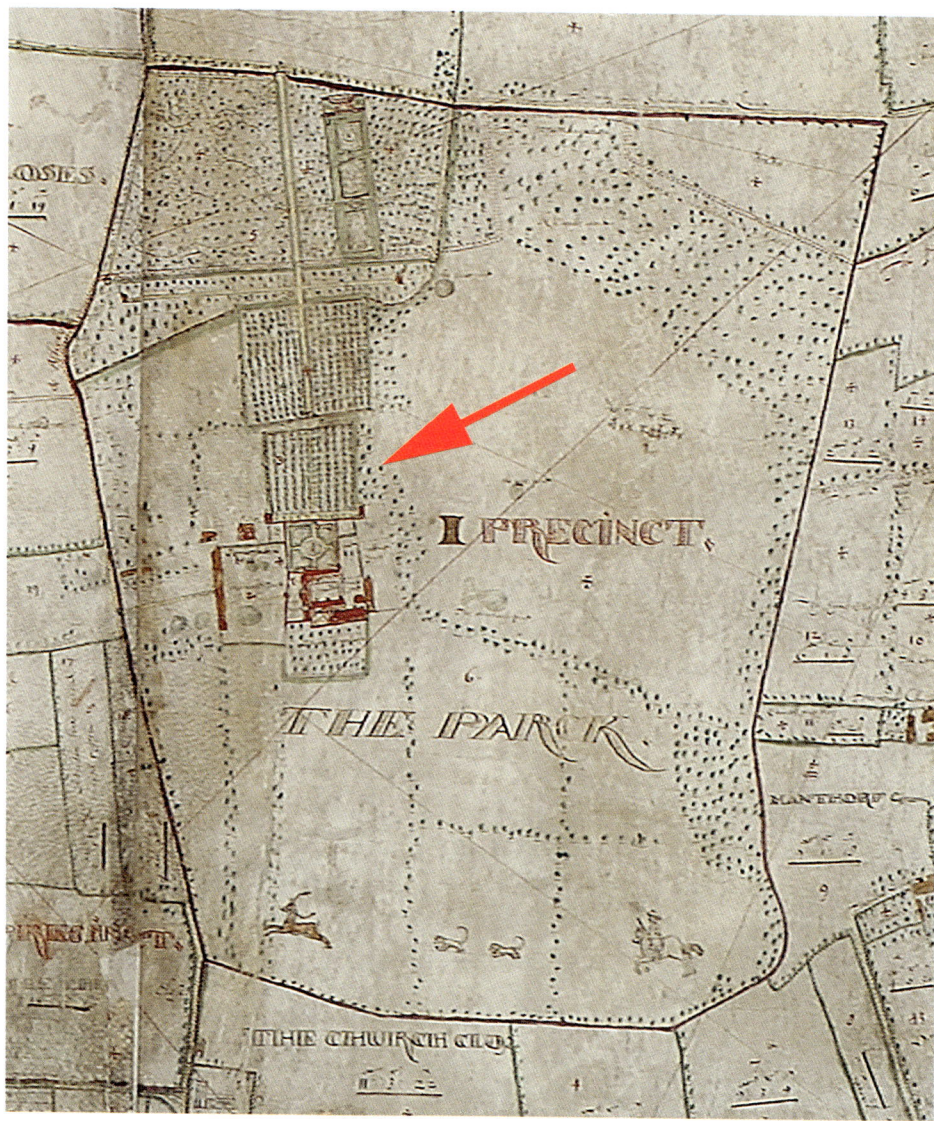

Figure 4.3 Somerleyton Hall, Suffolk and its gardens in 1652. To the north of the hall lay the Great Garden, and beyond this a transverse terrace with banqueting houses at each end. This provided a view across the North Orchard, which lay immediately to the north. Suffolk Record Office (Lowestoft) L295.

Italian gardens and was organised symmetrically around a long north–south axial path. Immediately beyond the Great Garden, overlooked by a transverse terrace and ranged either side of the axial walk, lay the extensive North Orchard, beyond which were other, less regular areas of planting. Rather similar, perhaps, were the gardens at Moor Park in Hertfordshire in the 1650s, as described by William Temple in his *Upon the Gardens of Epicurus* of 1685. Here there was a series of terraced gardens arranged down a slope below the house, the lowest of which was 'all fruit trees ranged about the several quarters of a wilderness which is very shady'.[18]

Jan Woudstra has emphasised that, at the royal palace of Hampton Court by the seventeenth century, 'fruit was present in varying forms in virtually every part of the garden'. Innumerable illustrations of country houses, including those published in Kip and Knyff's *Britannia Illustrata* of 1707, show that fruit trees were routinely trained, as fans or espaliers, against the walls of the ornamental as much as those of the productive gardens.[19] A lease for Harrold Hall in Bedfordshire, drawn up in 1653, bound the tenant 'From tyme to tyme [to] preserve and keepe the Orchyards, gardens, Cort yards and the Mounts and Walkes therein with prunninge, weedinge, new gravellinge and rollinge in such sort as the beauty thereof may be preserved and maynteined'.[20] The attached schedule described how the grounds included a garden containing '30 trees of wall fruit'; how there were 28 fruit trees 'in quarters'; and how there were '4 grass quarters encompassed with an apple hedge before the door opening out of the chief house eastward'. The term 'wall fruit' is an important one. While the trees trained against garden walls might include apples and pears, they were more likely to be peaches, apricots or nectarines. These were high-status fruit, grown by gentlemen rather than farmers, largely because they required walls for shelter and warmth, together with a considerable amount of management to ensure high yields.[21] They also required a high degree of luck in terms of the weather, and many landowners could doubtless have recounted experiences similar to those recorded by Sir John Wittewronge of Rothamsted, Hertfordshire, in his diary for August 1685: 'The Apricotts & peaches (by reason of the unseasonable wett weather) ripened very ill & backward the former not till the middle of August for the most part & many of them rotted, the peaches not till the latter end of Aug: & Septemb: they rotted also and fell off: not good … .'[22] The possession of peach, apricot or nectarine trees was thus one of the features that marked out major landowners from the rest of society, although the distinction was not an absolute one. Mary Birkhead's daughter, more 'middling sort' than a member of the landed elite, had an apricot and a vine in her garden at Thwaite in Norfolk in 1734 and in the garden of the neighbouring tenant farm, formerly Birkhead's own home, there was a single peach tree.[23] Significant displays of such fruit were, however, restricted to the gardens of large country houses.

Cherries and plums, generally coming into blossom earlier than apples and pears and thus more vulnerable to late frosts, were also often grown within walled gardens. A plan of

---

18 W. Temple, *Miscellanea: The Second Part* (London, 1690), p. 129.

19 J. Woudstra, 'Fruit Cultivation in the Royal Gardens of Hampton Court Palace 1630–1842', *Garden History*, 44/2 (2016), pp. 255–71.

20 BRO, TW685.

21 Bellamy, *The Language of Fruit*, pp. 46–54.

22 Williams and Stevenson, '*Observations of Weather*', pp. 22–3.

23 NRO, BRA 926/122.

the fruit trees growing in the gardens of Wormley Bury in Hertfordshire in 1741 reveals that there were seven nectarine trees, all of different varieties; 13 peach, all different; five apricots, all different; 17 plums in 11 varieties; 21 cherries in three varieties; and 12 pears, each a different variety. The nectarines and the peaches were partly standard and partly dwarf trees; the plums were mainly and the pears and apricots entirely on dwarfing stocks. Only the cherry trees were all standard trees.[24] Dwarf fruit trees seem, in general, to have characterised the walled gardens of the sixteenth, seventeenth and early eighteenth centuries. Other lists of fruit trees in manor-house gardens – from Sharnbrook and Hinwick in Bedfordshire, and Honing and Carleton Rode in Norfolk – suggest that, as at Wormley, peaches were roughly twice as numerous as nectarines and apricots, which were themselves present in roughly equal numbers, accompanied by variable numbers of cherry, plum and pear.[25] There were relatively few apples. These were instead planted as dwarf trees against the outside walls or, more usually, grown as standards beside walks, in shrubberies or in orchards.

The distinction between the fruit grown in walled gardens and that cultivated in orchards needs to be emphasised because a cursory examination of estate lists and memoranda dating to the seventeenth and early eighteenth centuries often gives the impression that apples were of little concern to the wealthy. In many cases, however, the lists are only of garden fruit, ordered from London nurseries, and maps show that great houses also had orchards in which apples and pears were grown. Where such lists do appear to include the trees growing in or destined for all parts of the grounds, apples and pears are usually better represented. The fruit trees ordered in 1672 for the new gardens at Ryston Hall in Norfolk, for example, included 24 varieties of apple and 18 of pear.[26] But, overall, apples and pears, and to an extent plums, constituted a higher *proportion* of the fruit grown by yeoman farmers, compared with the gentry and aristocracy.

Although gardens remained formal and geometric in layout well into the eighteenth century, their style changed in numerous and complex ways. In particular, from the late seventeenth century they became simpler in layout and often more extensive; walls became less prominent elements; and larger and larger areas came to be occupied by 'wildernesses' – blocks of ornamental woodland and shrubbery dissected by hedged gravel paths.[27] These, too, might sometimes be planted with fruit trees – in some cases, indeed, the line between an orchard and a wilderness may have been a fine one. At Stow Bardolph in Norfolk in 1712 the wilderness 'quarters' were planted with '14 pears, 14 apples, 14 plums, 7 cherries

---

24   Royal Institute of British Architects Library, London, Mylne Drawing Collection SC 122/21.
25   BRO, OR 2331/11 and X800/32; private collection; NRO, PD 254/60.
26   NRO, Mf/Ro219/1.
27   J. Bartos, 'Wilderness and Grove: Gardening with Trees in England 1688–1750', PhD thesis (University of Bristol, 2013); J. Woudstra, 'The History and Development of Groves in English Formal Gardens, 1600–1760', in J. Woudstra and C. Roth (eds), *A History of Groves* (London, 2018), pp. 67–85.

all for standard trees'.[28] At Houghton Hall in the same county the gardens laid out to the west of the house comprised a great lawn and tree-lined vista, flanked to north and south by extensive wildernesses. That to the south appears to have doubled as an orchard and, in part perhaps, as a kitchen garden.[29] Ralph Freman of Hamels in Hertfordshire planted apples and plums as part of his 'woodwork', apparently a kind of wilderness, in 1722.[30] He also planted apple trees in his park, again perhaps a common practice.[31]

The aesthetic role of orchards and fruit trees in the grounds of country houses in the period before the mid-eighteenth century should not be exaggerated, however. Their main purpose, even when prominently positioned, was to produce fruit for the household and perhaps for sale. Many landowners possessed several orchards, some lying more distant from the mansion and its ornamental grounds. Sir John Wittewronge of Rothamsted, Hertfordshire, refers to his 'Hop Ground Orchard', 'Lazarusses Orchard' and 'Warren Orchard' in his diary from the 1680s.[32] Many new varieties of fruit were first developed, recognised or named by estate gardeners, most notably the greengage, imported from France as the Reine-Claude plum but given its new name in honour of Sir William Gage by the gardener at his mansion of Hengrave Hall in Suffolk in the 1720s.[33] But orchards and fruit trees were also key elements of early modern designed landscapes, and perhaps deserve more attention from garden historians than they have usually received.

Fruit trees in country-house grounds after c.1760

From the middle decades of the eighteenth century a new style of garden and landscape design became fashionable, first among the most wealthy landowners, but gradually spreading to the broad mass of the local gentry. Under the direction of landscape designers such as Lancelot 'Capability' Brown, geometric gardens, walled enclosures and productive facilities were swept away from the walls of the mansion, so that it appeared to stand within a sweeping expanse of 'naturalistic' parkland.[34] Gardens *per se* did not cease to exist, but were now without enclosing walls, and were instead separated from the park by a sunken fence or ha ha, and they were simple and irregular or serpentine in layout. Such 'pleasure grounds' consisted of neat gravel paths winding through lawns and shrubberies,

---

28 NRO, HARE 5531 223 X 55.
29 C. Campbell, *Vitruvius Britannicus*, vol. 3 (London, 1725).
30 A. Rowe (ed.), *Garden Making and the Freeman Family: A Memoir of Hamels 1713–1733*, Hertfordshire Record Society 17 (Hertford, 2001), pp. xxxix, 28.
31 Rowe, *Garden Making and the Freeman Family*, p. 40.
32 Williams and Stevenson, 'Observations of Weather', pp. 34–5.
33 M. Askay and T. Williamson, *Orchard Recipes from Eastern England: Landscape, Fruit and Heritage* (Lowestoft, 2020), p. 77.
34 D. Brown and T. Williamson, *Lancelot Brown and the Capability Men: Landscape Revolution in Eighteenth-Century England* (London, 2016); J. Phibbs, *Place Making: The Art of Capability Brown* (London, 2016).

and were usually tucked away to one side of the mansion. All signs of useful production – kitchen gardens, dovecotes, fish ponds and the like – were banished from sight. But the wealthy still needed vegetables and fruit. Walled kitchen gardens continued to exist, although now in more hidden locations, usually screened by shrubberies or plantations and sometimes moved several hundred metres away from the house. Fruit continued to be espaliered against their walls and orchards were usually planted beside them. Indeed, although fashionable taste decreed that these features should not appear in the same view as the house, or interrupt the views from the house across the park – with its elegant trees, smooth contours and (where possible) a lake – spatial marginalisation did not reflect any lack of interest on the part of the wealthy. Maps leave little doubt that kitchen gardens and orchards were usually accessed directly from the pleasure grounds.[35] They were regularly visited, especially in the winter or early spring when, as Humphry Repton noted in 1806,

> a warm, dry but secluded walk, under the shelter of a south wall, would be preferred to the most beautiful but exposed landscape; and in the spring, when ... on the south border of a walled garden some early flowers and vegetables may cheer the sight, although every plant is elsewhere pinched with the north-east winds ... .[36]

Repton himself often laid out walks leading to, and around the outside of, kitchen gardens as part of his 'improvements', and at places such as Woodhill in Hertfordshire he recommended that space should be left to either side of the path running between the shrubbery screens and the walls to allow light to reach the fruit trees trained against the latter.[37] Even when kept at a respectable distance, in other words, kitchen gardens and orchards were a regular destination for a leisurely stroll.

Owners certainly spent lavishly on them. The walled garden at Salle in Norfolk cost £565 in the 1760s, that at Heacham in the same county nearly £900 in the following decade.[38] Lists of trees planted in gardens and orchards, and bills paid to nurseries, suggest that gentlemen amassed sizeable collections of fruit, with a wide range of varieties now grown in the kitchen gardens rather than in the walled gardens close to the mansion. The bills for fruit trees purchased for the Heydon estate in Norfolk between 1797 and 1801, for example, include 17 different varieties of peach alone.[39] Richard Milles, owner of North Elmham Hall in Norfolk, made a detailed list of the trees planted in his new kitchen garden in 1765. They included six different varieties of nectarine, 12 of peach, 19 of pear, 14 of plum, 13 of cherry and a medlar, but only one apple. In all, the North Elmham garden

---

35 Brown and Williamson, *Capability Men*, pp. 126–9.
36 H. Repton, *An Enquiry into the Changes of Taste in Landscape Gardening* (London, 1806), p. 16.
37 John Soane Museum, London, ms (163) 64/6/2.
38 NRO, MC 65/1; HEA 489.
39 NRO, BUL 11/89.

Figure 4.4 Old espalier pear tree in the kitchen garden at Cockley Cley Hall, Norfolk.

contained 98 individual trees, with a further 56 growing against the outside walls, or in adjoining slips.[40] When the new kitchen garden was constructed at Shotesham Hall in the same county in the 1780s the plan – drawn up by the architect John Soane, no less – specified the position of four varieties of nectarine, four of apricot, eight of plum, nine cherry, and no fewer than 15 peach.[41] As in previous periods, the more tender and exotic fruit were thus grown against garden walls, albeit now at some distance from the mansion, while apples – and many of the pears and plums – sometimes on the outside walls but mainly separately, in an adjoining orchard. But on the largest estates especially, where kitchen gardens were particularly extensive and often subdivided into a number of walled enclosures, apples on dwarfing rootstocks might be an important feature of the interior, trained against the walls as fans or espaliers (Figure 4.4). In 1791 the duke of Bedford thus bought 80 dwarf apple trees and 80 dwarf pear trees from Samuel Swinton's nursery in Sloane Street, London, explicitly for his new kitchen garden at Woburn Abbey.[42]

40   W. Roberts, 'Richard Milles' New Kitchen Garden', *Norfolk Archaeology*, 62 (1937), pp. 501–7.
41   NRO, FEL 1115, L5.
42   BRO, R3/2114/534.

Figure 4.5 The kitchen garden at Kimberley Hall, Norfolk. The heated wall, inserted into the existing garden by Capability Brown in c.1778. The fireplaces that provided the heated air for the internal flues can be seen to the left, at the base of the wall.

The importance of fruit trees in eighteenth- and early nineteenth-century kitchen gardens explains much about the latter's layout and construction. Most examples were rectangular in shape but a few took more adventurous forms, all apparently intended to increase the length of south-facing walls for the benefit of the fruit trees trained against them. That designed by the celebrated landscape gardener Richard Woods, a rival and contemporary of Capability Brown, at Newsells in Hertfordshire in the 1760s had a trapezoid shape, while the one he created at Hengrave in Suffolk in the 1770s featured a curving north wall.[43] Woods had a particular interest in kitchen gardens but similar designs appeared elsewhere. The garden at West Acre High House in Norfolk has a curving north wall, a modification of the original structure; that at Raynham in the same county is so trapezoidal as to resemble a truncated triangle in plan.[44] The creation of internal subdivisions also served to increase the overall length of south-facing walls. A particularly expensive feature of the more elaborate gardens were walls heated by an arrangement of fireplaces and flues. Capability Brown himself designed, in 1778, the fine example that still survives at Kimberley in Norfolk (Figure 4.5).[45]

---

43 F. Cowell, *Richard Woods: Master of the Pleasure Garden* (Woodbridge, 2009), pp. 207–8, 221.

44 T. Williamson, *The Archaeology of the Landscape Park: Garden Design in Norfolk, England, c.1680–1840*, BAR British Series 269 (Oxford, 1998), pp. 164–5.

45 Brown and Williamson, *Capability Men*, p. 127.

Through the later eighteenth and early nineteenth centuries garden fruit and orchards continued to loom large in diaries and memoranda books, suggesting that even quite wealthy owners had hands-on engagement with them. On 27 November 1770 James Coldham of Anmer Hall in Norfolk, for example, noted the trees he had recently planted: Breda apricot, Burée pear, St Germaine's pear, Admirable peach, Red Magdalen peach, Roman nectarine, both dwarf and standard Duke cherries, and greengages. On the south wall of the 'Mulberry Garden' were '3 peaches, names unknown'.[46] The diary of Nicholas Styleman of Heacham Hall in Norfolk contains numerous entries relating to his gardening interests. In June 1820, for example, he described how he had been 'busy all forenoon with Hardy and Discipline planting fruit trees in ye new garden and orchard'.[47] By this time, even quite minor country houses included extensive provision for fruit production. In 1820 the kitchen garden at Langham Hall in Suffolk covered 4 acres and was 'walled in with lofty brick walls in 4 divisions, covered with fruit trees in full bearing, and … Hot [internally heated] Walls for the forcing of fruit'.[48]

Victorian and Edwardian fruit growing

In the middle and later decades of the nineteenth century the gardens in the immediate vicinity of large houses became increasingly structured and architectural, and geometric features such as parterres and topiary returned to popularity. Orchards and kitchen gardens, while connected to and accessible from the ornamental part of the grounds, usually remained separate and distanced, but the interest shown by landowners in their fruit trees seems, if anything, to have increased still further. Apples now seem to have been grown more frequently within walled gardens, often trained on frames lining the principal paths as well as against the walls. New techniques for protecting or forcing the more delicate kinds of fruit were also developed, part of a more general enthusiasm for technology and gadgets that characterised the period. These included such things as the 'conservative wall' developed initially by Joseph Paxton at Chatsworth in Derbyshire – a kind of narrow glasshouse attached to south-facing walls of kitchen gardens, designed mainly to protect the peaches and other exotics growing against them from frost.[49] Fine examples survive at Somerleyton Hall in Suffolk. Thomas Rivers, who took over Rivers Nursery at Sawbridgeworth, Hertfordshire, in 1837, published his book *The Orchard House; or the Cultivation of Fruit Trees in Pots* in 1851, which described how to grow diminutive fruit trees in pots in small glasshouses.[50] These could be taken to the dining table for guests to pick their own dessert, or otherwise displayed. Experiments were also made in

---

46 NRO, MC 40/113.
47 NRO, Le Strange LA 34–7.
48 SRO, B, HA 520/2/34–7, 256D. B4.
49 *Magazine of Botany*, 12 (1845), pp. 180–4.
50 T. Rivers, *The Orchard House; or the Cultivation of Fruit Trees in Pots under Glass* (London, 1851).

Figure 4.6 Bromham House, Bedfordshire, 1903. The owner inspecting the Apple House, covered with reeds, one of many marketed in the decades either side of 1900 by the firm of Bunyards in Kent. Bedfordshire Record Office Z50/21/54.

improving the storage of apples. In 1844 the steward at Woburn Abbey was dispatched to Wrest Park in Bedfordshire to 'view the new Fruit Room. It is in the first year's trial and the gardener is very satisfied and is sending apples and pears still perfect to Covent Garden. There is circulation of air to carry off sweating and double windows and doors to guard against frost.'[51] Towards the end of the century some local landowners were purchasing the distinctive 'apple houses' marketed by Bunyard's, the Kent nursery company, with their walls of woven reed (Figure 4.6).

Above all, this was the great age of head gardeners, whose achievements were discussed and celebrated in publications such as the *Gardeners' Chronicle*. Many of the new varieties of fruit, and especially of apple, that were developed in the eastern counties in the nineteenth and twentieth centuries were the work of such men. The apple variety Desse de Buff originated in the gardens of Wrest Park in Bedfordshire; the Golden Noble was reputedly found and developed by the head gardener of the Stow Bardolph estate in Norfolk; Lady Henniker (an excellent dual-purpose apple) was discovered in 1873 by Mr Perkins, the head gardener at Thornham Hall in Suffolk, as a seedling growing in the

---

51 BRO, R3/4823.

discarded waste from cider-making; the cooking apple Lord Stradbrooke was raised by the head gardener at Henham Hall, near Wangford in the same county, by a Mr Fenn shortly before 1900;[52] the Aldenham Blenheim, a highly coloured version of the Blenheim Orange, was discovered just after the First World War by Edwin Beckett growing in the gardens at Aldenham House in Hertfordshire; and the cooking apple known as the Bushey Grove was developed on the nearby Bushey Hall or Bushey Grove estate by J.T. Goode in 1897.[53] There are numerous other examples.

Sales particulars and other sources attest to the phenomenal range of fruit cultivated in country-house orchards and kitchen gardens by the end of the nineteenth century. When the Pines estate at Mettingham in Suffolk was put on the market in 1896 the orchard contained a phenomenal range of apples, the sales particulars listing specimens of: Waltham Abbey Seedling, Lord Suffield, Royal Somerset, Yorkshire Greening, Court Pendu Plat, Tower of Glamis, Northern Greening, Early Harvest, New Hawthornden, Cellini, Mere de Ménage, Easter Pippin, Normanton Wonder, Aromatic Russet, King of the Pippins, Kathleen Pippin, London Pippin, Nelson Codling, Gravenstein, Duchess of Oldenburgh, Cornish Gilliflower, Doctor Harvey, Crofton, Kentish Pippin, Bedfordshire Foundling, Yellow Joist, Philadelphia Pippin, Ribston Pippin, Golden Russet, Delaware Apple, Hubbard's Pearmain, Reinette du Canada, Flanders' Pippin, Pope's Apple, Lemon Pippin, Stirling Castle, Alfriston Apple, Harwell Souring, Court of Wick, Scarlet Nonpareil, Never Fail, Winter Non-Such, Scarlet Pearmain, Worcester Pearmain, Golden Winter Pearmain, Knobby Russet, Rymer, Norfolk Beaufin, Harvey's Wiltshire Defiance, Blenheim Orange Pippin, Forge Apple, Striped Beaufin, Beauty of Kent, Pomona and Golden Harvey. There was also an impressive range of pears, including Fondante d'Automne, Duchesse d'Angouleme, Marie Louise, Beurré Diel, Comte de Lamy, Louise of Jersey, Williams' and Bon Chrétien, as well as plums and greengages. In all, the orchard contained 200 trees, but in addition the 'highly productive Kitchen Garden' contained further pears and apples.[54] Such a range was perhaps not the norm, but it was not unusual, either. In 1890 Mr Benjamin Stimpson of Salle Moor Hall in Norfolk established a new orchard of 2.5 acres (*c*.1 hectare) adjacent to an existing one, and his orchard notebook records how it was planted in 13 rows, each with 17 or 18 trees.[55] He placed an order with a nursery in East Dereham for 219 apple trees, 29 varieties in all; and for ten plums, in five varieties.

From the late nineteenth century the owners of large estates were increasingly challenged financially by agricultural depression, the advent of inheritance taxes and other changes, but many country houses continued to function as elite residences and, at least until the middle decades of the twentieth century, most continued to maintain their

---

52   Morgan and Richards, *New Book of Apples*, pp. 205, 218, 233, 237.
53   M. Clark, *Apples: A Field Guide*, rev. edn (Tewin, 2015), pp. 45 and 134.
54   SRO, L, 1117/285/29.
55   NRO, MC 561/87.

orchards and kitchen grounds. After the Second World War the majority were gradually neglected but, where decline has been gradual and active clearance has not occurred, the surviving remains indicate – as we would expect – collections of fruit more diverse than are usually found in farmhouse or commercial orchards. The kitchen garden at Cockley Cley in Norfolk lay beside the hall until the latter was rebuilt on a new site, some 400m to the north-west, in the early 1870s. The walls, of eighteenth- and nineteenth-century date, do not form a complete circuit, but bound the former garden only to the north and east. Successive editions of the Ordnance Survey 6-inch maps show that a small orchard occupied part of the southern section of the garden, its size and shape changing over time. The garden still contains an impressive range of fruit. The walls are lined with pears and plums, some obviously trained; a little inside are the remains of a parallel line of apples, while to the south-east are the traces of a nuttery comprising five old cobnut stools. Four apples, all Bramley's Seedlings, survive from the area of orchard. The apples growing parallel with the walls are more diverse and include examples of relatively common varieties such as Ribston Pippin, Dumelow's Seedling, Striped Beefing, Sturmer Pippin, Ellison's Orange, Yellow Ingestrie, Newton Wonder and Claygate Pearmain, but also ones that are locally uncommon, such as Mabbot's Pearmain, and rarer ones, such as Belle de Pontoise, John Standish and King of Tompkins County (a large American dessert apple sold by Daniels' nursery in Norwich in the decades around 1900).[56] All are grafted on dwarfing or semi-dwarfing rootstocks and, now nicely veteranised, were probably planted in the 1920s or 1930s. In addition, some 130m to the north-west of the kitchen garden, another area of orchard was planted in the 1880s or 1890s. This is now represented by a single apple tree that is almost certainly an early clone of Golden Delicious, a north American variety introduced to the UK by Bunyard's in the 1920s and probably planted here very soon afterwards.

Some 25km to the north, and also in Norfolk, two interesting collections of fruit trees survive at Houghton Hall. One, apparently planted in the 1950s, to judge from the evidence of aerial photographs, is located within the walled garden and comprises a neat grid of 24 apples spaced at intervals of 14 feet (*c.*4.3m) each way. It features Bramley's Seedlings, varieties developed by the Bedfordshire firm of Laxton's in the first half of the twentieth century (Fortune, Epicure, Superb) and a single Ellison's Orange. The second group comprises an orchard of 26 much older, mainly bush-planted trees immediately to the south of the kitchen garden and accessed directly from it. They are shown on aerial photographs from 1946, planted in a neat quincunx pattern. Today they appear more irregularly spaced because losses have disrupted the original layout, which perhaps dates from the 1920s. Most are apples; Bramley's Seedling predominates but there are examples of Crimson Bramley, Warner's King, Rosemary Russet, Lane's Prince Albert, Blenheim Orange, Allington Pippin, Lord Suffield and Lord Lambourne – all fairly common varieties

---

56   Identification by Bob Lever.

– and a single example of the locally rare Court of Wick.[57] There is also a medlar and a single cobnut, perhaps a survivor from a larger collection.

This pattern – a predominance of Bramley's, a wide range of fairly common varieties and a small number of more unusual types – can be paralleled elsewhere. The old trees recorded in 2003 growing in the outer slips of the garden at Wandlebury House in Cambridgeshire – sandwiched between the walls of the unusual polygonal garden and the ramparts of the Iron Age hillfort within which this is situated – are again dominated by Bramley's, accompanied by examples of Annie Elizabeth, Lane's Prince Albert, Newton Wonder, Blenheim Orange, Charles Ross, Howgate Wonder and Lord Derby, but also including the relatively rare Hambling's Seedling and Winter Queen. Even where country-house collections survive in a fragmentary condition they often include at least one rare or locally unusual variety. At High House, West Acre, in Norfolk, there are only three fruit trees remaining within the walled garden and six surviving from the orchard immediately to the south, but they include examples of two relatively uncommon American varieties, Wealthy and American Mother. Even quite minor country houses can usually boast one unusual or rare variety, like the Calville Rouge d'Hiver – well over a century old – at Plumstead Grange near Norwich.[58]

Orchards in the suburbs

The period between *c.*1870 and the Second World War saw the large-scale suburbanisation of many districts in eastern England, especially in Hertfordshire and Essex, the counties closest to London. Not only did the capital extend northwards and eastwards into the countryside, large towns in its orbit also experienced considerable growth. All this was in part a consequence of the inexorable increase of the nation's population, but it was also the result of improvements in transport that allowed people to live in less crowded conditions at a distance from their place of work and – in the inter-war years especially – of changes in the national economy. In the 1920s and 1930s the spread of the National Grid encouraged the development of new 'light' industries, such as printing and the manufacture of cars and aircraft in many small towns.[59] By 1941 Watford and Barnet in the south of Hertfordshire were 'largely dormitory areas for London', while other market towns in the south of the county had 'entered a new phase: fast and efficient transport to London and to the Midlands combined with a local labour supply have attracted many light industries and much of south-west Hertfordshire has thus become greatly industrialised'.[60] Much the same was true of the south-western parts of Essex. Before the passing of the Town and Country

---

57 Identification by Bob Lever.
58 Identification by Martin Skipper.
59 K. Hudson, *The Archaeology of the Consumer Society: The Second Industrial Revolution in Britain* (London, 1983).
60 L.G. Cameron, *The Land of Britain: Hertfordshire* (London, 1941), p. 336.

Planning Act in 1947 suburban sprawl was largely unregulated and occurred piecemeal; patterns of development were largely structured by transport networks. Up until the First World War house building tended to be concentrated close to railway stations; after the war, as car ownership spread, development was less constrained, although with a tendency to congregate close to arterial roads. This said, some large-scale, planned development also took place, most notably the Hertfordshire 'garden cities' of Letchworth and Welwyn.[61]

Suburbanisation was not, however, restricted to the areas in the immediate hinterland of the capital. Major towns and cities such as Bedford, Cambridge, Colchester, Ipswich and Norwich also experienced significant growth, as did many villages in *their* hinterlands, or with easy access to a railway station. 'Suburbs', in fact, are almost impossible to define, took many forms, and changed in character significantly over time. The term embraces Victorian terraces, inter-war 'semis' and opulent upper-middle-class residences set in spacious grounds, often in semi-rural or rural locations. All these diverse forms of housing are part of our story because their gardens often contained fruit trees, while the larger residences might boast true orchards in their grounds.

In small suburban gardens, as in the yards of rural cottages, a few small fruit trees might often be planted, although with space at a premium (and fruit now usually readily available from a local greengrocers) they were not a priority for many amateur gardeners, compared with flowers, soft fruit and vegetables. Already in 1911 F.H. Farthing was able to declare: 'how rarely does one see in the ordinary suburban back garden any real attempt to cultivate hardy fruit trees!', due in large measure to the fact that 'sixty feet by eighteen feet … is the customary space allotted by the builders of suburban middle-class homes'.[62] In the inter-war years the cultivation of both fruit and vegetables may have declined further: in *c.*1940 M. James, in his *Complete Guide to Home Gardening*, declared roundly that 'In the modern garden … flowers are of even greater importance in nearly every case, than are vegetables. Certainly, the smaller the garden the greater prominence is given to flowers … .'[63] Such practical texts all, however, provided some information about fruit trees, and make it clear that most small gardens contained them.

Farthing emphasised, as did other writers, how the ready availability of fruit on dwarfing rootstocks, and the training of these as fans or espaliers against walls and fences, made it possible to grow significant quantities of apples and pears even on quite restricted plots.[64] In his *Practical Gardening for Amateurs*, published in 1935, H.E. Hellier provided more advice, and described how

---

61 A. Rowe and T. Williamson, *Hertfordshire: A Landscape History* (Hatfield, 2013), pp. 268–94; A. Jackson, *Semi-Detached London: Suburban Development, Life and Transport 1900–1939* (London, 1973); T. Rowley, *The English Landscape in the Twentieth Century* (London, 2006), pp. 195–216.

62 F.H. Farthing, *Saturday in My Garden* (London, 1911), p. 317.

63 M. James, *Complete Guide to Home Gardening* (London, nd. *c.*1940), p. ix.

64 Farthing, *Saturday in my Garden*, pp. 317–22.

Much valuable research work has been carried out with a view to testing the influence of stocks upon the trees grafted on them, with the result that it has been conclusively proved that whereas some root systems encourage vigorous growth and delay fruiting others induce a dwarfing habit and encourage early bearing.[65]

He discussed the development by East Malling Research Station of the various 'M' rootstocks, recommending in particular Malling IX (M9) – described as 'extremely dwarfing' – for growing apples in the 'average villa garden', even varieties that were themselves naturally vigorous, such as Blenheim Orange or Bramley's Seedling. The cultivation of pears in small gardens was also now possible because 'the selected quince stock known as Malling A has proved to have a dwarfing effect'. As James put it, such trees were also 'easier to prune and spray regularly', and much easier to pick fruit from.[66]

Hellier provided a list of apples that he considered particularly suitable for small suburban plots. He recommended Gladstone, Beauty of Bath and Early Victoria as early varieties and James Grieve, Laxton's Fortune, Golden Spire and Grenadier for September picking. As late varieties he thought Ellison's Orange, Rev W. Wilks, Cox's Orange Pippin and Lane's Prince Albert excellent choices for small plots, and suggested Sturmer Pippin and Crawley Beauty for storing.[67] It is noteworthy that while some of these were relatively new varieties, introduced during the previous three decades, most were common types that had been grown commercially since the middle decades of the nineteenth century. For pears, similarly, a well-established range was mainly recommended, including Williams' Bon Chrétien, Louis Bonne of Jersey, Pitmaston Duchess, Doyenne de Comice and Conference. In c.1940 James produced a longer and slightly different list of recommended varieties, omitting Gladstone, Early Victoria, Golden Spire and Lane's Prince Albert from the apples, for example, but adding Blenheim Orange, Charles Ross, Duke of Devonshire, Newton Wonder and Laxton's Epicure.[68]

The extent to which fruit trees were planted in small suburban gardens in the first half of the twentieth century can cause confusion. Concentrations of old apple trees in suburban gardens are often said by local residents to be the remains of country-house, farmhouse or commercial orchards that existed before the land in question was developed for housing. Such stories are particularly common in Hertfordshire, not surprisingly given that it is the most suburbanised of the eastern counties. But they are seldom true. In Berkhamsted, for example, fruit trees in the gardens of houses in Cedar Drive, built in the 1930s, are said locally to be survivors from the orchard of Berkhamsted Hall, but the map evidence shows that this lay some 300m to the west and the houses were in fact built on what had been

---

65 H.E. Hellier, *Practical Gardening for Amateurs* (London, 1935), p. 212.
66 James, *Complete Guide*, p. 352.
67 Hellier, *Practical Gardening*, pp. 214–16.
68 James, *Complete Guide*, pp. 362–3.

open parkland. Trees behind houses on The Drive, Bengeo, supposedly originated in an earlier orchard but maps show that none existed here when the houses were erected in the 1930s. The same story is related to explain the old fruit trees in the gardens of houses in London Road, Knebworth, again built in the inter-war years on open fields, while the suggestion that fruit trees in gardens on Spencer Gate in St Albans were originally part of an orchard attached to Heath Farm is not borne out by the map evidence. Such stories arise, in part, from a widespread tendency to assume that fruit trees are older than they really are because they age and veteranise at a faster rate than most trees (discussed in more detail in Chapter 8). Some simply appear too old to have been planted to serve the house with which they are associated.

Keen hobby gardeners evidently grew apples, pears and other fruit on some scale in modest suburban gardens but small numbers of dwarf trees hardly merit the description of 'orchard'. As just noted, however, the term 'suburban', like 'villa' and 'middle class', was (and is) poorly defined, and in the later nineteenth and early twentieth centuries more substantial residences were also erected for wealthy businessmen and professionals, usually in rather more remote locations. Their design was heavily influenced by the ideas of a group of broadly 'Arts and Crafts' architects, including Phillip Webb, R. Norman Shaw, William Eden Nesfield, Detmar Blow and in particular Henry Voysey, all of whom drew heavily on vernacular farmhouse architecture, especially that of the Cotswolds and the Home Counties, for inspiration.[69] Similar houses were erected in some numbers on the coast, as grand retreats or retirement homes. Some of these residences were very large – comparable to small manor houses – but with the vital difference that they did not have an estate attached. They were houses in the country rather than country houses. The grounds of these places often featured orchards, or areas of garden so densely planted with fruit trees that they were effectively indistinguishable from them. Their wealthy owners sought not so much a home in suburbia but a life in the countryside: only as they were joined by others, often less wealthy, did the areas in question tend to become suburban. An orchard made a fitting accompaniment to a rural dwelling designed to look like a farmhouse. But, in addition, orchards fitted in well with the wider aesthetic of contemporary Arts and Crafts garden design, which – like the associated styles in architecture – involved a re-presentation and re-imagining of the 'traditional' and the vernacular. This was, moreover, a time when orchards, along with other aspects of rural life, were being romanticised in the paintings of popular artists such as Myles Birket Foster and, in particular, Helen Allingham.[70]

The famous garden designer Gertrude Jekyll advocated in 1899 the creation of 'orchard gardens' with irregularly scattered fruit trees in which the grass should be left rough,

---

[69] H. Barrett and J. Phillips, *Suburban Style: The British Home, 1840–1960* (London, 1993), pp. 80–91.

[70] I. Taylor, *Helen Allingham's England* (Exeter, 1990).

plentifully planted with daffodils and cowslips, and mown for hay once or twice a year.[71] In her book *Colour Schemes for the Flower Garden* (1919) she provided more details about the place of fruit in the garden. She described the importance of 'a beautiful fruit garden' adjacent to the main ornamental grounds and enclosed by walls against which peaches, vines and pears were trained, and which also contained ornamental flowers such as hollyhocks, Michaelmas daisies and hardy fuchsias. Such a garden would have a central area laid to turf and studded with bush pears and apples ranged around a central mulberry tree. In turn it would open onto an orchard:

> For what is more lovely than the bloom of orchard trees in April and May, with the grass below in its strong, young growth; in itself a garden of Cowslips and Daffodils. In an old orchard how pictorial are the lines of the low-leaning Apple-trunks and the swing and poise of their upper branches .... But the younger orchard has its beauty too, of fresh, young life and wealth of bloom and bounteous bearing.[72]

The landscape architect and garden designer T.H. Mawson, whose book *The Art and Craft of Garden Making* went through five editions between 1900 and 1926, described how 'More romances of fiction and song have been laid in an orchard than anywhere else, for, if rightly considered, it is the one part of the domain above all others which speaks of seclusion, peace, quiet and rest, a close commune with nature and rural pleasures.'[73] William Robinson devoted a whole chapter of his book *The English Flower Garden* (1913) to 'The Orchard Beautiful', which he envisaged as filled with fruit trees but also underplanted with 'Daffodils, Snowflakes, Snowdrops, wild Tulips'.[74]

Arts and Crafts writers were unanimous in their belief that these semi-ornamental orchards should be planted with large, spreading trees on vigorous rootstocks. Mawson recommended 'the older fashioned standard fruit trees' above 'dwarf bushes'.[75] William Robinson described how:

> When we plant for beauty we must have the natural form of the tree. Owing to the use of dwarfing stocks, fruit gardens and orchards are now beginning to show shapes of trees that are poor compared with the tall orchard tree. However much these dwarf and pinched shapes may appeal to the gardener in his own domain, in the orchard beautiful they have no place.[76]

---

71 G. Jekyll, *Wood and Garden* (London, 1899), pp. 181–3.
72 G. Jekyll, *Colour Schemes for the Flower Garden* (London, 1919), p. 140.
73 T.H. Mawson, *The Art and Craft of Garden Making*, 4th edn (London, 1912), p. 246.
74 W. Robinson, *The English Flower Garden* (London, 1890), p. 382.
75 Mawson, *Garden Making*, p. 247.
76 Robinson, *English Flower Garden*, p. 376.

It is noteworthy, however, that while they were keen to create orchards with a broadly 'traditional', farmhouse appearance, Arts and Crafts designers were not necessarily enthusiasts for ancient fruit varieties, Robinson memorably commenting that many domestic orchards were 'a museum of varieties, many of them worthless and not even known to the owner'.[77] For the most part, like those advising the owners of small suburban plots, they recommended well-established nineteenth-century varieties such as Bramley's Seedling. This said, by the 1920s some commercial nurseries consciously catered for suburban rural nostalgia, with Laxton's in particular offering collections of fruit trees with names such as 'The East Anglian Collection' or 'The Orchard Collection'.[78]

Garden orchards featured prominently in the grounds of houses designed by the leading Arts and Crafts architects, although few survive in recognisable form. Typical was that at Amersfort, a house designed in 1911 by the architect Ernest Willmott, which stands in the hamlet of Potten End near Berkhamsted in west Hertfordshire – safely distanced from London but a short distance from a station on the rail line leading to it. The main area of the grounds, typically for the period, featured a combination of strongly architectural features and irregular planting, on which Gertrude Jekyll herself advised. The main terrace walk, immediately below the main front of the house, was continued to the south as a broad path running through two extensive orchards, which together covered around a third of a hectare.[79] Extensive orchards similarly accompanied Kelling Hall and Happisburgh Manor, coastal retreats in north Norfolk, designed by the architects Edward Maufe and Detmar Blow respectively.[80] The former orchard has disappeared but the latter was carefully replanted in the 1990s. But, as already implied, orchards were more widely planted in the grounds of large houses in semi-rural or suburban situations in this period. Typical was a house in The Avenue, Ampthill, in Bedfordshire, advertised for sale in 1910:

> A most desirable and substantially built freehold residence known as High Knoll, built by the late Mr G Shaw for his own occupation in 1903. With stable, coach house and greenhouse, together with the ornamental pleasure and kitchen gardens which are most productive and contain upwards of 40 varieties of apple, pear, plum and other fruit trees … the whole embracing an area of about 1 acre, 16 poles and commanding extensive and unobstructed views towards the south.[81]

---

77   Robinson, *English Flower Garden*, p. 374.

78   Laxton's catalogues, Royal Horticultural Society, Lindley Library.

79   E. Willmott, *English House Design: A Review; Being a Selection and Brief Analysis of Some of the Best Achievements in English Domestic Architecture* (London, 1911), pp. 18–19.

80   P. Dallas, R. Last and T. Williamson, *Norfolk Gardens and Designed Landscapes* (Oxford, 2013), pp. 185 and 240.

81   BRO, HN7/1/AMP3.

Small collections of fruit trees in suburban gardens are not depicted on the 25-inch or 6-inch Ordnance Survey maps. But orchards are often shown in the grounds of larger residences, and also in areas more densely built-up, on building plots as yet undeveloped, some of which may have been leased to local market gardeners. Few have survived post-war development pressures, as they provide ideal sites for 'infilling' development. The loss of orchards from suburban areas represents, in fact, part of a wider and more worrying development. The 1947 Town and Country Planning Act was an important piece of legislation that served to save Britain from unregulated suburban sprawl. But, by limiting where housing development could take place, it intensified the density of building in areas that were zoned for development, leading to the destruction not only of orchards but also of other spaces where wildlife could once find a home close to human habitation – a theme to which we shall return in the concluding chapter.

Institutional orchards

One other type of orchard deserves a section of its own, not least because it includes some of the largest and most diverse examples surviving in the eastern counties today: those associated with institutions such as psychiatric hospitals and children's homes. There are sporadic references to orchards attached to almshouses and hospitals from an early date. At Braughing in Hertfordshire, for example, Thomas Jenyns left in his will of 1579:

> a Cottage with an Orchard, containing an Acre of Ground, for an ancient Couple to dwell in without payment of any Rent, on Condition to take Care of the Trees and Fruit, which the Minister and Church-wardens shall yearly distribute among the Poor of the Parish; and upon the Vacancy of the House, they shall put in others.[82]

Hospitals for the care of the indigent poor, such as St Giles Hospital in Norwich, appear to have been provided with orchards, as were some early workhouses.[83] In 1822, for example, there is a reference to an orchard at the workhouse in Wickhambrook in west Suffolk.[84] But there is some evidence that, by the middle and later decades of the nineteenth century, orchards of this kind were less common.

In particular, while the tithe apportionments of *c.*1840 often describe 'gardens' beside workhouses, they seldom note the presence of orchards. In a similar way, while the late nineteenth- and early twentieth-century Ordnance Survey 6-inch and 25-inch maps might detail rectilinear networks of paths in such locations, similar to those shown in country house kitchen gardens, orchards are usually absent. Those that are shown are small in area – like that beside Depwade Union Workhouse, Pulham, in Norfolk, which covered a mere

---

82   H. Chauncy, *The Historical Antiquities of Hertfordshire*, 2nd edn, vol. 1 (London, 1826), p. 449.
83   Blomefield, *Topographical History of the County of Norfolk*, 2nd edn, vol. 4 (London, 1806), p. 250.
84   SRO, B, FL 652/8/1.

640 square metres. Some workhouses had small farms as well as gardens attached, where the younger and healthier inmates were expected to work, making the apparent paucity of orchards more surprising. Perhaps the vindictive approach to the poor manifested by the New Poor Law did not encourage an excessive provision of anything as pleasurable as fruit, even if produced by the labour of the inmates themselves.[85] Whatever the explanation, surviving institutional orchards are almost exclusively associated with new forms of establishment that appeared in the late nineteenth or early twentieth century: psychiatric hospitals, children's homes and other places with long-term residents who were capable of regular work.[86] In many cases, orchards were part of more extensive farming enterprises largely manned by inmates, work on which was deemed to have a therapeutic or at least character-building role. There were particularly large numbers of such places in Hertfordshire and Essex because of their proximity to London and high local population densities. Although many of these places no longer serve their original purpose, having been sold off for residential development, their orchards sometimes remain.

Probably the first public psychiatric institution to appear in the region was the Three Counties Asylum at Arlesey in Bedfordshire – so called because it served Hertfordshire, Bedfordshire and Huntingdonshire – which was opened in 1860 and, at least by the 1880s, was provided with an orchard as well as kitchen gardens and a farm. It was followed ten years later by that established by the Metropolitan Asylum Board on a 143-acre (58-hectare) site at Leavesden, just to the north of Watford in Hertfordshire, again provided with its own range of food-production facilities.[87] Most of the psychiatric hospitals subsequently erected in south Hertfordshire and Essex – including Hill End in St Albans, opened in 1900, Napsbury in London Colney, opened in 1905, and Severals near Colchester, opened in 1913 – followed suit. The practice continued into the inter-war years. Cell Barnes, also in St Albans and opened in 1933, had a large farm and orchards, as did nearby Shenley (1934) and Harperbury (1936), although in the case of Shenley the orchard, together with the kitchen garden, predated the establishment of the hospital, having been associated originally with the country house (Porters Park) that it replaced.

Both Sarah Rutherford and Claire Hickman have ably discussed the landscapes associated with nineteenth-century psychiatric institutions. Rutherford in particular has emphasised how, even before the passing of the 1845 Lunatics Act – which made it a duty for counties and boroughs to provide asylums for their 'pauper lunatics' – some private asylums, but in particular the few public ones set up under the previous voluntary

---

85 D. Englander, *Poverty and Poor Law Reform in Britain: From Chadwick to Booth, 1834–1914* (Abingdon, 2013).

86 P. Higginbotham, *Children's Homes: A History of Institutional Care for Britain's Young* (London, 2017); K. Jones, *Asylums and After: A Revised History of the Mental Health Services: From the Early Eighteenth Century to the 1990s* (London, 1993).

87 M. Diplock, *The History of Leavesden Hospital* (Abbots Langley, 1990).

act of 1808, had been provided with farms, kitchen gardens and the like.[88] Phillipe Pinel's influential *Traité médico-philosophique sur l'Aliénation Mentale* of 1801, translated into English as *A Treatise on Lunacy* in 1806, advocated (among other things) the therapeutic value of 'interesting and laborious employment' and suggested that asylums should be provided with 'a sort of farm' to this end.[89] This chimed well with contemporary beliefs about the moral superiority of the countryside over the town and encouraged the establishment of asylums on sites well outside major cities such as London:

> The choice of a rural site allowed a more extensive site to be acquired than might be available in an urban setting, giving greater opportunities for recreational and employment space. The acquisition of adjacent farmland enabled the vocational therapy becoming associated with the ideas of moral treatment to be easily and conveniently undertaken.[90]

John Conolly and other contemporary writers on the subject believed that outdoor labour was superior in therapeutic value to that undertaken inside, although only for men.[91] Female patients generally undertook indoor work, in the laundry for example. As Rutherford and others have noted, however, farms and kitchen gardens were established not only for their therapeutic value. The food produced was seldom sold, but was instead consumed by the inmates. 'The asylum estate was essentially a closed market with a potentially large source of "free" labour which would otherwise be absorbing revenue rather than offsetting it.'[92]

Initially, at least, the therapeutic role of the orchard was thus limited to the opportunities for work that it provided and most examples were located at a distance from the main hospital buildings, together with the farmyards and associated 'dirty activities, offensive smells and unhygienic animals'.[93] But it is interesting that at a number of places, over time, new orchards were added, closer to the wards. At Leavesden, for example, the original orchards lay outside the main grounds, across a public road; but around 1938 a new one was planted only 100m from the main residential blocks. At Napsbury, similarly, the orchards were initially located some way to the north of the wards. But just before the

---

88 S. Rutherford, 'The Landscapes of Public Lunatic Asylums in England, 1808–1914', PhD thesis (de Montfort University, Leicester, 2003); C. Hickman, *Therapeutic Landscapes: A History of English Hospital Gardens Since 1800* (Manchester, 2013).

89 P. Pinel, *Traité médico-philosophique sur l'Aliénation Mentale* (Paris, 1801); translated into English as *A Treatise on Lunacy* (London, 1806).

90 Rutherford, 'Landscapes of Lunatic Asylums', p. 120.

91 J. Conolly, *The Construction and Government of Lunatic Asylums and Hospitals for the Insane* (London, 1847), pp. 78–9.

92 Rutherford, 'Landscapes of Lunatic Asylums', p. 226.

93 Rutherford, 'Landscapes of Lunatic Asylums', p. 180.

Second World War another was added to the south of the main range of buildings, beside the cricket ground. The implication is that these places were intended as more purely therapeutic spaces, calming areas in which patients could sit and walk. In fact, as early as 1891 Sir Henry Burdett, in his *Hospitals and Asylums of the World*, had recommended that the courts between hospital wards 'should be laid out as gardens, and orchards, and lawns'.[94] But such a concept seems, at least within the area studied, to have been only slowly accepted.

A number of orchards associated with psychiatric hospitals still survive. That at Shenley is now maintained by the Shenley Park Trust (the hospital was finally closed in 1998); the orchard that accompanied its sister institution, Harperbury, also survives, although in a sad and derelict condition and threatened with development. The most important examples, however, are the two associated with the Three Counties Asylum, just to the north of Letchworth in Hertfordshire. The hospital site has been redeveloped for housing but both orchards survive and are kept in excellent condition. One was apparently planted soon after the hospital opened in 1860.[95] It lay immediately to the west of the main block of wards, but this was probably because the hospital farm was itself positioned unusually close by. The other was established to the south-east of the principal range of buildings, replacing a football pitch. As in the cases just noted, this was planted shortly before the Second World War. The original orchard boasts an extensive range of apples, mainly dessert varieties but with some cookers, including 14 examples of Monarch, 24 of Charles Ross, 20 of Ellison's Orange and 13 of Worcester Pearmain, some perhaps dating back to before the First World War but many added later. A fine line of cobnuts is planted along its eastern edge. The orchard was extended to the south in the 1950s and 1960s, mainly with dessert varieties developed by Laxton's nursery in Bedford (which lies only 20km to the north-west) such as Lord Lambourne, Laxton's Fortune and Laxton's Superb. In contrast, the second orchard, planted in the late 1930s, is composed almost entirely of Bramley's Seedlings and with only a few other varieties represented, including Lord Derby, Gascoyne's Scarlet, Annie Elizabeth, Ellison's Orange, Lady Sudeley and Newton Wonder.[96] Most of the trees seem to be survivors of the original planting.

It was not only psychiatric hospitals that were provided with orchards. St Elizabeth's at Much Hadham in east Hertfordshire was established as a residential school for epileptics in 1903.[97] Although it lacked a farm, it was provided from the start with three orchards to the north of the main ranges of buildings. The school was run by the Catholic order of the Daughters of the Cross of Liège, and the Ordnance Survey 6-inch map surveyed in 1915

---

94 H.C. Burdett, *Hospitals and Asylums of the World: Asylum Construction* (London, 1891), p. 13.

95 J. Pettigrew, S. Rouse and R. Reynolds, *A Place in the Country: Three Counties Asylum 1860–1999* (Hatfield, 2017).

96 Identifications by Bob Lever.

97 <www.stelizabeths.org.uk/about-us/about-st-elizabeths/history-of-st-elizabeths/>, accessed 12 March 2020.

Figure 4.7 The orchard at the St Elizabeth's Centre, Much Hadham, Hertfordshire. Many of the larger old orchards, in Hertfordshire especially, are associated with late nineteenth- or early twentieth-century residential institutions.

shows that there was a small burial ground for the nuns at the southern end of the site, with a small mortuary some 140m to the north of it. At some point between the wars a fourth orchard was planted in the area between them, surely in part with symbolic intent. Only this southern orchard now survives, in remarkably good condition (Figure 4.7). More than 150 old apple trees remain, together with a few plums and areas of plum thicket, where suckers have spread outwards from lost rootstocks. The apples are reminiscent of the range found in the grounds of a country house, with just fewer than 30 different varieties represented among the older trees, including some relatively rare ones such as King of Tompkins County. Bramley's Seedlings make up a third of the trees, accompanied by other culinary varieties such as Peasgood's Nonsuch, Newton Wonder, Bismarck, Annie Elizabeth and Golden Noble. In all, culinary varieties account for well over half of the surviving trees, with dual-purpose types such as Gascoyne's Scarlet, Blenheim Orange, King of Pippins and Allington Pippin making up a further quarter. Dessert varieties such as Blenheim Orange, Beauty of Bath and Ribston Pippin are thus in a minority, probably accounting for not much more than a fifth of the older trees. Evidently, the orchard provided large numbers of apples for cooking, together with a significant minority that could be eaten raw, although we do not know what was grown in the three lost orchards or how far the surviving trees in this remaining one relate to what was present in its heyday, before the 1960s.

Figure 4.8 The fine orchard at The Oval, Harpenden, Hertfordshire. The orchard was planted soon after the children's home, then known as Highfield, was opened in 1913.

On the other (western) side of Hertfordshire, Highfield in Harpenden – now called The Highfield Oval, and the base for a Christian training organisation – was established as a residential institution by National Children's Homes in 1913, a short distance from the charity's Elmfield Sanatorium, which had opened in 1910.[98] Highfield was a replacement for the National Children's Homes' Bonner Road home in Bethnal Green, London, and its residential and other buildings were arranged around a central oval of grass. The orchard, which still contains more than 50 trees, occupies a triangular site to the east of the main area of buildings. It is adjoined to the west by another, smaller group of fruit trees arranged in four parallel lines, which originally lined a central path in a kitchen garden, now laid to grass. The orchard developed in stages, to judge from the evidence of Ordnance Survey maps and aerial photographs. The southern section is shown on the OS 6-inch revision of 1922 and was probably planted (together with another example, now gone, some 60m to the south-west) when the home was first established (Figure 4.8). The northern part was added some time in the post-war period. The earlier section is dominated by culinary (16 trees: Annie Elizabeth, Bramley's Seedling, Grenadier, Monarch, Newton Wonder, Queen, Warner's King) and dual-purpose varieties (three trees: Blenheim Orange and

---

98 <http://www.childrenshomes.org.uk/HarpendenNCH/?LMCL=moRAYW>, accessed January 2020.

James Grieve), with only a single dessert apple (Sturmer Pippin). Around a third of the trees are Bramley's Seedlings. Most of the trees probably date back to the original planting and none of the varieties represented was developed after 1893. The newer, post-war section is also dominated by culinary varieties, but is more varied in character. There are examples of Lane's Prince Albert, Peasgood's Nonsuch, Warner's King, Dumelow's Seedling and Edward VII, but only one Bramley's Seedling. There are two dual-purpose apples (both Alexander) and four dessert varieties, all types developed by Laxton's of Bedford, some 35km to the north. More important than the differences, perhaps, are the similarities between the two sections of the orchard, which are both dominated by culinary varieties. Interestingly, the surviving trees in the old kitchen-garden area show a more even balance between eaters, cookers and dual-purpose apples. Highfields was equipped with its own print works and bakery, where some of the older children received training. The kitchen gardens provided most of the vegetables consumed by the residents, even in the 1950s, and the orchard produced enough fruit to keep them supplied right through the winter. The labour of the permanent gardening staff was supplemented by that of the residents; in the 1950s teenagers could earn 2s 6d a month by working in the kitchen garden and orchard.[99]

It is important to emphasise that not every residential institution in the later nineteenth or twentieth century was provided with an orchard. They do not seem to have been a normal feature of boarding schools, nor are examples usually found associated with general medical hospitals. One possible exception is the small (c.0.2 hectare) orchard at Steppingley Hospital in Flitwick, just south of Ampthill in Bedfordshire. Steppingley was founded as an isolation and smallpox hospital in 1905 on land donated to Ampthill Rural District Council by the duke of Bedford, but it was converted into a long-stay unit for women in 1956 and, to judge from the size of the remaining trees (all with girths of less than a metre), the orchard was probably planted then (Figure 4.9).[100] It seems too small to have served much of a practical purpose, and was perhaps intended to have a mainly ornamental and therapeutic role, although the apples planted there include culinary as well as dessert varieties. On the whole, institutions in the period after c.1850 appear to have been provided with extensive orchards only where the residents were able and expected to work; most such places also had kitchen gardens and farms. Where residents were too infirm, too transient or too wealthy to provide a regular labour force, true orchards were rarely established.

Cambridge University colleges – among the oldest residential communities in the eastern counties – are interesting in this respect. Some at least seem to have had their own orchards in the medieval and early post-medieval periods, but by the nineteenth century

---

99 <https://www.youtube.com/watch?v=jMLzCLggcKA>, accessed 12 December 2019.

100 <http://bedsarchives.bedford.gov.uk/CommunityArchives/Steppingley/Steppingley-Isolation-Hospital.aspx>, accessed 12 December 2019.

Figure 4.9 The small orchard at Steppingley Hospital in Bedfordshire, probably planted in the 1950s.

they had, with the exception of that in the grounds of St John's, apparently gone. Pressure on space and the easy availability of produce from the market and the city's greengrocers presumably made their maintenance uneconomic. In fact, only two colleges – Homerton and Girton – have their own orchards today, of which the latter is the largest, covering 1.75 acres (*c*.0.7 hectares, Figure 4.10). It was planted some time after the college was founded in 1869 and does not appear on the first edition Ordnance Survey 6-inch map of 1886, although it is shown on the revision of 1904. It appears to be first mentioned in the college archives in the same year. The oldest trees, many probably from the original planting, are all culinary varieties – predominantly Bramley's Seedling but with small numbers of Northern Greening, Warner's King, Norfolk Beefing, Blenheim Orange, Bismarck, Peasgood's Nonsuch, Monarch, Dr Harvey and Dumelow's Seedling. There are also some pears (Conference, Pitmaston Duchess and Fondante d'Automne) and plums, as well as a fine cobnut walk along the northern edge of the orchard. Homerton orchard is smaller and appears to have been planted a few decades after the college took over the existing buildings (Cavendish College) in 1894. The presence of orchards at these two late-established colleges probably has two explanations. Firstly, unlike the older colleges in the centre of the city, these were built on virgin sites, allowing for the provision of spacious grounds. But, secondly, both were originally women's colleges, designed in a muted gothic

Figure 4.10 The orchard at Girton College, Cambridge, planted around 1895.

style, for which orchards may have seemed particularly appropriate, redolent both of antiquity and domesticity. Being less wealthy than the established colleges, production of fruit on site may also have made more economic sense.

Conclusion

We have devoted an entire chapter to garden orchards, and to orchards associated with institutions, in part because of their intrinsic interest and in part because, while they were always vastly outnumbered by orchards attached to farms or run as commercial businesses, their survival rate has, in general, been rather higher than that of these more mundane examples. They have, that is, steadily increased as a percentage of surviving orchards, and especially as a percentage of the larger remaining examples, as these other types have been steadily lost or degraded over the last half century. What underlay this process of loss, as well as its scale and geographical incidence, are matters to which we shall return in Chapter 6.

CHAPTER FIVE

Processing: cider, jam and canning

Introduction

The cropping period of an individual fruit tree is relatively short, and both seasonal gluts in fruits that could not be easily stored and methods of preserving those that could critically shaped early foodways and culinary practices. Eighteenth- and nineteenth-century texts record a number of local dishes using orchard fruit from various parts of eastern England.

Cherries, as we have seen, were grown on a significant scale on the dipslope of the Chiltern Hills from at least the seventeenth century, and were difficult to preserve in any quantity for extended periods of time. William Hone described in 1832 how in certain parts of Hertfordshire – he presumably had the west of the county in mind – people had for centuries made cherry pasties 'which are by them highly esteemed for their delicious flavour'.

> Entertainments called 'the pasty feasts,' in which the above mentioned 'niceties' shine conspicuous, are always duly observed, and constitute a seasonal attraction 'for all ages,' but more particularly for the 'juveniles', whose laughter-teeming visages, begrimed with the exuberant juice, present unmistakeable evidence of their 'having a finger in the pie'.[1]

In East Anglia, and especially in Norfolk, the apple variety known as the beefing is recorded from the late seventeenth century and, while it was being marketed right across England by commercial nurseries by the end of the eighteenth century, it remained (and to an extent remains) closely associated with Norfolk, although other kinds of beefing certainly existed, such as the Herefordshire Beefing.[2] It is a particularly hard, long-keeping apple, which can be left on the tree through the winter. Despite its rather attractive appearance it is not pleasant to eat raw, as its texture is rather dry and its flavour bland. However, when cooked in certain ways it becomes a real delicacy.[3] It was used, most famously, to make 'Biffins'. During the nineteenth century these were extremely popular, not least as a Christmas delicacy, as described by Charles Dickens in *A Christmas Carol*.[4] They were a Norwich

---

1 W. Hone, *The Year Book of Daily Recreation and Information* (London, 1832), p. 1203.
2 Hogg, *British Pomology*, pp. 146–7.
3 Askay and Williamson, *Orchard Recipes*, pp. 65–7.
4 C. Dickens, *A Christmas Carol* (London, 1858), p. 50.

Figure 5.1 Norfolk Beefing apples, ready for baking into 'Biffins'.

speciality, prepared by bakers in their ovens as they cooled after bread-baking. They were cooked whole, packed in straw, and gradually flattened and dried; then they were packed in boxes layered with sugar and sent to London fruiterers, or by post as gifts (Figure 5.1). As William White explained in 1845, 'The *beefin* apples are baked as a sweetbread, by the confectioners, and pressed flat, like small cakes, without breaking the skin, in which state they are sold for 6d or 9d per dozen.'[5] They are best made in brick ovens and changes in oven technology contributed to their demise, although they were available commercially until the 1950s. They were also made domestically, as Esther Copley described in her *Housekeeper's Guide or a Plain and Practical System of Domestic Cookery* of 1838:

> Have a baking wire on short feet, on which lay clean straw, then the fruit, then another layer of straw; set them in a cool oven, and let them remain in four or five hours; then take them out, press them in the hand very gently, to get them as flat as possible, without breaking the skins; put them again in a cool oven. If this process is repeated three or four times, they will become as flat and as dry as those which are sold at a high price in the pastry-cook's shop. To do them properly, requires two or three days.[6]

---

5 White, *Norfolk*, p. 37.

6 E. Copley, *The Housekeeper's Guide or a Plain and Practical System of Domestic Cookery* (London, 1838), p. 377.

Similar descriptions appear in other sources. Eliza Acton, writing in 1868, described how the Norfolk Biffin, a 'hard and very red apple', was 'most excellent when carefully dried; and most fine we would say when left more juicy but partially flattened, than it is when prepared for sale'.[7]

Many of the close associations of 'traditional' recipes with particular local areas appear, however, to be inventions or simplifications of nineteenth- or twentieth-century writers. The 'Bedfordshire Clanger' was an elongated pasty containing meat at one end and apple at the other, which was made by the wives of agricultural labourers and taken into the field as a midday meal. Recorded fillings include liver and onion, bacon and potatoes, and pork and onion: sage was often used as a flavouring.[8] The filling was enclosed in suet pastry and either baked or boiled in a cloth.[9] There is some discussion about whether the pastry was to be eaten or was just there to protect the filling. Clangers were certainly popular in nineteenth-century Bedfordshire but they were also enjoyed, from an early date, well beyond the borders of the county. Indeed, they were sometimes described as *Hertfordshire* Clangers, and in the west of that county as 'Trowley Dumplings', presumably after the hamlet of Trowley Bottom in Flamstead. Clangers are also known from Buckinghamshire and have even been reported in Huntingdonshire.[10] Perhaps more importantly, the Clanger shows how 'tradition', rather than being timeless and unchanging, is in reality in a constant state of development and flux. A number of sources make it clear that clangers could also be, and may in origin have been, entirely savoury in character: what we now think of as the traditional clanger was one type, the ''alf and 'alf', which may have developed quite late in the nineteenth century.[11] Moreover, the clanger continues to change and adapt. Revived in the 1990s by Gunns, a local baker with branches in Sandy, Biggleswade and Bedford, it is now available with a range of fillings, including Bombay Vegetable Curry with Mango.

The 'Potton Florentine' is another interesting case. An article in *Hone's Year Book* for 1832 described how at Potton in Bedfordshire and the surrounding villages, 'sixty years since', it had been the custom to consume the Apple Florentine at Christmas entertainments.

> This 'Florentine' consisted of an immensely large dish of pewter, or such like metal, filled with 'good baking apples,' sugar, and lemon, to the very brim, with a roll of rich paste

---

7   E. Acton, *Modern Cookery for Private Families* (London, 1857), p. 572.
8   C. Morsley, *News from the English Countryside, 1851–1950* (London, 1983), p. 259; L. Meynell, *Bedfordshire* (Wallingford, 1960), p. 68.
9   R. Croft-Cooke, *English Cooking: A New Approach* (London, 1960), p. 217; R. Mashiter, *A Little English Cookbook* (Belfast, 1989), pp. 28–31.
10 R. Cotchin, 'A Monumental Clanger', *The Countryman*, 87 (1982), pp. 45–6: H. Harman, *Buckinghamshire Dialect* (London, 1929), p. 143; D. Jones-Baker, *The Folklore of Hertfordshire* (London, 1977), pp. 190–1.
11 C.F. MacKay Brown, 'Some Bedfordshire Recipes', *Bedfordshire News*, 10 (1966), pp. 20–1.

covering – pie fashion. When baked, and before serving up, the 'upper crust' or 'lid,' was taken off by a skilful hand, and divided into sizeable triangular portions or shares, to be again returned into the dish, ranged in formal 'order round,' by way of garnish; when, to complete the mess, full quart of well-spiced ale was poured in 'quite hot, hissing hot'.[12]

But a florentine was a type of pastry that appears to have originated in France. It was introduced into England before 1570 and then continued to be popular throughout the country into the early nineteenth century. Why it became identified so closely with this Bedfordshire village remains unclear. Particular types of fruit also became associated, quite spuriously, with particular places. Wardens – a term used for a range of hard, long-lasting and often large culinary pears – have long been said to have originated in the Bedfordshire village of Old Warden and as early as the fifteenth century the Cistercian Abbey of Old Warden included three pears in its coat of arms. But wardens are recorded from all over the country in the previous centuries and the abbey seems to have adopted the fruit as a 'logo' simply because of its name. 'Warden' does not, in fact, allude to the place but derives from the Anglo-Norman word *warder*, meaning 'to preserve or maintain', alluding to the keeping qualities of the fruit.[13]

The real aim of local people was not, of course, to devise novel ways of rapidly consuming large quantities of ripe fruit, but rather to extend the 'season' during which it could be eaten. This explains, in part, the proliferation of varieties, which was intended both to prolong the period of cropping and to provide – in the case of apples and pears – fruit that could be preserved through the autumn and winter and, in a few cases, into the spring. But from an early date less durable fruit, such as plums and cherries, was also bottled or preserved in other ways, especially as jam. Apples and pears were also converted into beverages, which served both as nutrition and, more importantly, as a source of inebriation. And, from the eighteenth century, and in particular from the mid-nineteenth century, a number of such essentially domestic practices developed as large-scale commercial and industrial processes.

Aspall Cider

There is a fundamental distinction or division in orchard history between the east and the west of England. In the latter, cider was the most commonly consumed alcoholic drink from an early date. Orchards were accordingly more extensive than in the east and special varieties of apple, particularly suitable for cider-making, were developed. Almost certainly this reflects the fact that the arable acreage was low in the west and the small quantity of barley produced was, owing to the character of the soils and climate, of poor malting quality. With beer in comparatively short supply, cider filled the gap and was produced on

---

12   Hone, *Year Book*, pp. 1596–7.
13   Roberts, *The Original Warden Pear*; Askay and Williamson, *Orchard Recipes*, pp. 32–3.

innumerable farms. In the east, in contrast, an abundance of good malting barley ensured that beer was always the principal alcoholic drink. This is not to say that cider was never produced in the eastern counties. In 1713 and 1715, for example, it was being made at Hamels, a country house in east Hertfordshire, and in 1718 the new 'apple mill room' there was boarded with 'feather edged elm boards'.[14] The diary kept by Sir John Wittewronge of Rothamsted in the same county in the 1680s also contains numerous references to cider-making. In October 1687, for example, he recorded: 'The 7th beat my golden pippins, & the 8th some green pippin & squeezed them … of which made a runlett & hogshead with some other sorts of apples mingled with them. The 11th beat & made one hogshead of Cider of Marroms apples.'[15]

Sir John, like most later cider-makers in the eastern counties, thus used ordinary culinary or dessert varieties for his cider, often mixed together. On 12 November the following year he 'made a hogshead of Cider of several Sorts of Apples', and the day after 'another hogsheads of Cider of several sorts of Apples, most whereof were Goody Marron's apples'.[16] But he also grew 'Normandy apples', which were probably cider apples, and, while he often seems to have pressed these in combination with other varieties, on at least one occasion he used them alone.[17] How far the activities of such members of the gentry were mirrored in the farming population are less clear. Mary Birkhead of Thwaite in Norfolk, successively the widow of an artist and minor landowner and a wealthy lawyer and thus perhaps socially closer to that group than to the elite, recorded in 1734 how the apple called the Darnel Pippin, or Darling Pippin, was 'good for Kitchen uses and excelant for cyder to drink from Christmass to the spring'.[18] But documents such as probate inventories provide little indication that farmers generally possessed the equipment – cider mills, presses – required for cider-making. Moreover, some early commentators explicitly state that the produce of the orchards in particular areas was not used for cider-making. Arthur Young in 1804, describing the extensive orchards of west Hertfordshire, noted that 'none of the apples are for cider'.[19] Eight years earlier Nathaniel Kent, in his survey of Norfolk agriculture, described orchards as 'very few, and much neglected – consequently no cyder'.[20] Cider thus never became a 'traditional' drink in the east, but it was by no means unknown. Indeed, a number of large cider-making businesses developed in the region in the course of the nineteenth century and one – its history extraordinarily well documented in the company archive – in the eighteenth.

---

14 Rowe, *Garden Making and the Freeman Family*, pp. 6 and 87.
15 Williams and Stevenson, 'Observations of Weather', p. 53.
16 Williams and Stevenson, 'Observations of Weather', p. 69.
17 Williams and Stevenson, 'Observations of Weather', pp. 54, 68–9.
18 NRO, BRA 926 122.
19 Young, *Hertfordshire*, p. 143.
20 N. Kent, *General View of the Agriculture of the County of Norfolk* (London, 1796), p. 63.

Clement Chevallier arrived from Jersey and settled at Aspall Hall, just to the north of Debenham in Suffolk, in 1728, having inherited the property from his uncle.[21] Here he was involved in a range of enterprises, including farming, forestry and brick-making. He also derived a good income from renting land, and a more modest one from his ownership of the lordship of the manors of Aspall and Kenton, receiving 'fines' when properties were inherited or changed hands. But his main interest was, from the beginning, the production of cider. Running this wider portfolio of enterprises was necessary given that the apple harvest was by no means dependable, and that cider-making took up only a part of the year, leaving him free to exploit other business opportunities through the other months.

A friend, Edward Vernon, described in a letter to his brother how Chevallier,

> coming out of a Cyder country amongst other improvements of his estate he has been a great planter of Apples, many of them of the sorts in use for Making of Cyder in Jersey & has had a large Mill for that use brought from Hence & has I believe been at a great expense for becoming a large dealer in it.[22]

Jersey was, indeed, a 'Cyder country', where production of the drink had expanded rapidly in the course of the seventeenth century.[23] In 1788 Arthur Young described how Chevallier had immediately planted 144 apple trees, brought from Jersey, on two acres of land, and how in subsequent years, until 1743, 'he planted, by grafting, ten acres more, of various sorts'.[24] Chevallier's own account books show that he was planting apple trees at Aspall within a fortnight of taking up residence there in April 1728.[25] A letter written in 1760 to his friend the Reverend Morant of Colchester (the famous Essex historian, who himself hailed from Jersey) includes an account of the cider made at Aspall Hall in the autumn of 1760 and features a list of the varieties of apple used and the method of pressing.[26] The letter is heavily stained with inkblots, making transcription of the apple varieties difficult, but all appear to have French names.

The apple trees brought from Jersey would have taken several years to mature, and they cannot have contributed to the large quantities of 'cyder' (Chevallier always spells the word with a 'y') that were evidently being produced by Chevallier within a few years of his arrival. By 1729 around 1,700 gallons were being made each year at Aspall Hall, rising to 3,660 gallons by 1730 and reaching around 8,000 by 1731, before falling back again

---

21 This discussion of the history of cider-making at Aspall is based on research carried out by Patsy Dallas and funded by Barry Chevallier and the Aspall Cyder Company.
22 Private collection: Aspall archive, DC Box 1/2.
23 N. Jee, *Landscape of the Channel Islands* (Chichester, 1982), pp. 73–6.
24 A. Young, *Annals of Agriculture*, vol. 5 (London, 1786), p. 216.
25 Private collection: Aspall archive, DC Box 1/1, fol. 102.
26 Private collection: Aspall archive, DC Box 3/3, fol. 30.

sharply to less than 200 the following year, for reasons which remain unclear, and slowly recovering thereafter to reach 4,794 in 1736.[27] Chevallier seems to have made immediate use of existing orchards associated with Aspall Hall, but he also purchased fruit from many of his new neighbours. One of his account books provides a list drawn up in 1729 'of apples bought to make into cyder'.[28] It lists 22 individuals from whom very varying quantities of apples were purchased, some paid for in cash (totalling £25 14s 11d) and some in cider (146 gallons). His 'cyder accounts' provide further lists of people from whom apples were bought, totalling around 30 names in 1730 and 40 in 1734.[29] The sums spent rose and fell in line with production: they increased from £25 14s 11d in 1729 to £41 12s 5d in 1730, reaching £79 5s 6d in 1731, before falling back again to a mere £2 5s 0d in 1732. They then rose again, to £6 7s 8d in 1733, £47 15s 6d in 1734 and £57 5s 3d in 1736.[30] Most of his suppliers appear to have lived in the parish of Aspall, but some were in neighbouring villages, such as Thorndon and Earl Stonham.

Chevallier himself planted a range of English apple varieties, in addition to those brought from Jersey, to supply his cider business. This is clear from a list in the second of his account books of the varieties of apples growing in 1737/8 in his own 'nursery joining the dovehouse mote'.[31] Most are varieties that are relatively familiar from contemporary sources. The second row consisted of 'golden pipping', the Golden pippin; the third comprised 'golden pairmain', or Pearmain; and the fourth 'golden runnets', or Golden Reinette. Nonpareil was planted in rows 7 and 11. Others include Beefing (which seems a slightly odd choice as a cider apple), Holland Pippin, White Russetting, White Pippin, Hollow Crown and 'Jully Flower' (Gillyflower). A few are more obscure, however. 'Look no Further', planted in row 24, may well be the traditional Monmouth variety 'Seek no Further', recorded from 1700, and which was used as a cooking and eating apple as well as for making cider. The variety 'Good Wives', which was received from Peter Karsay, the local farmer and carter, is otherwise unrecorded, while the name of the 'large apple' planted in row 8 was presumably unknown even to Chevallier himself.

In a letter written in 1753 Chevallier praised the superiority of his Jersey apples over the local Suffolk varieties. In particular, he claimed that when he had been obliged to depend entirely on the latter he had needed to add sugar when making cider, something that was now – with the trees brought from his homeland in full production – unnecessary.[32] But, as noted above, he continued to use English dessert and culinary apples, many obtained from neighbours, as his principal ingredient even when the imported trees had matured.

---

27 Private collection: Aspall archive, DC Box 1/2, fols 4 and 5.
28 Private collection: Aspall archive, DC Box 1/1, fol. 89.
29 Private collection: Aspall archive, DC Box 1/2, fols 4 and 6.
30 Private collection: Aspall archive, DC Box 1/2, 4, fol. 5.
31 Private collection: Aspall archive, DC Box 2/1, fol. 84.
32 Private collection: Aspall archive, DC Box 3/1.

126 The Orchards of Eastern England

Figure 5.2 The 'Cyder House' at Aspall, Suffolk, constructed by Clement Chevallier in the 1720s, showing the cyder mill with its great stone trough, brought all the way from the Ilses de Chausse, off the Normandy coast.

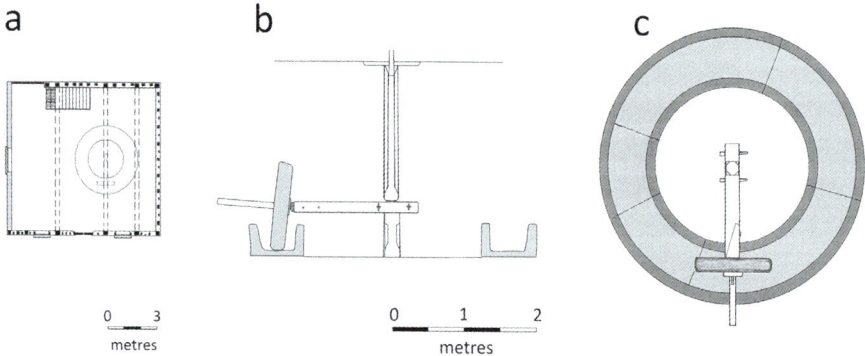

Figure 5.3 Clement Chevallier's cider mill and 'Cyder House' at Aspall, Suffolk. (a) Ground plan of the Cyder House. The building is timber-framed, plastered and rendered, apart from the west wall, which was rebuilt in brick (shaded solid grey) in the nineteenth century. (b) and (c) Elevation and plan of the cyder mill. Stone parts (wheel and trough) shaded grey.

As late as 1749 he wrote in a letter that 'the Cyder which I have is not wholly made with Apples of my own growth'.[33]

In 1728, the year of his arrival at Aspall, Chevallier built the two-story 'Cyder House', apparently by converting an earlier timber-framed building, probably a barn. Thirty loads of timber, felled in his own Aspall Wood, were specifically allocated to this building, which still survives. The accounts record payments for tiles, laths and lime at this time,[34] as well as the money paid for bringing '6 stones from Ipswich': that is, the stones making up the trough of the horse-powered cider mill, which also remains in place, a rare piece of industrial archaeology (Figures 5.2 and 5.3). The letter from Edward Vernon quoted earlier implies that this 'large Mill' was brought from Jersey, but in fact the stones making up the trough were initially quarried on the Iles de Chausey off the Normandy coast – 30km to the south-east of Jersey and under French jurisdiction. The quarries on the islands produced fine granite, widely used for building and for other purposes where exceptionally durable stone was required – as in a cider mill. The trough bears the inscription 'C C [for Clement Chevallier] 1728'.[35] The original oak cider press installed by Chevallier also survives in place, although the wooden screw was replaced with a steel one in 1922. Arthur Young, writing in 1786, described how it could produce four gallons from every bushel of apples.[36]

Apart from apples, a mill and a press, other things were required for the production of cider. As already noted, in the early years at least Chevallier usually added some sugar to the juice to aid fermentation, improve preservation and, in particular, increase the alcohol content. He often obtained this from London, having it shipped to Ipswich and then stored in a warehouse until it could be picked up by one of his men. This was presumably because he wished to have large quantities at the cheapest prices, imported directly from the West Indies. In October 1731 he asked Mr Grunchy, who acted as his London agent, to buy him the 'same sort of sugar … as you bought last year'. It was 'in a Hog which waid 15 hundredweights, 3 quarters 2 lib but I should like itt better in two half Hogs: it cost 30 shillings per hundredweight'.[37] On some occasions, however, he bought the sugar more locally, especially from a Mr Ray at Stonham.[38] The sums paid were large, between £20 and £23 a time – equivalent to over £3,000 today. He also purchased quantities of isinglass, initially locally but, as larger quantities were used, again from London, indicating that at least some of the cider he sold was clear rather than cloudy.[39]

---

33   Private collection: Aspall archive, DC Box 3/1, fol. 101.
34   Private collection: Aspall archive, DC Box 1/1, fol. 104.
35   Private collection: Aspall archive, DC Box 1/1, fol. 36.
36   Young, *Annals of Agriculture*, vol. 5, p. 216.
37   Private collection: Aspall archive, DC Box 1/2, item 31.
38   Private collection: Aspall archive, DC Box 1/2, items 66 and 67.
39   Private collection: Aspall archive, DC Box 1/2, items 31, 32, 41, 42, 108, 221, 223.

Most of Chevallier's cider was sold in casks described as hogsheads (usually around 66 gallons, but sometimes containing as little as 56) or half-hogsheads. These were expensive items, valued at between 4s and 7s each – around £30 in modern money – and were accordingly stamped with either 'CC' (Clement Chevallier's initials) or 'ɔɔcc' to aid identification. Customers were supposed to return them, whether or not they needed further supplies of cider, but the accounts for March 1738 include a list of customers who had failed to send them back.[40] Problems with non-return are referred to less frequently in the 1740s and 1750s in the surviving letter books, although as late as 1747 Chevallier was still sending stern letters on the subject to some customers. Given the difficulties of communication and transport, it is not surprising that casks often went missing. Some of the non-returners were private individuals, such as Francis Buxton of Kenninghall in Norfolk, but most were publicans, including John Cunningham of the Bowling Green, Badingham, William Blome of the Bell, Wilby, and Joseph Folger of the White Horse in Eye.

Chevallier was happy to sell on credit, and a list of debtors appears in his account book for 1738–42.[41] They include Thomas Summers, inn keeper of Debenham, who owed £7 7s 6d for cider received between September 1737 and September 1738, and William Wythe of the 'Angell' in Debenham, who owed £1 15s in 1739 for 35 gallons of cider. At times he considered suing defaulting debtors, as in the case of Mr Buckston, a Norfolk chapman, who owed him £3 18s in 1737. In August 1731 Chevallier wrote to one Mr Holborough, asking for payment for cider received by him and two other customers and refuting the suggestion that what he had supplied them with had been deficient in any way:

> Seeing it is seven months since I sent itt and have had no complaint till now that I asked to be payed but on the contrary I heard long after they received itt that they like itt well; itt is also strange that of sixty three Hogsheads that I have sold this year theirs alone should prove bad.[42]

As noted, by 1731 – a peak year – Chevallier was producing 7,827 gallons of cider annually, most of which was sold. Given that he usually charged retailers 14d a gallon and private individuals 16d, sales on this scale must have been bringing in something in the region of £500 *per annum*, a sum perhaps approaching £100,000 in modern money, although not all of this was profit. Large amounts of cider were held in store at Aspall Hall, ready for sale. A list of stock drawn up in 1737 lists livestock and grain with a total value of £181 10s (including a sow and pigs worth £1 10s), but cider worth £300.[43] The

---

40   Private collection: Aspall archive, DC Box 2/2.
41   Private collection: Aspall archive, DC Box 2/2.
42   Private collection: Aspall archive, DC Box 1/2, item 25.
43   Private collection: Aspall archive, DC Box 1/1, fol. 35.

scale of production varied, however – as noted – from year to year, and was at a very low level between 1740 and 1744. During this time cider was made for home consumption and for a few neighbours, but relatively little was sold commercially. This hiatus was apparently related to changes in the payment of excise duties; further changes in 1743 allowed Chevallier to fully resume his activities.[44] Once resumed, production seems to have remained at a high level until Chevallier's death in 1762, with the exception of poor cropping years such as 1753, when he seems to have produced only 40 hogsheads.[45] In 1762, the year of his death, at least 5,914 gallons were produced at Aspall. In short, although Chevallier made money from his woodlands, his brick kiln, his various farming activities and his role as a landowner and manorial lord, cider-making remained his most important income stream throughout the 40 years from the time he took over the estate until his death.

The success of the business was in large part a reflection of Chevallier's restless energy and enthusiasm. In the early years he was happy to send free samples, in bottles, to potential customers, accompanied by letters that emphasised the excellence of his product and – in the case of retailers – the money that could be made from selling it. Nor was he shy in exploiting personal contacts in the furtherance of his business. In February 1731 he wrote to one Captain Dumaresque, probably a relative, thanking him for the 'kind entertainment' he had received 'when last in Harwich'. Enclosed were letters to two other individuals whom, by implication, he had met while visiting the Captain, Robert Newton and John Stibbs. These informed the two gentlemen that each was to be sent '4 dozen and ½ Cyder which at 5 shilling [a] dozen is 22s 6d but they are to return ye bottles or pay for them according as they are worth'.[46] Chevallier asked the Captain to enquire of the men:

> How they like the Cyder tho I doo not dout but it is better than they ever had any and let 'em know for ye time to come if they or any other person have a mind to a Hogshead or a Hog and they provide bottles to bottle it when itt comes to them I'll send it them for 16d a gallon which makes such difference in ye price that with Advanttage they'll have in ye bottles not holding measure they may sell itt for eight pence a quart bottle and get as much per bottles as they doo now they'll also have ye Advantage of selling more.[47]

---

44   The changes in excise duty on cider in the eighteenth century are complex but see, in particular: H. Yeomans, 'Taxation, State Formation and Governmentality', *Social Science History*, 42/2 (2018), pp. 269–93; and D. Walsh, A. Randall, R. Sheldon and A. Charlesworth, 'The Cider Tax, Popular Symbolism and Opposition in Mid Hanoverian England', in A. Randall and A. Charlesworth (eds), *Markets, Market Culture and Popular Protest in Eighteenth-Century Britain and Ireland* (Liverpool, 1996), pp. 69–90.

45   Private collection: Aspall archive, DC Box 3/1.

46   Private collection: Aspall archive, DC Box 1/2, item 1.

47   Private collection: Aspall archive, DC Box 1/2, item 1.

As this letter shows, Chevallier was never shy in proclaiming the excellence of his produce to potential customers. Only to his brother does he ever appear more candid, describing in a letter sent with two dozen bottles of cider in 1741 that it was 'pretty good but not so fine as I wish it was'.[48]

Such was the scale of Chevallier's ambition that he occasionally made attempts to sell his cider in London, although these appear to have met with little success.[49] His market remained, for the most part, a local one. Most of the inns supplied were in the nearby market towns of Debenham, 2km to the south (the Ram, the Angel, the George); Eye, 9km to the north (the Angel, the Crown, the Queen's Head, the Half Moon, the Cross Keys at Little Lanthorn Green, the White Horse, the King's Arms and the Buck's Horn); and Framlingham, 12km to the east (the Duck and Mallard, the Blue Boar, the Dove, the Griffin, the White Horse, the White Hart and the Crown). He also had a few customers in Ipswich, 21km to the south (the White Horse Tavern, the Bowling Green near Friars Bridge) and in Harwich, across the county boundary in Essex (the King's Arms). The very large numbers of inns in these places is remarkable. Eye, with eight premises supplied, had a population, even in 1801, of only 1,734. But sales were also made to village inns and alehouses, including the Lion at Yaxley, the Stuston Drum, the Bell at Wilby ('near the church'), the Lyon at Brundish, the Fountain at Tannington, the Bull at Pettaugh, the Red Lyon at Laxfield, the Bowling Green at Badingham, the Swan at Worlingworth and the Ship at Woolpit, together with unnamed inns at Denham and Laxfield, and at Kenninghall in Norfolk. Almost all the outlets that he regularly supplied in the 1730s lay within a 12-mile (19km) radius of Aspall, and a high proportion within 8 miles (12km).[50]

Most of the inns supplied were thus in the centre of Suffolk, in an area extending from Yaxley and Stuston in the north-west to Framlingham in the south-east, and from Pettaugh and Debenham in the south-west to Laxfield in the north-east, but there were outliers in the extreme south of Norfolk, in Ipswich, and in Woolpit, near Bury St Edmunds. The lack of retail customers in west Suffolk – other than at Woolpit – is striking, and so too is their absence from anywhere to the east of Laxfield, Badingham and Framlingham. What is perhaps curious is the way that the places supplied mainly lay to the north and east of Aspall. Chevallier's place of production, that is, did not lie at the centre of the distribution, but asymmetrical to it, towards the south-west. There is no obvious reason for this, except perhaps the fact that – after Debenham – the nearest market towns in the area were Framlingham and Eye, lying to the east and north respectively, with most of the village inns supplied lying on roads leading to them.

His private customers, as opposed to those in the retail trade, were more widely scattered. They included in the 1730s a Mr Barker of the Hospital Yard, Norwich, and

---

48   Private collection: Aspall archive, DC Box 1/2, item 230.
49   Private collection: Aspall archive, DC Box 1/2, item 232.
50   Private collection: Aspall archive, DC Box 1/1, *passim*.

several individuals dwelling in Ipswich and in west Suffolk, including three in Bury St Edmunds.[51] In the 1740s the account book refers to buyers in Stowmarket, Saxmundham and Woodbridge. Although the quantities purchased by private customers were smaller than those delivered to inns, they were by no means negligible. In 1735 a Mr Dove at Eye received in one consignment no less than 35 gallons. In general, the market towns where large numbers of inns were supplied also had large numbers of private customers. Only occasionally are any details provided of their status or occupation. Mr Temple of Coddenham is described as a 'minister'; Mr Bothwright, Mr Negus and Mr Rix, all residents of Eye, were attorneys at law; Mr Tripp, also of Eye, and Mr Savage of Woodbridge were wig-makers; Charles Dowe of Eye was a brazier (i.e., a brass-worker) and Mr Dove was a draper. There were a number of doctors, a vicar, and several country houses, including Helmingham Hall. Two recipients are of particular interest. Mr Lovell of Claydon appears to have operated the toll gate on the turnpike road from Ipswich, and he seems to have received cider at a cheap rate, perhaps in lieu of tolls. More intriguingly, Mr Sikes of Saxmundham and Bury St Edmunds was the local Supervisor of Excise, and the letter Clement sent to him with a consignment of cider makes no reference to payment, simply stating: 'I send with this two half Ancors of Cyder which I hope will please you.'[52]

It seems that the 'core' area of Chevallier's business was supplied by his own wagon, perhaps on a regular round or rounds that embraced the three main towns and the neighbouring villages, while more distant customers – mainly private individuals – were supplied by independent carters. References in his letters indicate that he had 'an opportunity of sending to Ipswich once a week' using a neighbour, a carter called Joseph Karsay.[53] The same individual was sporadically used for trips to other, more distant destinations, such as Woolpit, in the west of the county, while from the mid-1730s one Samuel Ray of Saxmundham was employed on a number of occasions to make deliveries to Woodbridge. Distant customers might also be served, however, by using his own wagon to take a consignment to a place where it could be collected by a commercial carrier and then taken on to its destination. He thus used the Eye carrier to take cider to Mr Baker of the Hospital Yard in Norwich.

There seems little doubt that commercial production on the scale undertaken by Clement Chevallier was at the very least unusual, and in all probability otherwise unknown, in eastern England at this time. Cider does not, as already noted, appear to have been a major item of domestic production or consumption in the region during the sixteenth and seventeenth centuries, and Chevallier himself boasted in a letter that 'from the year 1728 to 1740, I made, & sold, more Cyder than any Person in the Neighbourhood could

---

51 Private collection: Aspall archive, DC Box 1/1.
52 Private collection: Aspall archive, DC Box 1/2, item 6.
53 Private collection: Aspall archive, DC Box 1/2, item 4.

have imagined'.⁵⁴ It may have needed an outsider like Clement Chevallier to realise the full potential for commercial cider production in the eastern counties.

After Clement Chevallier's death in 1762 the scale of cider production seems to have declined at Aspall, although by how much is difficult to ascertain, as the sources are less numerous and on the whole less detailed than those that remain from his own time. The best information comes from two surviving account books maintained by his son, Temple Chevallier, for 1767 and 1775.⁵⁵ The first contains virtually no references to cider beyond a single note of money received from selling 20 gallons. It is difficult to argue from negative evidence, however. The account book seems largely concerned with personal rather than business payments, suggesting that the latter were recorded in one or more other, now lost, books. The 1775 book is more interesting. It contains a memorandum which notes: 'Dec 9th 1775 finished making of Cyder and made about 48 hogsheads'. This is a substantial quantity, albeit below the levels of production in his father's best years. Yet there are few entries recording money received from the sale of cider and these never in large amounts. Instead there are numerous (around 25) entries for money received for 'cyder making', mostly for relatively small sums, usually less than 10s and almost always less than £1, with only two larger examples – one for £1 4s 4d and one for £2 4s 11d. Temple thus appears to have been making cider, but on a smaller scale than his father had done, partly for his own use and partly to sell. But he was also using the mill and press to process the apple crops of neighbours, receiving reasonable payment in return. Evidently, where the facilities required for cider-making were available, Suffolk people were ready to use them.

Chevallier's cider-making activities were noted by Arthur Young in 1788, and his orchards described as the finest Young had seen in Suffolk.⁵⁶ But neither are referred to in his *General View of the Agriculture of the County of Suffolk*, published in 1797, although the dairy at Aspall, which he also mentioned in 1788, was still going strong, Mrs Chevallier contributing several pages of observations on the management of dairy cattle.⁵⁷ By the time the Raynbird brothers published their book *On the Agriculture of Suffolk* in 1849 the Chevallier family's main claim to fame was as arable farmers, and especially through the development by John Chevallier of a strain of barley – the famous Chevallier barley – that produced yields around 10 per cent higher than other contemporary varieties, and which was particularly suitable for malting.⁵⁸ A valuation of Aspall Hall, drawn up in 1870, listed the 'cyder house' among the features of the property, and eight cider

---

54   Private collection: Aspall archive, DC Box 3/1.
55   Private collection: Aspall archive, DC Box 7/2 and DC Box 7/4.
56   Young, *Annals of Agriculture*, vol. 5, p. 216.
57   A. Young, *General View of the Agriculture of the County of Suffolk* (London, 1797), pp. 184–8.
58   W. and H. Raynbird, *On the Agriculture of Suffolk* (London, 1849), p. 186; private collection: Aspall archive, DC/9/6/5.

casks.[59] But by this time production was probably at a modest level, perhaps largely for domestic consumption.

The situation seems to have changed at the end of the nineteenth century, as cereal farming slipped into depression and the family turned to alternative forms of income. Henry Sparrow, born in 1891, described in his memoirs how he had been employed in the cyder house at Aspall in his mid-teens – probably around 1907 – and was soon put in charge of production, 'which was a great responsibility for me, being so young'.[60] The great trough in the cyder house was still in use, Sparrow describing how it could hold between 16 and 20 bushels of apples, which it took around an hour to crush. Buckets, shovels and other equipment were 'made of wood as no metal was suffered to touch the Cyder. The press was held together by pegs, no nails'. Cider was now being made on a scale comparable to that under Clement Chevallier, with as much as 17,000 gallons being produced in one particularly prolific season. The cider was stored in casks that had previously been used for port, rum, gin or brandy, and which were obtained from local spirit merchants. It was allowed to ferment down to dry (that is, until the sugars had been consumed) before being recasked and sugar syrup added. As in the eighteenth century, a mixture of apple varieties was used. What Sparrow described as 'real Cyder apples', grown in the orchards at Aspall, were one constituent. These were now West Country rather than French varieties, including [Sweet] Coppin, Woodbine, White Clover, Sweet Alford, Knotted Kernel, Kingston Black, Medaille D'Or, Strawberry Norman and Broadleaf Norman. But these were augmented with the more usual varieties of dessert and culinary apples grown in East Anglian orchards, some brought from 'as far as Cambridgeshire'.[61]

While production may have increased in the first years of the twentieth century as part of a policy of diversification more widely shared by farmers in this arable region at a time of agricultural depression, a further and more important stimulus came, as so often, from improvements in transport systems. The Mid Suffolk Light Railway was constructed in 1908, with Thorndon and Aspall Station located a little over a kilometre to the north of Aspall Hall.[62] An article in the *Suffolk Chronicle and Mercury* for 1914 described how production of cider at Aspall had been 'very considerably augmented since the construction of the Mid Suffolk Light Railway', so that John Barrington Chevallier had been induced to 'very considerably extend this phase of farming at Aspall Hall'.[63] Capital had been invested and a more modern press installed. Production was, on average, around 7,000 gallons per season. A new building had been erected to store casks beside the cyder house and a new orchard had been planted 'beside Aspall parish church'. The importance of the rail network

---

59 Private collection: Aspall archive, DRC/Box 20/21.
60 Private collection: Aspall archive, DC/Box 12/9.
61 Private collection: Aspall archive, DC/Box 12/9.
62 P. Paye, *The Mid-Suffolk Light Railway* (Upper Bucklebury, 1986).
63 Private collection: Aspall archive, DC Box 12/2.

is evident from surviving printed catalogues of Aspall products, that from 1916 assuring purchasers that prices paid included costs of transportation 'to any station GER or MSLR'. Casks of 4½, 6 or 8 gallons could be supplied, 'or larger if desired'; but jars and bottles, the latter in groups of a dozen, could also be sent.[64]

Expansion of production meant that, by the 1920s, larger quantities of apples were being brought in from the Cambridgeshire orchards and, while most of these were of the usual dessert or culinary types, the surviving account books record how cider-making varieties such as Madeleine and Bédan were purchased from the orchards of Charles Townshend at Fordham near Ely. The same accounts show a range of other things required for the production and selling of cider being purchased, including sugar, wooden boxes (from Waltham Cross in Essex), stone bottles (from Chesterfield), and wire netting 'for fencing apple trees', presumably against attack by rabbits (from a firm in Ipswich). Most of these goods, unsurprisingly, seem to have been brought to the nearby station by train.[65]

Production remained on this larger but still relatively modest scale through the middle decades of the twentieth century. The Aspall orchards were regularly restocked with trees, a sketch made in 1945 referring to the planting of cider varieties such as Kingston Black, Cap of Liberty, Morgan Sweet and Eggleton.[66] Cider-making was still based in the Cyder House, from the door of which sales were made to visiting customers. One, writing in 1972, recalled how, only a few years previously, 'The board at the gate said "Cyder" and looked promising. Chickens ran protestingly from the wheels as the car followed the drive to a wide lily-strewn moat … '. Things began to change rapidly, however, after the business was taken over by John Chevallier Guild, son of Perronelle Guild, John Barrington Chevallier's daughter. The *East Anglian Magazine* in 1972 reported how production had been significantly increased, from around 7,000 gallons of cider per annum to 22,000 gallons, together with 7,000 of apple juice. 'The key to this transformation lurks behind the Tudor barn [i.e., the Cyder House]; a great big glistening 20th-century machine which hungrily pulverises tons of apples a day, producing over 300 gallons of juice an hour', which had been imported from Switzerland. The year-long fermentation process was also being modernised. The old system, using 'a series of ancient wine hogsheads and casks', was being replaced by 'new oak vats holding 2,000 gallons each, and the old "jug, funnel and steady hand" system has given way to progress in the form of a bottling machine'. By this stage, the company was supplying retailers throughout England (as far north as the Lake District), including 20 outlets in London.[67] The Ordnance Survey 25-inch map of 1977 shows well over 27 acres (11 hectares) of land planted as orchard at Aspall, a figure that expanded still further through the 1980s, before contracting slightly to the present area. The Aspall Cyder

---

64 Private collection: Aspall archive, DC Box 12/4.
65 Private collection: Aspall archive, DC Box 12/7 and 12/8.
66 Private collection: Aspall archive, DC Box 12/10.
67 Private collection: Aspall archive, DC Box 12/16.

Processing: cider, jam and canning

Figure 5.4 The orchards at Aspall, Suffolk, in 2017.

Company continues to operate, although recently taken over by an American firm, and the cider works are still surrounded by extensive orchards (Figure 5.4).

Cider in Norfolk: Rout's and Gaymer's

We have devoted several pages to the story of Aspall cider, in part because of the wealth of documentary (and archaeological) evidence. But it was not the only place in the eastern counties where commercial cider production emerged. Although, as we have noted, cider-making was not a major domestic activity in the region, it was never entirely neglected and it may have increased in importance in the course of the nineteenth century, perhaps especially in south Norfolk. In 1845 White's *Directory* could describe how orchards were 'numerous ... especially on the south side of the county, where many of the farmers make cider for their own consumption, and some little for sale'.[68] One centre of production was the village of Banham in south-west Norfolk. In 1869 five individuals are listed in Kelly's *Directory* for the county as 'Cider Merchants and Manufacturers', of whom no fewer than three were in Banham – George Alderson, William Gaymer and Charles Murton – while a fourth, John Briggs, resided in the nearby parish of Kenninghall.[69] Two major cider-making businesses had their origins in the parish in the middle years of the nineteenth century.

---

68 White, *Norfolk*, p. 37.

69 E.R. Kelly, *Post Office Directory for Cambridgeshire, Norfolk and Suffolk* (London, 1869), Pt 2.

The firm of R. Rout and Son seems to have begun production in 1856 and met with some success, but in 1908 was acquired by A.J. Caley and Son, producers of mineral water, ginger beer and a range of other products – including Christmas crackers and chocolate – in Norwich. Nevertheless, the Banham works continued to produce cider and by the 1950s boasted a range of 10,000-gallon oak vats and 2,000 maturing barrels. It finally closed at the end of that decade.[70]

The other Banham firm, Gaymer's, was of much greater importance and appears to have originated rather earlier. Robert Gaymer (1738–1821) was a farmer in the parish and was probably producing cider on a small scale in the 1780s. This continued under his son John (1770–1843, known as 'Long John' because he was 6 feet 10½ inches tall).[71] An advertisement from the *Bury and Norwich Post* for 26 May 1800 described how he had inherited the trade secrets of his father-in-law, Joseph Chapman, which were 'the result of the last ten years practice and experience', and noted that 'the cydermaking business is carried on by the said John Gaymer at Banham aforesaid, by whom all orders will be thankfully received, and readily executed.' Joseph Chapman had described himself as a 'cyder merchant' in 1781.[72] John Gaymer's son, William, took over the tenancy of the Crown Inn in Banham but also farmed, the tithe apportionment of 1845 recording him as tenant of a little over 40 acres (16 hectares) of land in the parish.[73] The same year he was described in White's *Directory* as landlord of the Crown, 'cyder manufacturer' and farmer, and in 1854 as a 'victualler and cider manufacturer'.

William Gaymer was evidently producing cider on a significant scale, at one stage supplying colleges at Cambridge. But it was his son, another William (1842–1936), who really expanded the business, establishing a purpose-built cider factory at Banham complete with an engine house and hydraulic press (installed in 1870), cask and bottle store, and other buildings. In 1896 he began building a new factory beside the railway station at Attleborough, some 5 miles (8km) to the north, retaining the old Banham premises as a storage depot.[74] The new factory's railside location affirms, once again, the key importance of rail transport in the development of both orchards and orchard-related industries. Indeed, from the start the factory was provided with its own set of sidings, on 2 rods and 7 perches of land bought in 1896 for £81 11s. In 1912 the Great Eastern Railway purchased land from the company to extend the sidings, which would

---

70 O. Thompson, 'Notes Towards a History of Norfolk Cider' (2007), pp. 4 and 9, <http://www.cider.org.uk/Notes%20Towards%20a%20History%20of%20Norfolk%20Cider.pdf>, accessed 7 March 2021; M. Chandler, *A–Z of Norwich: Places, People, History* (Stroud, 2016); NRO, BR 266/85.

71 NRO, GAY 1/6/49; GAY 1/6/51; Attleborough Heritage Centre, 'History of Wm Gaymer and Son, Cyder Makers, Attleborough'; Thompson, 'Notes', pp. 5–9.

72 NRO, MC 297/8/1–26.

73 NRO, DN/TA 885.

74 NRO, GAY 1/6/47–57.

Figure 5.5 The Gaymer's cider factory at Attleborough in Norfolk, built beside the railway line in the 1890s, photographed from the air in c.1955. Note the extensive orchards.

mainly be used by Gaymer's.[75] The factory, which cost the substantial sum of £5,886, was a well-built brick structure with tall chimney and shaped 'Dutch' gables that was added to piecemeal over the following decades (Figure 5.5). The business expanded steadily, especially following its incorporation in 1906 as a joint-stock, limited liability company, although William Gaymer retained a majority holding and his son, William Chapman Gaymer (1882–1970), became managing director.[76] In the same year the company acquired a depot near Bishopsgate railway station in London. By the 1920s Gaymer's were producing for export as well as for home consumption, and in 1928 they received a royal warrant as purveyors to the royal household – perhaps a consequence of supplying the royal residence at Sandringham in Norfolk – followed by another in 1933. William Gaymer finally died in 1936 at the age of 94 and was succeeded as chairman by William Chapman Gaymer.[77]

Gaymer's factory was bombed in December 1940; an incendiary device landed in the paper store, leading to a fire that damaged, in particular, the bottling machinery and filtration plant. The following week the factory was heavily machine gunned.[78] In 1948 the damaged parts of the site were cleared and rebuilding commenced. The new works, which were of steel-frame construction, comprised over 60,000 square feet spread over three floors.[79]

75 NRO, GAY 2/1/31.
76 NRO, GAY 2/1/1.
77 NRO, GAY 1/6/47–57.
78 NRO, GAY 1/6/51.
79 NRO, GAY 1/7/16; GAY 1/1/16.

The cider was fermented in surviving portions of the original 1896 buildings, although in a block of 101 concrete tanks, holding in all half a million gallons, installed in 1949. It was then pumped into receiving tanks located in the new building, from where it passed through a chiller before being filtered. From here it was either pumped into tanker lorries for shipment elsewhere, or up onto the second floor, where it was bottled. The top floor was for cleaning and storing bottles, which were delivered by conveyor belt from the adjacent railway sidings and lorry-loading areas below.[80]

There were two cider mills and four presses capable of pressing two tons of milled fruit at a time. The natural yeasts in the apples were supplemented with cultured strains, and the cider fermented for four or five weeks before being filtered and some sugar being added, after which it was left to mature for about six months. It was then blended, prior to being bottled, in batches of 2,000 gallons.

Production rose, erratically, from around 1.5 million gallons yearly in 1930 to 2.4 million in 1940. Following the bombing in 1940 this fell to around 1.4 million, thereafter rising to a second peak of 2.34 million in 1948.[81] By the 1950s the company was exporting on a substantial scale to east and west Africa, South Africa and the USA, and its home sales rivalled those of the great West Country producers. The main varieties marketed in this period were VD Cyder, Two Star, Diamond, Gay Flag, Gay Sec and Olde English. Only a small proportion of the cider was now being transported by rail: most was taken to its destination by lorry.[82] In the 1950s 400 men worked in the factory, which was the largest employer in the area. By the 1970s the factory was capable of processing 250 tonnes of apples per week on a single shift, rising to 500 tonnes on 24-hour operation in peak periods.

Initially, there were no orchards in the area surrounding the factory. Planting began in 1933, however, and by 1946 they extended over an area of some 17 hectares, to which a further 1.8 hectares had been added by 1950, to judge from the Ordnance Survey 6-inch map surveyed in that year.[83] As was the case at Aspall, however, these supplied only a relatively small proportion of the apples used by the company. As a document drawn up in 1966 described, 'Gaymer's take thousands of tons of apples per annum from East Anglian growers and thereby provide a very useful outlet for some of the surplus apple crop'; Gaymers, even more than the Aspall company, used 'mixed varieties of dessert and cooking apples, and in this respect differs from the West County cyder manufacturers', with their dependence on specialised cider varieties.[84] In the 1970s the factory was taking nearly 6,000 tons of 'cull' apples each year from regional growers, of which most came from the

---

80   NRO, GAY 1/1/6.

81   NRO, GAY 1/1/16.

82   NRO, GAY 1/1/16.

83   NRO, GAY 1/2/2–7; GAY 1/6/56.

84   NRO, GAY 1/1/6.

area around Wisbech. In addition, between 2,000 and 3,000 tons were regularly imported from Kent.[85]

A wide range of varieties was bought from local producers. A surviving invoice from a Mr Blake of Wicklewood records the purchase of Warner's King, Ribstone Pippin, Mere de Menage, Dr Harvey, Norfolk Beefing, Blenheim Orange and Rollins, as well as quantities of pears.[86] Overall, however, the main culinary varieties used, at least in the 1970s, were Bramley's Seedling, Emneth Early, Grenadier, James Grieve, Howgate Wonder and Lord Derby; these accounted for around 75 per cent of the apples processed. A further 25 per cent comprised dessert varieties: Cox's Orange Pippin, Laxton's Superb, Worcester Pearmain and Egremont Russet.[87] As a report compiled in 1980 noted,

> Fruit is delivered in 18–20 tonne tipper loads and on receipt is inspected for rots, dirt, leaves, etc. and the proportion of culinary to dessert is checked. If necessary, a price adjustment is made on loads for poor quality, but in general terms, growers know what we expect and quality is not a problem.[88]

In years when the crop was poor, apples would also be brought in from the West Country or imported from France; in extreme need, concentrated apple juice would be imported from Switzerland.[89] In the 1970s ingredients were brought from Austria, Holland and Canada.[90]

The orchards beside the factory thus only ever supplied a small proportion of the apples used in Gaymer's cider. Indeed, in some periods the quality of the fruit they produced was so good that a proportion was sold for retail by Norfolk Fruit Growers of Wroxham.[91] They may always in part have been maintained for their symbolic importance, as a form of advertising. They certainly contained a wide range of varieties, including Bramley's Seedling, Norfolk Royal, Kingston Black, Sweet Alford, Royal Wilding, Chisel Jersey, Lord Derby, Strawberry Norman, Blenheim Orange, Medaille D'Or, Worcester Pearmain, Barnack Beauty, Ellison's Orange, Cox's Golden Pippin, Forge, Bulmer's Norman, Ribston Pippin, Knotted Kernel, Dabinette, Woodbine, Sweet Coppin and Laxton's Exquisite, as well as Oldfield Pears.[92] Some but by no means all of these (Forge, Kingston Black, Chisel

---

85   NRO, GAY 1/5/20.

86   NRO, GAY 1/6/53.

87   NRO, GAY 1/5/20.

88   NRO, GAY 1/5/20.

89   NRO, GAY 1/1/16, 19–21.

90   Transcript of oral history interview with Roy Woods, Gaymer's orchard manager 1975–88; Attleborough Heritage Centre.

91   Transcript of oral history interview with Roy Woods, Gaymer's orchard manager 1975–88; Attleborough Heritage Centre.

92   NRO, GAY 1/2/2–7.

Jersey, Dabinett, Sweet Coppin, Sweet Alford, Strawberry Norman) were cider varieties, not normally grown in eastern England.[93] As at the Aspall works, although to a lesser extent, some cider apples were thus used in the manufacture of the cider. But the main ingredients were the normal dessert and culinary varieties grown in eastern orchards.

In the immediate post-war period the company continued to flourish but in the mid-1950s demand for cider contracted and it began to experience financial problems.[94] In 1961 it was purchased by Showerings of Shepton Mallet in Somerset. The Attleborough works continued to operate under the name of William Gaymer and Son, with William Charles Chapman Gaymer acting as chairman from 1974, but the workforce declined to 164 in 1961 and to 135 by 1986, falling to 75 a few years later when the bottling plant was moved to Shepton Mallett. Allied Breweries acquired Showerings in 1968 and 'Coates Gaymer's Ciders' eventually became part of Allied Lyons PLC.[95] In 1992 a de-merger took place and The Gaymer Group PLC was established, but this was taken over by Matthew Clarke PLC in 1994.[96] In 1995 the factory was sold to Banham Poultry Ltd and since then most of the buildings, including the chimney stack, have been taken down. The orchards had already disappeared, grubbed out in the late 1980s to make way for industrial units, housing and playing fields.

Although Norfolk and Suffolk may have had the strongest cider-making traditions, some small producers existed in other counties in eastern England. In Hertfordshire, for example, Samuel Wright's Victoria Brewery was established in Walkern in 1870 (although local farmer Thomas Wright started malting barley in the village in 1790) and appears to have produced cider for a short period. But no other firm could rival the success or longevity of Gaymer's, the Aspall Cyder Company, or even Rout's.

Jam making and canning

The other main way in which fruit was processed in the region on an industrial scale was in the manufacture of jam. This developed at a rather later date than large-scale cider production, from the mid- to late nineteenth century, but it was similarly associated with by now familiar drivers: the improvement of transport systems, especially the railways, large-scale urbanisation in the Midlands and the North, and the growth of London. It was also encouraged by a decline, from the 1850s, in the price of sugar, which made the large-scale production and sale of jams and preserves economically viable. Improvements in food hygiene, which reduced anxiety about processed foods, were also a significant factor.[97]

---

93   NRO, GAY 1/6/54 and 56.

94   NRO, GAY 1/1/16.

95   NRO, GAY 1/1/20; GAY 1/5/20.

96   NRO, GAY 1/6/51.

97   D. Harvey, 'Fruit Growing in Kent in the Nineteenth Century', *Archaeologia Cantiana*, 79 (1964), pp. 94–108, at pp. 96–7.

The Chivers family settled in Histon in Cambridgeshire around 1817 and initially operated as farmers, growing wheat and barley. But in 1850 Stephen Chivers bought an orchard beside the new station on the Cambridge–St Ives line (opened in 1847) and laid some of his farm down to fruit trees, a total of 160 acres (65 hectares) by 1861.[98] To begin with, much of the fruit grown was sent, via Cambridge, to the market at Covent Garden in London, but he was soon distributing it more widely, and especially in the North and the Midlands. In 1870 Chivers established a distribution depot, under the control of his sons William and John, at Bradford in Yorkshire.[99] According to family tradition, much of the fruit sold there was purchased by local jam-makers, and the two young men persuaded their father that they should undertake this activity themselves, transporting the finished product rather than the raw materials. Accordingly, in 1873 the first Chivers' jam was produced in a small barn and two years later the Victoria Works was erected on the orchard site beside the railway and equipped with its own sidings. Initially the jam was put into stone jars but in 1885 the first glass jars came into use. Other forms of food processing soon followed, with marmalade, fruit jelly, lemon curd, mincemeat and Christmas pudding all being produced by 1895. In 1893 the first canned fruit in England was marketed by the company.[100] By this time Chivers' owned some 300 acres (*c.*121 hectares) of orchards

Figure 5.6 The Chiver's 'Victoria' factory at Histon, Cambridgeshire, photographed in 1900, soon after it had been completed.

---

98 *Journal of the Royal Agricultural Society*, 92 (1861), p. 143.

99 S. Burian, 'Benevolent Capitalists? A Study of Paternalist Authority in an Industrial Firm', PhD thesis (University of Cambridge, 1983); G. Horridge, *Growth and Development of a Family Firm: Chivers of Histon, 1873–1939* (Cambridge, 1983).

100 Wright and Lewis, *Cambridgeshire*, p. 99.

in the parish and had over 400 regular employees, bolstered by seasonal workers during peak times, and a substantial new factory had been erected containing the first automatic canning machinery in Europe, designed by the firm's engineer Charles Lack (Figure 5.6).[101] He also developed a range of other processing and sterilising equipment. H. Rider Haggard visited in 1902 and was impressed: 'The factory with its silver lined boilers, its cooling rooms, its patent apparatus for filling jars, its tramways, its printing and silver plating, packing case making, labelling, baking powder, mincemeat and lemonade departments etc. was a truly wondrous place.'[102]

The firm expanded steadily following its incorporation as a public company in 1901, exporting on a large scale, and by the 1920s the main processing buildings, fruit stores and ancillary plant sprawled over an area of more than 18 acres (*c*.7.5 hectares). The factory had its own water supply, produced its own electricity and manufactured its own cans; it also featured a paint shop, sawmill, smithy, carriage works and barrel-making workshop. By 1931 some 3,000 people were employed at Histon, and other factories had been opened at Huntingdon and in Montrose and Newry.[103] Chivers' was by now the largest canner of fruits and vegetables in England. The family continued to farm on a large scale but 3,000 of the 7,000 acres (1,200 of 2,800 hectares) they owned were devoted to orchards, principally planted with plums, and to soft fruit.[104] Much of the fruit they processed, however, continued to come from independent growers, mainly in the surrounding Cambridgeshire countryside.[105]

In the post-war years the company suffered from a lack of investment and in 1959 it was sold to Schweppes, who merged production with other similar companies they had acquired, including Hartley's, the Liverpool jam makers. In 1986 the old factory was demolished and its site partly developed as a business park. It was replaced with a new works, costing £5 million, by new owners Premier Foods. Jam was still produced, but now under the Hartley brand, alongside Gale's honey, Sun-Pat peanut butter and Smash instant potato. The factory has since changed hands a number of times and any association with the Chivers family, or with local fruit production, has been lost and most of the neighbouring orchards have disappeared.

In some ways the origins of the Wilkin's Jam Company, at Tiptree in Essex, mirrors that of Chivers'. Once again, the family's shift from arable to fruit farming preceded the agricultural depression, beginning as it did in the mid-1860s. It reflected the steady expansion of the London market and the proximity of Kelvedon railway station, some 6km

---

101 Wright and Lewis, *Cambridgeshire*, pp. 98–9.
102 H. Rider Haggard, *Rural England*, vol. 2 (London, 1906), p. 53.
103 *Proceedings of the Institute of Mechanical Engineers*, 121 (1931), p. 72.
104 *Journal of the Royal Agricultural Society*, 92 (1861), pp. 142–51.
105 Wright and Lewis, *Cambridgeshire*, pp. 98–9.

to the north-west of their farm.[106] In 1885 Arthur Charles Wilkin established the Britannia Fruit Preserving Company in the village, initially with plant comprising a portable engine, four copper pans and a fruit pulper, processing some 50 tons each summer.[107] By 1905 more than 200 tons of fruit were being grown by the family, of which half was made into jam. The factory had been expanded and was well-equipped and modern: 'lighted by electricity, and served by light trolleys running on tramways, which are laid throughout the building'.[108] The company's fortunes were augmented by the opening of the Kelvedon and Tollesbury Light Railway in 1904, part of the Great Eastern Railway, which ran for nearly 14km from Kelvedon to Tollesbury near Colchester. The line ran next to the factory, which was provided with its own sidings.

The company capitalised on its claims to produce good-quality products without additional glucose: 'freshly gathered fruit and no adulteration'.[109] It was in part a drive to ensure quality control that encouraged direct production of their own fruit, rather than a reliance on outside suppliers. By 1906 Wilkin and Sons had acquired over 800 acres (323 hectares) of land in the surrounding area, especially in the villages of Tiptree, Tollesbury and Goldhanger. The firm also leased much land, some located as far away as Dagenham, on the edge on London. The marked concentration of orchards in the locality, already clear on the second edition Ordnance Survey 6-inch maps surveyed around 1900, intensified significantly over the following decades. The firm's fortunes suffered briefly during the First World War but by 1926 it owned 1,000 acres (405 hectares) of land and employed 440 regular workers (Figure 5.7).[110]

Wilkin's were probably most famous for their strawberry jam but surviving accounts from 1932 show that a fairly wide range of top fruit was grown: eight varieties of plums (Cherry, Egg, Golden Gage, Green Gage, Mirabelle, Orleans, Purple and Victoria), three of pear (Doyenne, Pitmaston, Williams) and ten of apple (Allington Pippin, Blenheim Orange, Bramley's Seedling, Hyslop Crab, Crab Siberiense, Keswick, Lane's Prince Albert, Lord Derby, Newton Wonder and Wellington), as well as cherries, mulberries, prune damsons, quince and medlar. A list drawn up in the previous year suggests that other apple varieties were also cultivated – Eckville and Beauty of Bath – together with Rivers' plums. As well as fruit, honey from hives set in the orchards was sold on a substantial scale.[111] The period after the Second World War saw further expansion. Today, Wilkin

---

106 Information sheets, Tiptree Heritage Centre; 'Wilkins and Son: History', <https://web.archive.org/web/20141112223240/http://www.tiptree.com/goto.php?ref=y&sess=+A5E5147191D51+F18435A52+9+B581D1058+E+357+9+25F1D1758&id=14>, accessed March 2020.

107 *The Lady*, 11 April 1985.

108 *Essex Weekly News*, 2 December 1904.

109 Ibid.

110 'Harvest Home at Tiptree', company brochure, 1926; Tiptree Heritage Centre.

111 Tiptree Heritage Centre, Accounts, 1928, 1931, 1932.

Figure 5.7 Wilkin and Son's jam factory, Tiptree, Essex, and its orchards; undated photograph, early twentieth century.

Figure 5.8 The orchards at Tiptree today.

and Sons continues to produce preserves but the company also sells fresh fruit and runs tea rooms and a number of food-related businesses. Around 350 hectares of soft and top fruit, the latter including medlars, mulberries and quinces, are still grown in the orchards at Tiptree (Figure 5.8).

Wilkin's and Chivers' are the most famous fruit-processing companies in the eastern counties. But there were others, including the Elsenham Jam Company, based in the village of that name in north-west Essex, not far from the Hertfordshire town of Bishops Stortford. In 1890 a large fruit farm was established here by Sir Walter Gilbey, and the Elsenham Jam company was founded three years later.[112] It was taken over by Tony Blunt in 1959, when its jam was advertised as 'the most expensive ... in the world'. The factory and offices were destroyed by fire in 1969. Of more importance were the various canning and processing factories that were established in Wisbech, at the centre of the Fenland orchard district, from the second half of the nineteenth century, including the Wisbech Fruit Preserving Company Ltd, which began to trade in 1890, and Smedley's National Canning Factory, opened in 1924.[113] The latter, originally Wisbech Produce Canners, was the most long-lived and successful of these businesses, expanding rapidly through the late 1920s. By 1931 800 people were employed and, at peak periods, 500,000 cans produced each day, although these included vegetables from the Fenland farms as well as fruit from its orchards. The company passed through a number of hands after being sold by the Smedley family in 1968. The factory offices, in a Grade II listed Art Deco building on Lynn Road, still survive.

Conclusion

The foregoing brief discussion has demonstrated the importance of a number of businesses associated with the region's orchards. Their geography displays some surprising features. They were not as closely associated as we might have expected with districts in which fruit orchards were particularly extensive. A significant processing industry emerged, it is true, at Wisbech in the Fens; and, a little further south, Chivers' located their jam-making and canning business at Histon, in the heart of the fen-edge orchard district. But Rout's, Gaymer's, The Aspall Cyder Company, Elsenham Jam and Wilkin and Son were all located some distance from the main fruit-growing areas. Indeed, in the last two cases the presence of these firms encouraged significant increases in orchards in areas where they had formerly been sparse. While, as we have seen, the development of all these businesses was dependent, to a significant degree, on good transport links – and especially on those provided, from the middle of the nineteenth century, by the rail network – their location

---

112 <http://www.stortfordhistory.co.uk/guide2/sir-walter-gilbey/>, accessed 20 May 2020. ERO, D/DBi T1–27, E1, T/P 68/12/3.

113 PRO/TNA, BT 34/7/45/33049; BT 31/26038/16867; < https://www.gracesguide.co.uk/Smedley's>, accessed 7 November 2020.

seems to have owed most to accidents of history, and perhaps especially family history. The majority were closely associated with particular business dynasties and it is especially remarkable that, until its recent sale to an American company, cider production at Aspall had remained in the hands of the Chevallier family for nearly three centuries.

CHAPTER SIX

The recent history of orchards

The decline of orchards since the 1960s

The immediate post-war period witnessed, as we have seen, a continued increase in the area of orchards in the eastern counties that probably peaked in the mid-1950s and, in the case of Suffolk, the 1960s. Since then it has steadily contracted, as it has across the UK as a whole. It is often suggested that the decline in commercial fruit production was the consequence of Britain joining the European Economic Community in 1973, and the influx of imports this encouraged. But the chronology suggests that this is too simple. Rather than accelerating, the decline in the orchard area seems, if anything, to have slowed slightly following accession (Figure 6.1). The UK's changed trading arrangements with Europe certainly had an impact on the fruit-growing industry, and at the time were widely perceived as a serious threat to it. But their effects were complex and accompanied by a range of other negative factors.

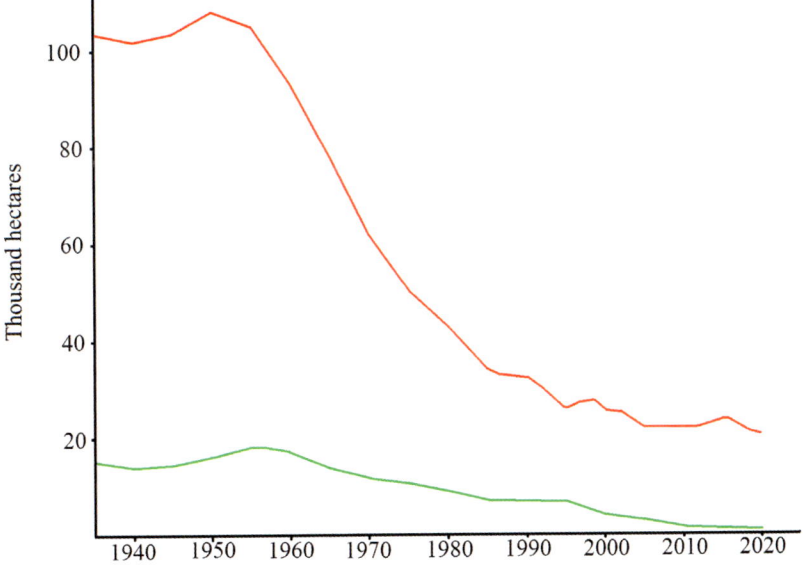

Figure 6.1 The decline of the orchard area in the post-war period. Red line: national area. Green line: eastern England. Source: the Agricultural Census. The figures include only commercial orchards on holdings of 1 acre (0.4 hectares) or more.

The removal of tariffs lowered the cost of fruit grown in Europe, which, for obvious geographical reasons, could be transported to Britain more cheaply than that from elsewhere in the world. Indeed, from an early stage in the negotiations over entry there were concerns, expressed in parliamentary questions and debates, about potential problems. French apples, in particular – and especially the infamous Golden Delicious (actually a north American variety) – were significantly cheaper than those produced at home, and in the eastern counties, as elsewhere, there was much resentment of the influx on the part of home producers. In 1979 the Market Traders' Association even tried to ban the sale of French apples, although in part as a protest against a French refusal to accept imports of English lamb.[1] But British fruit-growers had faced competition from foreign imports for over a century, especially from America and Canada. In 1932 import duties were imposed on European and American fruit, but not on that coming from New Zealand, Australia or Canada – apples from the latter country posing a major problem because they were produced in the same season as in Britain.[2] Imports continued to be a major concern into the post-war period. Leslie Clarke of the Essex Farmers Union, speaking in 1948 in a broadcast for the BBC, described how in recent years the industry had not only been obliged to 'compete with the cream of overseas fruit, but it was subjected to the depressing effects of large quantities of poor quality, badly graded stuff coming onto the market in glut years from scrub orchards'. The problem had, he believed, been exacerbated by wartime price guarantees, which had 'removed the price incentive to grow, grade and pack to the best possible standard'. 'With control fixed well below the price that the consumer was prepared to pay we have experienced the inevitable result of second rate fruit making the same price as good fruit.' In contrast, 'An overseas grower would produce and pack fruit which would stand the cost of transport and the vigilant eye of the export inspector. That gave a spur to good growing and packing which had not been applied to anything like the same extent in this country.'[3]

Such complaints about the poor quality of home-produced fruit, compared with that from foreign competitors, continued through the 1950s and into the 1960s. The December 1962 issue of *British Farmer* warned:

> World markets face a surplus of high grade apples and pears. Under these conditions there is no room for low grade fruit, which can bring loss to those who incur the expense of marketing, and depresses the price of better grades. It is purchased by certain retailers who buy it cheaply and sell dearly foisting it on to the public under the label 'English Apples', thus bringing our fruit into disrepute.[4]

---

1 East Anglian Film Archive, Norwich, ref. 216723: 'Look East: Apple Ban', 1979.
2 Short *et al.*, *Apples and Orchards in Sussex*, p. 108.
3 ERO, D/F 152/7/1.
4 PRO/TNA, MAF 302/39.

Foreign competition had thus been a problem for several decades before 1973, and a more serious threat to English orchards perhaps came from the workings of the EEC's Common Agricultural Policy. The CAP subsidies ensured that in many contexts more money could be made from a given area of land by growing barley, wheat or other arable crops than by cultivating top fruit. They also created an unsustainable level of fruit surpluses that, from the late 1980s, brought about strenuous attempts to reduce the extent of orchards by grant-aiding their removal.[5] A MAF press release in April 1995 described how 'English apple growers are delighted with the latest figure from Brussels showing that the target of between 10 and 15 per cent of the European Union apple orchards will be grubbed (30,000 hectares) leading to a significant reduction in European apples.'[6] Applications had already been received to grub out 2,400 hectares of British apple orchard, about 14 per cent of the national area. 'The 90% of English apple growers who are staying in the industry are pleased that the European surplus problem is being addressed by Brussels and are confident that more modern English orchards planted in the last few years will guarantee consumers even higher quality home grown apples.'[7] There was, nevertheless, widespread public disquiet at the policy, an article in the *Sunday Times* describing how:

> Up to a million apple trees are to be bulldozed because of a European scheme that rewards overproduction by European farm cooperatives. British farmers … say it is more economical to grub up their orchards and get compensation from European funds than to continue businesses that have been in the family for decades … . The bulk of the criticism by British producers is at the way the EU intervention scheme subsidises growers in other European countries for producing a glut of apples that nobody wants … .[8]

The problem of over-production was compounded by the fact that any decline in the orchard acreage was offset by steady improvements in yields. The larger commercial orchards now comprised, as noted earlier, low-growing trees on dwarfing or semi-dwarfing rootstocks, intensively sprayed with herbicides and pesticides. The old sprays of the inter-war years, generally using small air-cooled engines and sometimes home-made in character, were now superseded by a range of expensive machines, such as the portable sprayer with fixed nozzles developed by Seabrook of Chelmsford, or 'the Autoblast, where there is a substitution of air for water as a carrying medium for the insecticide or fungicide.'[9] Of particular importance was the liberal use of DDT (dichlorodiphenyltrichloroethane);

---

5   PRO/TNA, MAF 456/37.
6   PRO/TNA, MAF 456/38.
7   PRO/TNA, MAF 456/38.
8   PRO/TNA, MAF 456/38.
9   Norbury, 'Modern Developments', pp. 726–7.

and new synthetic phosphorus sprays, which for the first time provided an effective way of controlling red spider mite.[10] There were also significant increases in the amounts of nitrogen and potash applied. The modern orchard industry, in other words, followed the same high-input, chemical-based path as the rest of British agriculture through the 1950s, 1960s and 1970s, and with similar gains in yields. The Apple and Pear Development Council estimated in 1982 that old apple orchards produced 7 tonnes per hectare, whereas a new orchard would produce 20 tonnes.[11]

The effects of European Economic Community (EEC) membership were thus complex, and often worked in association with other factors to reduce the viability of commercial orchards. Interviews with retired growers and others, moreover, highlight a range of quite unrelated pressures that militated against profitable fruit growing. Of particular importance were labour costs and labour supply in an industry that remained, in comparison with other kinds of farming, largely unmechanised. The main reason given for the ending of commercial fruit growing in the 1960s and 1970s at Hill Farm, Walpole, in Suffolk, for example, was the difficulty of finding both pickers and, in particular, pruners. Alternative forms of employment were now available as the economy of rural areas became more diversified, with the development of industrial estates in the larger market towns, and there was a growing antipathy, especially on the part of the young, towards outdoor work.[12] Moreover, fruit-picking was a seasonal activity, often undertaken by women – a season's picking in Essex was said to provide enough money to purchase a washing machine.[13] But more and more women were now in full-time employment. A shortage of labour further increased the attraction of arable farming as an alternative use of the land, for this was now automated to an extent that fruit growing could not be.

Equally significant was the decline in the number of independent greengrocers and in the number of wholesale fruiterers supplying them, as the large supermarket chains steadily increased their market share, which in turn acted to suppress the prices paid to growers. In the half-century up to 2014 the number of greengrocers in the UK fell by 90 per cent.[14] A number of commercial orchards – such as that planted by the Byass family at Clophill in Bedfordshire in the early 1960s (mainly with Cox's and Bramley's but with Queen Cox, Egremont Russet, Grenadier and Worcester Pearmain as pollinators, all on dwarfing rootstocks) gradually declined through the 1980s and 1990s, in part because the number of greengrocers being serviced, some located as far away as north London,

---

10 Norbury, 'Modern Developments', p. 726.
11 PRO/TNA, MAF 302/154.
12 Pers. comm., Tony Gillet, Hill Farm Walpole, Suffolk.
13 Oral history interview with Andrew Tann, September 2020.
14 D. Sharpley and C. Powell, *A Brief History of Fresh Produce's Role in the UK Supermarket Revolution* (London, 2014), p. 8.

dwindled.[15] A number of commercial growers moved into the 'Pick Your Own' market in the 1970s and 1980s, but this became less popular through the 1990s.[16] In many cases, individual orchards were finally rendered unprofitable by some calamitous event, such as an attack of silverleaf on a plum orchard, or the 1987 gales, which levelled the remaining section of the orchard at Hill Farm, Walpole, the larger part of which had been grubbed out two decades earlier.[17]

While Britain's membership of the EEC, later the European Union, was unquestionably a factor in the steady decline in the commercial orchard acreage in eastern England over the last half century, it was only one of a number of influences. The heart of the problem was globalisation of food commodities, over-production and the dominance of the retail sector by a handful of huge supermarket businesses. Following the fall of the Iron Curtain in 1989 the trend towards tariff-free global trade accelerated, facilitated by improvements in packaging and the growth of container trade. The demise of many orchards should be seen as part and parcel of a more general reduction in the numbers of smallholdings and small farms and the inexorable rise of large, mechanised agricultural producers that has transformed rural life and landscape in the eastern counties since the war.

The decline of small orchards, 1945–1973

From the perspective of the ecologist, and certainly from that of the landscape historian, the late twentieth-century reduction in the overall orchard acreage needs to be distinguished from the decline in the number of small 'traditional' orchards, containing tall trees on vigorous rootstocks growing in permanent grassland, which began at an earlier date and had rather different causes. Direct government involvement in the details of agriculture and land-use planning, which had commenced in the inter-war years and accelerated during the Second World War, continued into the 1950s and 1960s, as both Labour and Conservative administrations sought to protect the farming economy and to guarantee and enhance food supplies. Successive governments maintained price controls for basic foodstuffs, including fruit and fruit products; farm prices were guaranteed; grants were made available for drainage, field amalgamation and other initiatives that would enhance productivity; and farmers were bombarded with official advice on how their practices could be improved. Farming became increasingly mechanised, with the widespread adoption of tractors, combine harvesters and other machinery, and increasingly dependent on pesticides and artificial fertilisers. The long depression in agriculture was over, and the industry was pervaded by a sense of optimism in the possibilities of scientific improvement and by a hostility to the old and the traditional. An unprecedented phase of agricultural modernisation was thus under way by the 1950s that, while certainly serving to ensure that

---

15   Pers. comm., Ms J. Byass, Clophill, Bedfordshire.
16   Pers. comm., John Everitt, Applebee Orchard, Bramerton, Norfolk.
17   Pers. comm., Tony Gillet, Hill Farm Walpole, Suffolk.

the population was adequately fed, had serious effects on the environment, as hedgerows were grubbed out, marshes drained and ancient pastures ploughed.[18]

These post-war changes had a number of negative impacts on old and, in particular, farmhouse orchards or, as Stamp described them in 1948, 'casual' orchards – 'generally left to look after themselves except for an occasional pruning', and in which 'any control of pests is the exception and spraying is almost unknown'.[19] There was a steady increase in the average size of working farms and thus a reduction in their overall numbers. Modern agriculture demanded significant scales of investment, whether in arable equipment or in facilities like milking parlours, so that farms became more specialised, concentrating on either arable or livestock – mainly the former in the eastern counties. But many farmers were unwilling or unable to make the required investment and sold up, and farms became amalgamated with neighbouring holdings, especially in arable districts. When the associated farmhouses were sold off as surplus to requirements the orchard might survive in the care of a new owner, often from an urban background, but it might just as easily be converted to a garden. In many cases, though, the orchard was separated from the farmhouse, grubbed out and absorbed into adjacent fields. In addition, a new generation of professional farmers of extensive arable acreages had little incentive to maintain old orchards beside their homes. They were unwilling, in this new world, to spend time pruning the trees or selling any small surplus of fruit, and they were as likely as anyone else to buy what fruit they needed from the local greengrocers or, increasingly, the supermarket. On top of this, in the new climate of agricultural modernisation there was a more generalised hostility on the part of government and the industry itself towards the older forms of orchard, including not only those of Stamp's 'casual' variety but also many of those that had come into existence during the great expansion which had taken place over the previous century.

This antipathy was based not only on the small size of such orchards but also on the location of many examples and the character of their planting. As Stamp put it in 1948:

> It is really only within the last two or three decades – particularly since about 1930 – that we have begun to understand scientifically the soil requirements of different species of orchard tree and also to realise that the most important factor of all is the climatic one of freedom from spring frosts. It is not too much to say that the bulk of British orchards, if not badly sited, do not occupy the best sites available.[20]

---

[18] J. Sheail, *An Environmental History of Twentieth-Century Britain* (London, 2002); A. Douet, *Breaking New Ground: Agriculture in Norfolk, 1914–1972* (Aylsham, 2015); M. Shoard, *The Theft of the Countryside* (London, 1980); R.A. Robinson and W.J. Sutherland, 'Post-War Changes in Arable Farming and Biodiversity in Great Britain', *Journal of Applied Ecology*, 39 (2002), pp. 157–76.

[19] Stamp, *Land of Britain*, p. 108.

[20] Stamp, *Land of Britain*, p. 109.

The sharp spring frosts of 1929, 1935, 1938, 1941 and 1945 continued to be remembered by growers for decades.[21] Their consequence, and that of other extreme weather events exacerbated by topography, was marked variability in yields from year to year, 'whereas consumers' demand is relatively constant'.[22]

In the post-war years, in a climate of increased state involvement and widespread concerns about foreign competition, small farm orchards – and old commercial examples, especially on smallholdings, established over the previous century – were thus regarded with hostility. Modernisation was required, of the kind that was transforming other sectors of the agricultural industry. Large orchards, managed according to the latest scientific approaches, were the future, and these required significant levels of investment. As Norbury explained in 1952:

> The capital investment in the industry is high; suitable land for fruit is anything from £100– £150 per acre. The planting up of such land with trees today costs another £100 per acre, looking after it until it comes into full production costs another £100 per acre at least – and then the cost of a packing house, grading machinery, cold stores and other equipment would not be much less than another £150 per acre ... .[23]

Grants for grubbing out derelict orchards had been introduced at the beginning of the war and were continued after the cessation of hostilities.[24] 'Derelict' orchards were defined as those which, 'on an average of the past four or five years', were 'no longer capable of bearing a crop worth marketing'.[25] The Ministry of Agriculture and Fisheries was insistent that the scheme should not be abused, in 1951 ordering that if an orchard was past bearing and was to be replaced by farmland then clearance could be grant-aided, but not if the intention was to restock with young trees.[26] There was, however, a limited take-up of the scheme in the eastern counties. In 1956/57, for example, only 132 orchards covering a total of 456.5 acres (184 hectares) were grubbed out in the whole of Bedfordshire, Cambridgeshire (and the Isle of Ely), Essex, Hertfordshire, Huntingdonshire (with the Soke of Peterborough), Norfolk and Suffolk. It is noticeable that their average size was only 3.5 acres (c.1.4 hectares), reflecting the fact that smallholdings and old domestic orchards were the target.[27]

The early 1960s saw continued hostility to old-fashioned orchards and further exhortations to grub them out. A press release by the Ministry of Agriculture, Fisheries and Food in October 1961 asked farmers, rhetorically:

---

21   Norbury, 'Modern Developments', p. 727.
22   Norbury, 'Modern Developments', p. 727.
23   Norbury, 'Modern Developments', p. 720.
24   PRO/TNA, MAF 55/51.
25   PRO/TNA, MAF 187/11.
26   PRO/TNA, MAF 137/11.
27   PRO/TNA, MAF 137/11.

> Is your orchard an asset or a liability? There is no doubt that quite a number of orchards – the smaller ones in particular – are likely to be an embarrassment to the owner rather than a source of gain … . In these days of fierce competition only the quality product can hope to find a paying market. … What can be done with these worn out orchards, those orchards which are so small that they do not warrant the expenditure on spraying tackle and equipment for grading and packing? What can be done with those mis-sited orchards where frost claims the crop three years out of four? What can be done to clear the rubbishy samples of fruit which not only clutter up the market but – worse – depress the price of first class sendings? There can only be one answer – grub out and put the land to more profitable use.[28]

Grants were now available to cover a third of the cost of grubbing under the Horticulture Improvement Scheme, backed up by free advice from the Ministry.[29] But uptake, although steady, continued to be unspectacular – in 1964 there were only 99 applications from Norfolk, Suffolk, Essex and Cambridge combined – and internal MAFF memos repeatedly urged the need to reduce the orchard acreage significantly, one in 1962/3 suggesting that the area occupied by culinary apples nationally needed to fall by 20 per cent – from 50,000 to 40,000 acres (*c.*20,230 to 16,187 hectares) – by 1971.[30] The NFU pressed hard for larger grants to remove 'uneconomic' apple and pear orchards, stating in a press release in November 1970 that this would result in 'at least 15,000 acres of the country's least viable fruit' being cleared:[31]

> The National Farmers Union, in continuation of its policy of bringing about the removal of uneconomic apple and pear orchards by means of more realistic grubbing grants, have been having consultations with the Minister of Agriculture on the early introduction of a substantial increased rate of grant for this purpose.[32]

The following year a new, improved grant was announced, a flat rate equivalent to the full standard cost of grubbing, again with the proviso that no replanting would take place for at least five years.[33] The uptake of grant aid significantly increased: in eastern Norfolk alone there were 174 applications to grub out orchards in 1972.[34] Moreover, many other examples were, throughout the 1960s and 1970s, removed without grant aid or perished gradually, through neglect or deliberate conversion to gardens and pony paddocks.

---

28   PRO/TNA, MAF 302/39.
29   PRO/TNA, MAF 302/40.
30   PRO/TNA, MAF 302/40 and 302/108.
31   PRO/TNA, MAF 227/252.
32   PRO/TNA, MAF 227/252.
33   PRO/TNA, MAF 183/389.
34   PRO/TNA, MAF 302/108.

By this time, of course, the story of the decline of small 'traditional' or quasi-traditional orchards was merging with the more general reduction in the orchard acreage, affecting even large commercial fruit farms, already described. But, while the two narratives become increasingly integrated over time, it is useful to keep them notionally distinct. In the eastern counties small old-fashioned orchards were being widely neglected, or even grubbed out, even in the 1940s, and their decline preceded that of the large commercial fruit farms by several decades.

Gardens and institutions

The post-war years, and especially the last five decades, have also seen the disappearance of other kinds of orchard discussed in previous chapters. Large psychiatric institutions, for example, gradually abandoned the practice of growing their own food. Rather than being seen as 'therapeutic', farm and garden work came to be regarded by most professionals advising the government as both exploitative and of little benefit in health terms. There were also financial benefits to be reaped from selling off the land formerly used for such activities. Indeed, as early as 1948 all hospital boards were urged to dispense with farms not regarded as essential. 'Advances in medical treatment and improvements in the supply of clean milk and vegetables have reduced the need for hospitals to have their own farms.'[35] But there was also opposition to this approach. As James Dance MP put it in a parliamentary speech in 1959: 'I think that the value of farms is undoubtedly apparent to the layman. It is obviously a good thing that people who suffer from mental sickness should have the peace and comparative quietness of working on the land, and the hard manual work involved is also beneficial.'[36] Some psychiatric institutions – such as Leavesden in Hertfordshire – continued to produce some food into the 1970s, although here as in other cases the orchards were neglected before other aspects of the home estate. But, as at all such hospitals, the production of food had effectively ceased by the end of that decade. Other kinds of institution likewise abandoned their farms, gardens and orchards in the post-war years, although the process was often a gradual one. At the NCC home at Highfields, Harpenden, in Hertfordshire, the existing orchard was extended after the end of the war; in 1945 the kitchen gardens still provided most of the vegetables required by the kitchens, grown in part with the aid of the children, while into the mid-1950s it was said that 'helping in the orchard is a popular task: enough apples are grown here in a good season to meet needs through the winter'.[37] But almost everywhere serious management of institutional orchards had ended by the 1970s.

---

35   Hansard: <https://hansard.parliament.uk/Commons/1958-04-22/debates/ff751ea9-ba17-411c-9132-48d87b9702d4/Hospitals(Farms)>, accessed 30 March 2020.

36   Hansard: <https://api.parliament.uk/historic-hansard/commons/1959/feb/11/mental-hospitals-farms>, accessed 28 March 2020.

37   National Children's Home, promotional film, 1954: <https://www.youtube.com/watch?v=jMLzCLggcKA>, accessed 9 March 2021.

In the 1980s and 1990s such orchards faced a new threat, as social policies turned against the very existence of large institutions, especially psychiatric hospitals, in favour of smaller, more dispersed units of care. Many of these places constituted prime sites for residential development. Their buildings might be converted into flats and houses, or they might be demolished and their sites developed for housing, but either way their orchards were usually an irrelevance. Only in a few cases, as we shall see, were they retained as 'features' within new residential areas.

The orchards associated with country houses – where these had not been repurposed and converted to serve some new, institutional use – were also increasingly neglected through the post-war years, as their owners came to rely more on supermarkets for fresh fruit and vegetables, and reduced their labour costs. And, in suburban areas, while small collections of fruit trees continued to be maintained in innumerable back gardens, the kinds of true orchard associated with large upper middle-class residences steadily declined. In part this was because of changes in lifestyles, including a growing dependence on supermarkets and a decline in the home production of such things as apple pies or jam. In part it was a consequence of the progressive 'infilling' of large suburban plots, for one of the consequences of the 1947 Town and Country Planning Act was that, by reducing the scope for suburban sprawl, it encouraged higher densities of houses in areas zoned for residential development, something that also led to the demise of many market gardens – with associated orchards – in suburban areas.[38]

Planting in post-war orchards

Another key issue that concerned post-war agricultural policy-makers, and which encouraged the grubbing out of old orchards, was the particular varieties of fruit, and the range of varieties, being cultivated. There was widespread official hostility to orchards crammed with many different types of apple and pear, especially where these included old varieties. This was fuelled in part by a rising enthusiasm for modern 'scientific' approaches and by the belief that some varieties of apple, pear and plum were particularly susceptible to fungal infections and other pests. In 1944 the government published lists of apples recommended for planting in new orchards. The 'Primary list' included only Bramley's Seedling, Cox's Orange Pippin, Edward VII, Grenadier, Laxton's Superb, Miller's Seedling and Worcester Pearmain; Laxton's Fortune and Lord Lambourne were also under consideration, pending the results of field trials. These varieties, nearly half of which had been introduced since 1900 and most since 1850, were considered 'sufficient for most districts', although it was agreed that

> there are places where other varieties are known to succeed and, in consequence, the nursery trade will arrange for the propagation of trees of the following varieties: Allington

---

38   T. Williamson, *An Environmental History of Wildlife in England, 1650–1950* (London, 2013), pp. 184–5.

Pippin, Beauty of Bath, Blenheim Orange, Charles Ross, Early Victoria, Ellison's Orange, James Grieve, Lane's Prince Albert, Lord Derby, Monarch and Newton Wonder.[39]

Where old orchards were not grubbed up, in other words, they needed to be replanted: they should all be made to conform to the standards of the most modern and productive. The range of fruit grown commercially had already been reduced during the inter-war years, and many of the older varieties had been replaced. But equally important had been the reduction in the number of different varieties cultivated within each orchard. As Leslie Clarke put it in 1948, 'in the east of the country we tend to plant big blocks of trees of one variety so that we can cultivate and spray with modern machinery.'[40] This does not mean that, on the larger fruit farms, four or more varieties of each fruit type might not be grown. When French's Farm in Hadleigh, Suffolk, was sold in 1984 the particulars described the older planting, from the mid-1930s, as featuring Cox's Orange Pippin with Emneth Early pollinators, and Conference pears with Williams pollinators, while a later planting made between 1945 and 1948 comprised blocks of Worcester Pearmain, Cox's, Tydeman's Early Worcester and Laxton's Superb apples, Oullins Golden Gage and Victoria plums and Conference and Doyenne du Comice pears (with Williams pollinators). In 1956/7 some of the Worcester Pearmains were top-grafted with Tydeman's Early Worcester. There were thus five varieties of apple, three of pear and two of plum, but this was a smaller range than could be found in most farm orchards – or even in those associated with many early smallholdings – and the different varieties were not intermingled, except in terms of the pollinators, but instead formed large blocks within an area of orchards extending, in this particular case, over some 50 hectares.[41] Many of the larger commercial enterprises were similarly planted. In 1961 31 acres (12.5 hectares) of 'well developed Orchard Land' were sold at Hay Green, Terrington St Clement, in the Norfolk Fens. They were planted with Cox's Orange Pippin, Worcester Pearmain, Beauty of Bath, Charles Ross and Bramley's Seedling apples, accompanied by Comice, Laxton's Superb, Early Market and Conference Pears.[42] Almost all of the varieties in these two orchards had, typically, been introduced since 1860, around half since 1890.

Large commercial orchards planted with extensive blocks of a limited number of varieties were thus already widespread by the 1940s, but there was general agreement that they needed to become the norm. In a globalised and scientific world there was no room for orchards in which a greater range, sometimes including older varieties and extensively intermixed, were planted in order to provide a long season for the benefit of the owner or

---

39 PRO/TNA, MAF 43/54.
40 ERO, D/F 152/7/1.
41 SRO, B, HE 503/11/449.
42 CRO, KAR 115/38/2/122.

to sell gradually in local markets. Leslie Clarke believed in 1948 that the system of price controls was partly to blame for their continued existence:

> This has led growers to keep poor and unpopular varieties of fruit trees on their farms because they made good money. Now I appeal to anyone who is listening and has some of these old things – put the saw through them this winter and either grub them out or top graft them to good kinds. It will pay you in the end, you know.[43]

W.P. Seabrook, the noted nurseryman and fruit-grower from Essex, voiced a view of older varieties that seems to have been widely shared when he wrote in December 1943 to Dr Taylor, the Commissioner for Horticulture:

> it is quite likely that some old varieties may be worth resuscitating but my father collected several hundreds and fruited them but combed them out some twenty years ago and I do not think he missed anything of real value. I have since gone through what he left and none appear to be of commercial value.[44]

The post-war decades thus saw a sustained attempt to reduce the range of varieties planted in commercial orchards and to limit the numbers present in any individual orchard. There was a particular emphasis on varieties with good resistance to pests and diseases, which seem to have posed a growing problem, presumably because of the increasing size of commercial orchards and the practice of planting large blocks of single varieties. In 1959 orders were issued by the Ministry of Agriculture for the complete grubbing up of all orchards infected with fire blight, a serious disease of apples and pears.[45] In 1963 there was even a suggestion that all Laxton's Superb pear trees should be grubbed out because they were particularly prone to the disease.[46]

Attempts to reduce the range of varieties grown in English orchards continued and intensified through the 1970s and 1980s. The Ministry of Agriculture, Fisheries and Food, in a letter sent to fruit growers in February 1981, insisted that:

> For the English fruit industry to survive it is vital that the number of varieties is reduced as a matter of urgency. Certainly the multiplicity of dessert varieties marketed during the September–December period is severely depressing prices. Fewer varieties, with improved continuity of supply, can be backed by increased promotion.

---

43   ERO, D/F 152/7/1.
44   PRO/TNA, MAF 43/54.
45   PRO/TNA, MAF 302/39.
46   PRO/TNA, MAF 302/39.

It is fashionable for some farm shops to offer a wide range of marginally commercial varieties. This, however, we believe to be counter-productive. The good, well run farm shop or PYO unit, providing good commercial varieties, at full retail prices, is the best ambassador the English fruit industry can have.[47]

The number of varieties being recommended had by now contracted still further: Cox's Orange Pippin, Discovery and Bramley's Seedling were now the officially preferred apples, Conference and Comice the recommended pears, and the only second-choice varieties suggested were the apples Crispin, Spartan and Idared, and even these were to be planted with caution. Research was being undertaken into the future viability of other varieties, but these were few in number – Golden Delicious, Worcester Pearmain, Tydeman's Early and Egremont Russet. 'Growers are strongly urged to consider grubbing varieties not listed above.'[48]

Again, government policies, at European Community or national level, only partly account for these developments. Changes in lifestyles and in attitudes to food – a decline in the amount of home cooking undertaken as a higher proportion of women entered full-time employment – coupled with the proliferation of ready-processed meals available from large supermarkets worked symbiotically to reduce demand for diversity. By the 1990s, for most consumers, 'apple' or 'pear' no longer meant a range of varieties with different tastes, uses and properties, but three or four basic types, some of them bland and predictable and more likely to be imported than home grown. As Andrew George, the Liberal Democrat agriculture spokesman, put it in 2004, 'the problem is the supermarkets like bland uniformity but it is the New World that provides bland uniformity.'[49] Gala apples, grown on a large scale throughout the world, were probably now the most widely consumed variety in the UK.

The rise of heritage orchards

By the 1970s a reaction was well under way against the impacts of modern farming. Publications such as Marion Shoard's *The Theft of the Countryside* (1980) and Richard Mabey's *The Common Ground* (1980) emphasised its deleterious effects not only on the environment but on the very quality of life.[50] The title of Mabey's book was, in 1982, adopted for a new organisation with a particular focus, founded by Angela King, Sue Clifford and Richard Deakin. Common Ground was not merely concerned with the conservation of species and habitats but was 'propelled by worries about widening gaps between nature and culture,

---

47 PRO/TNA, MAF 302/154.
48 PRO/TNA, MAF 302/154.
49 *The Independent*, 19 June 2004.
50 Shoard, *Theft of the Countryside*; R. Mabey, *The Common Ground: A Place for Nature in Britain's Future* (London, 1980).

between the special and the commonplace, increasing detachment from decision making'.[51] It was an alliance of nature conservationists and individuals from an arts background, and was to have a major impact on the history of orchards. By 1988 the organisation had begun its 'Save Our Orchards' campaign, 'intuitively recognising the richness of culture and nature held in the traditional tall tree orchard'.[52] Orchards were important because they formed a key aspect of 'local distinctiveness', that particular character of place that arose from the interaction of people, over long periods of time, with their immediate environment. The varieties of fruit grown in old orchards were themselves a vital aspect of this, and on 21 October 1990 the first Apple Day was held, at which members of the public could have their own fruit identified. In Angela King and Sue Clifford's words:

> Orchards are more than formal collections of fruit trees, they are a manifestation of our long relationship with fruit cultivation in different localities. They vary from place to place in the kinds of fruit, the varieties, size and disposition of trees, the domestic animals that are grazed beneath them, the soft fruits, flowers and other crops grown around them, the ways and times of pruning, grafting, picking and planting.[53]

It was the way that orchards represented a fusion of the natural, the cultural and the local that made them of particular importance:

> When you lose an orchard you sacrifice not simply a few old trees (bad enough, some would say) but you might lose for ever varieties particular to that locality, the wild life, the songs, the recipes, the cider/perry/cherry brandy, the hard but social work, the festive gatherings, the look of the landscape, the wisdom gathered over generations about pruning and grafting, about aspect and slope, soil and season, variety and use. In short the cultural landscape is diminished by many dimensions at one blow.[54]

Common Ground was a major influence on the burgeoning enthusiasm for orchards, not least through their publication of a range of books, pamphlets and advice notes.[55] But other organisations, only loosely connected, were also important, in the eastern counties as elsewhere, all reacting against both the destruction of old, wildlife-friendly orchards and the disappearance of old fruit varieties.

The Norfolk Apples and Orchards Project was set up in 1994 and in 2003 developed into the East of England Apples and Orchards Project (EEAOP), a registered charity

---

51 Clifford, 'Save Our Orchards', p. 32.
52 Clifford, 'Save Our Orchards', p. 33.
53 King and Clifford, 'The Apple, the Orchard', p. 73.
54 King and Clifford, 'The Apple, the Orchard', p. 75.
55 For a list and discussion see Clifford, 'Save Our Orchards'.

working across all of the seven modern eastern counties (that is, those covered in this book, together with Lincolnshire). The organisation has undertaken survey and research work but has mainly focused on the planting of new orchards and the identification and propagation of fruit varieties associated with the region. From the beginning it organised 'Apple Days', and more than 270 varieties of apple, pear, cherry and plum are now (as of 2021) grown in their nursery ground at Raynham in west Norfolk, propagated and sold to individuals, community groups and schools.[56] The organisation, established and still largely directed by Clare Stimson and Martin Skipper, also organises pruning and grafting workshops, many of which are taught by Bob Lever. Nor are they the only such group to have emerged in the region. The Hertfordshire Orchards Initiative (HOI) was established as early as 1991 by Martin Hicks and David Curry, the Cambridgeshire Orchard Group (COG) was founded in 2003 and the Suffolk Traditional Orchards Group (STOG) in 2009, with the Bedfordshire and Luton Orchard Group (BLOG) following in 2010. The most recent development has been the establishment, in 2017, of Orchards East, a project funded by the Heritage Fund, which has augmented existing endeavours in planting and the teaching of orchard skills but has, in addition, undertaken the mass of research and survey work on which this volume is largely based. It continues (again, as of 2021) to operate as a forum, research group and lobbying organisation.

The particular focus of these organisations, groups and projects has varied. Some are primarily concerned with the conservation of 'traditional' fruit varieties characteristic of the locality or region, and for these the kinds of rootstock on which the varieties are grafted is a secondary concern. Others are more interested in orchards as *habitats*, and thus emphasise the crucial importance of vigorous rootstocks, considered by some to be more likely to live to a ripe old age, veteranise and as a result provide the niches required for rare organisms, most notably saproxylic insects. Whatever the particular emphasis, members of the various orchard groups form a loose network of like-minded individuals with links to the county Environmental Record Centres and key national organisations such as the People's Trust for Endangered Species. A number of individuals from these groups, including in particular Peter Laws, Paul Read and Bob Lever, have worked on developing 'FruitID', an online fruit identification site designed to supplement the various books on the subject that have appeared over the last few decades, including, at a local level, *Apples: a Field Guide* by Michael Clark, warden of Tewin Orchard and Hopkyns Wood, the fine nature reserve donated to the Hertfordshire and Middlesex Wildlife Trust in 1984.[57]

Another Hertfordshire example – Stone's Orchard in Croxley Green – was given to Three Rivers District Council in 1983 and, from the early 1990s, was developed as a public open space by the parish council.[58] Tewin and Stone's orchards are two of several examples

---

56   Their excellent website provides details: <http://www.applesandorchards.org.uk/>, accessed June 2020.

57   For FruitID, see <https://www.fruitid.com/#main>, accessed 9 March 2021. Clark, *Apples*.

58   Pomfret, *Stone's Orchard*.

of old orchards in the eastern counties that have been given a new lease of life. That associated with Shenley psychiatric hospital in south Hertfordshire was – together with other features inherited from the old hospital and the country house that preceded it – taken over by a trust for the benefit of local people in 1992.[59] The two orchards associated with the Three Counties Mental Hospital at Arlesey in Bedfordshire were retained as the site was developed for housing following its closure in 1999, and are now beautifully maintained. Elsewhere, large institutions have survived, or have been repurposed, and their orchards are now cared for – and opened to the public on a limited basis – thanks to the hard work and enthusiasm of volunteers, as at St Elizabeth's, Much Hadham, in east Hertfordshire, or The Oval in Harpenden, in the west of that county. And wherever heritage organisations or local authorities managing country parks or similar facilities have inherited old orchards they have – over the last four decades – often conserved and augmented them, as, for example, at Wandlebury in Cambridgeshire or Mowsbury in Bedfordshire. A small but significant number of orchards in the eastern counties, including some particularly large and important examples, have thus been preserved for future generations. Indeed, it is only when owned by sympathetic organisations or private individuals dedicated to their conservation that orchards can be conserved once they have ceased to be commercially viable. There is little official protection even for the oldest and most biologically diverse. The 1967 Forestry Act specifically excluded orchards from felling regulations, allowing fruit trees to be cut down without a licence, although in rare cases specific examples have been conserved with the use of Tree Preservation Orders.[60]

Of equal interest to this shift in attitude to old orchards has been the upsurge, over the last two or three decades, in the planting of new examples (Figure 6.2). This has been spearheaded by EEAOP but supplemented by other groups, including, in recent years, Orchards East. 'Community' orchards have been planted by parish councils and community groups and by organisations such as the Museum of East Anglian Life at Stowmarket in Suffolk. Many private landowners have done likewise, motivated by concerns both for the region's heritage and for nature conservation, although grant aid, through Countryside Stewardship or from the Forestry Commission, has been limited. Noted early adopters include Kevin West of Attleborough in Norfolk, who, since the 1990s, has planted extensively both on his own land and in a new orchard established on rented property at Morley, fired by an interest in old varieties encouraged by EEAOP and by an enthusiasm for wildlife, including the fieldfares that flock to his orchards to consume the glut of unused apples.[61] Many of West's trees were supplied by Neil Thomas of Ranworth Trees, who, forced out of the supply of conventional fruit trees by cheap European imports, began from the mid-1990s to specialise in 'heritage' varieties, and especially those

---

59 See their website, <http://www.shenleypark.co.uk/shenley-park/>, accessed 30 May 2020.
60 PRO/TNA, MAF; oral history interview with Steve Scott.
61 Oral history interview with Kevin West.

The recent history of orchards 163

Figure 6.2 Planting a new community orchard at Great Wymondley, north Hertfordshire, in February 2020.

Figure 6.3 A magnificent orchard of heritage varieties, planted over 20 years ago and now in full bearing, at Sarratt in west Hertfordshire.

associated with Norfolk.[62] Other examples include the wonderful orchard planted by Roger and Anne Dudley, with more than a hundred different apple varieties, at Sarratt in west Hertfordshire (Figure 6.3).

From the 1990s new orchards have thus begun to appear in the landscape, reflecting the fact that orchards have themselves acquired new roles: as wildlife reserves and as symbols of continuity and place in a world that is changing rapidly. Yet the various community orchards and heritage collections planted over the last few decades have done little to reverse the overall decline in the number and extent of orchards, as the results of a large-scale survey, recently completed by volunteers, has revealed.

The current state of play

It is difficult if not impossible to ascertain the current state of orchards in the eastern counties without a systematic ground survey. Aerial photography can tell us little about the character of an orchard – the type of trees it contains, for example – and it can sometimes be hard, from the air, to distinguish orchards from other collections of well-spaced trees planted in a loose grid, such as plantations of cricket-bat willows, or to identify the small domestic examples. As part of the Heritage Lottery funded project Orchards East, a number of volunteers was accordingly recruited from across the eastern counties and invited to survey the orchards in their local areas. They were provided with standard survey forms and a map showing the locations of all examples recorded on the second edition 6-inch and 25-inch Ordnance Survey maps from *c*.1900, together with ones known from other sources: a provisional survey based on existing collections of aerial photographs undertaken by the People's Trust for Endangered Species (PTES) several years ago and, for some counties, similar surveys carried out over the last few decades by the Environmental Record Centres or local orchard groups. All were habitat surveys, concerned with the identification of older orchards featuring large and well spaced trees of the kind important for nature conservation. There is a high degree of duplication between the PTES data and the county surveys, but remarkably little overlap – less than 5 per cent – between the orchards recorded by these 'modern' surveys and those mapped in *c*.1900 by the Ordnance Survey. Volunteers were asked to examine all these sites on the ground and, in addition, to inspect and record any other orchards that they could discover within their allotted areas, which were based on modern civil parishes or urban areas. The record forms contained a range of questions about the current size, condition and character of those orchards that still survived, and about the kinds of land use that had replaced those examples that had disappeared. The survey was carried out by around 150 volunteers over four years between 2017 and 2020.

The survey has cast important new light on the orchards of eastern England, but it was by no means perfect in either design or execution, and some potential biases need to be briefly highlighted. Firstly, not all the survey forms were completed to the same standard,

---

62   Oral history interview, Mr Neil Thomas (formerly of Ranworth Trees).

or even fully completed at all, so that some aspects of the orchards examined are more reliably recorded than others. Secondly, not all orchards could be inspected on the ground, but only from outside – from a public road or adjacent land. Thirdly, and perhaps most importantly, while in one sense this was a random survey – volunteers were self-selecting – the areas surveyed were not distributed in a statistically random or geographically even manner. Districts in which orchard loss has been at a high rate – especially urban and suburban areas – are to an extent under-represented. So too, conversely and to a greater extent, are those areas – most notably in the Fens of Cambridgeshire and Norfolk – in which commercial orchards still survive in significant numbers. In the former case, volunteers were discouraged by the simple absence of orchards; in the latter by the abundance of large, intensive and uninteresting examples. The scale of these omissions should not be exaggerated, however. Many parishes in such areas were examined by volunteers and some additional survey work was undertaken, to fill obvious gaps, by members of the project team. Nevertheless, all these issues ensure that estimates of overall loss or survival, or concerning the loss/survival of particular types of orchard, need to be treated with caution, and can only be made within relatively broad confidence limits.

The results of the survey show, in a way that should cause little surprise after the discussion presented over the previous pages, that there has been a dramatic loss of orchards, and especially of old or 'traditional' examples, over the last few decades. In all, the sites of around 10,200 known examples were examined, a figure representing 35 per cent of the total targeted population of 29,200; the parishes surveyed by volunteers amounted to around 30 per cent of the land area of the eastern counties. Only 1,259 of the locations examined, or a little over 12 per cent, were considered to still be 'orchards' by the surveyors. In fact, a significant minority of these – nearly 7 per cent of surviving sites – do not really fulfil the 'official', Natural England definition of an 'orchard', in the sense that they contained fewer than five fruit trees growing in reasonable proximity. They have been included in the analysis because in some respects the sites they occupy still retain orchard-like characteristics. In addition to these known orchard sites, volunteers located a further 345 new orchards, omitted from the maps with which they had been provided. Around two thirds appear to represent community orchards or private amenity examples, planted since the 1980s; most of the rest, twentieth-century commercial enterprises, many of them intensively managed, and featuring closely-planted trees on dwarfing rootstocks. These collectively cover an area of 550 acres, probably indicating a figure of around 1,800 acres (c.730 hectares) of such orchards existing across the eastern counties overall.

Most of the orchard sites examined by surveyors were ones shown on the second edition Ordnance Survey maps of c.1900. Indeed, around 35 per cent of the orchards depicted by this source were surveyed. Of these, 7,682 had been destroyed and only 657, covering 612 acres (248 hectares), remained. This suggests that of the 23,890 orchards covering 19,400 acres (7,850 hectares) present at the start of the twentieth century around 1,900, covering perhaps 1,800 acres (c.730 hectares), survive today across the whole of the seven historic counties. A significant proportion of these, moreover, are no longer in any sense 'traditional' in character, having been re-planted with close-set trees on dwarfing rootstocks. Of course, as we have seen, a large number of orchards were added in the course of the twentieth century, a high proportion of which appear to have been recorded, over the last few decades, by the PTES study and the county surveys. Volunteers examined the sites of 1,813 of these twentieth-century examples, out of a targeted total of 5,200 (covering 6,500 acres, or *c.*2,600 hectares). Around 38 per cent by number, 40 per cent by area, still remained. The contrasting survival rates of the two groups is striking, but unsurprising, given that a significant proportion of the second comprises commercial orchards established over the last five decades or so, some still in production.

The latest official government figures, from 2019, suggest that there are now around 3,800 acres (*c.*1,540 hectares) of working commercial orchard in the eastern counties.[63] Some 230 orchards of this kind, covering 690 acres (280 hectares), were included in the examples recorded by the surveyors, representing collectively around 2,000 acres (810 hectares) of the government figure. Taking this overlap of datasets into account, the real area of orchards now surviving in the eastern counties, including domestic, institutional, redundant, derelict and community examples, can be tentatively estimated at around 8,000 acres (*c.*3,240 hectares). This is made up of 3,800 acres of working commercial examples and 4,200 of other, essentially non-commercial types. The great majority of all surviving orchards in the region, over 77 per cent, clearly originated in the period between 1900 and 1960. All these figures, we would emphasise again, should be treated with extreme caution. But they are probably broadly correct.

The figure of 8,000 acres represents around 40 per cent of the area occupied by orchards in the seven historic counties in *c.*1900. But it is an even smaller fraction of the peak that was attained after the five or six decades of subsequent expansion between 1900 and the mid-1950s. The maximum extent of the orchard area appears to have been reached, to judge from government figures, around 1955, when no less than 44,217 acres (17,895 hectares) of orchard was recorded within the six eastern counties. But this, like other government estimates of the orchard area, seems to have ignored a host of small, domestic or unproductive examples, concentrating instead on those of a commercial or quasi-commercial character: the area of orchards officially recorded from the eastern counties in 1899 – 13,555 acres (5,486 hectares) – is thus significantly lower than that shown on the Ordnance Survey maps made around the same time – a total of 19,400 acres (7,851 hectares). It seems likely that around half this number of 'non-commercial', domestic

---

[63] See 'Structure of the Agricultural Industry in England and the UK at June'; https://assets.publishing.service.gov.uk/government/uploads/system/uploads/attachment_data/file/927036/structure-june-eng-county-15oct2020.ods, accessed 20 November 2020. The area covered by the government figures is not entirely the same as the seven traditional counties used as the basis of our own study, including in particular the Peterborough Unitary Authority area, but overall the differences are small.

orchards still existed in 1955, for a decade later the Agricultural Census, unusually, recorded 'non-commercial' as well as 'commercial' examples, the former totalling, across the seven counties, some 3,417 acres (1,383 hectares). Allowing for such omissions, it seems likely that the peak orchard area in 1955 must have been around 48,000 acres (19,400 hectares), suggesting a decline of around 84 per cent in area in the six and a half decades that have passed between then and today. In reality the decline is probably greater, for many of the surviving orchards now cover only part of their original area or have been reduced to a handful of trees. This appears, from the survey results, to be particularly true of those examples planted before 1900, the category that has anyway, as we have seen, suffered the greatest reduction in area and numbers. Pre-1900 orchards account for many, although by no means all, examples of 'traditional' orchards, with old, tall and well-spaced trees growing in permanent pasture. Their wholesale loss is one of the main reasons why the suggested figure of 8,000 acres of surviving orchard is a poor guide to the current extent of this particular type of orchard in eastern England, which is probably no more than a third of this overall figure.

It is difficult to provide accurate figures for the kinds of land use that have replaced the lost orchards, in part because many examples are now occupied by a number of different land-use types and in part because of problems of definition, especially regarding old farm orchards that have been absorbed into gardens but which may retain a few old trees (Figure 6.4). In general terms, around 15 per cent by area appear to have become absorbed into gardens and 26 per cent have been built on. A further 23 per cent have been converted to arable and 10 per cent are now pasture (as many such cases represent pony paddocks, attached to former farmhouses, they are perhaps closer in character to 'gardens' than to true agricultural land). Around 10 per cent of orchard sites are occupied by woodland or plantations, either as a consequence of deliberate planting or through natural regeneration following abandonment and dereliction. In some cases, however – with the post-1900 orchards, targeted in part on the basis of the People's Trust for Endangered Species aerial survey – sites occupied by small plantations may have been misidentified as orchards and then mistakenly recorded on the ground as a change in land use by surveyors. Of the remaining sites, 7 per cent are now occupied by industrial or business premises and 9 per cent by miscellaneous 'other' forms of land use.

The high proportion of former orchards now occupied by housing and industrial/commercial premises – nearly 33 per cent – reflects not so much the scale of urbanisation in the eastern counties in the course of the twentieth century as the fact that many orchards lay within areas zoned for development under post-war planning legislation – within village envelopes or on the fringes of towns and cities. The figure has been inflated, however, by particular examples of development and urban growth, such as the expansion of Wisbech across the adjacent Fenland orchard area and the development of Southend at the expense of the south-east Essex fruit-growing district.

168 The Orchards of Eastern England

Figure 6.4 An old farmhouse orchard preserved, but integrated into a garden, in north Suffolk. The line between 'orchard' and 'garden' can be a very blurred one.

There are only slight differences discernible between the kinds of land use that have replaced orchards established before, and after, 1900. For the most part, orchards planted in the period before 1900, and those established in the course of the twentieth century, have suffered similar fates in similar proportions. There is, however, a noticeable contrast between the proportion of pre- and post-1900 orchards which are now occupied by housing: 35 per cent by number, 28 per cent by area, in the case of the former, but only 9 per cent by number, 11 per cent by area, in the case of the latter. A high proportion of pre-1900 orchards lay within or beside settlements, and have thus fallen victim to development pressures to a greater extent than those later examples, many of which were more remotely located. There are, however, some grounds for believing that biases in the survey may have underestimated the extent of the differences between the fates of pre- and post-1900 orchards.

Conclusion

After reaching a peak in the mid-1950s the overall orchard area declined in the eastern counties, although small, 'traditional' farm orchards had already been disappearing for several decades. The contraction of fruit growing was in part a consequence of EEC, later European Community, membership but, as we have seen, it had several other causes as well, including a more general globalisation of trade in food commodities, changes in lifestyles and employment patterns, and structural developments in the retailing sector, in particular the rise of the great supermarket chains. It is difficult to provide precise figures for the decline in the orchard area (or for the different kinds of land use that have replaced orchards) and it is freely admitted that there are a number of problems with the calculations and statistics presented in the foregoing pages. They convey a misleading impression of accuracy that obscures both the uncertain character of much of the data and, indeed, the problems inherent in defining what precisely we mean by an 'orchard' and in assessing the precise extent of lost or surviving examples. Nevertheless, tentatively and in broad terms, we might say that there are today around 8,000 acres (3,240 hectares) of orchard of various kinds in the eastern counties, compared with around 19,400 acres (7,851 hectares) at the start of the twentieth century and over 48,000 acres (19,400 hectares) in the mid-1950s. Among the surviving orchards, those dating from before 1900 have suffered greater losses than more recently planted examples, and in general 'traditional' orchards appear to have been eroded from the landscape to a greater extent than other types.

The orchard heritage of the eastern counties thus survives in a tenuous, fragmentary state, and closer inspection of the figures reveals little to disperse the gloom. Of the orchards recorded in the survey, 127 were intensive commercial enterprises and, while this accounts for only 8 per cent of the sample in numerical terms, considered as a proportion of the orchard area it is considerably higher, approaching a fifth. Almost certainly the real proportion is higher still, given the uncertainties in the evidence already outlined. While a few of these orchards apparently display some significance as wildlife habitats, most do not: in 80 per cent, for example, no fungi or wild flowers were visible owing to intensive spraying or the fact that trees were growing in bare ground (Figure 6.5). There was little evidence of dead wood on the ground or, indeed, in the trees themselves: intensive management involves the replacement of trees long before they display 'veteran' characteristics, although – in spite of what is sometimes suggested – even trees grafted on M9 or MM106 will eventually do so, if left to their own devices, and probably sooner than those on traditional, vigorous rootstocks (see Figure 3.10).

A further 7 per cent of surviving orchards, as already noted, had few trees and, strictly speaking, should perhaps not be regarded as 'orchards' at all; just under 20 per cent had significantly contracted since first mapped, in the sense that they had lost a half or more of their original treed area – a figure that rises to 27 per cent if only those orchards established before 1900 are considered. On top of all this, even relatively intact orchards often retain only a small proportion of trees that are more than six or seven decades old and, as we shall see, few orchards now contain trees planted before the First World War.

Against this generally negative picture we should, however, note that perhaps 235 of the recorded orchards, or 13 per cent, appear to have been newly planted over the last two decades or so, 48 of which were community orchards. Their numbers, too, may be

Figure 6.5 A typical example of a modern, intensively managed commercial orchard in Wisbech St Mary, north Cambridgeshire. The apples are closely planted and grafted on dwarfing rootstocks and will be replaced before they attain any great age; the ground beneath the trees is sprayed with herbicide and maintained as bare earth.

under-estimated in the sample, a consequence of surveyors' uncertainty about whether such features could be considered as 'real' orchards and the sparse coverage of the urban areas where many are planted: the scale of activities of EEAOP and other groups suggests an overall figure higher than the 150 or so community and school orchards that we would predict for the eastern counties as a whole by extrapolating up from the sample. EEAOP alone have, since 2003, supplied trees for over 300 community projects, as well as to large numbers of schools.[64] Moreover, many surviving orchards, especially the older domestic examples, are now cherished by owners and managed in a wildlife-friendly manner, again as a consequence of the efforts of EEAOP and other groups, and especially their promotion of our fruit heritage through regular 'Apple Days'. All this said, there is no doubt that orchards, including 'traditional' orchards, have fared badly in the eastern counties over the past half century or so.

---

64 EEAOP website, <https://www.applesandorchards.org.uk/about/what-we-do/>, accessed 15 November 2020.

CHAPTER SEVEN

Fruit varieties and the nursery industry

One of the reasons why people value old orchards, as noted in the previous chapter, is because they contain a range of fruit varieties far wider than that normally available today from food retailers or which can be obtained in the form of trees from most commercial nurseries. This, according to many, constitutes a precious cultural and perhaps genetic heritage. As also already noted, local apple and orchard groups now hold regular events in the autumn to which apples, and increasingly other fruit, can be brought for identification by experts. Various books have been published to aid fruit identification, again mainly of apples, although to an extent these have been superseded by the FruitID website, with its multiple deep-zoom photographs to assist identification.[1] Peter Laws and colleagues are also actively involved – along with members of the Horticultural Department at Reading University – in the DNA fingerprinting of the many thousands of fruit varieties known from England, especially apples, and in assessing such things as whether a single variety name may in reality embrace two or more cultivars or, conversely, whether the same cultivar might have been given different names in different regions.

There is thus much interest in and enthusiasm for old fruit varieties. Many of these are routinely described as 'traditional', even 'ancient', but this is true only up to a point and depends, crucially, on how we are using these difficult terms. In spite of their evocative names, many varieties are not in fact very old. Dangerous, too, is an emphasis on the essentially *local* character of particular varieties – the idea that they were restricted in their distribution and were created by communities deeply rooted in the soil of particular areas.[2] In reality, to fully appreciate the character of our orchard heritage we need to understand how the varieties grown in orchards changed over time, how people in the past obtained their fruit trees, and above all how the nursery industry has developed over the last three centuries or so in eastern England.

Sourcing fruit trees before 1750

Books on fruit and orchards written before the middle of the seventeenth century, such as William Lawson's *A New Orchard and Garden* of 1618 or the anonymous *Countryman's*

---

1   For FruitID, see <https://www.fruitid.com/#main>.

2   King and Clifford, 'The Apple, the Orchard', pp. 37–46.

Recreation of 1640, never seem to refer to commercial suppliers of fruit trees. Similarly, documentary evidence shows that even the wealthier individuals, living in the more economically advanced areas of the country close to London, routinely acquired young trees from friends and relatives, or scion wood that they (or their gardeners) grafted onto rootstocks. In 1627, for example, Sir Henry Chauncy of Ardeley in Hertfordshire was asked by Sir John Butler of Woodhall near Watton-at-Stone to provide him with 'some younge trees, of Apples, peares and wardens', as he was 'entending this winter (if God permit) to plant an orchyarde'.[3] Among the social elite such exchanges might be with people living at a considerable distance, as when in 1716 Ralph Freman of Hamels in Hertfordshire was sent '3 litle cherry trees' from Northamptonshire, almost certainly by his mother-in-law.[4] But commercial nurseries trading over wide areas were already developing in the first half of the seventeenth century – in the 1630s the Wrest Park estate in Bedfordshire was buying fruit trees from Mr Marshfield's nursery at Knightsbridge and Mr Grigson's in Twickenham.[5] Such nurseries proliferated with particular rapidity following the Restoration in 1660, part of the general economic expansion of the post-Revolutionary era.

Many authorities, most notably John Harvey, in his great study *Early Nurserymen* (1974), have nevertheless argued that, until the second half of the eighteenth century, the nursery industry remained focused on London and poorly developed in the provinces.[6] It is certainly true that in the late seventeenth and early eighteenth centuries wealthy landowners often sourced their fruit trees from London companies. Of particular importance was the Brompton Park nursery in Kensington, which was founded in 1681 by Roger Looker, Moses Cook, John Field and George London, and which (for example) supplied fruit trees to Wrest Park in Bedfordshire in 1694.[7] Other London firms also had a deep geographic reach. When Sir Roger Pratt planted his new orchard at Ryston in Norfolk in the 1670s he sourced his trees from the nurseries of John Alcock of London and Leonard Gurle of Whitechapel.[8] In the 1710s Ralph Freman of Hamels in east Hertfordshire purchased almonds, apricots, apples and cherries from Brompton Park;[9] in 1754 the Chambers family of Honing Hall in Norfolk bought nectarines, peaches, apricots, pears and cherries from the same nursery;[10] while as late as 1791 the duke of Bedford at Woburn in Bedfordshire paid £12 for 80 dwarf apple trees and £14 for 80 dwarf pear trees from Samuel Swinton's nursery in Sloane Street,

---

3   W.B. Gerish, *Sir Henry Chauncy, Kt; Serjeant-at-Law and Recorder of Hertford* (London, 1907), pp. 28–9.

4   Rowe, *Garden Making and the Freeman Family*, pp. xlv, 8.

5   BRO, L31/296.

6   J. Harvey, *Early Nurserymen* (Winchester, 1974).

7   BRO, L 31/297.

8   NRO, MF/RO 219/1.

9   Rowe, *Garden Making and the Freeman Family*, pp. 4, 15 and 31.

10 Private collection.

London.¹¹ But to an extent the prominence of London nurseries is a consequence of the nature of our sources, which are biased towards the larger landowners and thus reflect their particular needs and lifestyles. Many of the fruit trees purchased from London comprised the kinds of exotic 'wall fruit' that, as we have seen, large landowners – to a much greater degree than farmers – cultivated in their grounds. In addition, the latest and best varieties of apples and pears, the most prestigious and often those recently arrived from distant, foreign places, could only be obtained from fashionable London. At Wrest Park in 1694 one group of fruit trees was explicitly described as 'choice pears lately obtained out of France'.¹² The capital, moreover, was frequently visited by members of the elite. For those in Hertfordshire or the southern portions of Essex it could be visited regularly, and relatively easily, but those living further afield also regularly visited on business, because of political commitments, or socially during the 'season'. Here they will have seen the stock displayed at the great London nurseries and placed orders accordingly.

The over-representation of the social elite in the documentary record unquestionably obscures the extent to which a network of more local nurseries was developing from a relatively early date. In 1669 Joseph Blagrave described how 'very many of my Countrymen are so most abominably cheated and abused' by being sold substandard trees by 'our Nursery-men'.¹³ It is clear that he had local firms rather than the big London concerns in mind because, commenting on how most such enterprises were located in areas of fertile soil, he observed: 'for otherwise how could a man maintain his Wife and Children on two or three Acres of Ground, if it were not extraordinarily good?'¹⁴ Eight years later Henry Browne referred to the 'Gardeners and Nurserymen from all the West and South, towards Oxford, then towards Cambridge, and so all over England'.¹⁵ By 1732 William Ellis, who farmed at Little Gaddesden in Hertfordshire, could describe how he obtained fruit trees from small local nurseries at Redbourn (Hertfordshire) and Brentford (Middlesex) as if this was a normal thing to do. Interestingly, he echoed Blagrave's suspicion of those involved in the trade:

> In a Nursery, particular Care ought to be had on the Inspection of Trees, that none may be made Choice of that has a Canker or any Tendency thereto … . So no less Care is to be had in buying those that are well rooted. And not withstanding the common Cant of the Nursery-Gardeners, who often impose on the ignorant by telling them this or that Tree will grow, altho' but half or quarter rooted, give them no Credit.¹⁶

---

11 BRO, R3/2114/534.
12 BRO, L 31/301; L 31/303.
13 J. Blagrave, *The Epitome of the Whole Art of Husbandry* (London, 1669), p. 299.
14 Blagrave, *Epitome*, p. 304.
15 H. Browne, *Nurseries, Orchards, Profitable Gardens and Vineyards Encouraged* (London, 1677), p. 14.
16 Ellis, *Timber Tree Improved*, pp. 151–2.

Indeed, by this stage, commercial nurseries, almost all marketing fruit trees along with other plants, appear to have been well-established even in districts quite remote from London. In 1751, for example, an advertisement announced:

> To be sold at Long Melford in the County of Suffolk a choice collection of fruit trees and best stock propergated [sic] in the best manner consisting of about an hundred of sorts of fruit. Choice to be taken of twenty thousand plants. ... Whereas Timothy Constable of Long Melford, Nurseryman, is deceased NOTICE is hereby given that his widow and brother carry on the business. Whereas any gentlemen, ladies and others may furnish their gardens or orchards with great choice of fruit trees of the best kinds of by their humble servants, Elizabeth and Thomas Constable.[17]

At least by the early eighteenth century, in other words, a complex network of nurseries existed, some serving local consumers and some, based in London, a wider, national market. Yet people also continued, right through the eighteenth century, to exchange fruit trees or scion wood with friends and neighbours. When Clement Chevallier of Aspall Hall in Suffolk planted his new orchard in 1737/8 it was in part with trees grafted with material obtained from local individuals, such as Peter Karsey, the local carter, or the vicar of the nearby village of Winston.[18] Scattered references suggest that a knowledge of grafting was widespread. The rector of North Runcton in Norfolk, writing in the early eighteenth century, described how one of the trees in his orchard was 'a very coarse Rig setting but as the wind broak it's head in 1720 I grafted it with the best russeting'.[19] Mary Birkhead, as we have seen, was the wife of a minor landowner – a London artist who had purchased a Norfolk farm – and she described in her orchard book how the fruit trees at her daughter's house, planted in the 1720s, had been 'Raised, planted and preserved by my care', how she had grafted many of them herself and how she obtained young trees or scion wood from people in Gorleston, Beccles and elsewhere, evidently reciprocating the favour when required.

This said, the extent of reliance on the kind of specifically *local* exchange necessary to ensure the perpetuation of distinct local varieties should not be over-estimated.[20] By this time even farmers, William Ellis seems to suggest, frequented local nurseries. Indeed, it is possible that, too busy with a wide range of tasks to undertake their own grafting, they actually made more use of commercial nurseries than the aristocracy and upper gentry, who had time on their hands and trained gardeners at their disposal. Some of the 'middling sort', moreover, made use of London nurseries as much as they did of local ones. Mary Birkhead had London connections and the trees growing at the farm she had lived on with

---

17 SRO, B, 2326/3.
18 Private collection: Aspall archive, DC BOX2/1, fol. 84.
19 NRO, PD 332/20.
20 NRO, BRA 926/122.

her first husband, now leased to a tenant, and in her daughter's orchard, included several bought from the Brompton Park nursery; others were grafted with scion wood obtained from trees in her second father-in-law's gardens in Knightsbridge, themselves very probably obtained from a London supplier.[21] All this means that already, by the middle of the eighteenth century, national fashions rather than local traditions were shaping the character of the fruit trees planted in orchards and gardens. To some extent, indeed, varieties of orchard fruit already had an *international* character. In 1696 Richard Godfrey of Hindringham Hall in Norfolk lamented in a letter how the severe frosts were preventing the delivery of fruit trees he had ordered from Holland;[22] in the 1730s the de Nassau family were sourcing fruit trees, including apples and pears, for their house at Panshanger in Hertfordshire from across Europe, including from Bruges, Terneuzen and Tournai.[23] Even farmers planted varieties bearing names at least suggestive of distant origins. Ellis singled out the 'Holland Pippin' and the 'French Pippin' as being particularly popular among his Hertfordshire neighbours.[24] In short, the idea that, even in the period before 1750, people routinely obtained their fruit trees as scion wood from neighbours or friends living in the immediate vicinity, and that their orchards were therefore stocked with specifically local types traditional to the areas in question, needs to be treated with caution. For the period after 1750, when commercial nurseries proliferated and expanded, such a model becomes even harder to sustain.

The development of the nursery industry, c.1750–1840

Small commercial nurseries were certainly widespread in provincial areas by 1700, and in the course of the eighteenth century a number of much larger firms developed in locations distant from the capital. One of the earliest was that established by Thomas Rivers at Sawbridgeworth in Hertfordshire in 1735.[25] The site is clearly shown on Dury and Andrew's map of Hertfordshire, published in 1766, already apparently covering a large area of ground.[26] Rivers may have been attracted to the district by the fertile yet relatively tractable nature of the local boulder-clay soils, but especially perhaps by the ready market offered by the elegant villas that were already beginning to appear in the south of Hertfordshire and Essex, within easy reach of London. His nephew, John Rivers, acquired land at High

---

21 NRO, BRA 926/122.

22 NRO, Y/C 36/15/18.

23 HALS, DE/Na/F49.

24 W. Ellis, *The Modern Husbandman, Complete in 8 Volumes*, vol. 1 (London, 1750), vol. 1, pp. 138–9.

25 E. Waugh, *Rivers Nursery of Sawbridgeworth: The Art of Pomology* (Ware, 2009), p. 25; E. Waugh, 'Planting the Garden: The Nursery Trade in Hertfordshire', in D. Spring (ed.), *Hertfordshire Garden History Volume II: Gardens Pleasant, Groves Delicious* (Hatfield, 2012), pp. 177–201, especially pp. 191–5.

26 A. Macnair, A. Rowe and T. Williamson, *Dury and Andrews' Map of Hertfordshire: Society and Landscape in the Eighteenth Century* (Oxford, 2016), p. 106.

176 The Orchards of Eastern England

Figure 7.1 Extract from a map of 1833, showing the main 'public' area of Mackie's nursery ground in Lakenham, Norwich, which extended over some 48 acres (c.19.5 hectares). Much of the land is laid out on a functional grid plan but note the area of curving drives and fashionably serpentine planting around the entrance. This was evidently designed to display plants to the best advantage and thus to tempt potential purchasers. Norfolk Record Office TRAFF 1075e.

Wych in the parish in 1789, but whether this represents the purchase of property formerly rented or the acquisition of additional land remains unclear.[27] By the time the tithe map for Sawbridgeworth was surveyed in 1840 his son, another Thomas, owned several cottages in the parish, a scatter of other land, and the nursery ground, which covered over 21 acres (8.5 hectares) and which was occupied by his son, Thomas Rivers Junior.[28]

More surprising, perhaps, given its distance from London, was the development of the Norwich Nursery, recently researched by Louise Crawley.[29] In 1759 the Aram family took over John Baldrey's nursery in St Benedicts, Norwich, moving in *c*.1777 to a site in Lakenham, just to the south of the city, where the business remained until 1859. Around the same time William Aram was joined in business by John Mackie, who married Aram's daughter, and, following Aram's death in 1781, the firm was generally known as 'Mackie's'. After John Mackie's death in 1818 the nursery was run by his widow Sarah, whose achievements received fulsome praise, following her own death in 1833, in an obituary in the *Gardener's Magazine*.[30] The company was then run by their children, Frederick and Arthur Mackie, and after 1849 by Arthur alone. Under Sarah the company acquired, in addition to the Lakenham nursery, warehouses at 10 and 11 Exchange Street, Norwich, where most of the actual business was handled. By the start of the nineteenth century the company was operating over a wide area, its advertisements appearing in and its activities being reported by the *Ipswich Journal*, the *Cambridge Intelligencer* and the *Suffolk Chronicle*, and even by the *Stamford Mercury* in Lincolnshire. On occasions it supplied trees even further afield – to the Ffynone estate in Pembrokeshire in 1796 and to the Woburn Abbey estate in Bedfordshire in the 1830s.[31] In the company's 1833 catalogue Frederick Mackie thought it 'necessary to inform his friends at a distance' that it was possible to use the newly improved navigation between Norwich and Lowestoft to send orders, via transhipment to coastal vessels, 'as regularly and cheaply as can be desired' to London, the north of England and elsewhere.[32]

Mackie's business, like others in the period, was fully geared up to entice potential customers. Printed catalogues were issued and the Lakenham site was laid out almost like a modern garden centre (Figure 7.1). The diarist James Woodforde, vicar of Weston Longville, described how in May 1780 he walked 'Out of St Stephens Gates to Aram and Mackie's Garden. Walked over the Gardens and then paid him a bill for Fruit Trees

---

27 HALS, 28111.
28 PRO/TNA, IR29/15/86.
29 L. Crawley, 'The Growth of Provincial Nurseries: Norwich Nurserymen, c.1750–1860', *Garden History*, 48/2 (2020), pp. 119–34.
30 J.C. Loudon, *The Gardener's Magazine and Register of Rural and Domestic Improvement*, 9 (London, 1833), p. 751.
31 National Library of Wales, FFYNONE 2248; BRO, R3/2322 and 2326.
32 J. Harvey, *Early Nursery Catalogues* (Bath, 1972), p. 151.

&c. Gave also to the men working in the gardens 0.1.6.'[33] But visits did not need to be undertaken on foot. In 1811 Nicholas Styleman of Heacham in west Norfolk 'drove round both Mackie's nursery grounds and towards Lakenham'. The *Norfolk News*, reporting in 1849 on one of the horticultural shows held there, described how the nursery was 'encompassed by a drive of one mile in length' designed to display to best effect the fruit and forest trees and ornamental shrubs.[34] The business was sophisticated in other ways. In 1781 Woodforde described a personal visit from William Aram, who provided advice on how to protect fruit trees from ants (he described Aram, who died soon afterwards, as 'a very hearty man … very large and looks as if he was dropsical').[35] The company even appears to have operated some kind of mobile pruning service, to judge from payments listed in the decades around 1800 in the accounts of several estates – one as far away as Anmer, nearly 50km from Norwich, another at Heacham, 70km distant – to 'Mackie's man' for pruning fruit trees: references that also, perhaps, suggest that this specialist knowledge was not widely disseminated among or fully understood by gardeners at the smaller country houses in this period.[36] Although Mackie's and Rivers' were unquestionably the largest and most sophisticated nursery businesses in the eastern counties by the end of the eighteenth century, others ran them close. James Wood established his nursery at Huntingdon in 1742 and by the 1760s was supplying fruit trees not only to local customers such as Sir Robert Bernard of Brampton Park or Lord Sandwich of Hinchinbrooke but also to more distant ones, such as the Pymm family of Hazells in Bedfordshire and the bishop of Lincoln.[37] The firm continued to operate, as Wood and Ingram, until 1950.

As these large provincial firms developed and expanded through the later eighteenth and early nineteenth centuries smaller local nurseries continued to proliferate, springing up in or just outside every significant market town, although often we know little more than their names, as with the Hertfordshire firms of Abraham Fells and David Newton in Hitchin or the Hertford Nursery, located just outside that town.[38] In Norfolk the county town could boast several commercial nurseries in addition to Mackie's, including those run by the Roe family and, from 1796, that at Catton owned by the renowned horticulturalist George Lindley. In the wider county there was a major nursery at Mundford, a little to

---

33   R.L. Winstanley (ed.), *Parson Woodforde: Diary of the First Six Norfolk Years, 1776–1781*, vol. 3 (London, 1984), p. 44.

34   *Norfolk News*, 28 July 1849.

35   R.L. Winstanley, *Parson Woodforde: Diary of the First Six Norfolk Years, 1776–1781*, vol. 1 (London, 1981), pp. 186–7.

36   Williamson, *The Archaeology of the Landscape Park*, pp. 172–3.

37   J. Drake, *Wood and Ingram: A Huntingdon Nursery, 1742–1950* (Cambridge, 2008).

38   Waugh, 'Planting the Garden', p. 195; B. Howlett, *Hitchin Priory and Park: The History of a Landscape Park and Gardens* (Hitchin, 2004), pp. 56, 57 and 61.

the north of Thetford, run by William Griffin from before 1758 until at least 1809; it was subsequently taken over by one William Kedie. Even the more remote examples of these businesses held substantial quantities of trees, shrubs and other plants. When that run by Frederick Fitt at Hoveton in east Norfolk through the 1770s and 1780s went bankrupt in 1793 the stock included, besides ornamental shrubs and greenhouse plants, 'upwards of 20,000 forest and fruit trees'. All were to be sold 'exceedingly cheap, the proprietor being under the necessity of clearing the ground'.[39] Many of these smaller nurseries, such as the firm of Fenn and Laws in Beccles, Suffolk, were by the early years of the nineteenth century producing printed catalogues.[40] And many were likewise long-lived businesses, passing through several generations of the same family. William Woods appears to have established his nursery at Woodbridge in Suffolk in 1749. In 1798 it was being run by John and William Woods, and it continued to be run by members of the family until taken over by the firm of Notcutts in 1909.[41] The nursery run by Timothy Coleman in Long Melford in Suffolk, already noted, was continued after his death in 1751 by his widow Elizabeth and brother Thomas, and subsequently by his son, another Timothy Coleman, who was still proprietor in 1798.[42]

Some of these local firms supplied not only private customers but early commercial orchards. South Cambridgeshire, as we have seen, was beginning to emerge as a plum- and apple-producing district by the early nineteenth century. In 1826, following the death of its proprietor, James Wright, the stock of the Melbourn Nursery was put on the market, the bulk made up of over a thousand fruit trees, mainly plums and apples.[43] Thirteen years later, again following the death of its proprietor, the stock of a nursery at nearby Bassingbourn was auctioned off. It consisted entirely of '2000 Thrifty, dwarf and standard apple and pear trees. In sorts from 5 to 15 years old. The trees will be sold in half rows about one hundred in a lot; they were selected with great care by the late proprietor of the nursery, and we strongly recommend for early fruiting.'[44] There are references in the accounts of Norfolk and Suffolk estates to nurseries based in Wisbech, King's Lynn and Downham Market on the margins of the northern silt fens, whose presence may be related in large part to the rising importance of the area's fruit-growing industry.[45]

Small nurseries as much as the larger ones developed new fruit varieties – or marketed ones that had arisen spontaneously in their districts. James Coe was operating as a

---

39 *Norwich Mercury*, 11 February 1793.
40 NRO, WGN 5/3/10; IRO, B1 9.
41 T. Williamson, *Suffolk's Gardens and Parks: Designed Landscapes from the Tudors to the Victorians* (Macclesfield, 2000), pp. 144–5.
42 Williamson, *Suffolk's Gardens and Parks*, p. 145.
43 CRO, 296/B 693.
44 CRO, 296/B 727.
45 Williamson, *Archaeology of the Landscape Park*, pp. 170–4.

nurseryman in Bury St Edmunds by the 1760s and his business was continued into the nineteenth century by his son, Jarvis, who advertised regularly in the local press. In 1802 he boasted of his collection of 'Hot-house and Green-house Plants, seeds of all kinds, Flowers, Fruit Trees, Shrubs, and Herbaceous Plants'.[46] Jarvis, or Jervais as he is sometimes known, was responsible for developing at least two new varieties of plum: the St Martin, a culinary variety, and the Golden Drop, a fine dessert plum that was never very widely grown in England – it needs a good, warm summer to ripen to perfection – but which was being extensively cultivated in California and other warm regions by the end of the nineteenth century.[47] In a similar way, the Sturmer Pippin, a highly successful dessert apple, was first raised by the nurseryman Ezekiel Dillistone some time around 1800 in the Suffolk village of Sturmer, probably by crossing two well-established varieties, the Ribston Pippin and the Nonpareil,[48] and the lost Waltham Abbey Seedling was raised at Waltham Abbey by John Barnard in 1810.[49] Often, the more promising of such new varieties were taken up and marketed by one of the larger concerns. The apple known by the picturesque name of 'D'Arcy Spice' – noted for its sweet, firm, rather aromatic flesh – is traditionally said to have been discovered in the garden of Tolleshunt d'Arcy Hall near Colchester around 1785, but it may have earlier origins. The apple was marketed by John Harris of Bromefield under the name 'Baddow Pippin' around 1848, but from the 1850s it was being sold by Rivers nursery, over the county boundary in Hertfordshire, initially under the name 'Spring Ribston'.[50]

More importantly, in this commercialised and competitive world, varieties first developed in very distant parts of the country might be taken up and marketed by nurseries in eastern England. In 1790, for example, William Wood of Huntingdon introduced to the market a seedling of the Golden Pippin from Court of Wick in Somerset, under the name of 'Wood's Huntingdon' (now known as Court of Wick, the variety is still widely planted in gardens today). In the case of the larger nursery companies, indeed, the sheer number of different varieties on offer would have precluded any exclusive focus on local types. Mackie's printed catalogue from 1790 offered no fewer than 111 different kinds of apple alone.[51] Provincial and local nurseries were especially keen to emphasise that their fruit trees were derived from more fashionable parts, from London or abroad. The printed catalogue of pear and fruit trees produced by Mackie's in 1835 proudly stated that they had

---

46 *Bury and Norwich Post*, 13 January 1802, p. 2, col. 5.
47 *The Florist, Fruitist and Garden Miscellany* (London, 1854), p. 277.
48 B. Maund, *A Treatise on Orchard and Garden Fruits: Their Description, History and Management* (London, n.d. *c*.1851), p. 41.
49 R. Hogg and G. Bull, *The Herefordshire Pomona*, vol 2 (Hereford, 1885), plate 17, no. 2.
50 Morgan and Richards, *New Book of Apples*, p. 204.
51 John Mackie and Sons catalogue, 1790, <https://archive.org/details/JohnMackieSonsNorwichACatalogueOfForestTreesFruitTreesEvergreenAndFloweringShrubs1790/page/n85>, accessed 9 March 2021.

been selected from the great number of *New Varieties* raised by Mr LEONARD PHILLIPS, of the Exhibition of Fruit Trees, Vauxhall, near London, who among numerous honorary marks of approbation conferred upon him by Public Societies, &c. has been presented with two Gold Medals, for the merit he has shewn in his Establishment … .[52]

Any commercial emphasis on the specifically local was also eroded by the fact that fruit trees were often sent from one nursery to another, often over considerable distances, when they lacked sufficient stock to meet demand. In the 1760s Wood's nursery at Huntingdon was obtaining fruit trees from Hewitt's in London.[53]

Increasing commercialisation did not, of course, end the informal exchange of fruit trees or scion wood and, among the wealthy, this continued to operate over considerable distances, further casting doubt on the importance of specifically local varieties in orchards and gardens. In 1807 William Gunn of Smallburgh in Norfolk, the amateur architect and brother of the owner of Sloley Hall, despatched to Thomas Hearn of Buckingham 'some beefing plants, Ribstone pippins, and another non-pareil called the Summer, with instructions for planting'.[54] Between 1811 and 1838 Lord Bristol of Ickworth Hall in Suffolk corresponded regularly with the noted horticulturalist and botanist Thomas Knight, president of the Royal Horticultural Society and author of both *A Treatise on the Culture of the Apple and Pear* and *On the Manufacture of Cider and Perry*, and many of their letters concern the sourcing of fruit trees. In 1824, for example, Knight informed him that he had received from contacts abroad

Many varieties of fruit and some of great excellence which the public nurseries do not afford, or at least from which there is much uncertainty of obtaining them. I have pears which ripen in succession from October to May, all of the melting kinds and all nearly equally excellent which I received from a correspondent in Belgium … The Belgian pears are not only most excellent but the varieties are very productive many succeeding well as standard trees.

He promised to forward young plants of an Italian apple, the Mela Carla, in the autumn.[55]

The orchards of eastern England might, by the start of the nineteenth century, thus include fruit with very distant origins, so that, in 1815, in the village of Thwaite in Norfolk, a member of the Gamble family was able to make a list of the 'American Apple Trees' planted in their orchard or garden (Large Yellow Newtown Pippin, Bellflower, 'Gilpin or Carthouse', Redling, Pennock's Large Red Winter, Wine Apple and Green Newtown Wonder).[56]

---

52   SRO, I, HA 11/B1/9/1–13.
53   Drake, *Wood and Ingram*, pp. 14–15.
54   NRO, WGN 5/3/10.
55   SRO, B, 941/56/25.
56   NRO, BRA 926/ XXVIII/121/11.

Nurseries after 1840

The larger nurseries already discussed continued to flourish right through the nineteenth and, in many cases, into the twentieth century, while smaller firms continued to proliferate, some expanding to join the ranks of the big concerns. Rivers of Sawbridgeworth thus went from strength to strength. Under the direction of Thomas Rivers (1798–1877) – who took over the business in 1837 – the company became one of the foremost suppliers of roses and fruit trees in the country (provision of the two often went hand in hand, as both involved the skill of grafting).[57] It developed numerous new varieties of fruit, including the immensely successful Early Rivers' plum. A correspondent of Darwin, Rivers was particularly interested in the identification and classification of fruit, proposing the establishment of a pomological society in 1854 in part to ensure some standardisation of the names given to apple varieties in different parts of England.[58] The first meeting of the British Pomological Society was held the following year. Rivers also wrote numerous articles in horticultural journals and was the author of three books – *The Rose Amateurs' Guide*, *The Miniature Fruit Garden* and *The Orchard House, or the Cultivation of Fruit Trees in Pots Under Glass* – all evidently directed at a middle-class audience as much as at the owners and head gardeners of great estates.[59]

Rivers actively sought to establish improved varieties by both selection and deliberate cross-breeding, and was most successful with Early Favourite and Early Prolific plums. He also introduced a number of new plum varieties from abroad, such as Precoce de Tour and Reine Claude Diaphane, further selecting and breeding from them and often changing their names. In addition, Rivers oversaw the development of new varieties of cherry and, in particular, of pear, travelling to France and Belgium to collect varieties (especially of the soft *beurré* pears) which he then propagated and marketed. His son Thomas Frances Rivers developed the Conference pear, a mid-season dessert variety that is now the most widely grown in England. It was so named because it was first exhibited at the pear conference held by the Royal Horticultural Society in 1888 at Chiswick to discuss the threat already faced by commercial fruit growers from imported American and Canadian fruit.[60] In contrast, the company was not a great breeder of apples, although it was responsible for the varieties Rivers' Early Peach, Thomas Rivers, Rivers' St Martins, New Hawthornden and Rivers' Nonsuch. The nursery was also the first to market Cox's Orange Pippin, first grown as a seedling by Richard Cox in Buckinghamshire.

---

57   Waugh, *Rivers Nursery*, pp. 82–95.

58   Waugh, 'Planting the Garden', p. 194; Waugh, *Rivers Nursery*, pp. 95–100.

59   Rivers, *The Orchard House*; T. Rivers, *Miniature Fruit Garden; or the Culture of Pyramidal Fruit Trees* (London, 1840).

60   Waugh, *Rivers Nursery*, pp. 103–5; P. Read, 'The Rescued Orchard and the Rivers Heritage', in Waugh, *Rivers Nursery*, pp. 184–200.

Figure 7.2 Although Rivers Nursery at Sawbridgeworth in Hertfordshire was closed in 1987, much of the area occupied by fruit trees, supplying scion wood for grafting, still remains.

At its peak Rivers was a large business: in the years around 1900, 20,000 Early Prolific and Early Favourite bare-rooted plums were dispatched by the nursery each autumn.[61] By this stage, but perhaps much earlier, substantial beech hedges sheltered the main growing areas, in which the young trees were brought to maturity.[62] Young fruit trees were sent not only to private customers but to other commercial nurseries, such as Wood and Ingram in Huntingdon. By the end of the nineteenth century Rivers nursery contained two separate areas of glass houses: one behind Bonks Hill House, where the Rivers family had their home, and one on the southern edge of the nursery, beside the road from Sawbridgeworth to High Wych. As we might expect, the fruit cultivated within them mainly comprised exotics such as oranges, lemons, figs, grapes, peaches and nectarines. But apples were also grown, on dwarf 'paradise' rootstocks. Thomas Rivers described how 'a few delicious American varieties' benefited from the method, including Newtown Pippin, Northern Spy and Melon apple, as well as the Italian variety Mela Carla.[63] The company continued to operate until 1987. Parts of the nursery grounds survive, densely planted with fruit trees (Figure 7.2). The site has been studied, and is being actively preserved, by a dedicated group of volunteers, but faces an uncertain future.[64]

---

61   Waugh, *Rivers Nursery*, p. 42.

62   J. Fitzgerald, 'Hedges and their Importance on the Rivers Nursery Site', in Waugh, *Rivers Nursery*, pp. 180–2.

63   Rivers, *The Orchard House*, p. 71.

64   See Waugh, *Rivers Nursery*.

Figure 7.3 Mackie's nursery at Bracondale, just outside Norwich, photographed in c.1855 by Mackie's business partner, John Stewart.

In Norwich, Mackie's nursery also continued to flourish, at least for a time. In 1849 the business, now run by Arthur Mackie, acquired John Bell's nursery ground in Bracondale on the southern edge of the city and, by c.1855 (to judge from a photograph taken by Mackie's business partner John Stewart (Figure 7.3)), this was liberally provided with glasshouses and cold frames, apparently installed by the previous owner (to judge from a trade card from c.1830 and the tithe map of 1843).[65] 'Hothouse grapes' were among the products marketed by Mackie in the middle decades of the century.[66] The Bracondale site had doubled in size by the time the Ordnance Survey 25-inch map was made in the 1880s. The nursery's Lakenham site, meanwhile, continued to provide fruit trees, as well as forest trees and shrubs, with the Bracondale site specialising in bedding plants. Norwich was connected to the rail network in 1845 and by direct line to London four years later, and the nursery's advertisements made much of the 'great facilities for the speedy and cheap transit of nursery goods' thus provided. 'Large quantities of trees and other plants' could now be

---

65   Norfolk County Council, 'Picture Norfolk' archive, 727934; private collection; and NRO, N/S17/39.

66   Crawley, 'The Growth of Provincial Nurseries', p. 123.

Figure 7.4 One of the catalogues produced by Daniels Brothers of Norwich, presented as a magazine for the amateur gardener. By the late nineteenth century commercial nurseries were competing hard for the attention of middle-class customers.

sent to London free of carriage charge to the customer.⁶⁷ In 1859, after four generations of being run (often in partnerships) by members of the Mackie family, the nursery was sold to John Bell – previous proprietor of the Bracondale ground – and the family emigrated to America. Bell continued to trade until his death in 1870. The Bracondale site was then sold for housing, but part of the Lakenham ground became the Town Close Nurseries, operated by the Daniels Brothers.

The Daniels Brothers company, established by George and Charles Daniels in the 1870s, was based in Bedford Street, Norwich, and sold a wide range of seeds, bulbs and plants. They were responsible for introducing a number of new fruit varieties, including in 1890 the apple known as Vicar of Beighton, which had been raised as a seedling a few years earlier in the garden of the vicarage in the village of that name. The brothers went bankrupt in 1881 but soon recovered, building up an extensive business in East Anglia through the late nineteenth and early twentieth centuries. From the 1880s they made the most of their status as suppliers of plants to the royal residence at Sandringham, issuing annual catalogues with covers carefully designed to appeal to middle-class consumers (Figure 7.4).⁶⁸ They continued to trade for a century, much of their business involving the supply of fruit trees, until their nursery site was bought by Notcutts of Woodbridge in 1976.⁶⁹

The middle and later decades of the nineteenth century saw the emergence or development of several other major nursery companies, some of particular significance in the history of fruit trees and orchards. Lane's of Berkhamsted, in Hertfordshire, was established by Henry Lane around 1777 in St John's Well Lane and was continued by his son, also Henry. It expanded considerably under John Edward Lane from the 1840s, becoming one of the town's principal employers (Figure 7.5).⁷⁰ Lane had a number of business interests – he described himself as 'nurseryman, florist, hotelier and farmer'⁷¹ – but his main concern was horticulture. Some of his nurseries were located to either side of the town's High Street; others were in the outlying hamlets of Gossom's End and Potten End. The latter was known as 'Balshaw Nurseries', as it occupied ground rented from the charity of that name; much of the other land was leased from the Ashridge estate.⁷² By the time of his death in 1889 John Lane was renting 142 acres (58 hectares) from the estate, of which roughly half comprised nursery grounds and around 2 acres orchards.⁷³ He

---

67 *Cambridge General Advertiser*, 10 December 1845.
68 NRO, Acc 2009/369; 2022/23; Gressenhall Museum, Norfolk, garden ephemera collection; *London Gazette*, 23 September 1881, pp. 4834, <https://www.thegazette.co.uk/London/issue/25018/page/4834/data.pdf>, accessed 27 March 2021.
69 Crawley, 'The Growth of Provincial Nurseries', p. 127.
70 *Berkhamsted Review*, August 1974.
71 HALS, DE/Ls/P6.
72 Dacorum Heritage Centre BK 3906.111 and Prop AF 1–10; HALS, AH 248–50, 255.
73 Dacorum Heritage Centre BK 3906.360.9.

Figure 7.5 Lane's of Berkhamsted, in Hertfordshire, like a number of commercial nurseries, branched out into commercial fruit production in the late nineteenth century. Undated photograph of workers in the company's orchards at Berkhamsted.

also owned four public houses in the neighbourhood, various parcels of land, a number of houses and a further 13 acres of orchard, 'planted with trees (now in full growth)'.[74] From 1889 the company was run by Frederick Quincy Lane, who further expanded the fruit-growing side of the business.[75] By 1902 the company reputedly had 20,000 apple, pear, plum and cherry trees growing on 60 acres (24 hectares) of land, as well as 15 acres (6 hectares) devoted to cobnuts. Most of the fruit was sent to Manchester and neighbouring industrial towns – the orchards were only a short distance from Berkhamsted station, on the direct line to the north-west of England.[76] Such an involvement in both the nursery business and in commercial fruit production was mirrored by several smaller companies in the decades around 1900, including Taylor's of Kings Lynn in Norfolk.[77]

74 *Buckinghamshire Herald*, March 1890.
75 HALS, DE/Ls/B517.
76 *Berkhamsted Review*, July 1902: Dacorum Heritage Centre, 1116.04.
77 Information from Peter Woodrow; the Taylors were primarily seedsmen, established at Wiggenhall St Germans as early as 1770. There is a useful collection of material relating to them at Gressenhall Museum, near East Dereham, Norfolk.

Figure 7.6 Lane's Prince Albert, the fine cooking apple developed by Lane's of Berkhamsted in Hertfordshire.

Lane's declined in the 1920s and 1930s and closed shortly after the end of the Second World War. Although famous for its grapevines, which were exported to France, Germany and other wine-producing countries, the company was best known in England for an apple known as Lane's Prince Albert. This was discovered by Thomas Squire, a keen amateur gardener in Berkhamsted, growing in the garden of a house called The Homestead. He propagated the tree and named it 'Victoria and Albert' following the visit of the queen and the prince consort to the town on 26 July 1841. The apple was marketed from the early 1850s by Lane's as 'Britain's Latest Apple': it is a good-sized cooker, juicy and rather acidic, that has been very widely planted (Figure 7.6).[78] Lane's also put other apple varieties on the market, notably Oakland Seedling and Lane's Prolific.

The nursery that made the greatest contribution to new varieties in the eastern counties was, however, probably Laxton's of Bedford. The firm was founded by Thomas Laxton, who was born in Tinwell in the county of Rutland and worked as a solicitor before developing an interest in botany and, in particular, plant hybridisation, corresponding for a time with Charles Darwin. By 1879 he had moved to Bedford and set up business as a 'seed grower and merchant' in Harpur Street, where he concentrated in particular on developing new varieties of strawberry. But under his two sons, Edward Augustine Lowe Laxton and William Hudson Lowe Laxton, the family became more closely associated with the development of novel varieties of apple, pear and plum. The brothers went into business together – as Laxton Brothers – in Bedford in 1888. Using the breeding methods developed by their father they were responsible for producing no fewer than 22 new varieties of apple, eight of pear and 18 of plum (as well as further new types of strawberry). Originally based in Bromham Road in Bedford, they subsequently opened a shop at 63a High Street and by 1900 operated the 140-acre (57-hectare) Tollgate Nursery in Goldington Road.[79]

Some of the most successful fruit varieties in history, many still widely cultivated today, were produced by the company, mainly in the three decades between 1895 and 1925. The apples were mostly dessert varieties, such as Laxton's Superb (1897), Epicure (1904), Fortune (1904), Lord Lambourne (1907) and Laxton's Favourite (1925) (Figure 7.7). They were generally developed by cross-pollinating established varieties. Laxton's Fortune, for example – a sweet apple with a pale yellow skin mottled with flecks of red – was a cross between Cox's Orange Pippin and Wealthy; Lord Lambourne, a rather aromatic apple with greenish flesh and a golden skin, flushed maroon, was the result of crossing James Grieve with Worcester Pearmain. Catalogues suggest that these dessert novelties were largely developed with an eye to the domestic grower, although many were also cultivated on a commercial scale. The most successful of Laxton's plum varieties were perhaps Early

---

78 <https://www.fruitid.com/#view/670>.
79 B. Ricketts, 'The Laxtons in Bedford (1879–1957)', *Bedford Architectural Archaeological & Local History Society, Newsletter*, 82 (October 2008), pp. 14–28; <http://virtual-library.culturalservices.net/webingres/bedfordshire/vlib/0.digitised_resources/high_street_history_laxton.htm>, accessed 10 March 2021.

Figure 7.7 'Superb', first marketed in 1897, is one of the most successful of the apple varieties developed by Laxton's of Bedford.

Laxton, first marketed in 1916, a medium-sized yellow-skinned dessert plum with juicy, slightly pinkish flesh, which was a cross of Catalonia and Early Rivers', and Laxton's Cropper, a cross of the Victoria plum and the Aylesbury Prune, which is a fairly large, blue-black cooking plum, first marketed in 1906.[80] After several decades of success the business came to an end in 1957, when it went into voluntary liquidation and the shop and nursery were sold.

The Seabrook family, like the Lanes, were both commercial fruit growers and fruit breeders. They planted, as we saw earlier, vast areas of commercial orchard in central Essex from the late nineteenth century. But they also introduced many new varieties, of apple especially, in the late nineteenth and the first half of the twentieth century, which they propagated and sold to other producers and to the general public, including Monarch (1888); Excelsior (1921); Flame (1925); Seabrook's Red (1925); Garnet (1936); Opal (1936); Pearl (1938); Acme (1944); and Eros (1947).[81] Monarch was particularly successful. It was widely grown in the orchards of south and central Essex and was especially popular during the Second World War, as it is sweet when cooked and thus required little additional sugar.[82]

The numerous smaller nurseries and individual nurserymen that existed all over eastern England by the middle of the nineteenth century also continued to develop new varieties of fruit. The Brownlees' Russet, for example – an intensely flavoured, juicy and rather acidic dessert apple – was raised in 1848 by the Hemel Hempstead nurseryman William Brownlees.[83] The immensely successful culinary apple now known as Emneth Early, but originally as Early Victoria, was developed around 1897 by William Lynn of Emneth near Wisbech by crossing Lord Grosvenor and Keswick Codlin.[84] The nursery run by Mr Thorington of Hornchurch near London produced Sunburn and Edith Hopwood in the 1920s. In many cases new varieties continued to arise by chance, as we saw in the case of Lane's Prince Albert. The apple known as Discovery was found in 1949 by a Mr Dummer of Langham in Suffolk, growing from a Worcester Pearmain pip, and was marketed by Jack Matthews of Thurston, initially under the name Thurston August (it matures extremely early).[85] Some new varieties were developed by companies whose main interests lay in some other fruit-related industry. Chivers', the Cambridgeshire jam company, marketed the apples Histon Favourite from the 1860s and Chivers Delight from *c.*1920.

---

80 Ricketts, 'The Laxtons in Bedford'; R. Wildman, 'Laxton of Bedford: The Family and Firm', *Bedfordshire Magazine*, 23/182 (1992), pp. 244–7; S. Readman, 'Laxton of Bedford: Pioneers of Plant-breeding', *Bedfordshire Magazine*, 23/182 (1992), pp. 250–5; <http://virtual-library.culturalservices.net/webingres/bedfordshire/vlib/0.digitised_resources/high_street_history_laxton.htm>.

81 Morgan and Richards, *New Book of Apples*, pp. 183, 211, 213, 216, 244, 249, 251 and 266.

82 <https://www.fruitid.com/#view/723>, accessed 3 October 2020.

83 Morgan and Richards, *The New Book of Apples*, p. 195.

84 <https://www.fruitid.com/#view/567>, accessed 3 October 2020.

85 Morgan and Richards, *The New Book of Apples*, p. 206.

We have devoted several pages to the development of the nursery industry in the eastern counties because of the widespread tendency to see old fruit varieties as intrinsically 'local' and 'traditional'. In fact, while some fruit varieties will always have been propagated by grafts and exchanged on a casual basis between neighbours, commercial nurseries were already widely established by the start of the eighteenth century and by the end of that century offered a wide range of varieties for sale, most of which were available throughout the country. With the arrival of the railways, moreover, orders could be dispatched with ease to ever more distant customers. Fruit trees raised by the firm of Bunyard's of Kent, for example, were marketed throughout the eastern counties: their 1893 catalogue included testimonials from satisfied customers living as far away as Hingham, Banham and Ketteringham in Norfolk.[86] In an atmosphere of intense commercial competition, new varieties were introduced at an ever-increasing rate and the numbers supplied by the larger firms had, by the last decades of the nineteenth century, reached dizzying heights. Lane's catalogue for 1862 includes no fewer than 100 varieties of apple;[87] Daniels' were advertising 128 apple varieties by 1878;[88] Rivers were supplying 113 in 1861, rising to 132 by 1870 and reaching 161 by 1914.[89] Pearson's, based just outside the region in Nottingham, were advertising the same number in 1906;[90] Bunyard's of Kent were selling no fewer than 192 in 1894 and 179 in 1900.[91] It is against this wider background – the early development of commercial nurseries, the emergence of large provincial companies in the course of the eighteenth century and the intense competition for customers in the nineteenth – that we need to examine the character and development of the fruit varieties planted in the orchards of eastern England.

The early development of fruit varieties

Two main sources can be employed to investigate this topic. Firstly, there are a number of written records listing the types of fruit growing in orchards (and gardens) or acquired for them from commercial suppliers or private individuals. Most of these date from the nineteenth century but a significant number survive from before this time. Secondly, we have a substantial number of catalogues produced by commercial nurseries such as Mackie's, Rivers or Laxton's. There are relatively few of these dating to the period before *c*.1800, and several of those that do fail to provide names for the varieties being offered for sale: Mackie's 1790 catalogue and John Lindley's combined orchard plan and catalogue

---

86   Bunyard Fruit Catalogue, Royal Horticultural Society, Lindley Library.

87   Lane's Fruit catalogue, Dacorum Heritage Centre, no catalogue number.

88   Daniel Brothers, 'The Illustrated Guide for Amateur Gardeners' (Norwich, 1878); consulted at Gressenhall Rural Life Museum, Norfolk.

89   Rivers Fruit Catalogue, John Innes Library, Norwich.

90   Pearson's Fruit Catalogue, Royal Horticultural Society, Lindley Library.

91   Bunyard Fruit Catalogue, Royal Horticultural Society, Lindley Library.

of 1796 are the most useful.[92] The information we have is, however, numerically biased towards apples, which feature more prominently than other fruit in documentary sources for the simple reason that they were always the most numerous fruit planted in orchards, and these will be our principal concern in the discussion that follows. Moreover, we should also note at this point the important distinction between a particular variety of fruit, with a specific genetic character, and the name by which it is known at a particular time or place. As we have seen in the case of, for example, D'Arcy Spice, names might be changed for commercial or other reasons.

We may begin by considering the apples grown in orchards attached to farms and other relatively modest houses. In 1734 Mary Birkhead listed the fruit trees growing in the gardens and orchards of two properties in Thwaite in Norfolk – her daughter's new house and her own former home, a farmhouse now let to a tenant.[93] There were in all around 48 varieties of apple (there is a degree of uncertainty over whether some of the names listed are pears). What is immediately striking is how different they are from the kinds of apple found in orchards a century later, or which might be brought for identification at a modern 'Apple Day'. Indeed, only around four or five appear among the 140-odd varieties described in Clark's *Apples: a field guide*.[94] While perhaps 20 can be confidently and easily identified with fruit named in Mackie's catalogue of 1790, in George Lindley's catalogue of 1796 or in such nineteenth-century texts as Robert Hogg's *British Pomology* of 1851, and a further six can be so identified but with rather less confidence, the remainder are otherwise unknown.[95] The identifiable varieties can be divided into three broad groups. Firstly, there are ones with rather vague and descriptive names, such as Golden Pippin, Golden Pearmain, Nonpareil, 'Ariomatic Russeting' and Dutch Pippin, which, as we will see, appear regularly in other contemporary lists. Secondly, there are at least four that are today – and have been since the nineteenth century – generally considered as specifically 'Norfolk' or at least East Anglian types – Biefen (Beefing), Dr Harvey, 'Magiton' and 'Colman' (Magiton is presumably the Winter Majetin, described by Lindley as a 'Norfolk apple'; Colman is Lindley's Winter Colman or Norfolk Colman).[96] The third group, however, comprises varieties with names suggesting more distant origins, such as Keswick, Isle of Wight or Paris Apple; or which are known to be products of particular nurseries, such as the Spice Apple, raised at Brompton Park; or which are old varieties distinguished from those in

---

92 George Lindley, catalogue and plan of an orchard, 1796, NRO, COL 9/96; Mackie's catalogue for 1790, <https://archive.org/details/JohnMackieSonsNorwichACatalogueOfForestTreesFruitTreesEvergreenAndFloweringShrubs1790/>, accessed December 2019.

93 There are two notebooks, similar but not identical in content: NRO, BRA 926/121/2 and BRA 926/122.

94 Clark, *Apples*.

95 Hogg, *British Pomology*; R. Hogg, *The Fruit Manual: Containing the Descriptions and Synonyms of the Fruits and Fruit Trees of Great Britain* (London, 1860).

96 George Lindley, catalogue and plan of an orchard, 1796, NRO, COL 9/96.

the first category by having more distinctive, less vague or less generic names, such as Juliflower (July Flower) or Joaneting, and which are again recorded widely across England in the eighteenth century.[97]

This leaves no fewer than 22 varieties that appear to be otherwise unknown, and which do not seem to appear in Mackie's catalogue, Hogg or similar late eighteenth- or nineteenth-century lists. These, too, can be roughly subdivided. Some have names that refer to places well outside the eastern counties – Gottenbury (perhaps a version of Gothenburg?) Apple, Egypt Apple, Oxford Apple, 'Red Lyons, from France', Westbery Apple, Lincolnshire Apple, Arundel Apple, Welch Apple. Others bear names that are simply descriptive (Best Pearmain, Grey Pipen, White Apple, Sower Apple, Bloody Apple). A number have fanciful appellations, homely in character: the Good Housewife, Maid's Pippin, Lady's Longing. A few are named after individuals, such as Rivet's Apple or Jack Holland. These latter examples may represent well-established varieties now lost, which were developed and marketed by the individuals in question, but in some cases this seems unlikely. 'Mr Walker's Apple', for example, suggests perhaps the name of a neighbour. A local origin is certainly implied by the striking names of four of the varieties – Thwaite, Free Thorpe, Corton and Halvergate – all of which reference Norfolk or Suffolk villages lying within 20km of the orchards described by Birkhead.

A much shorter but slightly earlier list comes from Westmill in north-east Hertfordshire.[98] Drawn up in 1710, it itemises the various trees growing in the grounds of the parsonage house. There were ten apple trees of six varieties. Of these, Golden Pippin and Nonpareil again feature prominently but the others are more obscure. White Pippin may be an alternative name for the Norfolk Stone Pippin, but, if so, the variety was here a very long way from its supposed traditional home.[99] Spencer's Pippin is an obscure dual-use variety described by Hogg. The identity of the Spiced Russeting remains unclear.[100] The Girton Pippin is interesting because it bears, once again, the name of a village lying at no great distance – in Cambridgeshire, some 35km to the north. Rather different is a list drawn up of fruit planted in the rectory orchard at North Runcton in Norfolk in 1719–20.[101] In this case, the varieties are all easily recognisable from sources such as Mackie's 1790 catalogue or Hogg's volumes, and are mostly ones with rather vague and generic names such as Royal Pearmain, Golden Rennet (Reinette), Golden Pippin, Winter Pearmain and Golden Russeting. Lastly, we have a list of the apple varieties – nine in all – planted in 1753 in the new orchard (15 trees) and in 1758 in the garden (16 trees) of a house in Carleton Rode

---

97   Hogg, *British Pomology, passim*.
98   HALS, DP/120/3/1.
99   Hogg, *British Pomology*, p. 147.
100 Hogg, *British Pomology*, p. 272.
101 NRO, PD 332/20.

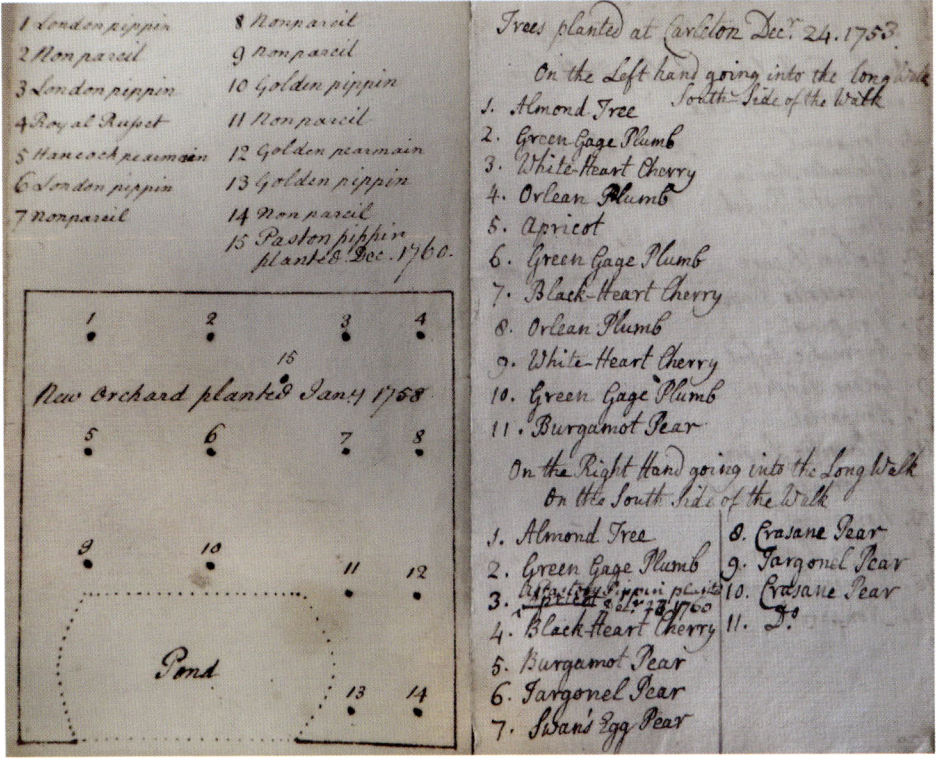

Figure 7.8 Plan of orchard and list of fruit trees, Carleton Rode, Norfolk, 1758. Norfolk Record Office PD254/60.

in Norfolk, probably but not certainly the vicarage (Figure 7.8).[102] Here the familiar, rather vague names predominate – 21 of the trees (68 per cent) are made up of Nonpareil, Golden Pippin, Golden Pearmain and Aromatic Russet, together with a single Royal Russet and three examples of London Pippin, both old varieties widely planted in England.[103] Others are more obscure. The Gloucester Pippin may be a synonym for Duchess's Favourite but this does not seem to be recorded before the end of the eighteenth century;[104] Hancock Pearmain is otherwise unknown, while the Paston Pippin, likewise otherwise unrecorded, is presumably of local provenance, the name referencing either the great Paston family, who owned extensive estates in north-east Norfolk until the early eighteenth century, or the village of Paston on the north-east Norfolk coast.

As noted earlier, the larger landowners in the later seventeenth and early eighteenth centuries often sourced most of their fruit from distant sources, especially London nurseries.

---

102 NRO, PD 254/60.

103 Hogg, *British Pomology*, pp. 128 and 175.

104 <https://www.fruitid.com/#view/552>.

But the earliest lists from country houses are, nevertheless, in some respects similar to those from middle-class homes, farms and parsonages. A list of varieties growing in or ordered for the orchard – all of which are probably, although not certainly, apples – was drawn up in 1660 at Ryston Hall in Norfolk.[105] Of the 12 varieties listed, only four or five can be identified with known types: Pomme Royale; Holland Pippin; Jenniting (Joaneting); Goe no Further (probably a synonym for King of Pippins); and Gilliflower.[106] Queene Pippin may be the Queen's that appears in Mackie's 1790 catalogue but most of the others are more difficult to identify. Some have names that appear descriptive (Peare Apple, Marygold, Strawberry), some perhaps of foreign origin (Margeriling). Others appear to be loose references to geographical origins, such as Suffolk Pippin. A second list from Ryston, dating from 1672 and apparently of trees to be ordered from the London nurseryman John Alcock, includes 49 apples of 17 varieties. Of these, six can be identified with fruit listed in the catalogues or described by Hogg or similar sources, such as the by now familiar Winter Pearmain and Golden Pippin, but also the more specific Kirton Pippin, Loan's Pearmain and Harvey (Dr Harvey, often said to be a Norfolk apple). A further two may be old synonyms for known varieties – Cardinal for the Api, Kentish Pippins for Kentish Fillbasket (although the latter is not otherwise recorded before 1782). But the rest have names that are otherwise obscure, including Duxans, Golden Doucet or Ducket, Lording Apple and Russet Pippin: one of these, Winter Russeting, appears in some of the other early local lists just discussed. There are, once again, a number with 'geographic' names, either general (such as Kentish Codling) or specific. One of the latter references a distant place (the Kirkham Apple, presumably named after Kirkham in Lancashire) but one appears to be more local: Wisbish Russetings, presumably from Wisbech, just over the county boundary in Cambridgeshire and, as we have seen, by the eighteenth century the centre of a major fruit-growing area.

Perhaps less interesting are the various apple varieties listed by Sir John Wittewronge of Rothamsted in Hertfordshire in diary entries in the 1680s. These are mainly familiar types such as 'Gilly Flower', Golden Pippin, Golden Russetting and Golden 'Runnett' (Reinette), but also include some with vague appellations such as 'Russet' and 'Russeting'; a few are mentioned by early printed sources (Red Streak, Apple John, Greening); some have apparently descriptive labels (Great Red, Green Pippin) or ones vaguely referencing foreign origins (Normandy Apple); and there is at least one with possible local origins, otherwise undocumented, and named after 'Goody Marrom'.[107] The appearance in this source of Red Streak, a West Country variety, and the 'Normandy Apple' reflects Sir John's interest in cider-making.

The orchard of English apples planted by Clement Chevallier at Aspall in Suffolk in 1737/8 (above, p. 125) is again largely dominated by familiar varieties already encountered in previous lists discussed, and which appear in later catalogues: 'Golden Pipping', or

---

105 NRO, MF/RO 218/7, 219/11, 220/1.

106 Hogg, *British Pomology*, p. 273.

107 Williams and Stevenson, *'Observations of Weather'*, pp. 9, 11, 17, 47, 52–4, 65.

Golden Pippin; 'Golden Pairmain', or Pearmain; 'Golden Runnets', or Reinette; White Russetting; Holland Pippin; and Nonpareil.[108] There were also examples of Beefing, White Pippin, Hollow Crown and 'Jully Flower' (Gillyflower), all of which again appear in at least one of the other lists. A few of the apples may, however, be local types, including 'Look No Further' and 'Good Wives'. Lastly, the apples planted at Hinwick House in Bedfordshire in 1740 similarly included types familiar from other sources, such as Golden Pippin, Holland Pippin, Non Pareil, Royal Russett and Golden Russet, together with some that are not, such as the otherwise unknown Pile's Russet.[109]

Although we have relatively few lists of fruit trees dating to the period before c.1760, a number of observations can usefully be made. Firstly, all the lists feature names that appear neither in the others nor in later sources. Some of these are shared with parishes, generally lying at no great distance – Halvergate, Thwaite, Free Thorpe ('Freethorpe'), Corton, Paston, Girton and Wisbech, among others. These may have been sourced from small local nurseries or – either as young trees or scion wood – from friends and neighbours, having perhaps originated as sports or seedlings in their own orchards. In a similar way, some of the apples named after individuals, such as 'Mr Walker', may well refer to the friends or neighbours from whom they had been obtained, rather than representing varieties named after nurserymen, which were standardised and widely available. Some of the names appear simply descriptive – Sower Apple – and while others may represent lost local varieties they may equally have been bestowed by individual owners or handed down as family traditions – Good Housewife, Lady's Longing.

Secondly, and perhaps more importantly, the majority of the varieties listed are not local to the eastern counties. Some are otherwise unknown, but have names – the Oxford Apple, the Paris Apple – indicating distant origins. Others are old types, such as the July Flower or London Pippin, that are widely recorded in the period across England. Even as early as this, in other words, only a minority of the apples growing in orchards in eastern England appear to be genuinely local. Perhaps the most interesting of these nationally available apples are a group, comprising a small number of recurrent types – Golden Pippin, Holland Pippin, Golden Russeting, Nonpareil, Aromatic Russeting, Golden Pearmain among them – that feature prominently in almost all of the lists. While these also appear in late eighteenth- or nineteenth-century books or catalogues, and many are recognised as defined varieties and still cultivated today, it is possible that in this period such rather vague names may have been used more loosely, for groups of apples with broadly shared characteristics of appearance, flavour, use, fruiting season or storage. Nonpareil and Golden Pippin thus feature particularly prominently (they were the only apples ordered for the gardens at Heydon Hall in Norfolk in 1755),[110] but the former, even when commercially

---

108 Private collection: Aspall archive, DC BOX2/1, fol. 84.
109 BRO, X800/32.
110 NRO, BUL 4/25/8, 605X8.

supplied, may have been a general term for a small, yellow and russetted dessert apple (that is, one in which much of the skin is rough, dull and brownish-yellow), and the latter one for an early-season, yellowish apple for culinary use. It is noteworthy, in this context, that Batty Langley's *Pomona* of 1729 listed only 35 types of apple 'worth our note, for the table or kitchen', most of which bore just these kinds of vaguely descriptive names (some even vaguer, such as 'Codlin' and 'Kitchen Apple'), with only a handful alluding to geographical origins or the individual who first raised or marketed them (Kirton Pippin, Kentish Pippin, Loan's Pearmain, Wheeler's Russet).[111]

The precise character of the common generic types such as Nonpareil or Golden Pippin is uncertain, but before the emergence of large nursery companies outside London, and at a time when many trees were bought from small local nurseries or were grafted from scion wood obtained from friends and relatives, we should not perhaps expect to find precise terminology or, indeed 'varieties' that shared precisely the same genetic characteristics: in 1734 Mary Birkhead remarked that 'I have frequently had the same fruit from several persons by different names.'[112] The rector of North Runcton in Norfolk bemoaned in 1720 how 'The true Aromatick Golden Russeting is so scarce in this Countrey that I perceive they give the name to any ordinary fruit if it have butt a Russett coat.'[113] It is noteworthy that when William Ellis discusses some of these 'varieties' he sometimes employs the plural, as when in 1732 he suggested that many existing orchard trees should be replaced by 'the Golden Rennets, Pippins, and Pearmains'.[114] In the late eighteenth and early nineteenth century strenuous attempts were made to systematise the classification of apple varieties in England that were manifested, in particular, in the publication of George Bradshaw's *Pomona Britannica* of 1812. But some echo of this older nomenclature may have lived on in the multiple subdivisions of what early lists had treated as a single variety of apple, such as the Nonpareil. In 1807 William Gunn of Smallburgh in Norfolk could refer to a 'non-pareil called the Summer'; one of the apples offered for sale by Mackie's in 1835 was described as 'a variety of the Nonpareil'; and some 40 different 'Nonpareils' are listed by Hogg in 1851. Some of these were clearly cultivars that had been recently developed by nurserymen, but others were perhaps the result of classifying as distinct varieties some members of what had formerly been considered a single, broader group of apples.[115]

---

111 B. Langley, *Pomona, or the Fruit Garden Illustrated* (London, 1729), p. 134. He devoted a separate section to western cider apples.

112 NRO, BRA 926 122.

113 NRO, PD 332/20.

114 Ellis, *The Practical Farmer*, p. 179.

115 NRO, WGN 5/3/10; IRO, B1 9; John Mackie and Sons catalogue, 1790, <https://archive.org/details/JohnMackieSonsNorwichACatalogueOfForestTreesFruitTreesEvergreenAndFloweringShrubs1790/page/n85>, accessed 10 March 2021; Hogg, *British Pomology*.

Of course, none of this is to deny that many of the fruit trees planted in eastern orchards before *c.*1750 were varieties in the modern sense, with specific shared genetic characteristics, which had been recently developed by or imported by the big London nurseries. Others probably represent products of small provincial nurseries, since lost or renamed. But many were perhaps something vaguer and more diffuse – or more local, informal and short-lived – in nature. Either way, the most striking feature of the apples named in such early lists is their unfamiliarity. Whether defined varieties propagated by commercial nurseries, short-lived sports and seedlings or broad families of fruit, they belong to a world distant from and very different from our own.

Fruit varieties in the late eighteenth and nineteenth centuries

In 1809 William Wilshere, with the assistance of Henry Hodgson, a Hitchin nurseryman, and another gardener called McIntosh, made a record of all the fruit, mainly apples and pears, growing in his garden and orchard at Hitchin in Hertfordshire.[116] This inventory was revised in September 1814, when some of the identifications were revisited.[117] He listed four Nonpareils, a Lemon Pippin and a 'supposed Lemon Pippin', three Ribston Pippins, a Winter Pippin, a French Pippin, two French Golden Pippins, a Hollow Crown Pippin ('a very good baking apple in November'), a Russet Nonpareil, two Norfolk Buffons (Beefings), a Spice Russet, a Margil, a Duncan Apple, a Catshead, a Bedford Seedling, a tree bearing smallish red apples and two others that could not be identified. The second list added Winter Pearmain and Spice Pippin.[118] Of equal interest is a list of trees planted in 1806 in the orchard of the rectory at Ayot St Lawrence in the same county. This includes 15 varieties: the omnipresent Golden Pippin, Nonpareil and Golden Rennet; Royal Russet; Syke House; Orange Pippin (Blenheim Orange); Beauty of Kent; Court of Wick; Russet Pearmain; Hollow Eyed Pippin, Bell's Pearmain ('a fine kitchen fruit keeps till June'), Bursdorff or Queens; Kentish Nonpareil; and Fair Maid of Wishford.[119] In the parsonage orchard in West Thurrock, Essex, in 1825 there were examples of Hawthorn Dean (Hawthornden), Ribston Pippin, Nonpareil Russet, Golden Rennet, 'Paradise Apple', Golden Pippin, Winter Pearmain, Lemon Pippin, 'Sykes' (i.e., Sykehouse) Russet and Royal Russet; while the orchard at Wood House, Kelvedon, was planted in 1831 with Abram Fairhead, Blenheim Orange, Court of Wycke, Hawthornden, Keswick Codlin, London Pippin, Nonpareil, Norfolk Biffen (Beefing), Ribston Pippin, Sach's Pearmain, Seek No Further, Wheeler's Russet and Winter Pearmain.[120] Lastly, the apple trees

---

116   HALS, 61181. Our thanks to Bridget Howlett for alerting us to this source.

117   HALS, 60158.

118   Hollow Crown Pippin is probably the old Norfolk variety Hollow Eyed Pippin; Spice Pippin is presumably different from the apple of that name exhibited at the Royal Horticultural Society show in 1897.

119   HALS, DP/10/1/3. Bell's Pearmain was listed in Scott's Orchardist of 1872, but seems otherwise unknown.

120   ERO, D/P 374/1/5 and D/DBm E/18; both lists are analysed in an excellent article by Neil Wiffen, '"An Account of Dwarf Apple trees Planted": A Scheme for Kelvedon', *Essex Journal*, 54/2 (2019), pp. 76–83.

planted in a new orchard at Hasketon in Suffolk in 1814 comprised 27 different varieties of apple.[121] More than a third were members of the familiar, rather standardised 'core' types, including Nonpareil (most numerous), Golden Rennet, Royal Russett, Golden Pippin, Winter Pearmain, French Pippin, Nonsuch and Golden Pearmain, or were the kinds of long-established but perhaps more closely defined variety frequent in earlier lists, such as London Pippin. These were accompanied by examples of Ribston Pippin, Sykehouse Russet, Wheeler's Russet, Scarlet Nonpareil, Hertfordshire Pearmain, Gray's Pippin and Red Bonum Magnum.

What these lists share in common, and what distinguishes them from the examples just discussed, is that they do not include many unique and perhaps very local 'varieties'. These had in large part been replaced by apples characteristic of other regions of England, or which had recently been developed there, but which were now being marketed nationally, such as the Blenheim Orange (Oxfordshire, 1740), Hawthornden (Midlothian, c.1780), Ribston Pippin (Yorkshire, 1707), Syke House Pippin (Yorkshire, 1780), Beauty of Kent (1790), Fair Maid of Wishford (Wiltshire, late eighteenth century), Court of Wick (Huntingdon, 1790) or Scarlet Nonpareil (discovered in Surrey in 1770 and soon marketed by London nurseries). A few had more distant origins, such as the 'Borsdorf', presumably the Edelborsdorfer, an old German variety introduced to England by the Brompton Park Nursery in 1785 and widely marketed thereafter.[122] Only a handful of the apples listed, such as the Sach's Pearmain and Abram Fairheads at Kelvedon, are difficult to identify. Yet at the same time most of the rather vague, general names that are common to many of the earlier lists both in eastern England and elsewhere – Golden Pippin, Nonpareil, Golden Russet, French Pippin and the like – continue to feature strongly. These are all, in other words, essentially lists of national rather than specifically local varieties, the products of a commercial industry, even if some of the individual specimens had been obtained from friends or neighbours.[123]

The eclipse of obscure and local types of fruit is even more marked in commercial orchards. A list of apple trees in such an orchard at Melbourn, Cambridgeshire, dating to 1826, is dominated by varieties first marketed throughout England during the previous century or so – Ribston Pippin, Downton Pippin (Wiltshire, 1806), Blenheim Orange, Hawthornden.[124] Here, even the common early types are limited to 'Dutch Apple Trees', French Pippin and Nonsuch. The identity of the Wiltshire Pippin is unclear, but it was evidently not local. A list of the trees growing at a nursery in the same village, drawn up

---

121 SRO, I, V5/11/4/.2.

122 For these identifications see Morgan and Richards, *New Book of Apples*; FruitID <https://www.fruitid.com/#main>; and Hogg, *British Pomology*.

123 Again, for these identifications, see Morgan and Richards, *New Book of Apples*, and FruitID <https://www.fruitid.com/#main>.

124 CRO, 296/B 661.

six years later, is similar, dominated by Hawthornden, Northern Greening, Joaneting, Alexander (introduced from the Ukraine in 1800), Midsummer Pippin (a synonym for Summer Golden), Golden Knob (from Somerset) and Lord Nelson (obscure but evidently recent).[125] There are a few of the common older types, such as London Pippin or Strawberry Cream, but once again nothing otherwise unknown and potentially local.

The disappearance of obscure or local types, well advanced by the start of the nineteenth century, was followed in its middle decades by another important change: the decline of the old 'generic' favourites such as the Nonpareil and Golden Pippin. Whether, as suggested earlier, such names really refer to 'varieties' in the modern sense matters less in the present context than the fact that they now became rare. Indeed, as early as 1851 Hogg observed that 'the Golden Pippin, and all the old varieties of English apple' had been 'allowed to disappear from our orchards' because they were 'not worth perpetuating, and their places supplied by others infinitely superior'.[126] Hogg and his colleagues at the Royal Horticultural Society were by this stage arguing that, whatever the value of local and old varieties in a domestic context, commercial growers needed to focus on a smaller number of varieties of proven worth, such as Ribston Pippin or Blenheim Orange.[127]

The apples sold from an unnamed Cambridgeshire nursery in 1874 were probably typical of the second half of the century, mainly comprising recently developed, nationally popular varieties: Ribston Pippin, New Hawthornden, Keswick Codling, Sturmer Pippin, [Cox's] Orange Pippin, Cox's Pomona, London Pippin and Bessie Poole (Nottingham, late eighteenth century).[128] Another commercial orchard, at Shefford in Bedfordshire, which was valued just after the First World War, contained 15 different types, but almost all had been introduced commercially over the previous century and most during the previous five decades: Allington Pippin (1870s), Lane's Prince Albert (1850), Bramley's Seedling (1867), Ecklinville (c.1800), Cox's Pomona (c.1825), Orange Pippin (c.1825), Gladstone (1868), Diamond Jubilee (1893), Gravenstein (introduced into England in the 1820s), Lord Derby (1862), Worcester Pearmain (1872) and Stirling Castle (1820s). Only Dr Harvey, Ribston Pippin and Warner's King pre-dated the nineteenth century.[129] This abandonment of older varieties appears to have occurred more slowly in domestic orchards, but this may in part be because the listed trees often included specimens of some considerable age. The orchard at The Pines, Mettingham, Suffolk, in 1896 contained 56 varieties, of which 41 were nationally popular types first introduced in the later eighteenth and nineteenth centuries (albeit sometimes bearing unfamiliar versions of their name, and in some cases now lost – like Harvey's Wiltshire Defiance). Fourteen were old varieties, but they were all

125   CRO, 296/B 693.
126   Hogg, *British Pomology*, p. 97.
127   Short et al., *Apples and Orchards in Sussex*, p. 90.
128   CRO, 296/B 932.
129   BRO, Z 740/108/10.

ones that had long been available from commercial nurseries throughout England, such as Norfolk Beefing, Hanwell Souring or Golden Russet. Only two of the names (Yellow Joist and Kathleen) are otherwise unrecorded and were probably synonyms used by, or short-lived cultivars introduced by, local nurseries.[130]

For, while interest in many of the older varieties dwindled in the second half of the nineteenth century, commercial nurseries continued to pour out new ones, in increasing numbers, to entice customers. The involvement of small local nurseries, as well as the major firms such as Rivers, in their development or propagation means that new, short-lived varieties of fruit, especially apples, constantly make their appearance, albeit at low frequencies, in our sources. The catalogue printed by Ewing's nursery in Norwich in 1853–4 thus included 'Colonel Harbord's Pippin', presumably developed in the gardens of that family at Gunton in Norfolk, and the 'Morningthorpe Pippin', which must have arisen in the south Norfolk village of that name.[131] Even lists of orchard fruit drawn up towards the end of the century can include some obscure names. Mr Benjamin Stimpson of Salle Moor Hall in Norfolk established a new orchard of 2.5 acres (*c.*1 hectare) in 1890, ordering 219 apple trees, 29 varieties in all, from a nursery in East Dereham (together with ten plums in five varieties).[132] The apples were mainly recently developed varieties such as Lord Grosvenor, or old but widely planted ones such as Dr Harvey and Nonpareil, but included four that are unfamiliar from other lists: Bird's Seedling, Holkham Red, Raynham Pearmain and Thetford Monarch. All were probably recent products of small commercial nurseries that never became successful. Holkham Red and Raynham Pearmain perhaps arose in the gardens of these estates. A plan of the orchard at Felmersham vicarage in Bedfordshire, drawn up in *c.*1870, similarly includes two varieties, out of a total of 11, that are otherwise obscure – Collins Pippin and Sloan Pippin – both again probably short-lived commercial products.[133] Most domestic orchards planted in the later nineteenth century were, however, dominated by easily recognised, modern, nationally marketed commercial varieties. That at High Knoll, Ampthill, in Bedfordshire, is typical. When the property was put up for auction in 1912 it was stocked with Lane's Prince Albert, Peasgood's Nonsuch, Gascoyne's Scarlet, Bramley's Seedling, Cox's Orange Pippin, Blenheim Orange, Newton Wonder, Worcester Pearmain, Fern's Pippin and Keswick Codlin.[134] There is little or no overlap between the varieties that feature in such lists and those which were recorded in eastern orchards a century and a half earlier.

---

130 SRO, L, 1117/285/29.

131 SRO, I, HA55/B1/22/19.

132 NRO, MC 561/87.

133 BRO, P93/28/2.

134 BRO, HN7/1/AMP3.

Twentieth-century developments

New varieties of apple continued to appear in the first half of the twentieth century, as we have seen, aimed at both commercial growers and the domestic market. But already, by the 1890s, some influential writers were becoming critical of the endless proliferation. As William Robinson put it:

> The English fruit garden is often a museum of varieties, many of them worthless and not even known to the owner. This is wrong in the garden, and doubly so in the orchard … . Too many varieties is partly the result of the seeking after new kinds in the nurseries. In orchard culture we should be chary of planting any new kind, and with the immense number of Apples grown in our country already, we may choose kinds of enduring Fame.[135]

The tide began to turn, and with some rapidity. At the start of the century Daniels' of Norwich regularly advertised around 100 apple varieties for sale but by 1910 this had dropped to 74 and by the 1920s to fewer than 60. Rivers' peak in offerings in 1906, of 161 varieties, had fallen to 147 by 1926, to 112 by 1931 and to 100 by 1935.[136] Pearson's, also peaking at 161 apple varieties in 1906, declined to 155 by 1908, 120 in 1911, 82 in 1919 and a mere 64 by 1921. There was then a slight recovery, with 78 varieties being offered for sale in 1927, but this was still less than half the number being advertised two decades earlier.[137] Bunyard's bucked the trend more dramatically, with numbers falling from 179 in 1900 to 114 in 1914 before recovering to 136 by 1929.[138] Nevertheless, the overall trajectory is clear enough, and continued into the post-war years. By the 1970s Daniels', for example, were advertising fewer than 25 different varieties of apple.[139] The shake-out mainly affected the older types and, given that the introduction of new examples continued, if at a declining rate, the ratio of new varieties to old increased steadily. Of the apple varieties offered by Daniels' in 1874 only 12 per cent were still available in 1917, 10 per cent in 1939 and just 1.5 per cent in 1974. The decline in older types was, in fact, occurring on some scale before 1900, owing to the large numbers of new varieties already being introduced in the late nineteenth century. Of the apple varieties offered by Lane's in 1862 only 27 per cent were still available in 1901. But the trend clearly escalated in the first half of the twentieth century.

While many established domestic orchards continued, in the inter-war years, to contain some old varieties, cherished by owners as they matured, commercial orchards became even more dominated by a relatively small number of comparatively recent types.

---

135 Robinson, *English Flower Garden*, p. 380.
136 Daniels Brothers Catalogues, Gressenhall Rural Life Museum.
137 Pearson's Catalogues, Royal Horticultural Society, Lindley Library.
138 Bunyard's Catalogues, Royal Horticultural Society, Lindley Library.
139 Daniels Brothers Catalogues, Gressenhall Rural Life Museum.

When, in 1920, the Ministry of Agriculture and Fisheries initiated a scheme to provide fruit trees for county council smallholdings, the list was short and almost all of the 11 varieties of apple offered had been introduced onto the market since 1860 – Bramley's Seedling (1867), Newton Wonder (1870), Gladstone (1868), Early Victoria (a.k.a. Emneth Early) (1899), Beauty of Bath (1864), Grenadier (1862), Worcester Pearmain (1872), Allington Pippin (c.1880), James Grieve (1893) and Rival (1920).[140] Only one – Lane's Prince Albert – was older, although not by much, having been introduced in c.1850. A large fruit farm at Willingham in Cambridgeshire in 1930 grew 11 different varieties of apple, but only one had been introduced before 1850.[141] As already discussed in Chapter 6, most commercial growers concentrated on a smaller range, usually comprising recently developed varieties. By this stage the Fenland orchards grew mainly Bramley's Seedlings, accompanied by only a small number of other types. An orchard in Upwell, put on the market in 1943, grew Bramley's, Newton Wonder and Grenadier; a 'capital fruit farm' in Walpole Highway for sale the following year grew Bramley's, Grenadier, Emneth Early, Newton Wonder, Lord Grosvenor and Allington Pippin.[142] Elsewhere in the Fens Bramley's might be accompanied by small numbers of similarly recent varieties, including Lord Derby, Lane's Prince Albert and Cockett's Red (1930).[143] Some of the larger fruit farms elsewhere in the east were concentrating on a more limited range of varieties – most strikingly, as we have seen, in the case of the COPO orchards at Cockayne Hatley in Bedfordshire, where Cox's Orange Pippins made up the bulk of the fruit planted, accompanied by small numbers of Ellison's Orange (1904), Worcester Pearmain, Bramley's, James Grieve, Newton Wonder and Beauty of Bath, partly to serve as pollinators.[144] There was much variation but, in the commercial orchards, fruit farms and market gardens of the inter-war years, a small number of varieties, mostly developed since the mid-nineteenth century, massively predominated over earlier types.

And, as we have also seen (above, pp. 156–9), in the post-war years this emphasis on a small number of well-tried, popular or newly developed varieties was actively encouraged by the Ministry of Agriculture, the National Farmers Union and professional bodies. Cox's Orange Pippin had become, by the 1950s, by far the most commonly planted dessert variety, Bramley's Seedling the most popular culinary apple. In east Suffolk, just four varieties – Cox's Orange Pippin, Bramley's, Worcester Pearmain and Laxton's Superb – accounted for two-thirds of the orchard acreage in 1951, falling only marginally, with the decline of Superb, over the following decade. The other third or so comprised a small range of types – Scarlet Pimpernel, George Cave, Beauty of Bath, Tydeman's Early, James Grieve,

---

140 BRO, AO N1/1.

141 CRO, K515/L/2069.

142 CRO, KAR 115/38/2/48.

143 CRO, 515/L/2069.

144 BRO, X604/36/8; BRO, PK1/4/102.

Egremont Russet, Laxton's Superb, Kidd's Orange Red – all of which had been introduced since 1870, and mainly in the 1920s and 1930s.[145]

Conclusion

The history of the apple varieties grown in orchards in eastern England is complex, in part because of the very real variations in the size, character and purpose of orchards themselves, but its broad outlines are nevertheless clear. In the period before the middle decades of the eighteenth century the fruit trees planted in the majority of orchards were sometimes obtained from distant sources – especially in London – but more often came from the local area. Some were purchased from small commercial nurseries, which were evidently more numerous in the provinces than we sometimes assume. Others were acquired from friends, family or neighbours, either as young trees or as scion wood for grafting. While true 'varieties', with a genetically distinct character, were certainly propagated in these ways, some of the names given to fruit, especially apples, in our sources appear general and descriptive, and may have been used to define broad types, with particular uses, properties or appearance, rather than representing 'varieties' in the modern sense. Others have names that suggest local seedlings, sports or cultivars, propagated over a limited distance and for only a short period before disappearing. In the later decades of the eighteenth century and the first of the nineteenth the rise of larger provincial nurseries and the proliferation of smaller ones saw both the disappearance of many local cultivars and the gradual eclipse of these common, generic types. At the same time, the most successful local and regional types now became more widely available. Varieties such as Norfolk Beefing, Dr Harvey, Blenheim Orange and Ribston Pippin were marketed everywhere.

The second half of the nineteenth century saw a flood of new varieties, developed or introduced by commercial nurseries, and the abandonment of most of the types commonly planted previously. By 1900 commercial orchards, and most newly planted domestic ones, were dominated by varieties first marketed less than 50 years before. Only a handful of earlier types, including Beefing, Dr Harvey, Ribston Pippin and Blenheim Orange, remained popular. By this time, commercial nurseries offered a phenomenal range of apple varieties. But all this changed after c.1900. The number of different varieties being marketed by nursery companies fell steadily through the early and middle decades of the twentieth century and the range cultivated commercially declined to an even greater degree.

The varieties of apple, and presumably those of other fruit, planted in the orchards of eastern England thus changed dramatically in the course of the last three centuries, and there was remarkably little overlap between the names appearing in lists drawn up in c.1750 and in c.1900. And this, in turn, raises obvious questions about the use of words such as 'ancient' and 'traditional' to describe the kinds of fruit encountered in old orchards today, a subject to which we will return in the next chapter.

---

145 SRO, I, HD 285/2/5.

CHAPTER EIGHT

The significance of orchards

The antiquity of fruit trees

As previous chapters have demonstrated, orchards have taken a variety of forms and were planted for diverse reasons over the centuries; and over the last few decades they have been lost from the landscape of eastern England, as from that of other areas, at a rapid rate. But, as we have also noted, since the 1980s there has been, to a limited extent, a reverse development. Many new orchards have been planted and old ones restored by private owners, community groups or heritage organisations. Orchards have gained new roles and new meanings. In particular, old examples have come to be valued as part of our cultural landscape and as repositories of ancient varieties of fruit, as well as for their biodiversity, as providers of an important range of habitats. These key roles are intimately associated with the age of their constituent trees. Old fruit trees provide habitats for rare or uncommon insects and fungi, and they were supposedly planted at a time before large commercial nurseries rose to dominance, suppressing the local fruit varieties that had been cherished for centuries by the populations of particular areas. As Sue Clifford has put it:

> The link with place may be so particular that the variety will only grow, or produce tasty fruit within a short distance. Apple trees, like most plants, are adapted to local conditions and do best where they originated. Coul Blush, Britain's most northerly (surviving) apple variety hails from Easter Ross and does well in northern and exposed situations, whereas D'Arcy Spice prefers the dryer, warmer summers of Essex and the south east. Apples are often named after the place they came from – Alfriston, Crawley Beauty, Cambusnethan Pippin, Carlisle Codlin … .[1]

Such attitudes are widely shared, with Brian Short and colleagues, for example, suggesting that '[l]ocal varieties … thrive in their native soil, and may even be less prone to disease' than when planted in other locations.[2]

We noted earlier how rapidly fruit trees age and 'veteranise' but provided few details, and with good reason. We have no clear idea how long most can grow for, nor how old they

---

1   King and Clifford, 'The Apple, the Orchard', p. 75.

2   Short *et al.*, *Apples and Orchards in Sussex*, p. 18.

must be to attain a particular size or acquire particular characteristics. Great claims are sometimes made for the antiquity of individual specimens but while these can sometimes be discounted using documentary evidence, this seldom allows us to establish very precise planting dates. Moreover, the fact that old trees tend to hollow significantly precludes dating them by counting their growth rings, something that would anyway necessitate felling or coring, the former certainly and the latter probably harmful to the tree (Figure 8.1). This particular problem also applies to veteran trees of other species, which have long been a source of interest and concern, and various non-invasive ways of ageing them have accordingly been developed based on measuring their circumference at the height of a person's waist (roughly a metre above the ground).

One method, developed by the arboriculturalist Alan Mitchell in the 1970s, suggests as a rough rule of thumb that for most species each inch of girth will, in the case of freestanding specimens, be equivalent to one year of growth; in the case of trees growing in woodland, to two years; and in the case of specimens growing in an 'intermediate' location (as in an avenue or small clump) to a year and a half. Mitchell noted, however, that the growth rates of 'most small-growing trees' soon fell below these figures.[3] A second method, developed by John White, is more complicated.[4] White emphasised, more than Mitchell had done, variations in growth rates over the life of a tree, which means that the relationship between age and circumference is not linear, as Mitchell's rough rule assumes. Trees start off by putting on girth slowly, grow vigorously through middle age, but then slow down again in 'senescence' or old age, as they hollow and their crown contracts. Moreover, growth rates will be significantly affected by soil conditions, proximity to other trees and other factors, as well as varying markedly between trees of different species.[5] White provided a useful table giving expected variations in growth rates between different kinds of tree, but unfortunately failed to include apples, pears, plums or cherries.

Fruit trees in orchards are growing, in effect, in what Mitchell regarded as an 'intermediate' location. In very broad terms, according to his rule we might therefore expect a tree that is 60 years old – that is, one that was planted around 1960 – to have a girth of around a metre, while one planted at the end of the nineteenth century ought to have a girth of around 2m. In the case of apple trees – the most numerous of the old trees found in orchards in eastern England – this approach does not work well. For younger trees, it is true, girth seems to provide a reasonable guide to age. Twelve apple trees growing in the walled garden at Houghton Hall in Norfolk, regularly spaced in a grid pattern and

---

3   A. Mitchell, *Collins Field Guide to the Trees of Britain and Northern Europe* (London, 1974), pp. 20–5.

4   J. White, 'What is a Veteran Tree and Where are they All?' *Quarterly Journal of Forestry*, 91/3 (1997), pp. 222–6. J. White, *Estimating the Age of Large and Veteran Trees in Britain*, Forestry Commission Information Note 250 (Edinburgh, 1999).

5   See also the discussion in G. Barnes and T. Williamson, *Ancient Trees in the Landscape: Norfolk's Arboreal Heritage* (Oxford, 2011), pp. 34–63.

Figure 8.1 The way in which fruit trees gain 'veteran' features at a rapid rate, compared with many other kinds of tree, also ensures that their life-span is relatively short. Examples like this apple tree in an old farm orchard at Saxmundham in Suffolk are easily brought down by strong winds.

already displaying some signs of veteranisation, were almost certainly all planted at the same time. They appear to represent a 'job lot' bought from Laxton's nursery in Bedford and comprise examples of Laxton's Fortune, Laxton's Epicure, Laxton's Superb and Ellison's Orange. Most have girths of between 0.7m and 0.85m, although with outliers ranging from as low as 0.5m to as high as 1.2m. Both the modal and the mean averages are 0.76m, which, following Mitchell's simple method, would give an age of around 45 years – suggesting, that is, that the trees were planted around 1975. In fact, aerial photographs suggest that they were planted between 1946 and 1960, some way off this predicted date. Four old apple trees at Oaklands Farm in Wymondham in the same county – two Rosemary Russets, a Sturmer Pippin and a Beefing – provide an interesting comparison. They are all that remain of an orchard first shown on the second edition Ordnance Survey 6-inch map of 1905, and described in sales particulars of 1911 as 'recently planted'. But they have girths of 1.1m, 1.2m, 1.2m and 1.3m, which according to Mitchell's method would suggest an age of around 70 years, rather than 120. Other apple trees, of comparable age but less securely dated, seem to display a broadly similar relationship between age and girth. Mitchell, as noted, suggested that his approach was unreliable when applied to small tree species, and the slight indications of increasing deviation over time from the age predicted by girth measurements may reflect the fact that, as White's more sophisticated approach asserts, growth rates of all trees reduce markedly in later life.

Differences in growth resulting from variations in the spacing of trees, in soil conditions and perhaps in modes of management all introduce further complications. And, with apple trees in particular, additional difficulties are presented by the fact that some rootstocks are more vigorous than others, while some varieties – most notably, Bramley's Seedling – put on girth faster than other trees, almost regardless of the rootstock on which they are grafted.[6] Some of the Bramley's planted at Applebee Orchard in Bramerton, Norfolk, in the 1980s already have girths of around a metre and are even starting to display some 'veteran' features. The figures given above for the various Laxton's apple trees planted in the 1950s in the walled garden at Houghton Hall omitted those for the Bramley's Seedlings that are inter-planted with them in the 'grid', and with which they are unquestionably coeval. Whereas the other trees, as noted, have girths ranging from 0.5m to 1.2m, with an average of 0.76m, the Bramley's Seedlings range from 1.3m to 1.6m, with an average of 1.4m. Growth rates for Bramley's seem particularly rapid in the moist, rich Fenland soils, where this variety has been widely planted over the last century. Girthing such trees is often problematic because of the local practice of pruning them low, 'bush' fashion, but examples planted in the inter-war period frequently have girths, measured at a height of around 0.5m, of as much as 2.5m. Other triploids may grow at comparable rates, at least if they are grafted onto vigorous rootstocks. Girth measurements can thus both under-estimate and over-estimate the age of trees.

---

6   Morgan and Richards, *New Book of Apples*, pp. 174–5.

Figures 8.2 This Rosemary Russet apple tree, planted around 1900, was broken by a gale in 2018. Given that virtually no heartwood remained – and that the thickness of the cambium and bark combined is less than 30mm – it is surprising that it lasted as long as it did.

It is unclear how long apple trees can grow once they have reached the 'senescence' phase, and this presumably depends on variety and rootstock type. Bramley's Seedling, as well as growing rapidly, can evidently live for long periods. The original Bramley's Seedling tree, planted as a pip in 1810, still survives at Southwell in Nottinghamshire.[7] A small number of other apple trees have been assigned a similar age, such as the 'Milton Wonder',

---

7   <https://www.fruitid.com/#view/490>, accessed 12 July 2020; Clark, *Apples*, p. 54.

in Milton, Oxfordshire. Such longevity must be rare, however. Most apple trees planted before *c*.1920 are now so hollow and veteranised that they are highly vulnerable to storm damage. One of the two Rosemary Russets in the orchard at Wymondham in Norfolk, just discussed, recently lost its head in a storm. It is so hollow that virtually no heartwood remains and the thickness of the cambium and bark combined is less than 30mm. It is surprising that it lasted as long as it did (Figure 8.2). The issue is complicated – as in the case of both the Southwell Bramley's and the Milton Wonder – by the ability of some old trees to regenerate, throwing up new trunks in the ruins of the old, something that may extend their lives significantly. But examples of such regeneration are vanishingly rare and it is likely that when orchards were more rigorously managed any collapsed trees were simply used as firewood. Few apple trees, in short, are more than 120 years old.

The growth patterns of orchard trees other than apples are more difficult to understand because of a paucity of dated examples. Pears can evidently grow at a rapid rate, similar to that of Bramley's Seedlings, and almost certainly live longer than apples, although much depends on rootstock and other factors. Cherries and plums are perhaps more straightforward. The orchard associated with the house now called Wheat Hill, but originally 'Monteagle', in Sandon in north Hertfordshire is interesting in this respect. It developed in stages. The house itself is first shown, with a small orchard immediately to the north, on the 1937 revision of the Ordnance Survey 6-inch map, but the main orchard that exists today, of *c*.1 hectare, first appears on the 1:25,000 map published in 1956, when it covered three times its current area; aerial photographs suggest that it was planted in the immediate post-war period. It originally comprised alternate lines of cherries and plums in a grid pattern. Today the plums have almost entirely disappeared; the handful of survivors are hollowed, dying and crumbling. The cherries are massive, some with girths of 2m, but are now also coming to the end of their lives; large numbers are already dead. In these conditions – on a light clay soil overlying chalk at no great depth – cherries can evidently reach an age of around 70 years, but little more (Figure 8.3). At this point they can attain a girth of 2m, although many apparently contemporary specimens at Wheat Hill are smaller. Plums, in contrast, are lucky to reach this age, by which time most will have attained girths of, at best, a little over a metre. Although, once again, soil conditions and specific varieties of fruit doubtless affect both growth rates and longevity, evidence from other sites suggests that these observations are more broadly applicable.

The fact that fruit trees veteranise early affects in turn our perception of particular orchards. Examples planted in the inter-war years, or even in the 1950s or 1960s, can look surprisingly ancient. A large (11-hectare) orchard in Rickmansworth in south-west Hertfordshire, located in what is still a surprisingly rural corner, although close to the M25, is a good example. Like that at Wheat Hill, it was originally planted with cherries and plums in alternate rows. The cherries are huge and ancient-looking, many with girths approaching 2m, and, like those at Wheat Hill, are clearly nearing the end of their lives. The plums have fared worse. Most of the original trees are dead and their rotting trunks are

Figure 8.3 Derelict cherry orchard, Sandon, Hertfordshire. Planted in the early 1950s and now approaching the end of its life, the orchard gives a false impression of antiquity.

Figure 8.4 Derelict cherry orchard, Rickmansworth, Hertfordshire. Full of dead wood and with areas of dense undergrowth, it is full of wildlife, in a way that it would not have been when heavily managed in its heyday in the 1960s and 1970s.

Figure 8.5 Large old Bramley's Seedling trees at Tewin Orchard, now part of a wildlife reserve owned and managed by the Hertfordshire and Middlesex Wildlife Trust. In spite of its ancient, 'traditional' appearance, the orchard was planted as recently as 1933 as a business venture by one William Stenning Hopkyns.

surrounded by thickets of suckers; or else they have gone altogether, their sites marked by concentrations of suckers alone. The grass has not been cut or grazed for many years and is rank, with many nettles, but is nevertheless herb-rich and of varied composition, at least in the more open areas. Ash and some oak are invading, particularly towards the south, and there are scattered specimens of elder. There are vast quantities of dead wood, heavily infested with insects. This is an evocative place, wild and ancient in appearance and rich in wildlife (Figure 8.4). But the orchard is not shown on the 1944 Ordnance Survey 6-inch map that was surveyed in 1938, first appearing on the 2½-inch of *c.*1960. It was presumably planted soon after the war; it may be younger than the authors.

Plums and cherries grow fast and die young. But even apple orchards, especially if dominated by varieties such as Bramley's Seedlings, can convey an erroneous impression of antiquity. This in turn encourages us to think of old or derelict orchards as being more a part of a lost, 'traditional' world than they really are. The wonderful Tewin Orchard, managed as part of a larger wildlife reserve by the Hertfordshire and Middlesex Wildlife Trust, is described in publicity material, websites and the like as a 'traditional village orchard', and considered a fitting place in which, among other things, to revive the ancient ceremony of wassailing, involving drinking, toasting or blessing the trees, singing and shouting, and generally making a loud noise – all practices traditionally carried out in January and intended to wake the trees and ensure a good harvest later in the year (Figure 8.5). Such a description, and such a 'traditional' use, seem reasonable given the huge size of its great spreading Bramleys. But the orchard was planted as recently as 1933 as a business venture by one William Stenning Hopkyns; his daughter, educated at the Slade art school in London, gave it to the Trust in 1984.[8] Tewin Orchard is one of the many places, including heritage orchards planted in urban parks, in which the custom of wassailing has been not so much revived as reinvented over the last two decades. Cynics might interpret all this, along with Morris dancing and folk singing, as nostalgia, and as middle-class escapism from the tedium and ugliness of modern life. But, as Edward Wigley has recently argued, like other reinventions of tradition, this one involves more than simple nostalgia: the wassailing ceremony has been mobilised, and adapted, to assert new forms of social identity.[9] Orchards, residing at the junction of nature and culture, seem a peculiarly appropriate locale in which to stage reinvented 'traditions'. But that does not mean that particular orchards should be considered as relics from a lost world of rural tradition, when they are evidently nothing of the kind.

Tradition and varieties

If even the oldest orchard trees are, for the most part, little more than 120 years old, then they were planted shortly before Queen Victoria's death, or shortly after it, at a time when – as we have seen – a large commercial nursery industry, marketing its products over extensive areas and issuing printed catalogues, had long been in existence. Not surprisingly, even a cursory examination reveals that the orchards of eastern England are overwhelmingly dominated by varieties developed during the nineteenth and twentieth centuries.

Many of the largest orchards planted before the middle of the twentieth century and still surviving in recognisable form are attached to institutions such as psychiatric hospitals or children's homes. The two wonderful examples at Fairfield in south Bedfordshire – formerly the Three Counties Mental Hospital – contain 15 different varieties of apple. Over two-thirds of these were developed or introduced by commercial growers and first appeared after 1850, and only two – Warner's King and Mere de Menage – originated before 1800. Both were freely available into the twentieth century from firms such as Laxton's (Bedford, where the company was based, lies only 15 miles (23km) to the east). The orchard planted in the 1920s at St Elizabeth's, the home for epileptics at Much Hadham in east Hertfordshire, contains 17 apple varieties, over half of which became available only after 1850. Here, five predate 1800 – Blenheim Orange, King of the Pippins, Reinette du Canada, Ribston Pippin and Keswick Codlin – but once again all were popular varieties, widely marketed into the twentieth century. They all appear, for example, in the catalogues produced in the 1920s by Rivers nursery, located less than 4km to the south-east, and from where the trees were almost certainly obtained. Orchards like these were clearly

---

8   Clark, *Apples*, p. 10.
9   E. Wigley, 'Wassail! Reinventing "Tradition" in Contemporary Wassailing Customs in Southern England', *Cultural Geographies*, 26/3 (2019), pp. 379–93.

planted with popular, dependable and widely marketed varieties. They do not contain, nor should we expect them to contain, anything local, rare or – in any meaningful sense of the word – 'traditional'. In a few cases, it is true, institutional orchards contain rather higher proportions of pre-nineteenth-century varieties. Trees probably surviving from the original planting in the 1890s at Girton College in Cambridge comprise 11 varieties of which no fewer than six originated before 1800: Blenheim Orange, Northern Greening, Dumelow's Seedling, Warner's King, and two specifically East Anglian types, Dr Harvey and Norfolk Beefing. But here, as already noted, we are perhaps dealing with a self-consciously 'archaic', traditional planting, and once again all the early types were ones that remained popular and were widely marketed by the principal nursery companies into the twentieth century.

Where old commercial nurseries still exist, the dominance of mid- to late nineteenth- and twentieth-century types is even more pronounced. The apples surviving from the original section of the county council smallholding at Jeacock's Farm in Tring comprise Bramley's Seedling, Annie Elizabeth (1867) and Lord Derby (1862). All but one of the 11 varieties of apple in the inter-war orchard at Orchard House, Blofield, Norfolk, originated after 1850 (nearly half the varieties were developed in, or after, the 1890s). The original trees at Tewin Orchard, in addition to the Bramley's Seedlings, are similarly dominated by varieties developed after 1850, such as Monarch, Grenadier, James Grieve, Laxton's Delicious, Newton Wonder, Howgate Wonder, Beauty of Bath and Ellison's Orange. Bramley's Seedlings are likewise accompanied by common or recent varieties elsewhere, such as Blenheim Orange at Redlands Farm, Ashwell, Hertfordshire, or Howgate Wonder at Walsoken, Norfolk. The small commercial orchard at Home Farm, Stow Bardolph, in Norfolk, which was planted between 1904 and 1927, is overwhelmingly dominated by Bramley's Seedling and Newton Wonder, with smaller numbers of Lord Derby, Warner's King and Worcester Permain. In none of these orchards do we find the kinds of tree that figure prominently in local planting lists dating to the period before the early nineteenth century. We look in vain for Nonpareil, Royal Pearmain, Golden Reinette, Winter Pearmain or London Pippin. Still less do we encounter otherwise unidentified types that might be examples of Lady's Longing, the Halvergate, or other obscure varieties that appear in our sources. The extent to which surviving commercial orchards were removed from 'traditional' culture, and from distinctly local planting practices, is most dramatically demonstrated by the case of the orchard at Redmayes Farm, Yaxham, one of the finest surviving examples in Norfolk. It was planted as a commercial venture in the 1920s and 1930s by a Mr Ormonde Knight, who hailed from Devon. In addition to common varieties such as Bramley's Seedlings, Allington Pippin, Annie Elizabeth, Beauty of Bath, Blenheim Orange and Newton Wonder, it contains a range of specifically West Country varieties, including Herring's Pippin, Hoary Morning, Tamar Valley Pear Apple and Venus Pippin, most of which are otherwise unrecorded in Norfolk.[10]

---

10   From a list in the possession of Mr Knight, copied by Martin Skipper of EEAOP.

There is little evidence that farmhouse orchards are much different. By the 1900s most farmers must have obtained their fruit trees, like everybody else, from commercial growers, or at the very least as grafts from neighbours who had done so. A number of farm orchards do seem to include, alongside familiar varieties, unidentifiable ones, like the 'Cats head' types in the orchard at Home Farm, South Elmham, in north Suffolk, but they are rare. The oldest trees, while often including varieties with pre-1850 origins, only very rarely include ones that were not being widely marketed at the start of the twentieth century – varieties such as Blenheim Orange, Sturmer Pippin, Carlisle Codling, Keswick Codlin, Ribston Pippin, Dumelow's Seedling, Striped Beefing and Rosemary Russet – and in most cases these are outnumbered by varieties first introduced by Victorian or Edwardian companies, especially Bramley's Seedling, Egremont Russet, Charles Ross, James Grieve, Newton Wonder, Lane's Prince Albert, Lord Derby, Beauty of Bath, Worcester Pearmain, Laxton's Fortune, Laxton's Superb and Bismarck.

There are some spatial patterns in the distribution of different fruit varieties found in orchards across eastern England but these are minor and appear to be related to the commercial dominance of particular nurseries. There is, in particular, a tendency for the main products of Laxton's nursery – apples such as Superb, Fortune and Lord Lambourne, plums like Early Laxton's – to be more frequent in orchards in Bedfordshire and north Hertfordshire, close to the company's base at Bedford, than elsewhere. But it is only a slight tendency, and Laxton's varieties can be found in large numbers even in Norfolk, with notable collections in orchards at Barney, Congham, Freethorpe and Bramerton, for example. Distribution patterns of this kind are rendered complex by the ways in which the more successful varieties developed by particular companies were often taken up and sold by others. Lane's Prince Albert appears if anything more common at a distance from its home in Berkhamsted in Hertfordshire, being widely distributed in East Anglia and Essex, not surprisingly given that by the early twentieth century it was also being marketed by companies such as Rivers of Sawbridgeworth and Daniels' of Norwich. There are signs that the apples Dr Harvey and Norfolk Beefing are more common in Norfolk and Suffolk orchards than in ones further west, but both varieties were widely marketed by the late eighteenth century and the latter is recorded as far west as Hitchin in Hertfordshire in 1809, among the trees growing in William Wilshere's orchard (Figure 8.6).[11] Any eastern emphasis in the distribution of these varieties may, to an extent, reflect the later assertion of 'tradition'. In the 1920s Laxton's, already catering for the nostalgia market, were advertising an 'East Anglian Collection' for sale, which included both of these varieties.[12] While it is thus clear that very broad regional variations in planting existed in England as a whole, born of climate, soil and the relative importance of cider-making, the idea that old orchards frequently contain examples of very old varieties of specifically local provenance should be

---

11 HALS, 61181 and 60158.

12 Laxton's catalogues, Royal Horticultural Society, Lindley Library.

Figure 8.6 The Norfolk Beefing, first referred to in the seventeenth century, remains a characteristic feature of East Anglian orchards but was already, by the start of the nineteenth century, being planted as far away as Hitchin in Hertfordshire.

treated with caution. The oldest orchard trees are almost invariably of the varieties popular, and widely marketed, in the decades around 1900. The obscure local types apparently referred to in our oldest sources – the Oxnead Pippin, the Freethorpe, the Girton Pippin – had, by this time, long gone. The veteran trees found even in old farmhouse orchards are, for the most part, a legacy of the late Victorian and Edwardian period – of an age of railways, the first cars, printed catalogues and public limited companies – rather than being a window on some more ancient, rural, 'traditional' world.

Orchards and biodiversity

The importance of orchards for biodiversity is to an extent debated. The great ecologist Oliver Rackham, as we have noted, fails to discuss them in his landmark book *The History of the Countryside*, roundly declaring that 'orchards, garden trees and other formal plantings are outside the scope of this book'.[13] This is a surprising comment, perhaps, given that such things as post-medieval plantations and planting in landscape parks are addressed. But Rackham's attitude is understandable. The trees planted in orchards are essentially introduced cultivars, and the habitat itself can survive only through regular and intensive interventions, including the replacement of lost trees. Left to their own devices, as we have

---

13   Rackham, *History of the Countryside*, p. 67.

seen, orchards eventually become treeless pastures (if grazed) or secondary woodland. More than any truly semi-natural habitat, orchards are self-evidently artificial, with no real sustainability. But over the last few years attitudes have changed, in part as a consequence of the efforts of organisations such as the People's Trust for Endangered Species. Ecologists are now more aware of the importance of orchards, perhaps especially for invertebrates, and Keith Alexander in particular has emphasised that the main orchard trees all have indigenous analogues – blackthorn for plum, wild cherry and bird cherry for cultivated cherry, and so on – and that, while many of the invertebrate species particularly associated with orchard trees may have arrived in Britain with the cultivated fruits themselves, some certainly pre-existed them, such as the large fruit tree bark beetle *Scolytus mali*.[14] Orchards, in Alexander's words, are 'an extreme form of wood-pasture'. Typically displaying a varied age structure, 'traditional orchards provide optimal wood-pasture conditions' of the kind demanded by saproxylic insects, in spite of their planted character and an inability to sustain themselves without human intervention. 'Although orchards might be viewed as cultural artifacts, or not somehow "semi-natural" and therefore not a conservation priority, this is very much a plant ecology viewpoint. It has no basis in fact.'[15]

Alexander's main interest is in insects, but as small-scale versions of wood-pastures orchards, especially those examples dominated by apple and pear trees, also provide habitats for a wide range of other organisms, including lichens and bryophytes. 'Traditional orchards' were, in fact, included in the 2006 UK Biodiversity Action Plan list, and in the revised list for 2011, of habitats considered to be of principal importance for the purpose of conserving biodiversity, and current advice notes emphasise the significance not only of their trees but also of the 'associated habitats including scrub, hedgerows, unimproved grassland, fallen dead wood, ponds and dykes. Much orchard wildlife depends on this mosaic.'[16] As we have seen, 'traditional orchard' is a term that is so elastic as to be almost meaningless, but in the official, English Nature view a traditional orchard may be defined as 'groups of fruit and nut trees planted on vigorous rootstocks at low densities in permanent grassland; and managed in a low intensity way…'. As noted earlier, the minimum size of an 'orchard' is taken as 'five trees with crown edges less than 20m apart'.

Lichens

Lichens are a symbiotic association between a fungus and an algae or, in the case of certain blue-green varieties, a bacterium. There are many different species, conventionally divided into three groups according to their growth habit – crustose, leafy and shrubby – and into

---

14   Alexander, 'Special Importance of Traditional Orchards', p. 13.
15   Alexander, 'Special Importance of Traditional Orchards', p. 14.
16   <https://hub.jncc.gov.uk/assets/2829ce47-1ca5-41e7-bc1a-871c1cc0b3ae#UKBAP-BAPHabitats-56-TraditionalOrchards.pdf>, accessed 10 March 2021.

four rather broader ones according to colour – greyish, greyish green, yellow and dark.[17] The algal partner can be free living, and the lichen name thus refers to the fungal partner. Lichens are slow-growing and long-lasting: those associated with ancient, undisturbed rocks can be hundreds of years old. Lichens reproduce sexually, through the fungal partner, which produces fruiting bodies. These eject spores which then need to germinate and find appropriate algal partners to form a new individual, although many lichens have in fact developed ways of ejecting spores and partner algae together. Reproduction can, however, also occur vegetatively, from fragments.

Lichens grow on soil and rocks but also on bark and wood, and 'the richest woodland for lichens is that associated with wood-pasture', including orchards.[18] 'Orchards are amongst the most favourable sites for lichen colonisation. As well as being wind-dispersed, lichen propagules, sexual (spores) and vegetative … are carried by birds and mammals visiting orchards for their rich pickings.'[19] Lichens throughout the UK have been adversely affected by a number of key environmental changes over the last two centuries. In particular, in the course of the nineteenth century high levels of industrial pollution reduced their diversity significantly, leading to the dominance in the worst affected areas of the monotonous greenish variety *Lecanora conizaeoides*. Successive Clean Air Acts and changes in fuel use have reduced levels of atmospheric sulphur dioxide considerably, allowing other lichen species to recolonise urban and industrial areas, and districts lying at a distance but downwind of them, although this has occurred only gradually. At the same time, moreover, rising levels of nitrogen in the agricultural environment have led to the increasing prominence of those lichen species well adapted to conditions of eutrophication, or nitrogen enrichment, leading in many places to the dominance of yellow-orange lichens such as *Candelariella reflexa* and *Xanthoria* spp.

In other areas of the UK the importance of orchards for lichen conservation has been clearly demonstrated and, in all, some 192 different lichen species have been recorded, nationally, occurring within them.[20] Research in Yorkshire, for example, in orchards located in the north of the county, distant from the more urban and industrial, and thus historically polluted, districts, has recorded high numbers of species. In seven sampled orchards, numbers ranged from 26 to 38, with a total across all orchards of 55 species. In Yorkshire as a whole 75 lichen species have been recorded in 23 orchards.[21]

In the east of England recorded figures are similar or higher. In Hertfordshire, for example, the ten orchards studied in 2011 by Powell, Harris and Hicks contained a total of

---

17   C.W. Smith, *The Lichens of Britain and Ireland* (London, 2009); F. Dobson, *Lichens: An Illustrated Guide to the British and Irish Species*, 5th edn (London, 2005).
18   J.R. Laundon, *Lichens* (Princes Risborough, 1986), p. 17.
19   Henderson, 'Lichens in Orchards', p. 78.
20   Henderson, 'Lichens in Orchards', p. 78.
21   Henderson, 'Lichens in Orchards', p. 78.

71 species, with an average of 34 species on fruit trees and a further 15 in other locations, including on gateposts and old machinery. The researchers emphasised, however, that all the species recorded were 'relatively common in a national context', although in several cases, such as *Arthopyrenia analepta*, *Hypotrachyna revoluta* and *H. afrorevoluta*, they had not previously or recently been noted in the county.[22] As might be expected, *Candelariella reflexa* was particularly common, as were other species associated with high levels of nutrient enrichment, including *Lecanora barkmaniana* (although again not previously recorded in Hertfordshire). Rather similar results have come from Cambridgeshire, where Val Perrin examined nine orchards. He found a total of 74 species, 59 of which were on the trees themselves, with individual orchards generally containing between 30 and 40 species. But these were again mainly common ones and, indeed, there was a significant overlap with those found in Hertfordshire orchards.[23] One orchard in Cambridgeshire, at Rummers Lane, Wisbech St Mary, had already been examined by Natural England as part of a wider investigation into the biology of orchards. It was found to contain a total of 44 lichen species: noticeably fewer than in most of the other orchards surveyed as part of the project elsewhere in the country (such as Slew orchard in Devon, where 80 species were noted).[24] In Bedfordshire, similarly, lichen communities in orchards appear to be dominated by relatively common species.[25] A survey carried out in 2011 of the highly overgrown remnants of a small plum orchard at Sandy in Bedfordshire – much encroached upon by an adjacent area of woodland – recovered some lichen species of interest, most notably *Strangospora ochrophora* – only the second record for the county – and *Arthonia didyma* – the first record. But neither came from the surviving fruit trees, the first being found on an elder and the second on an old hazel stool.[26]

The general absence of rare or unusual lichen species in orchards in eastern England was explained by Powell and colleagues as being in part a consequence of the high historic air-pollution levels to which much of the region – close to London and downwind of the industrial Midlands – was prone: conditions that have only recently improved, so that orchards are in the process of being colonised, but initially by relatively common and easily dispersed species. It is also possible that the high levels of chemical sprays used in the

---

22   M. Powell, A. Harris and M. Hicks, 'Lichen Ecology in Traditional Hertfordshire Orchards and the Implications for Conservation', *Transactions of the Hertfordshire Natural History Society*, 43/2 (2012), pp. 69–79, at pp. 71–3.

23   Quoted in Powell *et al.* 'Lichen Ecology', p. 74; see also V. Perrin, 'Cambridgeshire Orchard Survey: Phase 2 Survey, 2006–09. Traditional Orchards Habitat' (Peterborough, 2010).

24   M. Lush, H.J. Robertson, K.N. Alexander, V. Giavarini, E. Hewins, J. Mellings, C.R. Stevenson, M. Storey and P.F. Whitehead, *Biodiversity Studies of Six Traditional Orchards in England*, Natural England Research Reports 25 (Peterborough, 2007), p. 137.

25   Powell *et al.*, 'Lichen Ecology', p. 73.

26   S. Raven, 'Sandy Smith Nature Reserve – wildlife and history of plum orchard', unpublished report, The Greensand Trust (May 2012).

orchards in the past (most of those examined are no longer in commercial production) may also have led to a low point in lichen diversity from which they are only now recovering. Powell and his co-workers also drew attention to the generally dry conditions in eastern England, not conducive to large and diverse lichen populations, and to the fact that the trees in many of the commercial orchards surveyed were relatively young, ensuring that they were closer in character to recent secondary woodland than to ancient wood-pastures.[27]

Bryophytes

Rather more research has been published relating to the importance of orchards in the eastern counties for bryophytes – that is, small vascular plants such as mosses and liverworts. These are abundant in wood-pastures, even those isolated from other examples, suggesting that they might likewise be varied and plentiful in orchards – at least those dominated by apples and pears (plum trees and, in particular, cherry trees generally carry fewer bryophytes).[28] But once again, in the eastern counties at least, orchards do not appear to score quite as well as might be expected. A study by Whitelaw and Burton of five examples in Hertfordshire and Cambridgeshire, carried out in 2009–11 and concentrating on the flora associated with Bramley's Seedling trees, recorded 23 species of bryophyte, none of which were deemed 'unexpected for the habitat or area'; in fact, this figure represented only 17 per cent of the 135 species recorded by J.W. Bates and colleagues in a transect across England, embracing all types of habitat, carried out in 1997.[29] The numbers present in each orchard were variable, ranging from 10 to 21. Whitelaw and Burton argued that this reflected differences in planting and management more than in the age of the trees, which was 'not an important factor in explaining the variations'.[30] While older trees have had more time for colonisation to occur, past management methods in commercial orchards – including spraying, tar-washing and physical removal of bryophytes – ensured that 'the age of the tree and the length of time for which the bark has been available for colonisation may not be the same'.[31] This said, trees less than 30 years old were generally

---

27 Powell *et al.*, 'Lichen Ecology', pp. 73–4.

28 A. Oldén and P. Halme, 'Grazers Increase β-diversity of Vascular Plants and Bryophytes in Wood-Pastures', *Journal of Vegetation Science*, 27 (2016), pp. 1084–93; T. Kiebacher, C. Keller, C. Scheidegger and A. Bergamini, 'Epiphytes in Wooded Pastures: Isolation Matters for Lichen but not for Bryophyte Species Richness', *PLoS ONE*, 12 (2017), <https://doi.org/10.1371/journal.pone.0182065>, accessed 7 March 2021.

29 M. Whitelaw and M.A.S. Burton, 'Diversity and Distribution of Epiphytic Bryophytes on Bramley's Seedling Trees in East of England Apple Orchards', *Global Ecology and Conservation*, 4 (2015), pp. 380–7, at p. 382; J.W. Bates, M.C.F. Proctor, C.D. Preston, N.G. Hodgetts and A.R. Perry, 'Occurrence of Epiphytic Bryophytes in a "Tetrad" Transect across Southern Britain 1: Geographical Trends in Abundance and Evidence of Recent Change', *Journal of Bryology*, 19/4 (1997), pp. 685–714.

30 Whitelaw and Burton, 'Diversity and Distribution', p. 383.

31 Whitelaw and Burton, 'Diversity and Distribution', p. 385.

poor in bryophytes. The most diverse floras were found in orchards with large, spreading, well-spaced trees, independent of age. All of the orchards studied were of a similar inter-war age, with the exception of that in St Albans, planted in the 1980s. It is particularly striking that the number of species recorded from the latter (14) was higher than that from the 1920s orchard at St Elizabeth's at Much Hadham (10) and only slightly below the number from the highest scoring orchards.[32] Diversity of bryophytes, in other words, is poorly correlated both with the age of the trees and with that of the orchards in which they are growing.

As noted, the species recorded in this survey were modest in number and thought to be unremarkable, but the sample was comparatively small and heavily skewed towards commercial, or formerly commercial, orchards, and to bryophytes found on Bramley's Seedlings. Other studies have produced slightly different results. The number of species recorded by Lush *et al.* at Rummers Lane near Wisbech in Cambridgeshire – a large redundant orchard containing several different varieties of apple – was far higher, at 42, while research carried out by Stevenson and Rowntree in Cambridgeshire orchards has, in contrast to the investigations by Whitelaw and Burton, recorded a number of comparatively infrequent species, some new to the county, including *Hypnum cupressiforme* var. *heseleri* and *Antitrichia curtipendula*).[33] Work by Stevenson and associates in Norfolk has likewise recorded new species such as *Hypnum cupressiforme* var. *heseleri*.[34] Overall, the numbers of bryophytes recorded in Norfolk by Stevenson and Rowntree are higher than noted by Whitelaw and Burton, with no fewer than 40 found, for example, in the royal orchards at Flitcham.[35]

These contrasting results may be due to Stevenson and Rowntree's most interesting discovery: that different apple cultivars have different numbers, and species, of bryophyte associated with them, presumably ensuring that more mixed orchards will be more bryophytically diverse than the Bramley-dominated examples studied by Whitelaw and Burton.[36] Among other important observations made by these researchers were that age of tree probably is a factor in diversity – the difference in conclusions here perhaps reflects the fact that Stevenson and Rowntree's focus was more on 'traditional' than on recent or

---

32 Whitelaw and Burton, 'Diversity and Distribution', p. 382.

33 Lush *et al.*, *Biodiversity Studies*, p. 138; R. Stevenson and J. Rowntree, 'Bryophytes in East Anglian Orchards', *Field Bryology*, 99 (2009), pp. 10–18; N.G. Hodgetts, C.D. Preston and C.R. Stevenson, '*Antitrichia curtipendula* in a Cambridgeshire Orchard', *Field Bryology*, 89 (2006), pp. 8–9.

34 T.L. Blockeel and C.R. Stevenson, '*Hypnum cupressi-forme* var. heseleri (Ando & Higuchi) M.O.Hill (Bryopsida, Hypnales) in Norfolk. New to the British Isles', *Journal of Bryology*, 28 (2006), pp. 190–3.

35 Stevenson and Rowntree, 'Bryophytes in East Anglian Orchards', p.13.

36 Stevenson and Rowntree, 'Bryophytes in East Anglian Orchards', pp. 13–15; C.R. Stevenson, C. Davies and J.K. Rowntree, 'Biodiversity in Agricultural Landscapes: The Effect of Apple Cultivar on Epiphyte Diversity', *Ecology and Evolution*, 7 (2017), pp. 1250–8.

redundant commercial orchards, where bryophytes were more strenuously removed in the past; and that, rather than presenting similarities with parkland or similar wood-pasture environments, the range of bryophytes found in East Anglian orchards was closer to that associated with 'elder scrub and sallow carr', echoing the suggestions of Powell, Harris and Hicks that the lichens in Hertfordshire orchards most closely resemble those associated with young secondary woodland.[37]

Recent, unpublished surveys have tended to amplify rather than overturn these findings. Preliminary surveys of three Norfolk sites suggest a measure of variation related, in part, to the spacing of the constituent trees and, in consequence, the extent to which conditions were shaded and damp. A mere three species were thus recorded from trees within the warm, dry walled garden at Houghton Hall, and 12 in the adjacent, rather open orchard, but as many as 23 and 24 in more closely planted orchards on damp fenland soils at White House, Walpole Highway and Marshland St James respectively.[38] Again, there were indications that particular bryophyte species have an affinity with individual apple varieties, with *Homalothecium sericeum* being closely associated with the Blenheim Orange trees in the Houghton Hall orchard, for example. Nine orchards examined in Hertfordshire in 2017–18 contained between 12 and 20 species, but – despite differences in age and history – with significant similarities in the kinds of species present and also in average numbers.[39] A total of 35 species, 32 mosses and three liverworts were recorded across all the orchards, 30 of which were growing as epiphytes. Most of the orchards supported between 18 and 20 species, of which seven occurred in all nine orchards (the mosses *Brachythecium rutabulum*, *Bryum capillare*, *Cryphaea heteromalla*, *Orthotrichum affine*, *O. diaphanum* and *Hypnum cupressiforme* and the liverwort *Frullania dilatata*). Of these moss species, however, seven were each recorded in only one of the orchards. Of particular interest were the results from a large orchard of 'heritage' varieties at Sarratt, planted only 30 years ago. This already contained 15 species, suggesting that diverse collections of bryophyte species can develop in orchards with remarkable speed.

All this suggests that some of the claims made for the importance of orchards for both lichens and bryophytes have been exaggerated. Nevertheless, in the eastern counties orchards do unquestionably have an important role in the conservation of these taxa, given the extent of urbanisation in the south of the region and the dominance of intensive arable farming elsewhere, as well as the general paucity of old wood-pastures. As Powell *et al.* put it, 'orchards clearly support good, diverse lichen floras and are of considerable local importance in this respect' (Figure 8.7).[40]

---

37 Stevenson and Rowntree, 'Bryophytes in East Anglian orchards', p. 16.
38 Initial survey work by Julia Masson.
39 Initial survey work by Agneta Burton and associates from the Hertfordshire Natural History Society.
40 Powell *et al.*, 'Lichen Ecology', p. 69.

Figure 8.7 Old apple trees can carry rich collections of lichens and bryophytes.

Saproxylic insects

In terms of their fauna, orchards are principally important for their tree-associated invertebrates, and these may be divided into four broad groups: those associated with the canopy (the leaves, blossom, fruit and so on); those associated with the bark of the trees; species associated with roots and mycorrhizal fungi; and wood-decay species or saproxylics.[41] The Biodiversity Action Plan lists for the UK include three invertebrates that are associated principally with orchards. The noble chafer (*Gnorimus nobilis*) is dependent on the debris ('wood mould') produced within trees as their heartwood is broken down by fungi. Its larvae develop in the moist layers at the base of such deposits, within the hollowing trunk, feeding on the mould and producing distinct faecal pellets. In contrast, the apple-tree lace bug (*Physatocheila smreczynski*) is mainly found on the lichen growing on old apple trees, while the mistletoe marble moth (*Celypha woodiana*) depends on the mistletoe that is a feature of some old orchards, the larvae feeding on the leaves as the adults rest by day on trunks, flying only by night. These specialists, however, are accompanied by a number of other species of invertebrate that, while mainly found in wood-pastures, are also typical of old orchards. These include the lichen running spider (*Philodromus margaritatus*), the lackey moth (*Malacosoma neustria*) and the figure of eight moth (*Diloba caeruleocephala*).[42]

Of the species associated with old orchards, wood-decay species, especially beetles (Coleoptera), have attracted most attention, in part because true wood-pastures – the prime habitat for such species – are now so rare across much of the UK that orchards

---

41 Alexander, 'Special Importance of Traditional Orchards', p. 12.

42 Alexander, 'Special Importance of Traditional Orchards', p. 16.

potentially offer, in many districts, their best chance of future survival. Saproxylic species depend on the rotting wood within decaying trees, although to varying extents and in different ways. In the case of some species, the larvae feed on decaying wood and the adults on nectar. Some feed not on the decaying wood itself but on organisms that do.[43] The role of orchards in sustaining saproxylics is clear from a study of orchards in the Forest of Dean, which revealed that these contained an abundance of such species.[44]

Very little survey work has been undertaken in the eastern counties to assess how far orchards in this region, like those in the west of the country, are important habitats for invertebrates, and especially the extent to which they provide a home for saproxylic beetles. For this reason, 16 orchards of different kinds and ages were selected for detailed survey as part of the Orchards East project and two types of trap employed: interception traps, placed within the tree canopy throughout the spring and summer of 2019 (Figure 8.8); and traps baited with the pheromone of the female noble chafer. Not a single example of this species was recorded, in line with previous observations, suggesting that it is either extraordinarily rare or absent altogether from the eastern counties. But analysis of the insects recovered from the interception traps makes it clear that old orchards in eastern England, as elsewhere, can boast a rich insect fauna that includes, besides numerous relatively common species, a number that are nationally rare or scarce, including *Anisoxya fuscula*, *Atomaria lohsei*, and at least one new to the county in question – *Oligella foveolata* – the first Norfolk record, from an orchard in Marshland St James. One rather gruesome discovery, made among the insects trapped in the orchard at Houghton Hall in Norfolk, was the ant-decapitating fly *Pseudacteon formicarum*, which pupates in the head of its host and secretes a chemical that eventually severs the cord connecting the ant's head to its thorax.

Coleoptera generally made up between 30 and 50 per cent of the insects trapped, the numbers present in the sample orchards ranging from 6 to 161. There are few environmental explanations for this degree of variation, which must in large part be related to the character, and short duration, of the survey itself, which is still continuing. In most of the orchards studied saproxylics constituted between 20 and 40 per cent of the trapped insects and included a number of nationally scarce or rare species: *Tillus elongatus* and *Enicmus brevicornis* from Crapes orchard at Aldham in Essex; and *Triplax russica* from the west orchard at Fairfield in Bedfordshire. Saproxylics from other orders were also well represented. In the orchard at Home Farm, South Elmham St Michael, Suffolk, for example, the 18 saproxylic Coleoptera were accompanied by at least six essentially saproxylic flies (Diptera), such as *Asteia amoena* and *Sylvicola cinctus*.[45]

---

43 K. Alexander, 'The Invertebrates of Britain's Wood Pastures', *British Wildlife*, 11 (1999), pp. 108–17.

44 Alexander, 'Special Importance of Traditional Orchards', p. 14.

45 This discussion draws heavily on K. Alexander's lists and discussions; see in particular K. Alexander, *The Invertebrates of Living and Decaying Timber in Britain and Ireland: A Provisional Annotated Checklist*, English Nature Research Reports 467 (Peterborough, 2002).

Figure 8.8 A flight interception trap, used to capture flying insects in biodiversity surveys of orchards.

The fact that the highest numbers of saproxylic beetles generally come from the sites producing the highest numbers of trapped insect species overall suggests that results should be treated with great caution, but some observations can usefully be made. The highest numbers of saproxylic beetles come from two sites in the northern Fens, within the old orchard district around Wisbech, at Marshland St James (53 records) and White House, Walpole Highway (27 records); from the orchard at Houghton Hall (25); and from Home Farm, South Elmham (18). Raw numbers are, however, of less interest than the quality of the fauna, in terms of the scarceness or rarity of its constituent elements. To assess this, Fowles and Alexander have developed a 'Saproxylic Quality Index' (SQI), although this focuses on a limited range of Coleoptera because, as they explain:

> Many Coleoptera species occur within dead wood habitats that are by no means restricted to them. Such facultative species may be present on a particular site without any requirement for dead wood and hence their role in the evaluation of the importance of dead wood is limited. A primary aim, therefore, is to define a list of species in which there can be a high degree of confidence that their occurrence at a site relies solely on the presence of dead wood habitats.[46]

The SQI is calculated by totalling rarity scores for the saproxylic Coleoptera recorded from a site, dividing this by the number of such species recorded and then multiplying by 100. Almost all the eastern orchards examined had fewer than the 40 species that Fowles and Alexander recommended as the minimum for this form of analysis, but, based on a less reliable minimum of 25, the four outstanding sites were, once again, the two Fenland examples and those at Houghton and Home Farm South Elmham, all with SQI scores above 350. Only one of these – Marshland St James, with 53 saproxylic Coleoptera – really passes the minimum requirements, but this scored an SQI of 562, well above the 500 points indicative of 'national importance'.[47]

Most invertebrate conservationists place considerable emphasis on the low mobility of saproxylic invertebrates.[48] But, as Alexander has emphasised, this assumption has been subject to very little scientific testing.

---

[46] A.P. Fowles, K. Alexander, and R.S. Key, 'The Saproxylic Index: Evaluating Wooded Habitats for the Conservation of Dead Wood Coleoptera', *The Coleopterist*, 8 (1999), pp. 121–41, at p. 122.

[47] Fowles and Alexander, 'Saproxylic Index', p. 6.

[48] M.S. Warren and R.S. Key, 'Woodlands: Past, Present and Potential for Insects', in N.M Collins and J.A. Thomas (eds), *The Conservation of Insects and their Habitats* (London, 1990), pp. 151–211; J. Bratton and J. Andrews, 'Invertebrate Conservation; Principles and their Application to Broad-Leaved Woodland', *British Wildlife*, 2/6 (1991), pp. 335–44.

> The hypothesis is primarily based on the very consistent association between rich saproxylic assemblages, on the one hand, and historic woodland and wood-pasture sites, on the other … . The ecological explanation has been that these species evolved under continuous open forest conditions – a natural high density of suitable habitat, i.e. sufficient density of hollow trees – and there was not therefore selective pressure for relatively high mobility.[49]

The comparatively rich saproxylic faunas from the two Fenland orchards are thus of some interest, for the cartographic evidence leaves no doubt that until the twentieth century the areas they occupy comprised arable fields, while, in more general terms, before the large-scale planting of commercial orchards occurred in the district in the later eighteenth and nineteenth centuries, the local landscape was singularly deficient not only in woods, wood-pastures and plantations, but even in hedgerow trees. The drained marsh was from the start subdivided by ditches, rather than hedges, which were only sparsely lined with willows.[50] Not all Fenland orchards, it is true, boast the abundance of saproxylic Coleoptera recorded at Marshland St James. Only 27 species, as noted, were trapped at White House, Walpole, while English Nature's survey of the large example at Rummers Lane recorded 34.[51] These are, nevertheless, significant totals in regional terms. That the highest SQI score so far recorded from an orchard in the eastern counties should come from what has, for several centuries, been its least wooded and most sparsely timbered landscape is remarkable.

However, as Alexander has emphasised, conventional assumptions about low saproxylic dispersal rates

> Need to be tempered with known variations in mobility across the broad assemblage of 'saproxylics'. It is known, for instance, that certain species that are linked with highly ephemeral habitats such as dying or freshly dead woody material have a relatively high dispersal capacity, e.g. many bark beetles (Scolytidae) and certain longhorns (Cerambycidae) and jewel beetles (*Agrilus* species of Buprestidae).[52]

Alexander accordingly developed another scoring system, an 'Index of Ecological Continuity' (IEC), which was specifically based on a list of the species thought to be the remnants of the saproxylic beetle population characteristic of Britain's ancient, post-glacial natural woodland, fragments of which have survived in the refugia provided by deer

---

49   K. Alexander, *The Role of Trees outside Woodlands in Providing Habitat and Ecological Networks for Saproxylic Invertebrates: Part 1, Designing a Field Study to Test Initial Hypotheses*, Natural England Commissioned Report NECR225a (Peterborough, 2016), p. 13.

50   These comments are based on an examination of the available tithe maps and Ordnance Survey maps. See also Wade Martins and Williamson, *Roots of Change*, pp. 28–31.

51   Lush *et al.*, *Biodiversity Studies*, pp. 160–4.

52   Alexander, *The Role of Trees Outside Woodlands*, p. 13.

parks, wood-pastures and other habitats supposedly displaying strong continuity from the primaeval 'wild wood'.[53] In this context, it is striking that of the saproxylics recorded at the most abundant of the Fenland sites, Marshland St James, no less than 11 (20 per cent) feature on the list of species used to calculate the 'Index of Environmental Continuity'. Many have the highest rating of '3', ensuring that the overall score of 28 is enough to place the orchard in the 'national importance' category of sites displaying direct ecological continuity with the primeval grazed woodlands of remote prehistory – something which, for reasons already explained, is in this case completely impossible. This suggests that many of the saproxylics on the 'continuity index' can spread rather faster than is currently assumed, or can survive well enough in habitats other than wood-pasture. In this case, the most likely explanation is the very rapid dispersal of the relevant species through the northern Fens as orchards became widely established through the eighteenth, nineteenth and twentieth centuries, their trees (dominated in many cases by Bramley's Seedlings) soon displaying veteran characteristics. It is possible that the most important things we can learn from a study of saproxylics in eastern orchards relate to the complex patterns, and complex character, of 'environmental continuity'.

Either way, these very preliminary results suggest that in the eastern counties orchards are of significance for the conservation of saproxylic invertebrates, especially beetles, simply because there is a marked paucity in the region of genuine wood-pasture habitats.[54] Nevertheless, in national terms the numbers of species so far recorded do not compare well with orchards in the west of England studied by Alexander and others.[55] This is perhaps a reflection of the character of the wider environment in which the orchards are set – a critical factor, as Alexander and colleagues have argued.[56] Not only is the east of England deficient in old wood-pastures, there is a more general paucity of dead wood in what is mainly an arable and intensively farmed region. The numbers of saproxylic species is thus low overall, providing limited reservoirs from which orchards, evidently a prime habitat for them, can now be colonised.

---

53   K. Alexander, *Revision of the Index of Ecological Continuity as used for Saproxylic Beetles*, English Nature Research Reports 574 (Peterborough, 2004).

54   A full analysis will be written by Paul Read after this aspect of the 'Orchards East' project has been completed in 2021.

55   K. Alexander, 'A Remarkable Wood-Decay Beetle Fauna from a Group of Traditional Orchards at Colwall, Herefordshire', *The Coleopterist*, 19 (2002), pp. 11–14; K. Alexander, L. Bower and G. Green, 'A Remarkable Saproxylic Insect Fauna from a Traditional Orchard in Worcestershire – But are the Species Resident or Transient?' *British Journal of Entomology & Natural History*, 27 (2014), pp. 221–9; K. Alexander and P. Chandler, 'Rare Fungus Gnats (Diptera, Mycetophilidae) from a Herefordshire Cherry Orchard', *Dipterists Digest*, 17 (2010), pp. 25–6.

56   Alexander *et al.*, 'A Remarkable Saproxylic Insect Fauna from a Traditional Orchard in Worcestershire'.

Other flora and fauna

Turning briefly to other kinds of flora and fauna, the orchards of eastern England are perhaps less important. The diversity of their ground flora is very variable, with the number of species recorded in a dozen sample orchards surveyed as part of the Orchards East project ranging from 17 to 108. To some extent, the lower scores in this range reflect particular circumstances at the time of observation – the orchard at Houghton Hall in Norfolk, with only 17 species recorded growing beneath and between the trees, had just been mown. For the most part, indeed, the numbers were significantly higher, with half of the orchards having more than 50 species of plant recorded. The key factors influencing diversity, other than orchard size, appear to be the character of the surrounding landscape, the presence within the orchards of features such as ponds and damp areas, the degree of variation in the age of trees and in the density of planting, and forms of management. The last of these, reflecting the new attitudes to old orchards, can include both the deliberate sowing of wild flowers by owners, as at Ricebridge Orchard, Thorpe le Soken, Essex, or at Oaklands Farm, Wymondham, Norfolk, and the careful encouragement of what is naturally there by, for example, allowing plants to seed before mowing, as at Home Farm, South Elmham, Suffolk. Another factor is almost certainly past management. As we have seen, many orchards, including some of those associated with farmhouses, were intensively sprayed with herbicides in the past, or the ground beneath the trees was cultivated for vegetables or cut flowers.

The kinds of species present appear to be a function of soil type, past and present management regimes, density of trees and other factors. While the flora of many orchards can include species usually associated with hay meadows, such as oxeye daisy (*Leucanthemum vulgare*), cock's-foot (*Dactylis glomerata*) or common mouse-ear (*Cerastium fontanum*), or with long-established pastures found on the relevant soil type, these are usually outnumbered by woodland-edge or hedgerow species such as black horehound (*Ballota nigra*) or lords and ladies (*Arum maculatum*), and in particular by plants associated with roadsides, waste and cultivated ground, including plantains (*Plantago* sp.), fat hen (*Chenopodium album*), pineapple weed (*Matricaria discoidea*), prickly sow-thistle (*Sonchus asper*), thyme-leaved speedwell (*Veronica serpyllifolia*) or dark mullein (*Verbascum nigrum*). Sometimes woodland plants occur, including supposed 'ancient woodland indicators': primrose (*Primula vulgaris*) at Mayes Farm, Yaxham, Norfolk; primrose, bluebell (*Hyacinthoides non-scripta*), yellow archangel (*Lamium galeobdolon*) and barren strawberry (*Potentilla sterilis*) at Ricebridge Orchard; remote sedge (*Carex remota*) and primrose at Foxburrow Farm, Melton, Suffolk; sanicle (*Sanicula europaea*) at Wandlebury in Cambridgeshire; and dog's mercury (*Mercurialis perennis*) and primrose in the orchard at Home Farm, South Elmham. In many cases these plants are associated with the perimeter hedges, but in some places, where the orchard trees are closely spaced, they have spread more widely (the sanicle at Wandlebury has probably arrived from the adjacent area of woodland). There are occasional oddities, like the garden asparagus growing in Crapes orchard at Aldham in Essex, for example, which are apparently legacies of cut flowers or vegetables once cultivated between the trees.

It is thus comparatively rare for the ground flora within orchards in the eastern counties to resemble that of ancient, unimproved grassland. One exception is the tiny example at Steppingley Hospital at Flitwick in Bedfordshire, a County Wildlife Site, which features such plants as green-winged orchid (*Anacamptis morio*), adder's tongue fern (*Ophioglossum vulgatum*), pignut (*Conopodium majus*), quaking grass (*Briza media*), cuckooflower (*Cardamine pratensis*), black knapweed (*Centaurea nigra*) and oxeye daisy. In this particular case the orchard was planted only in the 1950s or 1960s, partly if not mainly for aesthetic or therapeutic reasons, on an area of existing grassland. The more mixed, rather random flora more usually encountered in orchards in eastern England presumably arises from an earlier history of spraying or ground cultivation, the proximity of old hedges, the presence of shaded areas and, above all, current management, based on regular or irregular mowing rather than grazing or hay cutting. The orchards selected for intensive study were, in this last respect, similar to the wider sample, surveyed in less detail as part of the Orchards East project. Out of a total of 1,690 examples that remain largely under grass, rather than being managed as bare ground or now occupied by scrub, only 144 (8.8 per cent) were recorded as being grazed and only 20 (1.2 per cent) were cut for hay. Surveyors recorded 482 (29 per cent) as 'rough grass', cut on a more irregular basis, while 1,044 were regularly mown, as lawn. In general, the ground flora of old orchards in the eastern counties is best described as moderately interesting but, once again, context is all. Given that permanent pasture is now rare across large parts of the region, orchards may often constitute grassy oases within extensive seas of arable.

Little can be said about the incidence of fungi in orchards – their short fruiting season precludes extensive survey work – but as well as moderately common varieties such as chicken of the woods (*Laetiporus sulphureus*), surveyors noted the presence of orchard specialists such as orchard tooth fungus (*Sarcodontia crocea*).[57] More is known about orchard molluscs, as a result of a survey of five Norfolk orchards carried out in 2005.[58] An orchard at Aldeby in the south-east of the county contained 12 different species but half were common and a further quarter 'frequent'. Three were classed as 'occasional' (the crystal snail (*Vitrea crystallina*), the radiated snail (*Discus rotundus*) and the smooth glass snail (*Aegopinella pura*)); there were no infrequent or rare species. The orchard at White House, Walpole Highway, in the Norfolk Fens produced 11 species. Again, there were no rarities, and of the three 'occasional' species, two – Draparnaud's glass snail (*Oxychilus draparnaudi*) and the field slug (*Derocerus reticulatum*) – were not found among the wood and litter on the orchard floor, or on the trees themselves, but beneath disused wooden

---

57 In an orchard in Wymondham, Norfolk.
58 R. Baker, D. Howlett and K. Clarke, 'Mollusc and Diatom Surveys 2005, Norfolk', unpublished report for the East of England Apple and Orchards Project (n.p., 2005); copy kindly supplied by Roy Baker.

Figure 8.9 Fieldfares are regular visitors to orchards in the autumn and winter months.

pallets. A similar pattern was repeated elsewhere, and only in the orchard at Mayes Farm, Yaxham, was a species classed as 'rare' – the worm slug (*Boettgerilla pallens*) – recorded. Orchards, in short, appear on the basis of this small amount of data to be of limited importance for mollusc conservation.

Old orchards can be havens for a wide range of mammals and – in the right conditions – amphibians, but in some cases it is hard to demonstrate that an area of unimproved pasture bordered by long-established hedges and studded with old trees would not be just as good a habitat. It might be expected that certain species of bat would be particularly associated with orchards – the common pipistrelle (*Pipistrellus pipistrellus*), the noctule bat (*Nyctalus noctula*) or others that roost in old, hollow trees – but hard evidence is currently lacking. Birds, however, are more closely connected with orchards, not surprisingly given the abundance of trees – and fruit. Traditionally, orchards were associated in particular with bullfinches, which in early spring will consume the buds of fruit trees, especially plums and pears.[59] The 1566 'Acte for the Preservation of Grayne', which allowed churchwardens to pay individuals for the bodies of pests and vermin thought to harm agricultural production, presumably included bullfinches among the 30 proscribed species for this reason (6,600 were killed over a period of 36 years in just one Cheshire parish – 452 in 1676 alone).[60] A single bullfinch can allegedly

---

59 I. Newton, *Finches* (London, 1972), p. 117.

60 R. Lovegrove, *Silent Fields: The Long Decline of a Nation's Wildlife* (Oxford, 2007), p. 85.

remove fruit-tree buds at the rate of more than 30 a minute.[61] Orchards are also important to the various species of birds that feast on windfall apples in the autumn and winter, and especially for fieldfares, which gather in large numbers not only in long-established orchards like that at Tewin in Hertfordshire, but also in ones more recently planted, such as the example at Attleborough established in the 1990s by Kevin West (Figure 8.9).

Past and present environments

Surveys of orchards in eastern England are continuing and the observations made in the preceding pages must be regarded as provisional. But on present evidence orchards appear to be of some importance for the conservation of many forms of wildlife, especially given the suburbanised or intensively agricultural character of much of the region, and seem to be of particular significance as a habitat for invertebrates, and especially saproxylic beetles, due in large part to the presence within them of abundant quantities of dead wood. To judge from the wider, less detailed survey carried out as part of the Orchards East project, around three-quarters of orchards in the eastern counties contain some or many trees with noticeable quantities of dead wood, and around half contain trees with significant holes. Yet how far this would have been true in the past is less clear. It is easy to assume that orchards have always been enduring and stable elements of the landscape, their constituent trees allowed to grow old and veteranise over the years, steadily accumulating populations of slow-colonising species. Some orchards, it is true, appear to have lasted for very long periods of time. That beside the farm called Clintons at Bury Green, Little Hadham, in Hertfordshire, shown on a map of 1596, survived until the 1970s or 1980s (Figure 8.10). But this may have been unusual, and it is clear that orchards were often more transient in character, coming and going from the landscape over the years. To quote some examples from Suffolk: in Brent Eleigh in 1725 three roods of arable were sold, 'part whereof formerly an orchard';[62] in Sudbury in 1802 four cottages in Eastgate Street were described as 'built on an orchard';[63] in Walsham le Willows in 1841 1.5 roods of land sold were described as 'sometime an orchard'; while in Stanton Upthorpe in 1856 a property was mortgaged that included an orchard 'now converted into meadow'.[64] Conversely, references to newly planted examples are also common: at Wickhambrook in 1653, for example, 1 rood of pasture 'now an orchard' was sold;[65] in Walsham Le Willows in 1819 one acre of land was described as a 'meadow late converted in to an orchard'.[66] To some extent, orchards simply expanded or contracted as the relative value of fruit and other agricultural commodities changed, or as

---

61 Newton, *Finches*, p. 116.
62 SRO, B, 754/1/177.
63 SRO, B, HC 539/C1/7.
64 SRO, B, TEM. 173/240.
65 SRO, B, EL 13/12/73.
66 SRO, B, TEM.173/261/6 (b).

Figure 8.10 The orchard at Clintons, Much Hadham, Hertfordshire, shown (above) on a map of 1583 and (below, arrowed) on the Ordnance Survey 6-inch map published in 1950. It finally disappeared, gradually developing into an area of garden, in the 1990s. Hertfordshire Archives and Local Studies Topographical Much Hadham/4.

new owners tried out novel ways of using particular parcels of ground. But in some cases it appears that when an orchard was grubbed out a replacement had already been established on a neighbouring site. The old one was perhaps being abandoned because of a build-up of disease or the incidence of a particular pathogen, such as honey fungus. One of the farms shown on a map of Ickleford in Hertfordshire surveyed in 1771 was provided with two orchards, one marked as the 'Old Orchard'.[67] By the time the first edition Ordnance Survey map was made a century later this had been grubbed out, but the other remained.

Even where orchards were persistent features, lasting for centuries, this does not mean that their constituent trees were routinely allowed to become old, hollow and veteranised. It is arguable that, as in our attitudes to 'semi-natural habitats' more generally, we often confuse and conflate the environmental character of several different things: old, 'traditional' orchards as they are today, with their tall, ancient and veteranised trees; such orchards as they would have been in the past, when they were managed on more commercial or at least more productive lines; and orchards recently planted, and as we expect them to develop over future decades. For what we think of as 'traditional' orchards may to some extent have appeared, to our ancestors, over-mature and undermanaged. In the case of some examples – abandoned commercial orchards such as that in Rickmansworth, described earlier – it is obvious that present levels of biodiversity are the consequence of abandonment and dereliction. When this particular example was a productive fruit farm in the 1950s, 1960s and 1970s, full of young trees and regularly sprayed with fungicides and insecticides, it would have had a far more restricted range of wildlife. But the same is probably true, albeit to a lesser degree, of most 'traditional' farmhouse orchards.

In particular, the kinds of very decaying tree that are the key feature of old, 'traditional' orchards were almost certainly rarer in the past. There are clear signs that trees were often taken down as their productivity declined, as Thomas Hitt specified in 1758: 'The reasons given for destroying old trees are generally these two, viz, the one for not bearing good fruit, and the other for bearing little or none.'[68] In a closely planted orchard, old trees, hollow and unstable, also posed a threat to their neighbours. A felled tree was not a wasted one, for there was always a demand for firewood in this fuel-hungry world.[69] It is true that some early writers – especially William Lawson – believed that fruit trees could live, and be productive, for very long periods – perhaps as much as a thousand years.[70] But documentary references suggest that trees in late senescence were often replaced. The Norfolk farmer Randall Burroughes recorded in his journal in February 1798 how one of his men had been employed 'digging and cutting two useless apple trees out of the orchard'.

---

67   HALS, DE/Ha/P1.

68   T. Hitt, *A Treatise of Fruit-Trees* (Dublin, 1758), p. 65.

69   For a discussion of early modern fuel supply in England, see P. Warde and T. Williamson, 'Fuel Supply and Agriculture in Post-Medieval England', *Agricultural History Review*, 62/1 (2014), pp. 61–82.

70   Lawson, *New Orchard and Garden*, p. 49.

Lease agreements commonly refer to the removal and replacement of old trees. One for a garden and orchard in Beccles in Suffolk, drawn up in 1786, reserved to the lessor 'all the old standard Apple trees now standing and growing upon the said premises together with the free liberty of ingress, egress and regress to cut down and stub up all such old decayed trees that shall have done bearing and to cut and carry away the same'.[71] Another, for Stone's Orchard in Croxley Green, Hertfordshire, from 1893, instructed the tenant to 'keep all trees properly pruned and when necessary substitute and plant young trees of good varieties'.[72] Contracts made with gardeners at country houses in the seventeenth and eighteenth century include similar provisions, as at Harrold Hall in Bedfordshire in 1653, where it was stipulated that 'in case any of the fruite trees either in the Orchyards or gardens shall happen to decaye from tyme to tyme to plant new trees of the Like goodnesse in the roome of such as shall see decay and to preserve and Cherish the same'.[73]

Our 'traditional' orchards in the past, in other words, when more intensively managed than today, may have contained fewer hollowed, veteran trees, and they would certainly have lacked much in the way of dead branches and the like. These would soon have been used for firewood. Indeed, early writers such as Ralph Austen emphasised the wood supplied by orchards almost as much as the fruit: 'It is well known how usefull and profitable they are from yeare to yeare, not only in respect of the *Fruits* but likewise for *Fuell*, by the prunings of the *Trees*, and *old dead Trees*'.[74] This argument should not be taken too far, however. Even commercial orchards, at least in the period before the Second World War, routinely allowed apple trees to remain for at least five decades, by which time they would be displaying some veteran characteristics – as the rapid spread of saproxylic beetles through the north Fens in the course of the twentieth century, noted above, clearly suggests. Nevertheless, we should be wary, when looking at the spreading, decaying, veteranised trees in a traditional orchard today, of imagining that the landscape was once full of such places. The reality is perhaps more complex.

In other ways old orchards today differ from those in the past. While many had permanent grassland between the trees, in some commercial orchards (and even in some of those attached to farmhouses) the ground was cultivated for vegetables or cut flowers. The regular manuring of fruit trees, by spreading dung around them, would have increased the growth of common herbaceous species such as dock and nettle, suppressing the rarer herbs: it was a practice recommended by William Lawson in 1618 and was still widespread in the nineteenth and twentieth centuries, when it is referred to in some lease agreements.[75] Nor should we forget that not only commercial orchards but also some farm

---

71   Wade Martins and Williamson, *Farming Journal of Randall Burroughes*, pp. 95–6; SRO, L, 109/E5/5.
72   Pomfret, *Stones Orchard*, p. 8.
73   BRO, TW685.
74   Austen, *Treatise on Fruit Trees*, unpaginated introduction.
75   Lawson, *New Orchard and Garden*, p. 41; Pomfret, *Stones Orchard*, p. 8.

ones were subject to very high applications of chemical fungicides and pesticides in the nineteenth and twentieth centuries. We might also note that part of the conservation value of orchards arises from the fact that much of the fruit they produce is today simply left to rot. In the past there would have been far fewer apples for fieldfares to feast upon.

Orchards, to summarise, are of some importance for nature conservation but largely when old and neglected; the more intensively managed orchards of the past almost certainly sustained a more limited range of flora and fauna. The new orchards being planted today will eventually provide important habitats, but it remains uncertain how far these will be superior to what might be supplied by other carefully chosen collections of trees, shrubs and herbs, appropriately managed.

Landscape significance

Landscape historians, archaeologists and others often emphasise the role of distinctive local and regional landscapes in providing a 'sense of place', which can give an important feeling of stability and connection in a rapidly changing world.[76] Historic, cultural features such as the shapes of fields, the abundance or otherwise of woodland, patterns of settlement and styles of vernacular architecture are at least as important in shaping distinctive countrysides as any 'natural' influences such as geology or topography. The distinction is, perhaps, a little artificial given that, to a significant extent, the 'cultural' is shaped by the 'natural', by the attempts of successive generations to make a living from the land. Some of the assessments of 'Historic Landscape Character' made by English Heritage and various local and regional agencies during the 1990s and early 2000s for areas within the eastern counties treat orchards as part of the historic environment, such as those for the Chilterns, including west Hertfordshire, and for south Bedfordshire,[77] but most pay them scant attention. Historians and archaeologists often describe landscapes as 'palimpsests' on which successive societies write their own histories, while usually only partly erasing the traces left by previous generations. But landscapes in which orchards formed a key element – ones that owed much of their distinctive 'character' to fruit production – were, for the most part, a nineteenth- and twentieth-century development. The 'prune' orchards of south Bedfordshire, for example, with which – to quote the relevant HLC – the area around Eaton Bray has 'an historical agricultural association', seem to have scarcely existed before 1860. Orchard *landscapes* like this were not timeless and traditional, but rooted in a real and comparatively recent world of agriculture and economics: one of railways,

---

76   Roberts and Wrathmell, *Region and Place*.

77   D. Green, 'The Changing Landscape of the Chilterns: Chilterns Historic Landscape Characterisation Project Final Report' (2009), <https://www.chilternsaonb.org/uploads/files/AboutTheChilterns/Historic Environment/The_Changing_Landscape_of_the_Chilterns.pdf>, accessed 7 March 2021, especially pp. 28 and 167; Albion Archaeology, 'The Chalk Arc Initiative: Historic Environment Characterisation' (2007), <https://www.bedscape.org.uk/BRMC/chalkarc/low-res-pds/CA-HEC.pdf>, accessed 7 March 2021.

urban expansion, agricultural depression and government policies. And, as that world has changed, so in most cases have orchards disappeared from such landscapes once again. In the parish of Eaton Bray itself, survey work by Steve Halton in 2005 recorded around 45 orchards of the 140 or more that existed in the 1950s; recent fieldwork by Anne and Colin Hall and Jane and Keith Tompkins, carried out as part of the Orchards East project, suggests that there are now around 26 surviving in recognisable, if generally derelict or declining, condition.

Quite how we should treat the orchards of such areas, and orchards more generally, in terms of planning legislation is a moot point, and not a matter to be discussed in any detail here. Both comparatively recent and relatively short-lived in nature, and yet important components of some local and regional landscapes, orchards raise in particularly acute form rather wider philosophical questions in conservation. Given that landscapes have primarily been shaped by practical considerations – by agriculture and industry – and are constantly changing, how do we decide which of their constituent elements are worthy of protection? Should they include those quite recent features that local people have but recently come to regard as 'characteristic'? If so, we are close to saying that the landscape as it exists today should be frozen in time and undergo no further change, a position as philosophically untenable as it is practically impossible. And with orchards we have the additional issue that they require active interventions to preserve them intact into the future, to prevent them developing into open pasture or secondary woodland. Individual orchards can certainly be conserved and protected. Whether this can or should be done at landscape scale is, perhaps, a different matter.

CHAPTER NINE

Conclusion

Orchards are tricky things to deal with. For well over a century they have been bathed in the mellow light of nostalgia, romanticised as elements of a timeless yet disappearing rural world. Even before that they had a symbolic significance, were embedded in myths of lost Edens, of golden ages of effortless production. The antiquity of particular orchards and of the individual trees within them is frequently exaggerated, in part because of the remarkable speed with which fruit trees grow and veteranise – and which thus, somewhat paradoxically, ensures their short-lived character. Exaggerated, too, is the antiquity of the fruit varieties found in old orchards and their supposed connections with a distinctly local past. Our primary purpose in this book has been to challenge some of these myths by placing orchards within a wider but more grounded range of contexts, historical and to an extent environmental. We are aware that in doing this we may have offended some orchard enthusiasts, not least a number of individuals on whom we have relied for much advice and information. But it is vital to emphasise that orchards are not timeless. They have histories as a group, and biographies as individuals.

Orchards were planted for the most part for good economic and practical reasons, although, as we have seen, they were from an early date frequently used as a part of ornamental landscapes. Indeed, even on humble farms they were clearly appreciated for their aesthetic qualities. Orchards were ubiquitous features of the medieval and early modern landscape, their fruits valued in a world in which other forms of sweetness were in short supply, and the overwhelming majority of farms possessed one, albeit usually occupying considerably less than 1 per cent of their overall area. Their produce was used in the household and sold locally but they also, as we have seen, had a number of other roles in the farm economy. Small numbers of fruit trees could also be found in the grounds of cottages and were occasionally planted within churchyards, beside almshouses and in other public or semi-public locations for the good of the poor. Larger orchards, boasting a more diverse range of fruit, were associated with the houses of the rich. It would, in short, have been difficult to walk far in the countryside in the pre-industrial period without stumbling upon an orchard.

On most farms, throughout history, orchards formed only a small part of the farm business. But even in the Middle Ages there is evidence for holdings on which fruit production played a more important role, while by the seventeenth century some districts in the eastern counties had begun to specialise in fruit production, with the area of farms devoted to orchards rising significantly, to 3, 4, or 5 per cent – most notably west Hertfordshire and the Fens around Wisbech. But it was only in the 'orchard century', which began in the 1850s, that commercial production really took off and orchards became a major feature of local landscapes. This development was fuelled by the growth of large urban markets and the appearance of new transport systems that allowed fruit to be taken to customers with relative ease. But it was further encouraged by a range of other factors, including agricultural depression, the emergence of new processing industries and the development of government policies designed to increase the numbers of smallholdings. Areas of incipient specialisation now saw sustained growth, and entirely new orchard districts developed, such as the 'prune' villages of south Bedfordshire. The 'orchard century' also saw a more general increase in the numbers of commercial orchards wherever environmental conditions were suitable for the specialised production of fruit. Initially the great expansion in orchards was particularly associated with small farms and smallholdings, as specialised fruit growing had been in earlier periods. But over time large fruit farms increased in importance, dominating the industry in many districts by the middle decades of the twentieth century. The 'orchard century' also saw the continuing importance of orchards as garden features – more accurately, perhaps, it saw something of a re-emergence, following a period in which they had been marginalised from designed landscapes, if not actually neglected, during the popularity of 'naturalistic' styles in the later eighteenth and early nineteenth centuries. It also saw the proliferation of large 'institutional' orchards attached to places such as psychiatric hospitals.

At the start of the 'orchard century' there was a marked contrast in the numbers and extent of orchards in the east and the west of England. In the latter region the principal alcoholic beverage was cider, and farms of necessity planted large quantities of apples and, to an extent, pears for making their own cider or for sale to professional producers. Although, as we have seen, cider was produced to some extent in the eastern counties, and sometimes on an industrial scale, beer was always the main alcoholic drink consumed, the difference between east and west largely reflecting variations in the availability of good-quality malting barley. But the expanding urban markets of the nineteenth and twentieth centuries required not cider apples but dessert or culinary varieties, which grew as well or better in the drier east of the country, and, while the orchard acreage in the eastern counties never reached the same levels as in Devon, Herefordshire, Gloucestershire or Somerset, the gap narrowed significantly in the course of the twentieth century.

For a range of reasons the area planted with fruit trees in the eastern counties thus grew at an extraordinary rate after 1850, reaching over 19,400 acres (7,851 hectares) by 1900 and around 48,000 acres (19,400 hectares) by c.1955. But, as we have seen, this relatively short burst of expansion then came to an end, the orchard bubble burst, and the acreage dwindled rapidly. In fact, small traditional orchards, associated with farmhouses, had been disappearing for decades, partly due to changes in the wider agricultural industry and partly because they were poorly suited to the new technologies of fruit production. From the early 1960s they were joined in their decline by their commercial neighbours, including the large fruit farms only recently established.

While, for reasons we have explained, precise figures remain elusive, in broad terms we might say that the orchard area in the eastern counties has now declined to around 8,000 acres (c.3,200 hectares), and much of what remains survives in a decaying and derelict condition. This rapid reversal in the fortunes of orchards has complex causes. Although Britain's accession to the European Community is sometimes blamed, the area occupied by orchards nationally was already falling fast at that time and if anything the rate of decline slowed after 1973. The Common Agricultural Policy certainly encouraged the grubbing out of orchards, either directly or indirectly, but they disappeared mainly as a consequence of wider and more complex forces: the inexorable globalisation of trade in food commodities; the rise of ever larger units of agricultural production; and the steady decline in small food-retailers and their replacement by powerful supermarket chains. Changes in lifestyles and in employment patterns also played a part. A similar collection of influences has, albeit over a rather longer period of time, worked to reduce significantly the range of fruit varieties available for sale. The inexorable loss of both orchards and fruit varieties should be understood as part and parcel of much wider changes taking place in our increasingly urbanised country, involving the decline of the small-scale, the local and the controllable and their replacement by the global, the impersonal and the unaccountable – by the alienating world of late capitalism.

Over the last few decades there has been an impressive reaction against the decline. New orchards have been planted, old varieties brought back from the brink. But in among the good sense and clarity of purpose myths have flourished. The moderately old has become confused with the ancient, the relatively recent and commercial with 'tradition'. It is, perhaps, worth emphasising that most of the really impressive orchards that survive in the eastern counties, and especially those open to the public on a regular if sometimes infrequent basis, are not small, traditional farmhouse orchards. They were typical creations of the 'orchard century', and mainly of the period after 1900. These include commercial orchards planted in the inter-war years, such as Crapes Fruit Farm, Aldham, Essex, with its wonderfully veteranised trees on dwarfing rootstocks; Mayes Farm, Yaxham, Norfolk, now a County Wildlife Site; Tewin Orchard in Hertfordshire, a nature reserve managed by the Hertfordshire and Middlesex Wildlife Trust; and Jeacock's Farm near Tring, in the same county. They also include the important institutional orchards at Girton College, Cambridge (c.1895); St Elizabeth's, Much Hadham, Hertfordshire (1920s); and The Oval, Harpenden (c.1913). In old farm orchards there are usually at best only a handful of veteran trees. These comparatively recent sites contain scores of them.

While the ecological importance of old orchards as habitats – especially for sustaining important groups of invertebrates – is undeniable, their particular and unique role in this respect has perhaps been overstated by some orchard champions or, at least, remains to be proven. Orchards, like other 'semi-natural habitats', are in a sense accidents of history. They may deliver important biological services but this was not the intention of those who planted them and much of their importance in this respect arises only once they have reached an over-mature if not derelict condition. It is, moreover, arguable that other habitats, arising by chance or deliberately designed for the purpose, would provide the same or greater benefits for wildlife.

Yet to argue that orchards may not be quite what many believe them to be is not, we would emphasise, to downgrade their importance or to denigrate the efforts of those who fight to preserve them. The old fruit varieties they contain, while perhaps seldom as ancient or traditional as sometimes assumed, represent a testimony to the skill and knowledge of generations of past nurserymen, a priceless legacy of varied tastes and textures that serves as a powerful antidote to the blandness of experience offered by most modern shops. And orchards themselves, perhaps uniquely as landscape features, manage to provide multiple benefits within a relatively small space and serve to combine both cultural and natural value. Their importance for wildlife thus epitomises, in crucial ways, the role of the wider landscape in conserving biodiversity. How we treat them crystallises with particular clarity an emerging debate in conservation circles. An earlier generation of ecologists, including people such as Oliver Rackham, saw the conservation of historical landscapes and of wildlife as working together. The various key habitats, such as ancient woods or heathland, as well as the environments more generally in which wildlife exists, were created by human actions. They were shaped over many centuries by successive forms of social and economic organisation, by technologies, needs and practices whose time has now, in many cases, passed. Indeed, what we think of as the 'natural world' in Britain, as in most of Europe – the particular range and balance of species in particular locations – is more a cultural artefact than anything truly 'natural', if by that difficult word we mean independent of human agency. Orchards form part of a wider pattern. But today, for many conservationists, such ideas and approaches are falling from favour. 'Rewilding' is the only game in town: the idea that biodiversity is best sustained by creating spaces, preferably extensive ones, in which nature can be left to its own devices, not by maintaining or restoring the various practices that shaped the countryside – an approach put into practice most famously on the Knepp estate in Sussex.

Such ideas are popular and fashionable and are beginning to shape conservation policy. But they have a range of dangerous implications seldom recognised. Rewilding by its very nature involves the destruction of the human landscape, of the physical structures and spaces that provide a direct link with a range of pasts. More importantly, the wholesale adoption of rewilding would, almost certainly, encourage further intensification of agriculture in the 'normal' countryside, safe in the knowledge that the work of sustaining biodiversity was being continued elsewhere – potentially leading to further impoverishment of the everyday environment both as a historic and cultural artefact and as a wildlife resource. Rewilded areas would be discrete and often remote, but wildlife and

Figure 9.1 Old orchards are of critical importance in sustaining biodiversity and important pieces of landscape history that provide a direct connection with our past. Yet at the same time they provide a range of sensual pleasures, from the tastes of obscure fruit varieties to the smell of spring blossom.

'nature' are principally experienced – especially by the poor, the old, the infirm – close to home, on country walks, in the park or in the garden.

Rewilding is an admirable objective and will play a major role in conservation in the future. But for the reasons just given it must not be allowed to monopolise our energy and attention. Conservation of the wider landscape, of nature living in a world shaped over centuries by human histories, is also essential. And that is why orchards are so important. They were, and are, created and maintained by human activities to a greater extent, arguably, than any other 'semi-natural habitat'. Yet they sustain species, especially saproxylic beetles, that have (in the eastern counties especially) few homes elsewhere. Even in terms of the commoner forms of flora and fauna with which they are associated, orchards take on a particular significance because – again, to a greater degree than other habitats – they have always been intimately associated with the places where people live, and now, in new and exciting ways, this is even more the case, with the appearance of community orchards, open to all, in villages, towns and suburbs.

Orchards thus have an important role in wildlife conservation. And, as should by now be clear, they have histories, variously short or long, that tie them to their particular localities. The fruit varieties they contain provide connections with a wider and older past, if one less ancient than is sometimes suggested. All orchards, moreover, come laden with yet older associations, providing a connection with our earliest, most essential myths. Our ancestors, even our recent ancestors, were surrounded by orchards. Their general disappearance over the last few decades represents a profound discontinuity with a long past. Above all, the direct and almost primordial sensory experiences that orchards provide – the tastes of the many varieties of fruit, the beauty of spring blossom, the sound of birdsong, the rough textures of old bark – constitute a powerful antidote to the blandness that characterises so much of modern life. To quote, once again, the words of William Lawson, orchards make 'all our senses swim in pleasure, and that with infinite variety, joined with no less commodity'.[1] We need orchards; we need to sustain a good number of those that remain, perhaps repurposed, where possible, as areas of conservation and public amenity; and we need to plant new ones, and spread the skills required to maintain them into the future. Such work is, as we have emphasised, already being carried out by activists and enthusiasts. It needs to continue, to broaden, to intensify and to receive the support and funding that it requires from society as a whole. And such endeavours need to be backed up by further research: the work set out in this volume represents only a beginning, an initial foray into an area of immense interest and importance.

---

1 Lawson, *New Orchard or Garden*, p. 56.

Bibliography

Books, articles and reports

Acton, E., *Modern Cookery for Private Families* (London, 1857).

Albion Archaeology, 'The Chalk Arc Initiative: Historic Environment Characterisation' (2007), <https://www.bedscape.org.uk/BRMC/chalkarc/low-res-pds/CA-HEC.pdf>, accessed 7 March 2021.

Alexander, K., 'The Invertebrates of Britain's Wood Pastures', *British Wildlife*, 11 (1999), pp. 108–17.

Alexander, K., *The Invertebrates of Living and Decaying Timber In Britain & Ireland: A Provisional Annotated Checklist*, English Nature Research Reports 467 (Peterborough, 2002).

Alexander, K., 'A Remarkable Wood-Decay Beetle Fauna from a Group of Traditional Orchards at Colwall, Herefordshire', *The Coleopterist*, 19 (2002), pp. 11–14.

Alexander, K., *Revision of the Index of Ecological Continuity as used for Saproxylic Beetles*, English Nature Research Reports 574 (Peterborough, 2004).

Alexander, K., 'The Special Importance of Traditional Orchards for Invertebrate Conservation, with a Case Study of the BAP Priority Species the Noble Chafer *Gnorimus nobilis*', in I.D. Rotherham (ed.), *Orchards and Groves: Their History, Ecology, Culture and Archaeology* (Sheffield, 2008), pp. 12–18.

Alexander, K., *The Role of Trees outside Woodlands in providing Habitat and Ecological Networks for Saproxylic Invertebrates: Part 1, Designing a Field Study to Test Initial Hypotheses*, Natural England Commissioned Report NECR225a (Peterborough, 2016).

Alexander, K. and Chandler, P., 'Rare Fungus Gnats (Diptera, Mycetophilidae) from a Herefordshire Cherry Orchard', *Dipterists Digest*, 17 (2010), pp. 25–6.

Alexander, K., Bower, L. and Green, G., 'A Remarkable Saproxylic Insect Fauna from a Traditional Orchard in Worcestershire – But are the Species Resident or Transient?' *British Journal of Entomology & Natural History*, 27 (2014), pp. 221–9.

Anon., *The Fruiterer's Secret* (London, 1664).

Askay, M. and Williamson, T., *Orchard Recipes from Eastern England: Landscape, Fruit and Heritage* (Lowestoft, 2020).

Austen, R., *A Treatise on Fruit-trees, Showing the Manner of Grafting, Setting, Pruning, and Ordering of them in all Respects* (Oxford, 1653).

Bagenal, N.B. (ed.), *Fruit Growing* (London, 1939).

Baker, R., Howlett, D. and Clarke, K., 'Mollusc and Diatom Surveys 2005, Norfolk', unpublished report for the East of England Apple and Orchards Project (n.p., 2005).

Barnes, G. and Williamson, T. *Ancient Trees in the Landscape: Norfolk's Arboreal Heritage* (Oxford, 2011).

Barnes, G., Saunders, D.G. and Williamson, T., 'Banishing Barberry: The History of *Berberis vulgaris* Prevalence and Wheat Stem Rust Incidence across Britain', *Plant Pathology*, 69/7 (2020), pp. 1193–202, <https://bsppjournals.onlinelibrary.wiley.com/doi/abs/10.1111/ppa.13231>, accessed 8 March 2021.

Barrett, H. and Phillips, J., *Suburban Style: The British Home, 1840–1960* (London, 1993).

Barrow, E. and Hulme, M., 'Describing the Surface Climate of the British Isles', in M. Hulme and E. Barrow (eds), *Climates of the British Isles, Past, Present and Future* (London, 1997), pp. 33–61.

Bartos, J., 'Wilderness and Grove: Gardening with Trees in England 1688–1750', PhD thesis (University of Bristol, 2013).

Batchelor, T., *General View of the Agriculture of the County of Bedford* (London, 1813).

Bates, J.W., Proctor, M.C.F., Preston, C.D., Hodgetts, N.G. and Perry, A.R., 'Occurrence of Epiphytic Bryophytes in a "Tetrad" Transect across Southern Britain 1: Geographical Trends in Abundance and Evidence of Recent Change', *Journal of Bryology*, 19/4 (1997), pp. 685–714.

Beavington, F., 'The Development of Market Gardening in Bedfordshire, 1799–1839', *Agricultural History Review*, 23/1 (1975), pp. 23–47.

Belcham, L., *A History of the Land Settlement Association: With Particular Reference to its Newbourne Estate* (Newbourne, 2014).

Bellamy, L., *The Language of Fruit: Literature and Horticulture in the Long Eighteenth Century* (Philadelphia, 2019).

Blackburne-Maze, P., *The Apple Book* (London, 1986).

Blagrave, J., *The Epitome of the Whole Art of Husbandry* (London, 1669).

Blockeel, T.L. and Stevenson, C.R., 'Hypnum cupressiforme var. heseleri (Ando & Higuchi) M.O.Hill (Bryopsida, Hypnales) in Norfolk. New to the British Isles', *Journal of Bryology*, 28 (2006), pp. 190–3.

Blomefield, F., *An Essay towards a Topographical History of the County of Norfolk*, 2nd edn, 11 vols (London, 1805–10).

Bone, Q., 'Legislation to Revive Small Farming in England 1887–1914', *Agricultural History*, 49 (1975), 27–40.

Bowyer, M., *'We Have to Deal with the Farmers': Episodes in the History of North Hertfordshire in the 19th and 20th Centuries* (Cambridge, 2010).

Branch Johnson, W., *Industrial Archaeology of Hertfordshire* (Newton Abbot, 1977).

Brassley, P., Lambert, A. and Saunders, P. (eds), *Accounts of the Reverend John Crakanthorp of Fowlmere. 1682–1710*, Cambridge Record Society 8 (Cambridge, 1988).

Bratton, J. and Andrews, J., 'Invertebrate Conservation: Principles and their Application to Broad-Leaved Woodland', *British Wildlife*, 2/6 (1991), pp. 335–44.

Brown, D. and Williamson, T., *Lancelot Brown and the Capability Men: Landscape Revolution in Eighteenth-Century England* (London, 2016).

Browne, H., *Nurseries, Orchards, Profitable Gardens and Vineyards Encouraged* (London, 1677).

Bullein, W., *The Government of Health* (London, 1595).

Burdett, H.C., *Hospitals and Asylums of the World: Asylum Construction* (London, 1891).

Burian, S., 'Benevolent Capitalists? A Study of Paternalist Authority in an Industrial Firm', PhD thesis (University of Cambridge, 1983).

Bush, R., *Tree Fruit Growing*, vol. 1 (London, 1951).

Butcher, R.W., *The Land of Britain: Suffolk* (London, 1941).

Cameron, L.G., *The Land of Britain: Hertfordshire* (London, 1941).

Campbell, C., *Vitruvius Britannicus*, vol. 3 (London, 1725).

Catt, J. (ed.), *Hertfordshire Geology and Landscape* (Welwyn, 2010).

Chandler, M., *A–Z of Norwich: Places, People, History* (Stroud, 2016).

Chapman, G., *Chapman's Homer: The Iliad and the Odyssey*, ed. Jan Parker (Ware, 2002).

Chauncy, H., *The Historical Antiquities of Hertfordshire*, 2nd edn, 2 vols (London, 1826).

Clark Hall, J.R., *A Concise Anglo-Saxon Dictionary*, 4th edn (Cambridge, 2000).

Clark, M., *Apples: A Field Guide*, rev. edn (Tewin, 2015).

Clifford, S., 'Save Our Orchards: One Insight into the First Two Decades of a Campaign', in I.D. Rotherham (ed.), *Orchards and Groves: Their History, Ecology, Culture and Archaeology* (Sheffield, 2008), pp. 32–42.

Clutterbuck, J., *Agricultural Notes on Hertfordshire* (London, 1864).

Conolly, J., *The Construction and Government of Lunatic Asylums and Hospitals for the Insane* (London, 1847).

Cook, M., *The Manner of Raising, Ordering, and Improving Forest and Fruit-Trees* (London, 1676).

Copley, E., *The Housekeeper's Guide or a Plain and Practical System of Domestic Cookery* (London, 1838).

Corfield, P., 'From Second City to Regional Capital', in C. Rawcliffe and R. Wilson (eds), *Norwich Since 1550* (London, 2004), pp. 139–66.

Cornille, A., Giraud, T., Smulders, M.J.M., Roldán-Ruiz, I. and Gladieux, P., 'The Domestication and Evolutionary Ecology of Apples', *Trends in Genetics*, 30/2 (2014), pp. 57–65.

Cotchin, R., 'A Monumental Clanger', *The Countryman*, 87 (1982), pp. 45–6.

Cowell, F., *Richard Woods: Master of the Pleasure Garden* (Woodbridge, 2009).

Crawley, L., 'The Growth of Provincial Nurseries: Norwich Nurserymen, c.1750–1860', *Garden History*, 48/2 (2020), pp. 119–34.

Croft-Cooke, R., *English Cooking: A New Approach* (London, 1960).

Crossley, A., *Apple Years at Cockayne Hatley: The History of Coxes Orange Pippin Orchards ('COPO')* (Cockayne Hatley, 1999).

Currie, C., 'Fish Ponds as Garden Features', *Garden History*, 18 (1990), pp. 22–33.

Dallas, P., 'Seventeenth-century Garden Earthworks at Grange Farm, West Dereham', *Norfolk Archaeology*, 45 (2007), pp. 188–97.

Dallas, P., Barnes, G. and Williamson, T., 'Orchards in the Landscape: A Norfolk Case Study', *Landscapes*, 16/1 (2015), pp. 26–43.

Dallas, P., Last, R. and Williamson, T., *Norfolk Gardens and Designed Landscapes* (Oxford, 2013).

Dickens, C., *A Christmas Carol* (London, 1858).

Diplock, M., *The History of Leavesden Hospital* (Abbots Langley, 1990).

Dobson, F., *Lichens: An Illustrated Guide to the British and Irish Species*, 5th edn (London, 2005).

Douet, A., 'Norfolk Agriculture, 1914–1972', PhD thesis (University of East Anglia, 1989).

Douet, A., *Breaking New Ground: Agriculture in Norfolk, 1914–1972* (Aylsham, 2015).

Drake, J., *Wood and Ingram: A Huntingdon Nursery, 1742–1950* (Cambridge, 2008).

Edmund, M., 'Nicholas Dixon, Limner; and Matthew Dixon, Painter, Died 1710', *The Burlington Magazine*, 125/967 (1983), pp. 611–13.

Edwards, A.C. and Newton, K.C., *The Walkers of Hanningfield: Surveyors and Mapmakers Extraordinary* (London, 1984).

Ellis, W., *The Practical Farmer or Hertfordshire Husbandman* (London, 1732).

Ellis, W., *Chiltern and Vale Farming* (London, 1733).

Ellis, W., *The Timber Tree Improved* (London, 1738).

Ellis, W., *The Modern Husbandman, Complete in 8 Volumes* (London, 1750).

Ellis, W., *The Compleat Cyderman: Or, the Present Practice of Raising Plantations of the Best Cyder Apple and Perry Pear-Trees* (London, 1754).

Emmison, F.G., *Elizabethan Life. Home Work and Land. From Essex Wills and Sessions and Manorial Records* (Chelmsford, 1976).

Englander, D., *Poverty and Poor Law Reform in Britain: From Chadwick to Booth, 1834–1914* (Abingdon, 2013).

Evans, J., *The Endless Web* (London, 1954).

Farnell, M., 'The Neglected Aylesbury Prune', *Buckinghamshire and Bedfordshire Countryside* (March 1972), pp. 14–16.

Farthing, F.H., *Saturday in My Garden* (London, 1911).

Fitzgerald, J., 'Hedges and their Importance on the Rivers Nursery Site', in E. Waugh (ed.), *Rivers Nursery of Sawbridgeworth: The Art of Pomology* (Ware, 2009), pp. 180–2.

The Florist, Fruitist and Garden Miscellany (London, 1854).

Fowles, A.P., Alexander, K. and Key, R.S., 'The Saproxylic Index: Evaluating Wooded Habitats for the Conservation of Dead Wood Coleoptera', *The Coleopterist*, 8 (1999), pp. 121–41.

Fuller, T., *The History of the Worthies of England* (London, 1662).

Garner, R., *The Grafter's Handbook*, 6th edn (London, 2013).

Gee, M., *The Devon Orchards Book* (Wellington, 2018).

Gerish, W.B., *Sir Henry Chauncy, Kt; Serjeant-at-Law and Recorder of Hertford* (London, 1907).

Giles, J.A. (trans.), *Matthew Paris's English History from 1235 to 1273*, 3 vols (London, 1854).

Gissing, T., 'Polstead Cherries', *The Phytologist*, 2 (1857–8), p. 326.

Gooch, W., *General View of the Agriculture of the County of Cambridge* (London, 1811).

Gordon, D.I., *A Regional History of the Railways of Great Britain, Vol. 5: The Eastern Counties*, rev. edn (Newton Abbot, 1977).

Green, D., 'The Changing Landscape of the Chilterns: Chilterns Historic Landscape Characterisation Project Final Report' (2009), <https://www.chilternsaonb.org/uploads/files/AboutTheChilterns/HistoricEnvironment/The_Changing_Landscape_of_the_Chilterns.pdf>, accessed 7 March 2021.

Griffin, C.J., '"Some Inhuman Wretch": Animal Maiming and the Ambivalent Relationship between Rural Workers and Animals', *Rural History*, 25/2 (2014), pp. 133–60.

Haggard, H. Rider, *Rural England*, 2 vols (London, 1906).

Haggard, H. Rider, *Regeneration: Being an Account of the Social Work of the Salvation Army in Great Britain* (London, 1910).

Harman, H., *Buckinghamshire Dialect* (London, 1929).

Harvey, D., 'Fruit Growing in Kent in the Nineteenth Century', *Archaeologia Cantiana*, 79 (1964), pp. 94–108.

Harvey, J., *Early Nursery Catalogues* (Bath, 1972).

Harvey, J., *Early Nurserymen* (Winchester, 1974).

Hellier, H.E., *Practical Gardening for Amateurs* (London, 1935).

Henderson, A., 'Lichens in Orchards', in I.D. Rotherham (ed.), *Orchards and Groves: Their History, Ecology, Culture and Archaeology* (Sheffield, 2008), pp. 76–85.

Hickman, C., *Therapeutic Landscapes: A History of English Hospital Gardens Since 1800* (Manchester, 2013).

Higginbotham, P., *Children's Homes: A History of Institutional Care for Britain's Young* (London, 2017).

Hitt, T., *A Treatise of Fruit-Trees* (Dublin, 1758).

Hoare, A.H., *The English Grass Orchard and the Principles of Fruit Growing* (London, 1928).

Hodge, C.A.H., Burton, R.G.O., Corbett, W.M., Evans, R. and Searle, R.S., *Soils and their Use in Eastern England* (Harpenden, 1984).

Hodgetts, N.G., Preston, C.D. and Stevenson, C.R., 'Antitrichia curtipendula in a Cambridgeshire Orchard', *Field Bryology*, 89 (2006), pp. 8–9.

Hogg, R., *British Pomology: Or The History, Description, Classification, And Synonyms Of the Fruits and Fruit Trees of Great Britain* (London, 1851).

Hogg, R., *The Fruit Manual: Containing the Descriptions and Synonyms of the Fruit and Fruit Trees of Great Britain* (London, 1860).

Hogg, R. and Bull, H.G., *The Herefordshire Pomona*, 2 vols (Hereford, 1876–85).

Homans, G.C., *English Villagers of the Thirteenth Century* (Cambridge, MA, 1941).

Hone, W., *The Year Book of Daily Recreation and Information* (London, 1832).

Horridge, G., *Growth and Development of a Family Firm: Chivers of Histon, 1873–1939* (Cambridge, 1983).

Howlett, B., *Hitchin Priory and Park: The History of a Landscape Park and Gardens* (Hitchin, 2004).

Hudson, K., *The Archaeology of the Consumer Society: The Second Industrial Revolution in Britain* (London, 1983).

Hunter, J.M., *For the Love of an Orchard* (London, 2010).

Infante-Amate, J., 'The Ecology and History of the Mediterranean Olive Grove: The Spanish Great Expansion, 1750–2000', *Rural History*, 23/2 (2012), pp. 161–84.

Jackson, A., *Semi-Detached London: Suburban Development, Life and Transport 1900–1939* (London, 1973).

James, M., *Complete Guide to Home Gardening* (London, n.d. c.1940).

Janick, J., 'The Origins of Fruits, Fruit Growing and Fruit Breeding', *Plant Breeding Review*, 25 (2005), pp. 255–320.

Jee, N., *Landscape of the Channel Islands* (Chichester, 1982).

Jekyll, G., *Wood and Garden* (London, 1899).

Jekyll, G., *Colour Schemes for the Flower Garden* (London, 1919).

Jones, K., *Asylums and After: A Revised History of the Mental Health Services: From the Early Eighteenth Century to the 1990s* (London, 1993).

Jones, R. and Dimiz, M.A., *Twentieth Century Land Settlement Schemes* (London, 2020).

Jones-Baker, D., *The Folklore of Hertfordshire* (London, 1977).

Kain, R.J.P. and Prince, H., *The Tithe Surveys of England and Wales* (Cambridge, 2006).

Kelly, E.R., *Post Office Directory for Cambridgeshire, Norfolk and Suffolk* (London, 1869).

Kent, E., *Sylvan Rambles, or a Companion to the Park and Shrubbery* (London, 1825).

Kent, N., *General View of the Agriculture of the County of Norfolk* (London, 1796).

Kiebacher, T., Keller, C., Scheidegger, C. and Bergamini, A., 'Epiphytes in Wooded Pastures: Isolation Matters for Lichen but not for Bryophyte Species Richness', *PLoS ONE*, 12 (2017) <https://doi.org/10.1371/journal.pone.0182065>, accessed 7 March 2021.

King, A. and Clifford, S., 'The Apple, the Orchard, the Cultural Landscape', in S. Clifford and A. King (eds), *Local Distinctiveness: Place, Particularity and Identity* (London, 1993), pp. 37–46.

King, A. and Clifford, S., *Community Orchards Handbook* (Totnes, 2008).

Kirby, T., 'Railways', in T. Kirby and S. Oosthuizen (eds), *An Atlas of Cambridgeshire and Huntingdonshire History* (Cambridge, 2000), section 68.

Kitchen, F., *Settlers in England* (London, 1947).

Lake, J., 'The English Pays: Approaches to Understanding and Characterising Landscapes and Places', *Landscapes*, 8/2 (2007), pp. 28–39.

Langley, B., *Pomona, or the Fruit Garden Illustrated* (London, 1729).

Laundon, J.R., *Lichens* (Princes Risborough, 1986).

Lawson, W., *A New Orchard or Garden* (London, 1618).

Lee, J.R., Woods, M.A. and Moorlock, B.S.P., *British Regional Geology: East Anglia and Adjoining Areas*, 5th edn (London, 2015).

Leward, K.H. (ed.), *Calendar of Close Rolls, Henry VII: Volume 1: 1485–1500* (London, 1955).

Lindley, G., *A Guide to the Orchard and Kitchen Garden; or an Account of the Most Valuable Fruit and Vegetables Cultivated in Great Britain* (London, 1831).

Loudon, J.C., *The Gardener's Magazine and Register of Rural and Domestic Improvement*, 9 (London, 1833).

Lovegrove, R., *Silent Fields: The Long Decline of a Nation's Wildlife* (Oxford, 2007).

Lush, M., Robertson, H.J., Alexander, K.N., Giavarini, V., Hewins, E., Mellings, J., Stevenson, C.R., Storey, M. and Whitehead, P.F., *Biodiversity Studies of Six Traditional Orchards in England*, Natural England Research Reports 25 (Peterborough, 2007).

Mabey, R., *The Common Ground: A Place for Nature in Britain's Future* (London, 1980).

MacKay Brown, C.F., 'Some Bedfordshire Recipes', *Bedfordshire News*, 10 (1966), pp. 20–1.

Macnair, A., Rowe, A. and Williamson, T., *Dury and Andrews' Map of Hertfordshire: Society and Landscape in the Eighteenth Century* (Oxford, 2016).

Markham, G., *The English Husbandman* (London, 1613).

Martin, E. and Satchell, M., *Wheare Most Inclosures Be. East Anglian Fields, History, Morphology and Management*, East Anglian Archaeology 124 (Ipswich, 2008).

Mashiter, R., *A Little English Cookbook* (Belfast, 1989).

Masset, C., *Orchards* (Aylesbury, 2012).

Maund, B., *A Treatise on Orchard and Garden Fruits: Their Description, History and Management* (London, n.d. *c*.1851).

Mawson, T.H., *The Art and Craft of Garden Making*, 4th edn (London, 1912).

Meynell, L., *Bedfordshire* (Wallingford, 1960).

Mitchell, A., *Collins Field Guide to the Trees of Britain and Northern Europe* (London, 1974).

Moore, J.P., 'The Impact of Agricultural Depression and Landownership Change on the County of Hertfordshire, c.1870–1914', PhD thesis, University of Hertfordshire, 2010.

Morgan, J. and Richards, A., *The New Book of Apples* (London, 2002).

Morsley, C., *News from the English Countryside, 1851–1950* (London, 1983).

Mosby, J.E.G., *The Land of Britain: Norfolk* (London, 1938).

Mudge, K., Janick, J., Scofield, S. and Goldschmidt, E., 'A History of Grafting', *Horticultural Review*, 35 (2009), pp. 437–93.

Newton, I., *Finches* (London, 1972).

Noble, C., 'Norwich Cathedral Priory Gardeners' Accounts 1329–1530', in C. Noble, C. Moreton and P. Rutledge (eds), *Farming and Gardening in Late Medieval Norfolk*, Norfolk Record Society 61 (Norwich, 1997).

Norbury, C.P., 'Modern Developments in Fruit Growing', *Journal of the Royal Society of Arts*, 100/4881 (1952), pp. 719–34.

Norden, J., *The Surveyor's Dialogue* (London, 1608).

Oldén, A. and Halme, P., 'Grazers Increase β-diversity of Vascular Plants and Bryophytes in Wood-Pastures', *Journal of Vegetation Science*, 27 (2016), pp. 1084–93.

Page, W. (ed.), *Victoria County History, Bedfordshire*, vol. 2 (London, 1908).

Page, W. (ed.), *Victoria County History, Hertfordshire*, vol. 4 (London, 1914).

Pam, J., 'Essex Agriculture: Landowners' and Farmers' Responses to Economic Change, 1850–1914', PhD thesis (University of London, 2004).

Parhill, G. and Cook, G., *Hadleigh Salvation Army Farm: A Vision Reborn* (Hadleigh, 2008).

Paye, P., *The Mid-Suffolk Light Railway* (Upper Bucklebury, 1986).

Paye, P., *The Wisbech and Upwell Tramway* (Tarrant Hinton, 2009).

Peake, A.S., *The Life of Sir William Hartley* (London, 1926).

Perren, R., *Agriculture in Depression 1870–1940* (Cambridge, 1995).

Perrin, V., 'Cambridgeshire Orchard Survey: Phase 2 Survey, 2006–09. Traditional Orchards Habitat' (Peterborough, 2010).

Perry, P.J., *British Farming in the Great Depression: An Historical Geography* (Newton Abbot, 1974).

Petitt, G.H.N., *The Land of Britain: Cambridgeshire and the Isle of Ely* (London, 1941).

Pettigrew, J., Rouse, S. and Reynolds, R., *A Place in the Country: Three Counties Asylum 1860–1999* (Hatfield, 2017).

Phibbs, J., *Place Making: The Art of Capability Brown* (London, 2016).

Pinel, P., *Traité medico-philosophique sur l'Alienation Mentale* (Paris, 1801); translated into English as *A Treatise on Lunacy* (London, 1806).

Pollegioni, P., Woeste, K., Chiocchini, F., Del Lungo, S., Ciolfi, M. and Olimpieri, I., 'Rethinking the History of Common Walnut (*Juglans regia* L.) in Europe: Its Origins and Human Interactions', *PLoS ONE*, 12/3 (2017), <https://doi.org/10.1371/journal.pone.0172541>, accessed 7 March 2021.

Pomfret, M., *Stone's Orchard, Croxley Green* (Croxley Green, n.d.).

Powell, M., Harris, A. and Hicks, M., 'Lichen Ecology in Traditional Hertfordshire Orchards and the Implications for Conservation', *Transactions of the Hertfordshire Natural History Society*, 43/2 (2012), pp. 69–79.

Rackham, O., *The History of the Countryside* (London, 1986).

Raven, R., 'Sandy Smith Nature Reserve – Wildlife and History of Plum Orchard', unpublished report, The Greensand Trust (May 2012).

Raynbird, W. and Raynbird, H., *On the Agriculture of Suffolk* (London, 1849).

Read, P., 'The Rescued Orchard and the Rivers Heritage', in E. Waugh (ed.), *Rivers Nursery of Sawbridgeworth: The Art of Pomology* (Ware, 2009), pp. 184–200.

Readman, S., 'Laxton of Bedford: Pioneers of Plant-breeding', *Bedfordshire Magazine*, 23/182 (1992), pp. 250–5.

Repton, H., *An Enquiry into the Changes of Taste in Landscape Gardening* (London, 1806).

Ricketts, B., 'The Laxtons in Bedford (1879–1957)', *Bedford Architectural Archaeological & Local History Society, Newsletter*, 82 (October 2008), pp. 14–28.

Rippon, S., *Historic Landscape Analysis: Deciphering the Countryside* (London, 2004).

Rivers, T., *Miniature Fruit Garden; or the Culture of Pyramidal Fruit Trees* (London, 1840).

Rivers, T., *The Orchard House; or the Cultivation of Fruit Trees in Pots under Glass* (London, 1850).

Roberts, B. and Wrathmell, S., *An Atlas of Rural Settlement in England* (London, 2000).

Roberts, B. and Wrathmell, S., *Region and Place: A Study of English Rural Settlement* (London, 2003).

Roberts, M., *The Original Warden Pear*, rev. edn (Bedford, 2018).

Roberts, W., 'Richard Milles' New Kitchen Garden', *Norfolk Archaeology*, 62 (1937), pp. 501–7.

Robinson, R.A. and Sutherland, W.J., 'Post-War Changes in Arable Farming and Biodiversity in Great Britain', *Journal of Applied Ecology*, 39 (2002), pp. 157–76.

Robinson, W., *The English Flower Garden* (London, 1890).

Rotherham, I.D., 'An Introduction to Orchards and Groves', in I.D. Rotherham (ed.), *Orchards and Groves: Their History, Ecology, Culture and Archaeology* (Sheffield, 2008), pp. 6–10.

Rotherham, I.D. (ed.), *Orchards and Groves: Their History, Ecology, Culture and Archaeology* (Sheffield, 2008).

Rowe, A. (ed.), *Garden Making and the Freeman Family: A Memoir of Hamels 1713–1733*, Hertfordshire Record Society 17 (Hertford, 2001).

Rowe, A. and Williamson, T., *Hertfordshire: A Landscape History* (Hatfield, 2013).

Rowell, C.W., 'County Council Smallholdings, 1908–1958', *Agriculture*, 60 (1959), pp. 109–14.

Rowley, T., *The English Landscape in the Twentieth Century* (London, 2006).

Rutherford, S., 'The Landscapes of Public Lunatic Asylums in England, 1808–1914', PhD thesis (de Montfort University, Leicester, 2003).

Sabin, C.W., 'Agriculture', in W. Page (ed.), *Victoria County History, Kent*, vol. 1 (London, 1908), pp. 457–71.

Sanders, R., *The Apple Book* (London, 2010).

Scarfe, N.V., *The Land of Britain: Essex* (London, 1936).

Seabrook, W., *Modern Fruit Growing* (London, 1933).

Seabrook, W., *Fruit Production in Private Gardens* (London, 1942).

Sharpley, D. and Powell, C., *A Brief History of Fresh Produce's Role in the UK Supermarket Revolution* (London, 2014).

Sheail, J., *An Environmental History of Twentieth-Century Britain* (London, 2002).

Shoard, M., *The Theft of the Countryside* (London, 1980).

Short, B., 'The South-East: Kent, Surrey and Sussex', in J. Thirsk (ed.), *The Agrarian History of England and Wales Vol. V, I, 1640–1750* (Cambridge, 1984), pp. 270–316.

Short, B., May, P., Vine, G. and Bur, A.-M., *Apples and Orchards in Sussex* (Lewes, 2012).

Silva, G.J., Souza, T.M., Barbieri, R.L. and de Oliveira, A.C., 'Origin, Domestication, and Dispersing of Pear (*Pyrus* spp.)', *Advances in Agriculture*, 20 (2014), pp. 1–8.

Smith, A. Hassell, 'The Gardens of Sir Nicholas and Francis Bacon: An Enigma Resolved and a Mind Explored', in P. Roberts (ed.), *Religion, Culture and Society in Early Modern England* (Cambridge, 1994), pp. 125–60.

Smith, C.W., *The Lichens of Britain and Ireland* (London, 2009).

Spangenberg, J.E., Jacomet, S. and Schibler, J., 'Chemical Analysis of Organic Residues in Archaeological Pottery from Arbon Bleiche', *Journal of Archaeological Science*, 33/1 (2006), pp. 1–13.

Stamp, L. Dudley, *The Land of Britain: Its Use and Misuse* (London, 1948).

Stanyon, M., 'Papermaking', in D. Short (ed.), *An Historical Atlas of Hertfordshire* (Hatfield, 2011), pp. 80–1.

Stevenson, C.R. and Rowntree, J.J., 'Bryophytes in East Anglian Orchards', *Field Bryology*, 99 (2009), pp. 10–18.

Stevenson, C.R., Davies, C. and Rowntree, J.K., 'Biodiversity in Agricultural Landscapes: The Effect of Apple Cultivar on Epiphyte Diversity', *Ecology and Evolution*, 7 (2017), pp. 1250–8.

Taigel, A. and Williamson, T., 'Some Early Geometric Gardens in Norfolk', *Journal of Garden History*, 11/1–2 (1991), pp. 1–111.

Tate, W.E. and Turner, M., *A Domesday of English Enclosure Acts and Awards* (Reading, 1978).

Taylor, C., *Village and Farmstead: A History of Rural Settlement in England* (London, 1983).

Taylor, H.V., *The Apples of England* (London, 1948).

Taylor, I., *Helen Allingham's England* (Exeter, 1990).

Temple, W., *Miscellanea: The Second Part* (London, 1690).

Thirsk, J. (ed.), *The Agrarian History of England and Wales, Vol. V, 1640–1750* (Cambridge, 1984).

Thompson, F.M.L., 'An Anatomy of English Agriculture, 1870–1914', in B.A. Holderness and N. Turner (eds), *Land, Labour and Agriculture 1700–1920* (London, 1991), pp. 211–40.

Thompson, O., 'Notes Towards a History of Norfolk Cider' (2007), <http://www.cider.org.uk/Notes%20Towards%20a%20History%20of%20Norfolk%20Cider.pdf>, accessed 7 March 2021.

Turner, G.J. (ed.), *A Calendar of the Feet of Fines relating to the County of Huntingdon, Levied in the King's Court from the Fifth Year of Richard I. to the End of the Reign of Elizabeth, 1194–1603* (Cambridge, 1913).

Tusser, T., *A Hundreth Good Pointes of Husbandry* (London, 1557).

Upcher, H., 'Norfolk Farming', *Transactions of the Norfolk and Norwich Naturalists Society*, 16 (1946), pp. 37–105.

Wade Martins, S. and Williamson, T. (eds), *The Farming Journal of Randall Burroughes of Wymondham, 1794–99*, Norfolk Record Society 58 (Norwich, 1995).

Wade Martins, S. and Williamson, T., *Roots of Change: Farming and the Landscape in East Anglia c.1700–1870* (Exeter, 1999).

Wade Martins, S. and Williamson, T., *The Countryside of East Anglia: Changing Landscapes, c.1870–1950* (Woodbridge, 2008).

Walsh, D., Randall, A., Sheldon, R. and Charlesworth, A., 'The Cider Tax, Popular Symbolism and Opposition in Mid Hanoverian England', in A. Randall and A. Charlesworth (eds), *Markets, Market Culture and Popular Protest in Eighteenth-Century Britain and Ireland* (Liverpool, 1996), pp. 69–90.

Ward, A.J., *The Early History of Papermaking at Frogmore Mill and Two Waters Mill, Hertfordshire* (Berkhamsted, 2003).

Warde, P. and Williamson, T., 'Fuel Supply and Agriculture in Post-Medieval England', *Agricultural History Review*, 62/1 (2014), pp. 61–82.

Warren, M.S. and Key, R.S., 'Woodlands: Past, Present and Potential for Insects', in N.M. Collins and J.A. Thomas (eds), *The Conservation of Insects and their Habitats* (London, 1990), pp. 151–211.

Waugh, E., *Rivers Nursery of Sawbridgeworth: The Art of Pomology* (Ware, 2009).

Waugh, E., 'Planting the Garden: The Nursery Trade in Hertfordshire', in D. Spring (ed.), *Hertfordshire Garden History Volume II: Gardens Pleasant, Groves Delicious* (Hatfield, 2012), pp. 177–201.

Wheeler, D. and Mayer, J. (eds), *The Regional Climates of the British Isles* (London, 1997).

White, J., 'What is a Veteran Tree and Where are they All?' *Quarterly Journal of Forestry*, 91/3 (1997), pp. 222–6.

White, J., *Estimating the Age of Large and Veteran Trees in Britain*, Forestry Commission Information Note 250 (Edinburgh, 1999).

White, W., *A History, Gazetteer and Directory of Norfolk* (Sheffield, 1845).

Whitelaw, M. and Burton, M.A.S., 'Diversity and Distribution of Epiphytic Bryophytes on Bramley's Seedling Trees in East of England Apple Orchards', *Global Ecology and Conservation*, 4 (2015), pp. 380–7.

Wiffen, N., '"An Account of Dwarf Apple trees Planted": A Scheme for Kelvedon', *Essex Journal*, 54/2 (2019), pp. 76–83.

Wigley, E., 'Wassail! Reinventing "Tradition" in Contemporary Wassailing Customs in Southern England', *Cultural Geographies*, 26/3 (2019), pp. 379–93.

Wildman, R., 'Laxton of Bedford: The Family and Firm', *Bedfordshire Magazine*, 23/182 (1992), pp. 244–7.

Wilkerson, J.C. (ed.), *John Norden's Survey of Barley Hertfordshire. 1593–1603*, Cambridgeshire Records Society 2 (Cambridge, 1974).

Williams, M.H. and Stevenson, J. (eds), *'Observations of Weather': The Weather Diary of Sir John Wittewronge of Rothamsted 1684–1689*, Hertfordshire Record Society 15 (Hertford, 1999).

Williamson, T., *Polite Landscapes: Gardens and Society in Eighteenth-Century England* (Stroud, 1995).

Williamson, T., *The Archaeology of the Landscape Park: Garden Design in Norfolk, England, 1680–1840*, BAR British Series 269 (Oxford, 1998).

Williamson, T., *Suffolk's Gardens and Parks: Designed Landscapes from the Tudors to the Victorians* (Macclesfield, 2000).

Williamson, T., *Rabbits, Warrens and Archaeology* (Stroud, 2007).
Williamson, T., *Environment, Society and Landscape in Early Medieval England* (Woodbridge, 2013).
Williamson, T., *An Environmental History of Wildlife in England, 1650–1950* (London, 2013).
Williamson, T., Liddiard, R. and Partida, T., *Champion. The Making and Unmaking of the English Midland Landscape* (Exeter, 2012).
Willmott, E., *English House Design: A Review; Being a Selection and Brief Analysis of Some of the Best Achievements in English Domestic Architecture* (London, 1911).
Winstanley, R.L. (ed.), *Parson Woodforde: Diary of the First Six Norfolk Years, 1776–1781*, vol. 1 (London, 1981).
Winstanley, R.L. (ed.), *Parson Woodforde: Diary of the First Six Norfolk Years, 1776–1781*, vol. 3 (London, 1984).
Wittering, S., *Ecology and Enclosure: The Effects of Enclosure on Society, Farming and the Environment in South Cambridgeshire, 1798–1859* (Oxford, 2013).
Wormwell, P., *Essex Farming, 1900–2000* (Colchester, 1999).
Woudstra, J., 'Fruit Cultivation in the Royal Gardens of Hampton Court Palace 1630–1842', *Garden History*, 44/2 (2016), pp. 255–71.
Woudstra, J., 'The History and Development of Groves in English Formal Gardens, 1600–1760', in J. Woudstra and C. Roth (eds), *A History of Groves* (London, 2018), pp. 67–85.
Wright, A.P.M. and Lewis, C.P. (eds), *A History of the County of Cambridge and the Isle of Ely: Volume 9, Chesterton, Northstowe, and Papworth Hundreds* (London, 1989).
Yeomans, H., 'Taxation, State Formation and Governmentality', *Social Science History*, 42/2 (2018), pp. 269–93.
Young, A., *Annals of Agriculture*, vol. 5 (London, 1786).
Young, A., *General View of the Agriculture of the County of Suffolk* (London, 1797).
Young, A., *General View of the Agriculture of the County of Hertfordshire* (London, 1804).
Young, A., *General View of the Agriculture of the County of Essex*, 2 vols (London, 1807).

Websites

Bedfordshire Libraries Website (information about Laxton's of Bedford), <http://virtual-library.culturalservices.net/webingres/bedfordshire/vlib/0.digitised_resources/high_street_history_laxton.htm>
Bishops Stortford History website, <http://www.stortfordhistory.co.uk/guide2/sir-walter-gilbey/>
East of England Apples and Orchards Project website, <https://www.applesandorchards.org.uk/about/what-we-do/>
FruitID, <https://www.fruitid.com/#main>
Hansard, <https://hansard.parliament.uk/Commons>
John Mackie and Sons, Norwich Nurserymen, Catalogue, 1790, <https://archive.org/details/JohnMackieSonsNorwichACatalogueOfForestTreesFruitTreesEvergreenAndFloweringShrubs1790/page/n85>
Le Maistre, F., a list of Jersey Cider Apples, <http://www.theislandwiki.org/index.php/Jersey's_numerous_cider_apple_varieties>
National Children's Home, promotional film, 1954, <https://www.youtube.com/watch?v=jMLzCLggcKA>
Shenley Park Trust Website, <http://www.shenleypark.co.uk/shenley-park/>
Suffolk Traditional Orchard Group, 'Cobnuts in Suffolk,' <https://issuu.com/suffolkbis/docs/stogan__6_cobnuts_in_suffolk_v3_aug?ff=TRUE&e=25146667/41601866>
Tiptree Heritage Centre website, <https://web.archive.org/web/20141112223240/http://www.tiptree.com/goto.php?ref=y&sess=+A5E5147191D51+F18435A52+9+B581D1058+E+357+9+25F1D1758&id=14>
UK Government Agricultural Statistics, <https://assets.publishing.service.gov.uk/government/uploads/system/uploads/attachment_data/file/183104/defra-stats-foodfarm-landuselivestock-june-results-england-1900series111129.xls> and <https://assets.publishing.service.gov.uk/government/uploads/system/uploads/attachment_data/file/927036/structure-june-eng-county-15oct2020.ods>

Index

Entries in *italic* refer to the illustrations

Abbots Langley, Herts 47, 64
agriculture 25, 151–3, 241
agricultural depression, effect on fruit growing 56, 60, 62, 71, 133
agricultural surveys 15, 167 *see also* government statistics
Apple Days 160, 161, 170
apple houses 100, *100*
apples 5, 7, 10–11, 39, 94, 99, 210–11, 213 *see also* fruit varieties; *Malus* spp.
    Aldenham Blenheim 101
    Allington Pippin 70, 73, 102, 112, 113, 143
    Annie Elizabeth 70, 103, 112, 113, 114
    Aromatic Russet 101, 195, 197
    Beauty of Bath 79, 82, 105, 112, 113, 143, 157
    Belle de Pontoise 102
    Bismarck 112, 113, 116
    Blenheim Orange 101, 102, 103, 105, 112, 113, 114, 116, 139, 143
    Bramley's Seedling 12, 13, *13*, 72, *72*, 79, 81, 82, 85, 102, 103, 105, 112, 113, 114, 115, 116, 139, 143, 156, 157, 159, 209–10, 221
    Brownlees' Russet 191
    Bushey Grove 101
    Calville Rouge d'Hiver 103
    Charles Ross 85, 103, 105, 112, 157
    Court of Wick 101, 103, 180
    Court Pendu Plat 82, 101
    Cox's Orange Pippin 69, 75, 79, 85, 105, 139, 156, 157, 159, 182
    D'Arcy Spice 180, 193
    Darnel Pippin (Darling Pippin) 123
    Desse de Buff 100
    Discovery 85, 159, 191
    Dr Harvey 45, 101, 116, 139
    Dumelow's Seedling 102, 115, 116
    Edward VII 115, 156
    Egremont Russet 85, 139, 159
    Ellison's Orange 102, 105, 112, 139
    Emneth Early (Early Victoria) 72, 78, 105, 139, 157, 191
    Forge 101, 139
    Gala 159
    Gascoyne's Scarlet 112, 113
    Golden Delicious 69, 85, 159
    Golden Noble 100, 112, 113
    Golden Russet 101, 197
    Gravenstein 101, 201
    Grenadier 72, 85, 105, 114, 139, 156
    Hambling's Seedling 103
    Harvey's Wiltshire Defiance 101, 201
    Holland Pippin 125, 175, 196, 197
    Hollow Crown 125, 199
    Howgate Wonder 103, 139
    James Grieve 75, 79, 85, 105, 115, 139
    'Jully Flower' 125, 194
    Kentish Pippin 101, 196, 198
    Keswick (Keswick Codlin) 143, 191, 193, 199, 201, 202, 214
    King of Pippins 101, 112, 113
    King of Tompkins County 102, 112, 113
    Kingston Black 133, 134, 139
    Knotted Kernel 133, 139
    Lady Henniker 100
    Lady Sudeley 79, 85
    Lane's Prince Albert 73, 82, 102, 103, 105, 115, 143, *188*, 189, 204
    Large Yellow Newtown Pippin 181
    Laxton's Epicure 102, 105, 189
    Laxton's Fortune 102, 105, 112, 156, 189
    Laxton's Superb 69, 79, 112, 139, 156, 157, 189, *190*
    Lemon Pippin 101, 199
    London Pippin 101, 195, 197, 199, 200, 201
    Lord Derby 70, 82, 103, 112, 139, 143
    Lord Lambourne 102, 112, 156, 189
    Lord Stradbrooke 101
    Lord Suffield 101, 102
    Medaille D'Or 133, 139
    Mela Carla 181, 183
    Mere de Ménage 101, 139
    Monarch 85, 112, 114, 116, 191
    New Hawthornden 101, 182

Newton Wonder 72, 78, 102, 103, 105, 112, 113, 114, 143
Norfolk Beefing (Norfolk Beaufin) 101, 116, 119–21, 139, *217*
Northern Greening 101, 116
Peasgood's Nonsuch 112, 113, 115, 116
Queen Cox 85
Ribston Pippin 85, 101, 102, 112, 113, 139
Rosemary Russet 85, 102, *210*
Scarlet Nonpareil 101, 200
Seek no Further 125
Spartan 85, 159
Strawberry Norman 133, 139
Striped Beefing (Striped Beaufin) 101, 102
Sturmer Pippin 85, 102, 105, 115, 180
Sweet Alford 133, 139
Sweet Coppin 133, 139
Tydeman's Early Worcester 157, 159
Waltham Abbey Seedling 101, 180
Warner's King 102, 114, 115, 116, 139
White Pippin 125, 194, 197
Winter Majetin 41, 193
Winter Queen 103
Woodbine 133, 139
Worcester Pearmain 69, 75, 78, 79, 82, 83, 101, 112, 139, 156, 157, 159
apricots 93, 94
Arts and Crafts style 106–8
Aspall Cider
  apples used for 124, 125, 133, 134
  cider making 124, 127, 134
  Chevallier, Clement 124, 129–30, 131, 174, 196
  cyder house, the *126*, 127
  orchards at 124, 125, 132, 135, *135*
  production 124–5, 128–9, 132, 133
  selling 128, 130–1, 134
Austen, Ralph 10, 236

Banham, Norfolk 135, 136
barberry (*Berberis vulgaris*) 9
Barron, Archibald 11
Batchelor, Thomas 32
Bedfordshire and Luton Orchard Group 161
Bedfordshire Clanger 121
bee-keeping 41, 79–80
beer 123
biffins 119–21
biodiversity, importance of orchards for 5, 161, 164, 169, 217, 233, 237, 241–2, 243
  amphibians 232
  birds 232–3
  bryophytes 221–3

fungi 231
ground flora 230–1
invertebrates 218, 224–29
lichens 218–21
mammals 232
management for 230
molluscs 231–2
Birkhead, Mary 35, 36–7, 40, 44, 123, 174, 193
Blofield, Norfolk *68*, 69, 215
Blomefield, Francis 44
British Pomological Society 182
Brompton Park nursery, Kensington 172, 175
budding 10
Bullein, William 46
Bunyard's nursery company 51, 102, 192, 203
Burlingham, Norfolk 67, 69
Burroughes, Randall 32, 35, 42, 44, 235

Cambridgeshire Orchard Group 161
Carleton Rode, Norfolk 39, 194, *195*
'champion' regions *23*, 25, 32
Channons Hall, Norfolk *90*, 91
cherries 5, 8–9, 11, 23, 37, 39, 46–9, *50*, 54, 59, 80–1, 93–4, 119, 122, 182, 211, *212*, 213, 218, 221
cherry orchards 12, 24, 46–9, 53, 64–5, 66, 89
cherry timber 49
Cheshunt, Herts 53
Chevallier, Clement *see* Aspall cider
Chivers jam company 62, 73, 141, *141*, 142
  orchards at 141, 142
cider 122–3, 240 *see also* Aspall Cider; Gaymer's; R. Rout and son
Clarke, Leslie 80, 148, 157, 158
climate 21
Clutterbuck, James 48
Cockley Cley Hall, Norfolk 102
commercial orchards 2, *3*, 13, 19, 71, 84, 86–7, 158, *170*, 200, 203, 204, 215, 240
  early 45–54
  factors influencing location 25–6, 56, 66, 73–5
  fruit farms 85–6
  management of 77–80, 84–5, 87, 149–50, 169, 221, 235, 236
Common Ground 159–60
  'Save our Orchards' campaign 160
community orchards *163*, 170, 243
conservation 159, 242–3
  rewilding 242–3
Cook, Moses 49
Cottenham, Cambs 51, 62, 78
country-house orchards 19, 88–9, 99, 156, 239, 240
  fate of 102, 117–18

fruit trees in wider grounds 93
functions 95
in glasshouses 99
in walled gardens 93–4, 96–7, *97*, 98–9, 173
layout 91
location of 91
management of 93
planting in 101–3
see also moated sites, orchards on
Cox's Orange Pippin Orchard 75–7
Crapes orchard, Aldham, 225, 231, 241
Cubitt family 71

Daniels' nursery 186, 192, 203, 216
Dengie peninsular, Essex 53

East Malling Research Station 11, 82, 105
East of England Apples and Orchards Project 160–1, 162, 170
Eaton Bray, Beds 57, *58*, 59, 237–8
Ellis, William 22, 25, 35, 48, 49, 173, 174, 175, 198
Elsenham Jam Company 145
Ely, Cambs 77–8
enclosure 25, 26, 57, 64
European Economic Community 147, 150, 151, 169
  Common Agricultural Policy 149, 241

farmhouse/domestic orchards 2, *2*, 13, 19, 28–32, *33*, 216, 239
  additional functions of 41, 43
  layout of 35–6, *36*, 37, *38*, 39
  location of 33, 53
  management of 44, 236
  planting of 35–6, *36*, 37, *38*, 39–40, 54
  removal of 151–5, 240
  sale of produce from 32, 44, 54
  value to owner 33, 44, 88, 170
Farthing, F.H. 104
Fens, the *see* fruit-growing districts
firewood 43, 235, 236
Flaunden, Herts 48
Forestry Act (1967) 162
Freman, Ralph 95, 172
fruit
  consumption of 40
  quality of 148
  storage and preservation of 40–1, 100, *100*, 119, 122, 140 *see also* jam making
  value of 33–4
fruit-growing
  as diversification from arable farming 49, 52, 56, 62, 85

competition from abroad 148, 149, 151
over-production 149, 151
trade with Europe 148
under glass 99, 182, 184
fruit-growing districts 4, 46–7, 239–40
  Essex 53, 59–60, 83–4
  Fenland 50–2, 54, 62–3, 72–3, 77–8, 240
  requirements for 26–7
  south Bedfordshire 55, 57, 59, 237, 240
  south Cambridgeshire 52, 63–4, 72, 73, 179
  south-east Hertfordshire 53
  west Hertfordshire 46, 49, 54, 64–5, 240
FruitID 161, 171
fruit-processing industry 72, 140–6
fruit trees
  aging of 207, 209, 235
  best planting sites 22
  exchange of between friends and relatives 44, 172, 174, 175, 181
  growth patterns 211
  longevity 5, 106, 206–7, 210–11
  management 10, 12 *see also* orchard management; pruning
  means of sourcing 171–5, 195, 205 *see also* nursery industry
  planted by cottages 29
  planted in churchyards 29
  planted in hedgerows 40, 48, *48*, 49
  pollination 12, 41
  preferred conditions 21, 22, 23–5
  propagation 10
  replacement of 235, 236
  senescence 210, *210*, 235
  timber from 49
  veteranising 5, 6, 106, 161, 206–7, *208*, 209, 211, 239
  vigour 11, 12
fruit varieties 10, 171, 239
  abandonment of older 200–5
  conservation of 161
  decline in numbers of 3, 156–9, 201, 203, 204, 205
  descriptive names 193, 195, 196, 197–8, 205
  development of 100–1, 179–80, 182, 189, 191, 192
  distribution of 216
  early 192–9
  genetics of 11–12, 198, 199, 205
  geographic names 193, 194, 196, 197
  heritage 162, *163*
  late eighteenth- and nineteenth-century 199–202
  local names 193, 194, 195, 196, 197
  lost 193, 194, 199
  nineteenth- and twentieth-century 203–5, 214, 215, 216–17

proliferation of 101, 122, 180, 192, 202, 203, 205
recommended by government 156, 204
short-lived 199, 202, 205
systematisation of 198
widespread 200
with disease resistance 158
see also apples; apricots; cherries; nectarines; nuts; peaches; pears; plums
fruiting season, length of 40, 119, 122
Fuller, Thomas 45
funding for orchard removal 153–4

garden design 88, 91–2, 94, 95–6, 99
Gaymer's 136–40
    apples used 139–40
    orchards at 138
geology 22, 23, *23*, 24 see also soil types
globalisation 151, 169, 241
Gooch, William 50
government policies 151, 159, 240
government statistics 21, 65
grafting 10, 174 see also top-grafting
grapes 183, 184, 189
grazing of orchards see orchard management

Hadleigh, Essex 60
Hamels, Herts 95, 123, 172
Harrold Hall, Beds 93, 236
Hartley's jam makers 66, 142
Hasketon, Suffolk 37, 39
hay, cut from orchards 41, 77
Hellier, H.E. 104–5
heritage orchards 159, 162, *163*, 164
Hertfordshire Orchards Initiative 161
Hethel Hall, Norfolk 89
Histon, Cambs 62, 73, 141
Historic Landscape Character 237
historiography 1–2, 5
Hitchin, Herts 39, 69
Hoare, Arthur 22
Home Farm, South Elmham 37, 216, 225, 227, 230
Home Farm Colony 60
Hone, William 119
honey 41, 80
Honing Hall, Norfolk 71, 172
Houghton Hall, Norfolk 95, 102, 207, 209, 223, 225, 227, 230
Hoxne Hall, Suffolk *89*, 90

industrialisation 65, 103
institutional orchards 2, 19, 109, 155–6, 214–15, 240
    Cell Barnes psychiatric hospital, Herts 110

Depwade Union Workhouse, Norfolk 109
Girton College, Cambridge 116–17, *117*, 215, 241
Harperbury psychiatric hospital, Herts 110, 112
Hill End psychiatric hospital, Herts 110
The Highfield Oval, Herts 114, *114*, 115, 155, 162, 241
Homerton College, Cambridge 116–17
Leavesden psychiatric hospital, Herts 110, 111, 155
Napsbury psychiatric hospital, Herts 110, 111
St Elizabeth's residential school for epileptics, Much Hadham, Herts 112–13, *113*, 162, 214, 222, 241
Shenley psychiatric hospital, Herts 110, 112, 162
Steppingley Hospital, Beds 115, *116*, 231
survival of 117–18
therapeutic value of 110, 111, 115, 155
Three Counties Asylum, Beds 110, 112, 162, 214

jam making 140 see also Chivers jam company; Hartley's jam makers; Wilkin and Sons jam company
Jekyll, Gertrude 106–7, 108

Kent, Nathaniel 123
Ketteringham, Norfolk 46
King's Langley, Herts 47, 64, 69
Knight, Andrew 29
Knight, Thomas 181

labour, availability of and cost 48, 65, 150
Land Settlement Association 70
Land Settlement (Facilities) Act (1919) 67, 70
Land Utilisation Survey 20
Lane's of Berkhamstead, nursery and fruit-growers 186–7, *187*, 188, 203
Lawson, William 35, 41, 88, 171, 235, 236, 244
Laxton's nursery, Beds 108, 189
Lindley, George, nurseryman 37, 178, 193
livestock in orchards 42
    poultry *43*, 59, 79, 85–6
    sheep 59
Long Ashton Research Establishment 75
Lunatics Act (1845) 110

Mackie's nursery, Norwich *176*, 177–8, 184, *184*, 186
Malus spp. 7 see also apples
Marham, Norfolk 46
market gardening 53, 59–60, 70
markets for fruit 26, 53, 55, 60, 66
Markham, Gervase 35, 41
Marshland St James, Norfolk 223, 225, 227–9
Mawson, T.H. 107
Mayes Farm, Yaxham 230, 232, 241
medlar (*Mespilus germanica*) 9, 37, 79, 96, 103, 143, 145

Melbourn, Cambs 179
Meldreth, Cambs 64
Ministry of Agriculture and Fisheries 82, 158, 204
moated sites, orchards on 89, *89*, 90–1
mulberries (*Morus*) 9, 37, 39, 107, 143, 145
Museum of East Anglian Life 162

nectarines 71, 93, 94, 96, 97, 172, 183
Norden, John 48
Norfolk Apples and Orchards Project 160
Norfolk Fruit Growers, Wroxham 139
North Elmham Hall, Norfolk 96–7
North Runcton, Norfolk 39, 194
Norwich, Norfolk 45–6
nursery industry
    commercial customers 179, 183
    international 175, 181, 182
    London 172–3, 174
    marketing 177, 179, 180, *185*, 186, 192, 216
    provinces 173–4, 175, 177–9
nut grounds 89
nuts 40
    cobnuts 9, *38*, 39
    Corylus avellana (hazel) 9
    filberts (*Corylus maxima*) 8, 35–6
    walnuts (*Juglans* spp.) 9, 35–6, 40

orchard management *see also* commercial orchards; farmhouse orchards
    grazing 13, 42, 59, 77, 79
    pest control 79, 80–1, 82, 149–50, 169, 221
    pesticides 80–1, 149, 220, 237
    see also pruning
orchards
    aesthetic value of 44, 54, 88, 95, 106–8, 239, 244
    ancient appearance of 211, *212*, 213, 239
    as habitats 5, 7, 161, 164, 169, 170, 217–18, 224–5, 241–2, 243 *see also* biodiversity, importance of orchards for
    as part of larger farms 47–8, 54, 59 *see also* farmhouse orchards
    as places of recreation 44
    association with settlement 29, 30
    attitudes to 235, 239
    conservation of 161–2, 238, 244
    conversion to arable 82
    cultural and symbolic value of 4, 44, 106–8, 160, 164, 213–14, 237, 239, 242
    decline in 3–4, 147, 151, 165, 167, 169, 240–1
    definition of 165, 218
    derelict 169, 211, *212*, 213, *213*, 237, 238, 241
    density 15, *16*, 65–6, 67, 86
    distribution 15, *16*, *18*, 25, 30, 65–6, 67, 73, 86
    expansion of 15, 27, 55–7, 59–66, 67, 71, 73, 82–5, 240
    factors influencing location 25–6, 30, 56, 66, 73–5
    importance in daily life 4, 239
    in towns 45–6, 109
    in wartime 82–3
    interplanting 41, 46, 51, 54, 77–9, 87, 236
    land use replacing 167–8
    longevity of 19, 233, *234*, 235
    new 170, 233, 241, 244
    organisations related to 160–1
    other uses of 41, 43, 79–80
    peak of 82, 147, 167
    replacement of 235
    replanting of 157
    requirement for maintenance 5, 7, 44, 217
    security of 33–4, 90
    size of 31, 32, 47, 51
    surveying of 164–6, 225
    surviving 165–6, 169, 241
    transient in nature 233, 235
    see also commercial orchards; community orchards; country-house orchards; farmhouse orchards; heritage orchards; institutional orchards
Orchards East 1, 161, 162, 164
Ordnance Survey maps, depiction of orchards on *17*, 18–19, 20

peaches 71, 93, 94, 183
pears 7–8, 11, 39, 94, 211 *see also Pyrus* spp.
    Conference 105, 116, 157, 182
    Doyenne de Comice 105, 143, 157
    Fondante d'Automne 101, 116
    Laxton's Superb 157, 158
    Pitmaston Duchess 105, 116, 143
    Wardens 122
    Williams' Bon Chrétien 101, 105, 143, 157
People's Trust for Endangered Species 161, 164, 166, 167, 218
plum orchards 57, *58*, 59
plums 5, 8, 11, 52, 93, 94, 211, 213 *see also Prunus* spp.
    Aylesbury Prunes 57, 59
    cherry plums 8
    damsons 8
    Golden Drop 180
    greengages 8, 11, 95, 143
    Laxton's Cropper 191
    mirabelles 8
    Victoria 143, 157
    Willingham Gage 52

ponds 42, 230
Potton Florentine 121–2
price controls 83, 148, 151, 158
pruning 10, 12–14, 81, 82, 178
    bush 12–13, *13*, 42, 81, 82
    cordon 14, 84
    espalier 14, 97, *97*, 104
    fan 14, 97, 104
    half-standard 82
    open centre 12–13, *13*
    pyramid 14
    spindle 15
    standard 12, 42
Prunus spp. 8, 49 *see also* plums
Pyrus spp. 7 *see also* pears

quinces 35, 37, 39, 143, 145

railways 55, 57, 60, 62–3, 64, 66, 73–4, 133, 143, 184
Redgrave Hall, Suffolk 91
retail sector, changes in 150, 151, 169, 241
Rivers Nursery, Herts 99, 175, 177, 182–3, *183*, 192, 202, 203, 214, 216
Rivers, Thomas 99, 175, 182
Robinson, William 107
rootstocks 49, 209
    crab 10, 82
    dwarfing 11, 81, 84, *84*, 94, 104
    extremely dwarfing 82, 105
    intermediate 11
    'M' 11, 82, 85, 105, 169
    paradise 10, 11, 14, 42, 82, 183
    quince 11, 82
    vigorous 11, 42, 54, 161
R. Rout and Son 136
Rummers Lane, Wisbech St Mary 220, 222, 228
Ryston Hall, Norfolk 94, 172, 196

Sarratt, Herts 47, 64, 164, 223
Saxmundham, Suffolk 39
scion wood 10, 172, 174
Seabrook, William 158
settlement patterns 25–6
shelter belts 34–5, 85, 183
Shotesham Hall, Norfolk 97
smallholdings 56, 59, *68*, 70, 204
    establishment of by county councils 67, 69
    importance of orchards to 69, 80
    Jeacock's Farm, Tring *68*, 69–70, 215, 241
social changes 159, 169, 241
soft fruit 9, 46, 79, 82, 86

soil types 22, 23, *23*, 24, 30, 50, 54, 57, 63–4 *see also* geology
Somerleyton Hall, Suffolk 91–2, *92*, 99
Southend, Essex 53, 60
Standon, Herts 31–2
Stone's Orchard, Herts 161, 236
Stow Bardolph, Norfolk 39, 94
Stowmarket, Suffolk 46
suburbanisation 103–4
suburbs 104
    fruit trees in 104–9, 156
    orchards in 109, 156
Suffolk Traditional Orchards Group 161

tenure 25, 30
Tewin Orchard, Herts 161, 213, *213*, 214, 215, 241
Tiptree, Essex 61, 142
tithe documentation 15, 18, 47, 53
tithes 41, 43–4
top-grafting 11, 83
Town and Country Planning Act (1947) 103–4, 109, 156
transport, improvements in 26, 27, 55, 103, 133, 240 *see also* railways
Tree Preservation Orders 162
Tusser, Thomas 29

urbanisation 26–7, 55 *see also* suburbanisation

Walsoken, Norfolk 51
Wandlebury House, Cambs 103, 162, 230
War Agricultural Committees 82
weather, impact on fruit crops 21–2, 153
    frost pockets 22
White House, Walpole Highway 223, 227–8, 231
Whitehead, John Alexander *74*, 75–7
Wilkin and Sons jam company 61, *61*, 142–3, 145
    orchards at 143, *144*, 145
William Seabrook and Sons 71, 84, 191
Willingham, Cambs 51, 52, 62, 73, 78, 79
Wisbech, Cambs 24, 50, 72
    processing industry at 145
Wisbech and Upwell tramway 63, *63*
Witham Fruit Packers 85
wood-pasture 5, 218, 223, 224, 229
'woodland' regions *23*, 26, 32
Wormley Bury, Herts 94
Wrest Park, Beds 100, 172, 173
Wyboston, Hunts 70

Young, Arthur 41, 42, 47, 53, 123, 124, 127, 131